Renowned Goddess of Desire

Renowned Goddess of Desire

Women, Sex, and Speech in Tantra

LORILIAI BIERNACKI

OXFORD
UNIVERSITY PRESS
2007

OXFORD
UNIVERSITY PRESS

Oxford University Press, Inc., publishes works that further
Oxford University's objective of excellence
in research, scholarship, and education.

Oxford New York
Auckland Cape Town Dar es Salaam Hong Kong Karachi
Kuala Lumpur Madrid Melbourne Mexico City Nairobi
New Delhi Shanghai Taipei Toronto

With offices in
Argentina Austria Brazil Chile Czech Republic France Greece
Guatemala Hungary Italy Japan Poland Portugal Singapore
South Korea Switzerland Thailand Turkey Ukraine Vietnam

Published by Oxford University Press, Inc.
198 Madison Avenue, New York, New York 10016

www.oup.com

Library of Congress Cataloging-in-Publication Data
Biernacki, Loriliai.
Renowned Goddess of desire : women, sex, and speech
in Tantra / by Loriliai Biernacki.
p. cm.
Includes bibliographical references and index.
ISBN 978-0-19-532782-3; 978-0-19-532783-0 (pbk.)
1. Women in Tantrism. 2. Kamakhya (Hindu deity)—Cult. 3. Tantric
literature—India, Northeastern—History and criticism. I. Title.
BL1283.842.B54 2008
294.5'514082—dc22 2006100015

9 8 7 6 5 4 3 2 1

Printed in the United States of America
on acid-free paper

For my mother and father,
Mary and Ivan Biernacki, and
for Nīlasaraswatī, the Blue Goddess of Speech

Acknowledgments

This book benefited greatly from the comments and the support of a number of colleagues, friends, and students who read drafts of parts of the manuscript. I would like to mention especially Kathleen Erndl, Fred Smith, Karen Pechilis, Elissa Guralnick, David White, Nina Molinaro, Bob Lester, Barbara Fox, Faye Kleeman, Michelene Pesantubbee; also especially Nicole Castillo and Matt Swoveland who prepared the index; Chip Horner, Norah Charles, Tracy Pintchman, Rita Sherma, Greg Johnson, Shree Maa of Kamakhya, for her wisdom and for arranging wonderful hospitality in Calcutta, Delhi, and Assam; the Das family, including Baiti Das, Jiten and Jyoti Das, Minu, and Mithu, and Riju, Pinky and Pippali Das, and especially Biju Das, for their tour?guiding finesse; Khuki, Achuta, Mahadeva Sharma, Neelima and Sanjay Agarwal. My heartfelt thanks goes also to Sri Sri Karunamayi and Ravi Venkata and Anitha Gowtam for their moral support.

I would also like to acknowledge the Wabash Center for funding that allowed me to journey to India in the summer of 2004. And I would like to offer my grateful appreciation to my editors at Oxford University Press, Cynthia Read and Gwen Colvin, and my copyeditor Renee Leath.

Additionally I would like to thank my colleagues in the Department of Religious Studies at the University of Colorado for their support throughout this process, particularly, my colleague Terry

Kleeman for his unfailing support and guidance. I'd like to thank also especially Jeff Kripal, who has been a guide and a very wise super-vīra, in a multitude of ways. Finally, I especially want to acknowledge DJ Zupancic for help and inspiration throughout.

Contents

Note on Transliteration

Standard diacritical marks have been used for transliterations of Sanskrit words throughout this book, with the exception of names of persons from the colonial and postcolonial period, contemporary place names, and also for words where the sources (in English or vernacular) ignore diacritics. So, for instance, references to the nineteenth-century Hindu saint Ramakrishna and his disciple Gauri Ma are written without diacritical marks, as are references to the sixteenth-century Koch king Naranarayan.

Renowned Goddess of Desire

Introduction

The Goddess on the Blue Hill of Kāmākhyā

In a well-known and delightfully graphic metaphor from India's classical philosophical tradition, *prakṛti,* the feminine principle, or nature, is likened to a dancing girl. As she dances, her physical charms seduce the male spirit, *puruṣa,* into the web of *māyā,* an unending circuit of desire, birth, and death. The purpose of her dance, actually, is finally to dance him into boredom. She helps him to understand his true nature by dancing and dancing until his desire to watch this beautiful woman dance finally reaches a point of satiation. He gets bored with the dance, and recognizing this, she gracefully withdraws.[1]

This image of the dance is exclusively scripted from the point of view of the male spirit, *puruṣa. Prakṛti*'s dance functions solely to serve his ends, both to delight him in the short term and ultimately to lead him to an enlightenment that finally entails his bored rejection of her. But what might her dancing look like from the other side of the lens? Does the primordial female as dancer live only to please and then wait for the male spectator to become bored and reject her dancing?

In the northeast region of India, in the state of Assam, a popular story suggests another angle to view the image of the dancing woman who weaves an illusory web of *māyā* with her dance. The Goddess of Great Illusion, Mahā-Māyā, the Tantric goddess who resides on the blue hill of Kāmākhyā, also dances.[2] Known also as Kāmākhyā Devī, she dances in her temple at Kāmākhyā, in Assam. She dances for her own pleasure, with no spectators, when the temple doors are closed, so that no one can see her dance.

The priest Kendukalai, however, gains her favor because of his great devotion toward her and is allowed to watch her nightly dance. He, unfortunately, tells the king, Naranarayan, of her dancing, and as a consequence incites the king's desire. Under pressure from the king, and to gain his favor, Kendukalai arranges to have the king watch the goddess dance through a crack in the wall. The goddess, of course, realizes what is going on and kills the unfaithful priest,[3] while the king and all his descendants are cursed to never be able to have the sight (*darśana*) of the goddess at Kāmākhyā.[4] To this day, the story goes, when the king's descendants come near the temple, they must carefully keep a distance and hold an umbrella as a screen between themselves and the temple.[5]

Both of these women dance, and in dancing, spin an enchanting web of motion for those who watch. Yet the two stories differ in how they present why and for whom the woman dances. In the classical Sāṃkhya story, the woman dancing serves the male *puruṣa*'s interests. *Prakṛti*, the primordial female, exists to fulfill his goals; she herself is simply an object, first inciting his desire and delight, and then his bored rejection. He is the center of the story, the subject viewing the world, and the dancing revolves around his needs and desires.

As the image of *prakṛti* in the metaphor avers, frequently woman in Hindu culture is represented or imagined as object, the object of male desire and male property (as we also find in the histories of Western cultures). As with *prakṛti*, her existence is meant to enhance and serve the interests of the other half of the species. And while a number of scholars have suggested that locating a sense of female empowerment and feminism in Hinduism depends upon establishing women's agency,[6] a generally typical view of woman presents her as the "second sex," dependent upon male governance. It may not be necessary to repeat here the often-quoted verse from Manu that stipulates that a woman never be allowed independence, but instead that she should be governed by her father in youth, her husband in the prime of life, and her son in old age.[7]

When the goddess at Kāmākhyā dances, however, she dances for herself, for her own delight. When she chooses, she may grant a vision of her dancing to her devotee, but this vision of her dance is hers alone to give, and may not be taken without her consent, at least not without dire consequences. The difference that the story of the goddess at Kāmākhyā encodes is a shift in the role of the woman. The vantage point of subjectivity shifts to her as woman, as a woman dancing. This goddess displays a subjectivity[8] where she controls the space of her dancing. Her actions tell us loudly that she understands her body as her own, not the property of a male guardian or spectator. That is, neither she nor her dancing serve the interests of either the king or the priest.[9]

Certainly, this representation of this goddess is not a common representation of women. She is a goddess, and beyond that, not a goddess who defers to her spouse. We might compare her iconographic representation to a well-known image that we find of the Goddess of Wealth, Lakṣmī, where Lakṣmī, who is frequently represented as about a third of the size of her husband, sits at his feet massaging them. In contrast, the goddess Kāmākhyā sits on top, her consort Kāmadeva below, in a spatial relation that illustrates her power.

The goddess Kāmākhyā is especially well known as a Tantric goddess. That is, often her devotees subscribe to a path designated as Tantra, a movement whose origins are not entirely clear, but which likely began around the fifth century CE, has continued through the present day, and has spanned a variety of religious traditions, including especially Hinduism and Buddhism. Tantra, in general, involves elaborate ritualization, and the traditions associated with the goddess at Kāmākhyā tend also to involve the elements of Tantra known as the "left-hand," the ritual praxis associated with the use of illicit substances such as liquor, and incorporating a rite involving sexual union. As her name literally translates, the "Renowned Goddess of Desire," the Tantric goddess at Kāmākhyā is, not surprisingly, especially associated textually with the Tantric rite of sexual union. Thus, when we find references in Tantric literature to rites of sexual union, we also often find reference to the worship of the goddess at Kāmākhyā, and Kāmākhyā itself as the preeminent place for the practice of these rites.

Now, typically, we find that representations of goddesses follow a pattern of bifurcation into benevolent goddesses who are married and subordinate to a male husband, and malevolent goddesses who are independent from male control and imagined as fierce.[10] In this case, the goddess Kāmākhyā, the Goddess of Love, is certainly benevolent; she could in no way be classified as a fierce deity. Yet she nevertheless manages to maintain her independence. She incorporates elements of the "fierce" goddesses, such as the acceptance of blood sacrifice, and, at the same time, she does not get carried away on a violent rampage, as Kālī often does in stories when she kills in battle, but then cannot stop her rage. Kāmākhyā's embodiment as a goddess of love, on the other hand, suggests benevolence, and her rage at the priest has a limit, as we saw in the story above; she does not also kill the king. Thus in a curious way, she manages to elude the dichotomy of these two categories, which typically hold good elsewhere.

Powerful females in Hinduism often come in the shape of Tantric goddesses. And we at times find the suggestion that powerful goddesses, on occasion and in specific contexts, translate into empowered women.[11] In fact, the image of the powerful female as Tantric goddess has made her a particular object for appropriation by specific Western groups. For instance, as Rachel McDermott notes, some advocates of Western feminism have seen in the dark goddess Kālī a model for advancing feminism in the West.[12]

However, even as we find these images of powerful goddesses in Tantra, it is not expressly apparent that the Tantric focus on the goddess has resulted in what we (as Western scholars) might recognize as an overt valorization of women in Hindu society, or even in the context of Tantra.[13] Even given the widespread popular understanding of Tantra as generally espousing congenial attitudes toward the empowerment of women, a careful examination of Tantric texts reveals that they do not always reflect images of respect toward women or a recognition of women as subjects in the way that we see men as subjects.[14] In fact, as we see below in chapter 1, one of the circa seventeenth-century texts analyzed here itself explicitly brings up the topic of whether women can act as agents and subjects within the Tantric rite. Certainly, the issue of woman's subjectivity is a charged topic, one that extends across the colonized and post-colonial third world, and in the West as well.[15]

This book addresses the representation of woman's subjectivity within one Tantric context. Drawing from a group of texts associated with Kāmākhyā, we find unexpected portraits of women and attitudes toward women. Even as they are mixed within a contradictory potpourri of other views, these images afford an intriguing recognition of women as subjects. A primary goal of this book is to present these alternative images of women that we find. Aligned with this are two other goals that this book aims to fill. I want to demonstrate that Tantric literature is by no means monolithic in its views, particularly in its views of women. That is, that Tantric literature is quite diverse and attention to this diversity may be fruitful in advancing our understanding, particularly about women's various roles in Tantra. And, specifically in appendix 1, I address the variety of attitudes toward women that we find among different Tantric texts.

Also, with this book, I especially address the problem of "talk" about women. What does it mean to read "talk" about women in books written by men in the seventeenth century, and what does it mean for *us* to talk about women who lived centuries ago, when these women themselves are silent? Thus, throughout this book I attend to "talk" about women: how this talk confines and defines notions of women's subjectivity, and with this, women's ability, or not, to speak and, finally, the implication of women's bodies in their speech.

The evidence I analyze for this study are all Sanskrit texts; all date to the fifteenth through eighteenth centuries and are located in the region of northeast India, and they have been, so far, not included in the current discussion in Western scholarship on women's roles in Tantra. The image of women they offer counters the picture of woman as object serving male interests, which the image of *prakṛti* we saw above presents. These texts borrow from other Tantric texts, and at the same time we find that they present something new; we find in them an articulation of an alternative attitude toward women, which contrasts not only with what we find generally in Hindu texts but also with what we find generally in other Tantric texts as well. Appendix 1 discusses the sources used in great detail, and appendix 2 offers a synopsis of the primary text I use, the *Great Blue Tantra* (*Bṛhannīla Tantra*).

Representations of Women

Given both the gaps in our historical understanding of northeast India in the fifteenth through eighteenth centuries, and the materials we do have available,[16] and given that these Tantric texts, which tell us that they contain secret information, are not necessarily normative in their views, it is difficult to ascertain to what degree these Tantric texts influenced public attitudes toward women.

To illustrate the difficulty here we may draw from an example taken from a different context. In her research on rivers, Anne Feldhaus notes that the view given by women, especially lower-caste women, diverges dramatically from that given by male Brahmins (and presumably, though not certainly, Brahmins or higher-caste males would have been the ones writing the late medieval texts utilized for this study). She notes that her male informants and her female informants often presented entirely disparate descriptions of the same slice of a riverbank.[17] One wonders if the texts we have here similarly miss whole slices of life because they were likely authored by only one particular segment of society, and that if lower-caste women had been authors of these texts, they might have given an entirely different perspective.

This problem is further complicated by the fact that these texts, which purport to be secret texts revealing ritual and social practices connected with the Tantric rite of sexual union, are just the sort of behavior that tends not to be recorded in public records in any case. Further, it would be difficult to argue that the evidence I present here records in any verifiable way women in their own voices,[18] or even to assess the degree to which what we find in these textual sources was reflected in historical practices. What we do have are images of women from Assamese histories, portraits gleaned from the British, and records left by the extraordinarily successful devotional movement to Viṣṇu that began in the fifteenth century. These sources offer evidence that can help to corroborate and explain what we find, but the evidence tends to be circumstantial.

This book does not propose to reconstruct actual practices from the historical context of seventeenth- or eighteenth-century Tantric circles in northeast India. Certainly, it may help us to know that a woman, Prathameśvarī, ruled in an area of this region in the early eighteenth century and may have supported some of the writers and readers of the texts consulted here with her patronage of goddess-centered Tantra. We offer here instead a study of the textual *representation* of women. That is, we address the propagation of discourse. By this I mean that we look at the ways in which women are talked about and how this talk functions as a means for constructing identities in a network of social relations that can be read as encoding relations of social power. I address the method I use in greater detail below.

As I note in chapter 2 regarding the rite of sexual union, with only textual sources as evidence, we actually only ever see "talk" about women, always a step (or more) removed from women's actual lives. What we find reveals the contours of the shadows left by women. Not the voices of women speaking, but, on the other hand, neither simple fabrication. Rather, we see traces reflected in an image, a representation of woman configured through a lens.

If the attention to discourse only indirectly offers us a portrait, one lens into this world, what it presents is nevertheless extremely valuable, both for the insights it offers as discourse and for the very challenge it presents to normative representations of women. That is, these texts reflect the emergence of a *discourse* addressing social relations between the genders, and I suggest that their importance lies in the difference, as discourse, that they offer to normative classifications.

In conjunction with this, part of my goal involves a dialectical engagement with these texts. When I first began this study with the arduous work of reading through a number of Sanskrit texts that have not yet been translated, I initially expected to find what I had encountered elsewhere in both primary[19] and secondary sources—occasional references to woman, mostly venerating her as a cosmic principle, especially as the goddess Kuṇḍalinī in the spine. However, I was surprised.

Instead I discovered interesting deviations from other Tantric representations of women. A few examples are the subtle rescripting of women as "pure spirit" instead of the more typical image of woman as body and matter, a striking deviation from the more usual male as spirit and female as body that we have come to expect from writing before the twentieth century in both India and the West.[20] Also we find images of women as gurus, as we see in chapter 1; images where woman takes the role of subject rather than object, as we see in chapter 2; and a move away from a notion of woman as objects for male gain, as we see in chapter 3.

As many specialists in Tantra know, Sanskrit Tantras are frequently not the most aesthetically appealing literary specimens. They often present a frustrating hodgepodge of elements, discussions that abruptly trail off, long and obscure (sometimes purposely so) descriptions of rites and *mantras*, at times embellished with confusingly incorrect grammar. Many of the insights I found most compelling were casually woven through a mishmash of complex ritual prescriptions in a literary form quite alien to twenty-first-century Western literary expectations. The insights and positive images of women gleaned from these texts are in no way glaring or highlighted. Hidden in some respects in these texts, and never presented with the eloquence of a writer like the brilliant eleventh-century thinker, Abhinavagupta, they are, nevertheless, striking enough to present irresistible evidence for thinking about how both we and these authors from the fifteenth through the eighteenth centuries might map gender.

So even as these images of women do not dominate within the complex profusion of diverse elements and topics we find in these texts, their very deviance from normative representations makes them especially interesting as a point of study. This study then is not a study of these texts as a whole. I particularly focus on those elements that lend themselves to a theoretical engagement on issues of gender.

So in some cases, as for instance, in chapter 3, which addresses the wife as the preferred partner for the Tantric rite of sexual union, I focus explicitly on the unusual presentation of the wife as the partner precisely because it offers a contrasting view of woman and one that offers space for conceptual reflection on issues of gender, even though it is admittedly only found in two of the eight texts I consult here.[21]

Along these lines, one major goal of this study is to tease out the deeper theoretical implications inherent in these representations of woman. The first chapter, most explicitly, details representations of women in a straightforward fashion. However, the following chapters all offer greater reflection upon how what we find in these texts may impact our own ways of thinking about gender, as well as how our ways of thinking about gender might apply to the insights offered by these texts, especially as implicated in notions of women's speech.

Specifically, we see particular, and in some cases uncommon, views of gender that may help us to think about gender for the West. For instance, in chapter 1, alongside the more common and typical understanding of gender as a male-female binary, we see also a model that offers the category of women as one among four other groups, a separate group classed along with the four other castes. Thinking of gender in these more complicated terms may help to rescript our own ideas away from an agonistic model, which the notion of two often entails.[22]

Similarly, in chapters 2 and 3 we note how the rite of sexual union is configured to move away from a model where women function as objects for male gain or male property. And, in chapter 2, where we examine the rite of sexual union, we note also a shift away from a model of male ascetic mastery over the body and over women. Interestingly, while much Tantric practice promises precisely a mastery over the body and the physical elements, the practice of revering women, which I discuss in chapter 1, does not offer magical power over the body or the elements, but simply promises eloquence in speech.

In chapter 4 we examine a myth that discusses the birth of the feminine *mantra* (*vidyā*). In this myth we find that feminine speech is "bodied" speech, incorporating a fusion of the word and the dancing-bodied goddess named by the word, a fusion that entails a disruption of the notion of the logocentricity of language. And in chapter 5 we see a myth where the Blue Goddess of Speech is silenced through male violence. With this we find a way of viewing the violation of woman that does not either blame or stigmatize the woman for being the object of male violence. These visions from a precolonial period in India offer food for thought in our own twenty-first-century attempts to think and rethink gender.

We also notice a coherency that gets articulated in different registers—on the level of explicit statements on woman and women, on the level of ritual gesture, and on the level of narrative, that is, in stories that reflect images of woman. Thus, we see that what the "Kālī Practice" discussed in chapter 1 encodes prescriptively, in its eschewal of all rules except treating women with respect, the rite addressed in chapter 2 encodes gesturally, for instance, through the ritual placement of male and female bodies. Likewise, the story of Vasiṣṭha, with its repudiation of male ascetic mastery, which we address in chapter 2, metaphorically enacts this through narrative.

Throughout, I address this issue of representation from two angles, from what these texts say about women and from what they say about goddesses. Both of these angles are important, especially since at times we find the suggestion that the two categories are incommensurable.[23] At this point I will describe the forms these representations of women take.

How Women Are Represented as Subjects

I mentioned earlier that the particular strand of Tantra I discuss here presents an exception to what we find elsewhere in Hindu Sanskrit sources, and even to what we find in Hindu Tantric sources. This different attitude toward women gets recorded in three distinct ways. The first is relatively straightforward; it consists of explicit pronouncements. This includes statements that explicitly include women in active and important roles, such as women as gurus. This also includes statements enjoining that women should be initiated. The examples I draw from expressly affirm a space for women as actors in any case textually, and for women occupying socially important roles traditionally only available to men.[24] Here one might also mention rites like that which we find in the *Sarvavijayi Tantra*, a text mostly concerned with herbal spells, which at one point, however, clearly addresses a woman practitioner, telling her how to perform a ritual, using a variety of substances like lemons, lotus flowers, and so on, in order to get control over her husband and make him her slave.[25]

The second manner in which women are recognized as subjects consists of explicit statements according either respect or importance or both to women.[26] For instance, as we see in chapter 1, we find textual prescriptions for treating women with respect and which declare women's particular facility in mastering *mantras* as a reason for treating women with respect. Also included in this second category are physical, gestural statements of reverence for women, such as bowing to a woman, which, incidentally, we do not find in earlier, more well-known texts such as the *Kulārṇava Tantra* or the *Kaulajñānanirṇaya*. I link the physical gesture with the statement of praise since these types of statements are proximate in the texts. These I discuss in chapter 1 and again in chapter 2 in the context of a version of the rite of sexual union that works to recode attitudes toward women and diverges from earlier presentations of the rite.

In this second category, women are not depicted expressly as actors, but are talked about in terms that praise women and prescribe that the practitioner should treat women in ways that respect women's bodies and wishes. This again, is not common in earlier Tantric texts like the *Kulārṇava Tantra* or the *Kaulajñānanirṇaya*. This, I suggest, places women in the role of subject, through the view, however, of the texts' (likely, though not certainly, male) authors.

The third category consists of images we find of women and the feminine via story. An analysis of these stories, especially focusing on the attitudes toward females, in this case goddesses, reveals much of interest regarding male responses to the feminine and women. Most of these stories come from the *Bṛhannīla Tantra* (the "*Great Blue Tantra*"), a long text and the primary text consulted for this study. A synopsis of this text is included in appendix 2. The characters in these stories, as we often find elsewhere in Tantric literature, are composed almost exclusively of otherworldly personages, gods, goddesses, and demons. At the same time the stories present templates for human behavior. Just as the myth of the god Śiva's beheading of the god Brahmā more generally acts as a prototype for human behavior for the sect of the skull-carrying Kāpālikas,[27] similarly the stories we encounter, of Vasiṣṭha in chapter 2, of the gods in chapter 4, and of the Blue Goddess of Speech in chapter 5, instantiate a prescriptive model that would presumably be adopted by the human devotees of these deities.

One interesting feature to note here is that some of these images surprise us. For instance, in chapter 5 we address the story of how the Goddess of Speech turns blue. In this story, while the Blue Goddess of Speech functions as an independent goddess, not the consort of another male god, she also is not a fierce goddess, nor a physically impervious or powerful warrior goddess.[28] Rather, the myth depicts her frailty—without making her a consort of a male god—and counsels a humane way of treating a woman, in this case the Blue Goddess of Speech, who is unable to fend off male violence.

In what follows below, first we briefly look at the Sanskrit texts consulted for this study. These are addressed in much greater detail in appendix 1, and I offer a synopsis of the primary text used, *The Great Blue Tantra* (*Bṛhannīla Tantra*), in appendix 2. Following this I offer a brief description of each of the book's chapters. After this I address methodological issues, including the question of how to read texts for images of gender when the texts are presumably not authored by women and the methodological influences for this study.

Sources

The texts I cite here are all Sanskrit Tantric texts—titularly self-identified as Tantras, and also contain explicitly Tantric elements[29]: ritual prescriptions, discussion of the six Tantric acts,[30] emphasis on *mantras*, aspects they share with other Tantric texts. They are also generally classified as Tantric texts in the extant scholarship.[31]

However, the group of texts I analyze here, and especially the *Bṛhannīla Tantra*, offers an uncommon view of women, and, along with this, a systematic and coherent cultivation of a respectful attitude toward women. This attitude is designated as part of a specific practice centered around women called the "Kālī Practice," which I discuss below. This view and attitude toward women is not typically presented among the many and various texts generally classified as Hindu Tantric texts in Sanskrit, even as we at times in some earlier Tantric texts see snippets reflecting inchoate precursors to elements of the view we find in the texts consulted here. In appendix 1 I discuss the texts used here and the differences they present to other texts. And, of course, the group of texts consulted here offers a view that differs from classical Sanskrit texts, such as, for example, Manu's *Dharma Śāstra* and what we find in Vedic Sanskrit texts.[32] I should emphasize that these texts, like many other Tantric texts, probably had several compilers and certainly present a tangled weave of all sorts of ritual, social, and philosophic prescriptions.

The main text I draw from for this study is: (1) *Bṛhannīla Tantra* (BT), a 256-page text based in part on an earlier and shorter published version entitled the *Nīla Tantra* (NT).[33] I analyze this long text extensively and draw most of the myths I discuss below from this text. Appendix 2 offers a synopsis of the *Bṛhannīla Tantra*. I also draw from a selection of other texts, especially in outlining the "Kālī Practice" in chapter 1. These texts include:

2. *Cīnācāra Tantra* (CT)
3. *Gandharva Tantra* (GT)
4. *Gupta Sādhana Tantra* (GST)
5. *Māyā Tantra* (MT)
6. *Nīlasarasvatī Tantra* (NST)
7. *Phetkāriṇī Tantra* (PhT)
8. *Yoni Tantra* (YT)[34]

These texts share a number of formal features, suggesting that we understand them in terms of a particular historical movement. Their common features pertain to:

(a) location. I discuss this in greater detail in appendix 1.

(b) approximate dating. I discuss this also in greater detail in appendix 1.

Further, all the texts consulted include some mention of "left-handed" Tantra, that is, specifically, the inclusion of the five substances known as the Five "Ms." The "Five Ms" are a list of five socially illicit elements used in the transgressive ritual. Each of the words in Sanskrit begins with the letter *m*. The list includes meat (*māṃsa*), fish (*matsya*), liquor (*madya*), parched grain (*mudrā*), and sexual intercourse (*maithuna*). In chapter 3 I also discuss an interesting variation of this list of five substances found in the BT, but not elsewhere among Tantric texts.

Most of these texts consider the pilgrimage site of Kāmākhyā in Assam as preeminent, and include a panegyric to Kāmākhyā.[35] As we see in chapter 2, the story where Vasiṣṭha learns the rite of sexual union as part of the practice of revering women takes place in Kāmākhyā. Also, the title for the *Bṛhannīla Tantra*, which translates as the "Great Blue Tantra," refers on the one hand to the Blue Goddess of Speech, but is also likely a reference to the Blue Hill (*Nīla parvata, Nīlācala*) in Kāmākhyā, particularly since this text references the blue hill in Kāmākhyā.[36] In the myth that tells of the genesis of Kāmākhyā, the god Śiva, in his grief over the death of his wife Satī, wanders all over the continent of India, carrying his wife's dead body on his shoulders while the god Viṣṇu sneaks behind him chopping off the limbs of Satī's corpse one by one, to remove the visible emblem of Śiva's grief. As the limbs fall to earth, the sex organ of the goddess Satī lands in Kāmākhyā. Where it falls the earth turns blue and becomes known as the Blue Hill.

Another common feature we see is a particular practice that entails getting rid of all rules except for one: treating women with veneration and respect.This practice, called the "Kālī Practice," is discussed in chapter 1.

We see also one unique verse, replicated across several texts within this genre, but which I have not come across elsewhere either in general Hindu sources or in general Śākta sources, such as the *Devī Māhātmya*. This verse reads "women are Gods, women are the life breath." Notably, many of these texts reference the *Devī Māhātmya* and some, such as the *Māyā Tantra* (3.12–3.20) directly quote the *Devī Māhātmya*.[37] Nor have I found the verse elsewhere among Hindu Tantric sources—and not even in much earlier Tantric sources such as the *Kulacūḍāmaṇi Tantra* (KCT) or the *Kulārṇava Tantra* (KuT), from which some of these eight texts borrow extensively. Given the verse's repetition across several texts, and given that many of these texts do borrow from older sources, what is probably most interesting is the singular absence of this verse elsewhere among older Hindu Tantric sources, and particularly its absence in other "left-handed" Tantric texts not from this time period. While the verse is not reproduced in all of the texts consulted here, it nevertheless nearly always accompanies, when it is found, the elements of the "Kālī Practice," which we find in these eight texts.

Also with some variation, and greater or lesser frequency the same goddesses keep popping up. Particularly important are Nīlasarasvatī (the Blue Goddess of Speech), Tārā/Tāriṇī, and Kālī.

Finally, one more point of interest—these texts have not been translated yet into English, or other European languages,[38] however all of them have been published in India. Several have been published multiple times; for instance, the *Bṛhannīla* and its earlier version, the *Nīla Tantra*, has been published five times since the 1880s, and the *Gandharva Tantra* four times. That none are manuscripts suggests that at least for an indigenous audience they have been considered important enough to merit space on the printed page—and from a publisher's point of view, an expectation of an audience in India interested in buying these texts, an expectation voiced also in the eminent Tantric scholar V. V. Dvivedi's mention of the popularity (*lokapriyatā*) of several of these texts.[39]

In appendix 1 I discuss in much greater detail the sources consulted for this study, and why I chose these texts and not other Tantric texts. Briefly here, I examined a number of other Tantric texts in the course of this research and found that Tantric texts are by no means uniform in their attitudes toward women. One finds a variety of views and some of the differences may be attributable to when and where the texts were written. Earlier texts in particular present important differences from a later text like the BT. For instance, a number of earlier texts, such as those referenced by David White in his superb study on Tantra,[40] present images of women that are more tangibly ambivalent, with women as dangerous devouring females. In appendix 1 I compare the texts consulted here to other Tantric texts and locate these texts within the context of other Tantric writing, as well as discuss how the historical context of the time and region may have facilitated what we find in these texts.

The Cast of Goddesses

All of these texts are framed as a dialogue between the god Śiva and his wife Pārvatī. Nearly always the role of the interlocutor is limited to a simple question that occasions a long discourse given usually by the god Śiva. Within this outer frame we sometimes find stories recounted where the goddess is instructing a god, either Śiva or Brahmā or a sage, usually Vasiṣṭha or Nārada. Vasiṣṭha is important because, as we saw earlier, he has a crucial role in the propagation of the sexual practice associated with Kāmākhyā. The presence of Nārada indicates a Vaiṣṇava connection.[41] Also, occasionally the frame itself has the goddess instructing the god Śiva.[42] In this respect we also at times find traces of older versions cropping up where the primary narrator of a text shifts without warning and we suddenly have the goddess giving instruction to Śiva, which is often then swallowed up in another gender-bending shift where the male god abruptly becomes the narrator again.[43] These confused traces, these moments where the voice of authority shifts its gender not only suggest that the texts were compilations transformed through various incarnations but also that some of these texts' redactors had conflicting ideas about which gender could most appropriately reveal the teachings of these secret Tantras.

The bulk of these texts are devoted to ritual prescriptions; some space is also given over to telling myths about deeds performed by the goddesses and gods. In most of the myths presented, it is primarily a goddess who wields the power and who saves the gods from all sorts of calamities, with an occasional exception. I discuss one particular exception in chapter 5 where Viṣṇu fulfills the role of saviour. More specifically, however, not all goddesses fulfill this role. Rather, only a few goddesses possess incomparable sovereignty, chiefly, in this group of texts, Nīlasarasvatī (the Blue Goddess of Speech), Tārā/Tāriṇī, and Kālī. These three particular goddesses, the Blue Goddess of Speech, Tārā/Tāriṇī, and Kālī are seen as a unity. One should never, the BT declares, see these three goddesses as separate from one another unless one wants to risk going to hell (BT 22.171). Tārā/Tāriṇī and Nīlasarasvatī/Nīlā here (BT 2.46) and elsewhere are seen as nearly identical, both in the visualizations of these two and in the frequent interchange of their names, although the Blue Goddess of Speech is on occasion visualized with blue eyes, unlike Tārā.[44] Though the BT enjoins us to see these three as one, Kālī appears to be slightly less identified with these two goddesses; Tārā and the Blue Goddess of Speech are usually visualized as young and full bodied, while Kālī is more frequently imagined as unattractively skinny. In appendix 2 I give a long visualization of the Blue Goddess of Speech, also called Tāriṇī in this context. Also of interest, we find that the "Kālī Practice" mentioned above, for the CT, should be followed in the worship of Kālī and Tārā, whereas in the worship of Bhairavī and Sundarī, a different procedure applies (CT 2.37–2.38). Also, the Blue Goddess of Speech and Tārā are frequently glossed as the "Goddess of Great Illusion," Mahā-Māyā, and this name is also connected to the goddess Kāmākhyā, the "Renowned Goddess of Desire."

Occasionally added to this list are Tripurā, Aniruddha-Sarasvatī (the unstoppable Goddess of Speech), Annapūrṇā, the Goddess of Food, and the goddess Kāmākhyā as a form of both Kālī, Tripurā, the Goddess of Great Illusion, that is, Mahā-Māyā, and, less frequently, Bhairavī. One also finds references to the well-known list of ten goddesses, the *daśamahāvidyā*. The story of the birth of the feminine *mantra* (*vidyā*) likely refers to this group of goddesses, and indeed Tārā, Tripurā, and Kālī are often members of this list, yet as a group of ten they are only occasionally mentioned and not central to the ritual procedure, while the Blue Goddess of Speech, Tārā, and Kālī are specifically and consistently accorded a place of eminence.

Contents of the Chapters

Briefly here I will summarize the contents of the chapters that follow this introduction. In chapter 1 we address women as actors within the context of the group of texts consulted here. In particular, I examine a form of Tantric practice, named the "Kālī Practice," represented in these texts from the fifteenth through eighteenth centuries, which attaches importance to women's abilities in spiritual pursuits—acknowledging women as practitioners and as gurus and which advocates treating women with respect.[45] The representation of women as actors suggests a social space beyond the text, and interacting with the texts, which, in turn, influences the writers of these texts to incorporate women in these roles in the writing. In a circuit of mutual influence, this writing both sanctions these attitudes toward women and directs the readers of these texts to implement these images of women as gurus and practitioners. While we must acknowledge that these textual representations of women acting in powerful, socially important roles remain textual images, nevertheless they institute a discourse, a kind of "talk" about women that sets up the terms for redefining women's identities in ways that point to women as subjects.

In this chapter I also present evidence that suggests that the model for understanding the veneration of women in these texts finds a parallel in the veneration of the Brahmin. This model, which likens women as a class to the Brahmin, is important especially because it offers a model of gender that is not based upon a binary. Of the five chapters in this book, this is the most straightforward in its presentation of evidence, since it uses explicit statements about women's position in society.

The rite of sexual union is a part of the "Kālī Practice" discussed in chapter 1. Chapter 2 addresses the Tantric rite of sexual union as we find it in the BT. In this chapter I present a case against the current prevalent scholarly notion that sex in Tantra universally functions to construct women as objects for male gains. I suggest that we find in this group of texts a configuration of the Tantric rite that reimagines its Tantric attitude toward women. Rather than a scenario where women are the means through which male practitioners attain some goal, the rite depicted here functions to place the woman in the subject position. In this context we also find that the rite moves away from a notion of ascetic mastery over the body and women.

This chapter also especially explores the theoretical dimensions of what it means to portray a rite involving sex in a textual source. As Raheja and Gold note in their research on women's songs, language about sex—what one male informant called "obscene" language—was frequently used in women's songs to "voice potent critiques of prevailing gender ideologies."[46] In the somewhat different context explored here, "talk" about sex functions also to reconfigure gendered hierarchies. This chapter is consequently very much about how we enact identity, and especially about how sex and language—and language about sex—gets employed in this process.

Chapter 3 analyzes an uncommon practice found in the BT and the GT, which prefers the wife as partner in the Tantric rite of sexual union. Through this particular representation of the rite we see that what is "transgressive" about the wife as partner is a disruption of normative relations between the genders. This disruption recodes the rite of sexual union as a social subversion and one that occurs in terms of gender. That is, the articulation of the female as an unassimilable difference, rather than the act of sex with one's wife, is what makes this rite "illicit." Especially in this chapter I discuss the representation of woman as the sign of what is different from the male, and that the responses to this difference in this rite are not to erase the difference by making women fit into the bipolar categories of either independent "witches" or docile, dependent "good wives." The bipolar categorization keeps these two categories separate and opposed. Here in this chapter we find how in the rite with the wife the two categories come to be integrated. This chapter indirectly addresses the issue of women's speech, through looking at underlying ways that meaning gets constructed through this rite, which offers an alternative to a bipolar system of categorization. Related to this, and a consequence of it, is that the advocacy of the wife as partner in the Tantric rite of sexual union undoes the more typical coding of women as male property.

Chapter 4 takes up issues addressed in chapter 2 with language about sex, and in chapter 3 with the identity of the wife as a faithful wife, a *satī*. Specifically, chapter 4 examines feminine magical speech, the *vidyā*. We look at a myth in the BT, which tells the tale where the Blue Goddess of Speech gives birth to the feminine word, twelve goddesses who are bodied speech (*vidyā*). Here we explore the relationship between the female body and language coded as feminine. In this context feminine magical speech, as *vidyā*, links both with notions of the body and with bodied feminine speech as performative speech. Here also we examine some of the BT's statements about the feminine principle of nature, and how in the BT both nature and speech coded as feminine undermine a notion of logocentricity. The vision that the BT presents here is an interesting and uncommon valorization of nature as feminine (*prakṛti*), which is otherwise in the classical Indian tradition devalued as insentient matter.

Chapter 5 expands the discussion of women's speech by looking at a myth in the BT that literally enacts the silencing of the Goddess of Speech. With this myth, which tells the tale of how the Blue Goddess of Speech became blue, we see an implicit discourse on violence toward women. What we find in this precolonial myth is a poignant sensitivity to the problem of violence toward women and how this violence makes speech an impossibility. A mute world ensues. Especially, this myth offers the possibility of an alternative response to violence toward women. To flesh out the differences this myth's response proposes, I compare it to a British response to violence toward women in the colonial period.

Chapter 5 suggests a notion of woman as subject by taking the perspective of the woman in instances of violence toward women. The myth from the BT told here subverts our initial narrative expectations. That is, the story of an abduction of a woman typically unfolds a tale of masculine heroics, where the male hero, through his prowess, wins back the woman as prize, which, as we cannot help noting, encodes the woman throughout as property, object as prize. Instead, the story in the BT takes a different tack, one that shifts to the perspective of the woman and her response, her feelings and anxieties about loss incurred through male violence on her person. In this sense we see the subjectivity of woman by seeing the story with its ramifications through her eyes.

Within this book, this chapter in particular offers what A. K. Ramanujan sees as a thematic element of women's stories, that is, stories told for and to women. The defining element of women's stories is that they address concerns that women have, as opposed to men's concerns.[47] Here, the story focuses on violence to women, but, more than this, in this context, the notion of violence and defilement is especially coded as a theme that concerns women: the loss of physical beauty. The resolution the tale offers is particularly humane, and one that recognizes women as subjects rather than objects in the drama of violence.

Following a short conclusion are two appendixes. Appendix 1 offers a detailed analysis of representations of women across a spectrum of Tantric texts, to help situate the texts selected for this study. Appendix 2 gives a synopsis of the *Bṛhannīla Tantra*, the primary text used for this study.

Each of the chapters in this book addresses a distinct though related manifestation of women's subjectivity, especially as it becomes configured within issues of speech about women and the relationship between women's speech and their bodies. Two of the chapters here, chapter 3 on wives as the preferred partner for the rite of sexual union, and chapter 2 on this rite, which is a focal part of the Kālī Practice, explicitly address women's identity constructed through sexuality. As Doranne Jacobson and Susan Wadley note, the themes of "female chastity and control of sexuality . . . are crucial elements of any discussion of women in India,"[48] and I think that the link we find in the group of texts used here between the rite of sexual union and a reimagining of women's status is not merely coincidental, but an integral connection. And, as

I note in chapter 2, this connection emerges explicitly for the author of the BT, where we find a link between the rite of sexual union and an ethic against war. In this sense the construction of gender participates in a larger social and political discourse.

One point I should make here: while I would not rule out the possibility of reading some portions of these texts' depictions of rites and stories involving women as metaphors for an esoteric practice cultivating a relationship with the goddess or women as an inner principle, such as the *kuṇḍalinī*,[49] the portions I have selected to analyze appear to be best read as exoteric rites involving real people, that is, women, and cultivating external behaviors and attitudes toward these other breathing, bodied humans. Unlike some texts from the Śrī Vidyā tradition, or some elements of the nondual Śaiva traditions from Kashmir that do, in fact, more readily lend themselves to an esoteric reading of inner experience and goddesses, the portions of these texts I focus on appear most coherent if one reads them as talking about actual rites involving sexual practice.[50] For these particular texts, adopting wholesale a method for reading that esotericizes as metaphor the rites involving women may avoid the uncomfortable suggestion that rites involving sex may have actually occurred, but it does not do justice to these particular texts; what such a reading does is, from the very outset, exclude even the possibility of seeing these texts as traces marking the imprints of women as actors in this late medieval society.

Methodology

To make my method clear it may be most transparent to begin by saying what I am not doing. First, and probably most important, I am not looking for, or trying to recover, women's voices. This focal strategy of much feminist work is eloquently argued by Miranda Shaw in her work on women's roles in Tibetan Buddhism. Outlining her strategy and goals for her study on women in medieval Buddhism, she tells us,

> One of my operative principles is to view women as active shapers of history and interpreters of their own experience rather than as passive objects or the victims of history. Women had powers of assent and dissent and were users and interpreters of symbols, performers and innovators of ritual and meditation practices, writers and teachers, religious specialists, and enlightened preceptors. My intent has been insofar as possible to discover and present the agency,

> creativity and self-understanding of the women of Tantric Buddhism. . . . Thus this study participates in an effort to recover women's own religious writings, views, practices, and self-understanding.[51]

Shaw offers us with her work texts written by women and historical accounts of women's views of Tantric practices. By recovering women as writers of texts Shaw gives us images of women that overturn stereotypes of women as passive, as objects used by male Tibetan practitioners. This attempt to afford women agency by recovering their views, through their own words, is an important strategy in feminist studies on gender, one that is widely used, and one that I fully support, but one that is not particularly suited for the sources I draw from. This ambiguity of the textual sources is not, however, the primary reason why my strategy and goals differ from Shaw's.

Yet in any case, to elucidate one difficulty encountered in recovering women's voices from my anonymously authored texts, it may be useful to draw from an argument that Wendy Doniger makes. For Doniger, gender is both too simple and too blurry a category when it comes to mapping the complexity of human relations. Men can at times feel and think and write like women and women can feel and think and write like men, making it very difficult to determine whose gendered voice we hear in an anonymous text. For Doniger, "it is time to stop asking whose voice is the author of the text"[52] because the problems associated with the search are legion. For my group of texts, which reflect complex and at times contradictory images, prescriptions, and stories, and which likely had multiple anonymous authors, the problem is further exacerbated.

Separate from this concern, and more to the point, with this study I especially focus upon the role that discourse plays in the construction of female identity, a different sort of project than one seeking to present women's voices. That is, the goals and strategies of this book are different from those of Miranda Shaw's admirable and eloquent work especially because my interest in these texts is less in finding and authenticating the voices of women in these texts and more in examining the dynamic of "talk" that maps the world into the categories of gender in the first place.

By discourse I mean models that direct the coding of the terms into a syntax, both linguistic and social, which orders the relations between the terms. So words like "women" (*striyaḥ*) and "the rite of sexual union" (*latā sādhana*, *maithuna*) form elements of a conceptual framework, which affectively prescribes the interaction between these terms. In my use of discourse especially I want to highlight that, as used here, discourse allows for a fluid interaction between the opaque and yet assumed presence of persons beyond the purview of the text interacting with, internalizing, and negotiating identities through the text's articulations of identities. Here I find useful a definition that Raheja and Gold give in articulating my own approach: "A discourse-centered approach' to language and culture has been proposed as a perspective capable of encompassing attention to the agency of particularly positioned speakers and actors, to the relationship between culture as a system of shared meanings and culture as a set of contested and negotiated meanings."[53]

Further, in my use of the notion of discourse, I want to highlight as well how a discourse emerges through specific pronouncements, through stories told in the texts, or through prescriptive discussions of how one should act, both ritually and nonritually. In this sense discourse is a kind of "talk" that enfolds within it a complex world of relations. I would stress as well that the idea of discourse, especially conveyed through specific stories, entails the possibility of negotiating and shifting identities. Here again Raheja and Gold are helpful when they suggest that discourse "views societies not primarily in terms of structural fixities but in terms of the processes through which relationships are constructed, negotiated, and contested."[54]

Keeping this in mind, I can begin to address here what I *am* doing. One primary strategy I employ for this project is especially to highlight areas where these medieval texts contest received portraits of women's identities, in the process negotiating new ways for us as scholars in the twenty-first century to be open to the diversity of women's images. So, for instance, I note in chapter 1 where the model of women does not follow the more typical gender binary, and which does not lump women in with the lowest caste, *śūdras*, but rather where the model is rewritten. Similarly, chapter 2 explores a story in the CT that offers a model of spiritual practice that rejects the pervasive stereotype of practitioner as ascetic. Likewise, in chapter 3 the practice with the wife as partner for the rite of sexual union offers a model that subverts the more generally pervasive view of wives as property. Of the five chapters in this book, the myth related in chapter 4 offers less by way of a contesting model in its constructions of gender than the other chapters, since it relies upon a gendered binary model in its assumptions about speech. However, even given the implicit binary model, the myth addressed here, along with some of the BT's conceptual pronouncements on nature (*prakṛti*, always feminine and aligned to matter), undoes the negative stereotype more typically attached to women's speech and suggests a challenge to a logocentric opposition of the word and the flesh. The myth explored in chapter 5 offers a renegotiation of women's identity by offering an atypical, and, we might add, uncommonly humanistic, example for addressing violence to women.

I would add that I am not offering intentionally provocative readings of these texts; rather, I select specific elements from these texts, which add provocative food for thought for our own analyses of gender. One of my goals is to tease out the ramifications of the ideas and representations of women, and especially to map out representations of women's abilities to speak, or not.

Having said all this, I should add that this project in one respect follows in Shaw's footsteps. That is, in chapter 1 I give evidence for the recognition of women as gurus and as practitioners, something that Shaw finds in the Tibetan Buddhist context, even as the primary impetus of my work apart from chapter 1 lies more in highlighting the creative reconfigurations of gender by my texts' authors. In short, however, this project seeks to complement both the work by Shaw, as well as a number of other excellent studies that draw from folk traditions, Sanskrit texts,[55] vernacular texual traditions, and contemporary traditions and insights gained from fieldwork, which offer us other models of women through women's voices. Ann Grodzins Gold and Gloria Goodwin Raheja's work on rural north India and Kathleen Erndl's work have been helpful examples for this author, and much other fine work in this regard exists.[56]

My other goal with this book is to address the problem of "talk" about women. That is, what does it mean to talk about women, for us today, and for our (presumably) male authors on the other side of the world, several centuries ago, when the women we talk about are not the authors and speakers of this talk?[57] Thus, the overarching hermeneutic that drives this project and emerges within each of the chapters below is a return to the question of women's talk and especially how we find that women's bodies are complicit in the "speaking" and the lack of speaking that women do.

Each of the chapters below addresses the problems entailed in "talk" of or about women and how this talk necessarily is implicated in women's bodies. Underpinning my hermeneutic are models and insights drawn especially from the work of Rajeshwari Sunder Rajan and Judith Butler. With this, I begin from the premise that the models of "imagined" women inform and form the practices that "real" women engage in.

As Sunder Rajan articulates it:

> Our understanding of the problems of "real" women cannot lie outside the "imagined" constructs in and through which "women" emerge as subjects. . . . Culture then, viewed as the product of the beliefs and conceptual models of society and as the destination where the trajectory of its desires takes shape, as by which these are structured, is the constitutive realm of the subject. As a result, culture

> appears as the chief matter and consequence of dominant ideological investment, powerfully coercive in shaping the subject; but since it is also heterogeneous, changing and open to interpretation, it can become a site of contestation and consequently of the reinscription of subjectivities.[58]

My contention here is that these Sanskrit texts, written by presumably male authors, nevertheless stand as products reflecting and producing conceptual models about women for this period. As cultural products they shape understandings of women and as a consequence, as Sunder Rajan points out in the quote above, they in turn may also contribute to shaping the articulations of identities women make of themselves. Even as texts provide the terms used in the articulation of self-identities, we also find that these identities are challenged and reconceived. What is especially key about the Sanskrit texts I draw from here is the way they also reinscribe and transform the images we see of women's subjectivity. Thus, I especially dwell upon the implications that arise from the shifts in the models the texts give. These shifts alert us to the fact that Tantric literature is diverse; this diversity extends to its representations of women, and this very diversity points to the places where we might find challenges contesting women's images and rescripting women's identities.

I should note here also that I use the terms *subject* and *subjectivity* not so much as a designation of some sort of "real" entity—certainly there are considerable philosophical and cultural problems entailed in assigning this notion to a nonmodern, non-Western context. So, instead of this study being about real or historical subjects, I, rather, point to a designation that signifies a slippery but rhetorically and linguistically effective and prevalent category. That is, we deal here with representations, imagined constructions that nevertheless have the power to engender certain types of behaviors, and that here particularly take on positive coding as venerable, powerful persons within a world of social interactions.

With this, I do not make the larger claim of women expressing agency; that would go beyond the evidence available here. Further, however, I think that Butler's problematization of the idea of a subject as originating agent in acts of speech is useful in thinking about the problems entailed in notions of agency. Butler suggests that our legal system imputes agency to the speaker where it does not in fact exist. She suggests that speech, rather, always functions as a recirculation of other speech, already spoken, inflected with variations in each of its speakers. Thus speech does not point to an originating subject of that speech, but instead to a subject who participates in an already given speech.[59] Given the nature of our Tantric texts, with many authors and with statements borrowed from elsewhere, incorporated and variously inflected, her comments seem especially apropos. Her problematization of the notion of the subject as agent is one that is incorporated in the demarcation of the limits of this study. With this, my contention is also that understanding women through representations of them, rather than through an idea of agency, in its own way also deconstructs a notion of women as "the victims of history" as Shaw offers in the quote above.

Further, I focus especially on language, "talk" about women and the ways in which women are able to speak, or not, because, like Butler, I see language and the representations of women and their identities in language as fundamental in marking out the possibilities for women. That is, the representations we have of women set the very terms of the possible for the roles that women can take. As Butler puts it,

> Who are "we" such that without language we cannot be, and what does it mean "to be" within language? . . . If the subject who speaks is also constituted by the language that she or he speaks, then language is the condition of possibility for the speaking subject, and not merely its instrument of expression. This means that the subject has its own "existence" implicated in a language that precedes and exceeds the subject, a language whose historicity includes a past and future that exceeds that of the subject who speaks. And yet, this "excess" is what makes possible the speech of the subject.[60]

Thus, women as subjects in the texts I draw from are situated in a language that is not their own, and yet the identities of women are constituted through this language that precedes and excludes them. However, this language that exceeds the woman as subject also offers something more in its very ability to exceed the intended meanings of each of its particular iterations. As Butler suggests, the power of language to enable subjectivity derives from its variations, from the differences it proposes from other particular instances of language. I would suggest that especially in the differential of images that arise, in the inflections that we find within the representations of women we may also recover a subjectivity for women. For this reason also I am specifically interested in bringing to light other models for women's roles, models that upset business as usual and offer a greater diversity of possibilities for the ways we can imagine women.

In this understanding, my analysis is framed with a critical theoretical lens that views the notion of subjectivity as a set of relations and necessarily in flux. Identity is, I suggest with these readings, malleable and scripted, and especially gendered identity is constructed through the representations of discourse.

My reading is feminist insofar as it allows us new portraits, portraits that shift the underlying differentials of power encoded in the ways that relations between the genders get represented. What it affords is an image of the subject not founded upon the notion of a universal male subject but rather suggests the possibility of recognizing a variety of female images.

Thus, this book is not an attempt to recover women's voices, but it does attempt to propose a subjectivity for women, a subjectivity woven within textual representations of women, and especially one that emerges through the differences these texts offer in their stories and their pronouncements. With this, we see how the indigenous voices in these texts mapped their own strategies of rewriting women's identities. The differences from other Hindu texts and other Sanskrit Tantric texts that we find in these texts' images of female identity suggest we and they—our authors from the fifteenth through eighteenth centuries—might at times imagine gender identity in terms other than those to which we, or they, have been accustomed. This reading of women's subjectivity is not, I suggest, merely a twenty-first-century importation. As we see in chapter 2, at certain places it would be hard not to ascribe some awareness to these texts' authors themselves of how discourse may be used to reconfigure identity and, in particular, gender identity.

To illustrate this point, a story that Jan Schoterman recounts from the *Bṛhadyoni Tantra*, a larger recension of the *Yoni Tantra* used in this study, is apt. This story tells of the god Kṛṣṇa's birth on earth and how he began wearing the peacock feather.[61] The amorous god Kṛṣṇa who is depicted frequently as the young lover, playing his flute, luring the young cow-herding women to dance with him in the forest at night, is ubiquitously iconographically depicted with a flute and a peacock feather. The story tells us that Kṛṣṇa is in reality a woman, the Goddess of Great Illusion, Mahā-Māyā.

While in heaven she desires to take birth on earth, and she comes down to earth in the male form of Kṛṣṇa. When she comes down to earth she must hide her yoni, her sex organ, so she hides it in the tail of the male peacock, making its brilliant colorful design. When Kṛṣṇa is a young boy he sees the tail of the peacock and recognizes his yoni, his female sex organ, hidden there, and so dons the peacock feather on the top of his head.

This gender-bending twist on identity encodes more than one interesting theoretical supposition. Especially important for our purposes, we note that gender is not particularly fixed, but instead rather malleable. Beyond this, this story offers a surprising coding of being, particularly for us in the twenty-first century, accustomed as we are to Freudian conceptions of gender, in that it recognizes the female sex organ not as a hole, a lack, as Freud suggested, but rather as a surplus of being that defines the female. In this sense, Kṛṣṇa is fully himself only when he recovers what was missing, his female sex organ. In proposing the basis of Kṛṣṇa's identity—Kṛṣṇa's "real" identity—as female, this recoding slyly posits reconfiguring the feminine as the "real" or normative mode of identity. With this it offers a way of reframing female identity away from mere object. This precolonial tale does not explicitly invoke theoretical language to make a case for understanding a different model of female being, nor does Schoterman in his retelling explore the implications, yet the tale employs discourse, story as narrative, to rewrite the way we understand gender.

I

The "Kālī Practice"

Rereading Women's Roles in Tantra

Does a woman herself worship the *yoni*?

—Pārvatī's question to Śiva, *Yoni Tantra*

On the peaks of the holy mountain, Mount Kailas, the center of the world, the god Śiva and his wife Pārvatī discuss the secrets of Tantric practice. In the middle of talking about a Tantric rite that involves worshiping a woman, the usually diffident and domesticated goddess Pārvatī asks her husband this curious question about women worshiping. "Should she herself worship the woman or with the male seeker [worship]?"[1] The god's reply to the question is, "the form of the *yoni*,[2] which is *jaganmayī*—that which makes up the whole world—should be worshipped by the male seeker and the *liṅga*, the male organ, should be worshipped by her, . . . By the mere worship of these two, one becomes liberated while in the body."[3]

Does a woman participate in worship or is she only the object of worship? If she does worship, what or whom should she worship? Pārvatī's question here presumes the worship of the *yoni*, that is, the worship of the female, as the normative practice. Her question seems to suggest that women and men, as equal actors in Tantric ceremonies, would perform the same normative ceremony of worshiping the *yoni*. So she asks, "Does a woman herself worship the *yoni*?" that is, does a woman participate in the Tantric ceremony the same way that a man does, where she would worship a woman?

Śiva replies to the contrary, and the question disappears.[4] The very question, however, signals that something is awry.

Typically in Sanskrit Tantric *textual* sources, we find that women are the objects of male worship, but not worshipers themselves. Hindu Tantric texts generally assume a male perspective, male practitioners, and a male audience, as we see in well-known texts like the *Kulārṇava Tantra* and the *Kulacūḍāmaṇi Tantra*.[5]

In light of this general relegation of women to a passive role, Pārvatī asks an odd, even inconceivable, question. Are women, she asks, actors or agents in the Tantric context? In the heady Tantric quest for magical powers and enlightenment, do women themselves engage in ritual worship? Or are they merely passive objects, simply used by men in a male-dominated conquest for magical powers and otherworldly states?

Textually, we commonly see women represented in transgressive, "left-handed" Tantras as preeminently suppliers of potent fluids, menstrual blood, and conduits for male ecstatic (and enstatic) experience. David White, in particular, compellingly argues for the position that women especially were the suppliers of fluids, for "left-handed" Tantra. On the other side, in the "right-handed" traditions, which do not employ liquor, meat, or sexual rites, usually woman is displaced by the metaphor of feminine imagery. She is an inner principle, the goddess within the (male) practitioner. She is an energy, which rises up the spine of the practitioner to join in ecstatic unity with the god Śiva in the practitioner's head. One sees the focus on women as an inner principle in esoteric, inner forms of "right-handed" worship, for instance, in some fine scholarship addressing the Abhinavaguptian corpus of Tantric texts.[6] In this case, as bodied living females, women are absent.

The question, of course, is a charged one, if only because the Tantric proclivity for goddesses has been on some fronts understood as a reclamation of feminine power, and the answer to whether the "goddess is a feminist," to borrow from the title of an important exploration of this topic, is one that that can and will be used by feminists today in creating strategies for social change.[7] I discuss this elsewhere in appendix 1, but it probably bears at least mentioning here as well. At least a part of the confusion about women's roles in Tantra I suspect stems from a tendency to consider Tantra as a single monolithic category. That is, Tantric texts are by no means uniform in their attitudes toward women, and different texts from different times and places offer different perspectives on this question of women's roles.

Pārvatī's Question

We return to Pārvatī, the text's interlocutor, a goddess and wife of the god Śiva, who asks here a jarring question. She suggests that we consider the uncommon possibility that women may actively participate in the Tantric rites described here, in ways that construed women as peers of men, rather than mere objects, and as having the same goals as men. In her question, Pārvatī presumes that since the worship of the *yoni* leads to enlightenment for the male, the same will hold true for the woman. Her question asks us to reconsider how we have understood women's roles.

Śiva's response, in any case, affirms her suggestion that women functioned as actors. While women do not perform worship exactly as men do, Śiva, nevertheless, emphasizes women as active participants. Only by the worship of *both*—that is both men *and* women worshiping their respective opposite genders—does one reach enlightenment in the body (*jīvan mukti*).[8]

This chapter addresses the theme of women as actors in Tantra. I suggest that a particular form of Tantric practice, named the "Kālī Practice," presents a textual view of women we do not often see: one that recognizes women's spiritual competence. We see women as gurus and their skill in the practice of *mantras* extolled,[9] and women are placed in the subject position, recognizing the wishes women may have in the daily business of living life.

The "Kālī Practice"

This particular form of Tantric praxis we find in a group of texts from the fifteenth through eighteenth centuries prescribing "left-handed" Tantric rites, including the use of liquor, meat, and the rite of sexual union along with a particular focus on women, is named variously in the texts as the "Kālī Practice" (*Kālī sādhana*), the "Great *Mantra* Practice" (*mahāmantrasādhana*), and the "Chinese Way" (*cīnācāra*), and, rarely, the "Śākta Conduct" (*śāktācāra*). The "Chinese Way" is the most common expression used in these texts. This is not to suggest that this nomenclature in any way indicates actual Chinese practice. This last expression—*cīnācāra*—sometimes translated as the "Tibetan method"[10]—looks suspiciously like a species of medieval "orientalism" where a repressed exoticism and eroticism is, within official discourse, in the space of the written text, displaced and projected outward onto someone else, in this case onto the neighboring Chinese.[11] For the sake of convenience I will refer to this practice throughout as the "Kālī Practice." This nomenclature is preferable to "The Chinese Conduct/Way" or "The Tibetan Way," even though the praxis is most frequently named this in the texts, since so much of Chinese and Tibetan Tantric practice does not in the slightest resemble this particular praxis and it would be confusing and misleading to label this practice with a contemporary national identity. The "Great *Mantra* Practice" and the "Śākta Conduct" are also not as frequently used to name this praxis as is "Kālī Practice," and since the essence of the practice revolves around the worship of primarily three female goddesses, Kālī, the Blue Goddess of Speech, and Tārā, taking this particular name from the texts captures the general impetus of the praxis best.

Five key elements make up the "Kālī Practice":

(1) The practice centers on women: seeking out women and treating women with respect.

(2) The practice is especially a mental practice; therefore, none of the ordinary rules for time, place, or purity apply.

(3) A rite that involves the worship of women, frequently incorporating the rite of sexual union, but at times simply limited to the worship of living women without including the rite of sexual union, particularly in the case of the worship of the young girl (*kumārī pūjā*) where sex is not included.[12]

(4) The praxis involved in the "Kālī Practice" explicitly goes beyond the limited time and place of the rite. The attitude of reverence and respect toward women should be maintained constantly, twenty-four hours a day. I suspect this particular rule is especially important in ritually habituating an attitude, which shifts the position of women and the relation to women, in contrast to what we see in an earlier text like the *Kulārṇava Tantra* (KuT), where, after the conclusion of the rite, normative hierarchies are reinstated, both with respect to gender and caste.

(5) Finally, the goddess is viewed as embodied in living women. Along with this final point, I also address that it is not simply that women who are worshiped in a rite are considered divine, but rather that women as a category are revered, whether worshiped or not. Further, as a category, women get assimilated to Brahmins. This last point in particular is structurally key to the shift these texts present for women since, as I discuss below, it moves away from a binary model of gender.

This chapter demonstrates and explores a particular Tantric view of women. This "Kālī Practice" especially proposes an alternative view of women that, I suggest, facilitates shifting attitudes toward women. All these five elements of the "Kālī Practice" are not present in some of the most commonly referenced Tantric texts in Western studies of Tantra, especially "left-handed"

Tantric texts that have been translated into English, such as the much earlier *Kulārṇava* Tantra, from the tenth through thirteenth centuries, the *Kālikā Purāṇa*, from the ninth through eleventh centuries, and the *Kaulajñāna Nirṇaya*, also from the ninth through eleventh centuries. As I note in the introduction, there is a coherency among the texts referenced here in that they are late, from the fifteenth through the eighteenth centuries, and they are associated with the northeast region of India. That earlier Tantric texts do not incorporate these elements listed above suggests that attitudes toward women shifted over time, though by no means do all late "left-handed" texts similarly exhibit these characteristics. Again, in appendix 1 below I discuss some of the differences in views of women that we find in various Tantric texts.

In reading Western scholarly literature on Tantra, one usually finds two salient arguments employed, which mitigate against construing Tantric traditions as recognizing women as subjects. The first often runs: Yes, Tantrics venerated the goddess, but this veneration did not actually carry over into a veneration of actual living women. The second usually goes: Yes, women were necessary to the Tantric rite, but only as vehicles for male attainment. They were conduits of power, vehicles that males used to obtain especially potent magical powers. However, outside the limited sphere of the rite, their importance dwindled.[13]

These views certainly accurately portray a specific body of Tantric literature, especially that produced several centuries earlier and in different locations than the texts I draw upon here.[14] We find here in this group of eight texts also an alternative view—including, for instance, the notion that women are especially skilled in perfecting *mantras*, that women at times are gurus, and a reconfiguration of the status of women as a whole class. This reconfiguration both extends to living women and is not confined to the limited time and space of the rite.

For Western women today, Rachel Fell McDermott notes that the symbolism of Kālī "offers healing in a male-dominated world,"[15] a trend that she sees expanded on some fronts via the new Internet culture.[16] In a variety of ways this twenty-first-century Western image of Kālī appears constructed out of thin air. Yet, in an unexpected way, this use of Kālī may not be entirely inconsistent with the advocacy of respect toward women that we find in the "Kālī Practice." I should also add here that, using some of the texts that I use for this study, and some others, Madhu Khanna also comes to a similar conclusion as mine here, that we find attitudes of respect toward women in some Śākta texts.[17] And, similarly, Edwin Dimock's research on the Sahajiyās in the Bengali region in the fifteenth through seventeenth centuries also supports the claims for women's roles as teacher that I make here.[18]

One more point to keep in mind, just as the Kālī of the twenty-first-century West is in some respects an imagined construction, proliferating especially through written words on the Internet, what we address here are also written words proliferated through Tantric texts. As such, both are *representations* of how one should respond to women. Both are necessarily fraught with the inevitable contortions of any form of representation. With this, it is beyond the purview of the evidence to make claims regarding the actual historical behavior of actual women or male Tantric practitioners. We can only recover a semblance of the "what really happened" through the refractory lens of the text, and we also need to keep in mind that the views presented here only form one element in what is otherwise an unwieldy and often contradictory potpourri of practices and views in these texts.

Also, as I mention in the introduction, I use the terms *subject* and *agency* here not so much as a designation of some sort of "real" or existentially autonomous entity—certainly there are considerable philosophical and cultural problems entailed in assigning these notions to a nonmodern non-Western context. Nor do I use them to designate a sovereign, intact self that exists prior to any relation to a world outside itself. So, instead of pointing to real or historical subjects, I rather point to a textual portrayal that signifies a slippery but rhetorically and grammatically effective and prevalent category.

Even with these limitations, these textual sources help us to reconstruct indirectly an alternative picture of women, even if not dominant, and especially so since they present such a striking contrast to what we find elsewhere in textual representations of women in Hinduism.[19] So, for instance, we find clear textual references to female gurus (NST 5.70; GST 2.18ff.), something not present even in earlier Tantras such as the *Kulacūḍāmaṇi Tantra* (KCT) or the *Kulārṇava Tantra*, from which some of these eight texts borrow extensively, let alone in a more normative Hindu text like Manu's *Dharma Śāstra*. This difference, which recognizes living women as venerable, may be read as representing a shift in attitudes toward women as a class.

However, further than this, I make a different sort of argument than one that hinges upon the reconstruction of seventeenth-century Tantric practice. Rather, I suggest that we understand the "Kālī Practice" as a form of representation of which the value lies perhaps most in terms of its historical value as a reference to the propagation of discourse. These texts reflect the emergence of a *discourse* addressing social relations between the genders, and I suggest that its importance lies in the challenge, as discourse, that it presents to normative classifications.

In this chapter we first briefly look at the texts that present the "Kālī Practice." Following this we address the notion of the gender binary and how we find an alternative model as well in these texts. We then briefly examine Pārvatī's role in asking the question of women's agency. After this we discuss the different elements of the "Kālī Practice" as well as specific instances of women in venerable positions, women as proficient with *mantras*, and women as gurus. Finally, I conclude with evidence that suggests that the model for understanding the veneration of women in these texts finds a parallel in the veneration of the Brahmin.

Binaries

The dialogue between Śiva and Pārvatī we saw above frames gender in terms of a binary. This model probably originally derives from the well-known classical cosmological and philosophical system of Sāṃkhya, with its notion of male as spirit (*puruṣa*) and female as matter and Nature (*prakṛti*). In the model here, male and female are two elements of a binary, and this notion of a binary reflected in gender pervades throughout these texts.[20]

However, working against this notion of a binary, we also find inscribed within these texts a separate, different model of the relation of women to men, one that constructs women as comparable to a particular caste. In this case women are not the lesser member of a binary, but rather, women function as one group among several.

In some ways the notion of caste appears to be just as fundamental a division to Indian society as the gender divide. A contemporary anthropologist, Anjali Bagwe, titled a recent book *Of Woman Caste*, where she draws from current colloquialisms that represent women as a caste group.[21] Apart from this, a designation of women as akin to one of the castes is something we find elsewhere in Sanskrit texts, as early as the Vedas, where we find women lumped in with the lowest of the four castes, the servants (*śūdras*).[22] In the earlier, classical representations, the primary division among humans has to do with which caste one belongs to. In this context all women and some men get grouped into this lowest class of persons, the servants. So in terms of ritual praxis, women are not treated as members of the caste to which their (blood) father or male guardian belongs, but rather as a whole group they are treated as members of the lowest caste of males.

In contrast, the suggestion we find here instead is that women as a group form a separate caste apart from the lowest servant caste and that this special caste of women ought to be treated more like Brahmins than like servants (*śūdras*). This grouping does not take into account differences among women, just as it does not take into account differences among Brahmins. In this configuration, women as a separate class, like Brahmins, warriors, and so forth, possess innate capacities that elevate their status as a whole class. When a text extols women's competence with *mantras* and advocates respecting them, women here begin to move up, just as, historically, redefining the collective identity of a particular caste subgroup facilitated an upward move along the continuum of the caste system for that group. Notably, we find here that in certain respects, the treatment accorded women—as a class—at some places in these texts parallels that of the highest caste, the Brahmin.

From our own view in the twenty-first-century West, perhaps the most salient element of this reconfiguration is that it affords a competing model of gender difference. While it certainly elides the no doubt real differences of status and wealth among different women, nevertheless, the presence of an alternative model, women as one group among several, presents an alternative to the nearly universal construction of women as the second sex, the perennially inferior member of a gender binary. So the view here is not like one particularly common and dominant view found in America, where the means of overcoming the gender binary is through an emphasis on the individual. In the American case the individual is of primary significance, and, consequently, gender is a contingent and secondary category assigned to the individual, and one capable of being transcended. Indeed, it is frequently argued that we ought to transcend gender as a category in order to achieve the goals of equality. This blanket equality of the individual is a different model than the model of women as one group among several.

Nor is the difference that gender makes in this alternative model like a view often found in French feminism,[23] modeled on a duality based on a gender essentialism, although, as I note above, we also find more commonly a binary model in these texts, encoding an essentialist gender binary. Neither do these texts propose a binary that then also allows space for a third neuter gender, though this is common enough in Indian texts elsewhere. Rather, in this particular alternative model, women are one group among five, which include Brahmins, warriors, merchants, servants, *and* women. The groups are generally hierarchically ordered with Brahmins at the top and servants at the bottom; women in this case form a fifth and are likened to the Brahmins, rather than being lumped in with servants.

Social classification often implies a social functionality and this functionality typically encodes hierarchies of value. Setting women off as one group among several affords a reconsideration of their social functionality, and one that in this case shifts their social value, as a class. That the classification includes more than three is important, because it tends to diffuse relationships away from an oppositional model, something that a number of scholars have noted.[24]

Both models, a binary and women as one category among several, operate throughout these texts, and a binary model is certainly much more pervasive in general. On the other hand, the presence of an alternative competing model helps to circumvent the familiar and inherent problematic dialectic of the binary—which unfolds as center and margin, self/other (male/female, mind/body, etc.). The writers of these texts do not try to integrate these two different models. No authorial voice notices the disjunction between these separate models. They coexist without comment.

On the other hand, an alternative model of women as one of five groups offers ways of thinking about gender that a view of two precludes. It offers a view that, by its contrast, may shed light on our own twenty-first-century understandings of gender. While this Indian model appears to still incorporate an essentialist model of women, which does not account for differences among women, nevertheless it does offer a move away from an idea of gender as a binary, which in turn affords a structural problematization of the idea of woman as the other of maleness.

A binary insinuates a structural pattern where normative (male) identity is established through the exclusion of what is not normative, that is, through the exclusion of female by relegating her to the "other" category. This entails definitionally a devaluation of the nonnormative other; this devaluation is what founds the possibility of a valued normative identity.[25] To put this another way, implicit in the structure of a binary is the notion that the two categories are opposed, and one of the two usually predominates. Further, implicitly the dominant category defines itself by what it is not, by what it excludes. This is one of the lessons Hegel so profusely iterated, that a binary implicitly incorporates an agonistic relationship. A multiplicity, on the other hand, diffuses the intensity of opposition (unless all the "others" are lumped again together, just as we see that the classical Hindu tradition lumps women and servants together). It may be that the stipulation of women as one class among a multiplicity (that is, they are comparable to Brahmins, but not lumped together with them) contributes to their greater valuation as a class of persons in these texts.

Docile Domestic Pārvatī

One more point should be addressed here that has to do with the identity of our interlocutor. Perhaps we might have expected a question about women's roles in the Tantric rite to come from the mouth of the dark, fiercely independent goddess Kālī. Kālī, after all, is well known for her warrior independence; she wreaks havoc on the battlefield in the *Devī Māhātmya* and for the authors of the

Great Blue Tantra (BT) here as well, Kālī is the ultimate causal agent. The gods Brahmā and the others praise her as the source of the world. They sing:

> We bow to you, O great ruler, who is the form of the supreme bliss. You have come on the water for the sake of protecting our life-breath. Homage to you, homage to you, homage to you, homage and more homage. Homage to you o great fierce Goddess, Homage to you who are the night of time. Without you o supreme fierce Goddess, we would be dead ghosts. Protect us, protect us, O supreme one, who is the vidyā (magical feminine speech), who is the womb of all the creatures in the three worlds. O, slayer of Madhu and Kaiṭabha, o destroyer of the demon Nisumbha, you give the Gods their powers to rule. O goddess, homage to you, the beloved of Śiva.[26]

After this hymn of praise the goddess Kālī gives the gods Brahmā and the others the boons to create the world and so on (BT.12.19). Brahmā in this case is confused on how to go about creating the world. He asks, "What form should creation, maintenance and so on take?"[27] In this case Kālī even supplies the material substance by giving him the dust from her feet. "Take the dust from my feet; that is a good material [for creation]."[28] Kālī is a supreme goddess, both transcendent insofar as she leaves the messy work of creation to Brahmā and the other gods, and immanent insofar as she supplies the "stuff" to make the world.

But Pārvatī herself? Pārvatī, the unobtrusive, pliant wife of Śiva mostly plays second fiddle to her husband. If we apply Wendy Doniger's bifurcation of goddesses into Goddesses of the Tooth and Goddesses of the Breast,[29] Pārvatī definitively figures as the latter, as an anything but independent and fierce goddess. In general, the *Yoni Tantra* presents no exception to this image of Pārvatī. We have only to note the disproportionate amount of speech she and her husband each have—her single stanza questions that then evoke several pages of discourse in reply by the male god—to realize how peripheral her role as actor is.

At the same time, in a well-known myth Kālī is Pārvatī's alter ego, the fierce black goddess whom Pārvatī expels and rejects from her body and persona in order to be more fair skinned in the eyes of her judging husband. Here, as if drawing upon her dark expurgated half, she musters the suggestion that women might have a role as actors in the ritual arena. Moreover, at times her determination to acquire the Tantric teachings includes extreme measures, such as when she threatens to commit suicide unless Śiva gives her the teachings. She says to the god Śiva, "O ruler of Gods, if you do not reveal to me this method [for the "Southern Kālī"] I will give up my life right in front of you.

Don't doubt this."[30] And we see the same stanza again when she wants to know about the supreme principle behind the cosmos (*tattva*).[31]

If the relations between gods at times mirror social human roles, then what might this be saying about a woman's role in Tantra? Does Pārvatī's question suggest that we might expect that human wives would force their husbands to reveal secret teachings? Especially, we should remember here that Pārvatī's human counterpart would not be the wild and independent *yoginī* about whom we so frequently hear, but rather the ordinary, generally deferential housewife. This is important because it shifts us away from an image of a woman who actively engages Tantric practices as only the exception, the exotic, the wild, the extraordinary woman. Pārvatī is not a model for the exceptional woman, but for the everyday housewife.

The Key: Women Are Gods

The "Kālī Practice" centers around women. With this, we find both the worship *of* women and worship *with* women. Thus first, the practitioner should make seeking out women a priority. We see in the god Śiva's instructions on the practice that he says, "Having abandoned everything, O Goddess, the aspirant should make great effort to seek out the company of women."[32] The texts establish a mythological precedent for the power of this practice. So the great god Śiva himself says, "I have become Śiva only by being connected with woman."[33] Further, we find that the great gods Rāma and Kṛṣṇa also have acquired whatever greatness or status they have only because they worshiped women. "By having worshipped the yoni of Rādhā, Kṛṣṇa attained the state of being Kṛṣṇa. Śrī Rāma, himself, the lord of Jānakī worshipped the yoni of Sītā, and having killed [the demon] Rāvaṇa, together with all his clan, again came back to the city of Ayodhyā dwelling there happily."[34]

Of course, other versions of Kṛṣṇa's dalliance with Rādhā do not include the mention of Kṛṣṇa's ritual worship of the yoni of Rādhā. Nor do we find in Vālmīki or Tulsidas's versions of the *Rāmāyaṇa* the suggestion that Rāma performed this rite. For this practice, however, the worship of women is especially important. This involves ritual worship of women, and also a cultivation of reverential mental attitudes toward women. "One should not at all have hatred towards women; rather one should worship women,"[35] and "one should not criticize women; one should increase one's love for them."[36] Here the word *love* is not the word *kāma*, which connotes lust and sexual desire, but rather the word *prema*, which connotes love as emotional attachment. This practice is, of course, nevertheless complexly coded. Also in the "Kālī Practice" the worship of women includes the rite of sexual union,[37] but, at the same time, it is not limited to it.

The practice contains much else besides this. We should also note, for instance, that the attitude of reverence toward women is inculcated outside the rite of sexual union as well and also toward all women, even women with whom one has no relations. So the practitioner here, "having bowed down to a little girl, to an intoxicated young woman, or to an old woman, to a beautiful woman of the clan (*kula*), or to a contemptible, vile woman, or to a greatly wicked woman, one should contemplate on the fact that these [women] do not appreciate being criticized or hit; they do not appreciate dishonesty or that which is disagreeable. Consequently, in every way possible one should not behave this way towards them."[38]

In this way the BT establishes a respectful attitude toward women,[39] and in this context not just toward a desirable woman with whom the male aspirant might perform the rite of sexual union, but toward all women, including a woman who is *kutsitā*, vile and contemptible, and whom one does not worship or engage with in the rite of sexual union. At this point the BT iterates "women are Gods, women are the life-breath."[40]

Now when does this contemplation happen? This bowing and this contemplation is what one does on a morning walk. That is, the morning schedule for the practioner is the following:

> Having gotten up in the morning, the knower of *mantras* bows to the clan tree. Having done this, and having meditated on the guru in the lotus in the head, he should visualize [lit., remember] that [guru] as a flood of nectar. He should then worship him [the guru] as free from illness using however, mental items for the worship. Beginning in the root *cakra* up to the *cakra* at the top of the head he should contemplate on his personal mantra [here, lit., the feminine *vidyā*]. Shining like ten million suns, with a form which is a flood of nectar, that effulgence which pervades through the covering [or roof, top of the head of the person], he should imagine this in his own body. The eight trees are *śleṣmātaka*, *karañja* tree, the *rudrākṣa* tree, lemon tree, banyan tree, the orange-blossomed *kadambakā* tree, the bilva tree and the tree called "no sorrow." These are declared in this way in another Tantric text, O Goddess. Then having bowed down to a little girl, to an intoxicated young woman, or to an old woman, to a beautiful woman of the clan (*kula*), or to a contemptible, vile woman, or to a greatly wicked woman, one should contemplate on the fact that these [women] do not appreciate being

criticized or hit; they do not appreciate dishonesty or that which is disagreeable.[41]

Thus the practitioner gets up in the morning and bows to the special tree of the clan. This particular bowing does not involve a mental visualization as does the next thing he does in the morning, which is to visualize the guru. Hence, if we reconstruct his morning, he walks outside to the "clan tree" and then visualizes the guru and contemplates on his main personal *mantra.* He then bows to the women mentioned in the quote above and then he reflects upon the fact that these women do not appreciate being lied to or hit, as we saw above. Here we see that this part of the "Kālī Practice," incorporated into the morning walk, is also not connected with the performance of the rite of sexual union, but is rather part of a habitual morning contemplation.

The worship gets extended further, even to the females of other species, of birds and animals. "The females of beasts of birds and of humans—these being worshipped, one's ineffective, incomplete deeds always become full of merit."[42] What this does is to encode and highlight the female as a separate class. It also makes it clear that the rite of worship does not necessarily entail the rite of sexual union.

The reverence of women takes a particular form that is also commonly practiced outside of this special "Kālī Practice," as well, in the worship of a young girl who is considered a manifestation of the goddess. The worship of a young girl (*kumārī pūjā*), which is publicly performed, is still performed regularly today in the temple at Kāmākhyā and, incidentally, is performed by both men and women.[43] This rite, the worship of a young girl, incorporates the same attitudes of reverence toward women; many of the texts used here also focus on it extensively.[44] It also does not include the rite of sexual union.[45]

As I noted above, we also find that this practice also involves worshiping *with* women. Thus, the *Celestial Musician Tantra* (GT) tells us, "Together with a woman, there [he should] reflect [on the mantra or practice]; the two of them together in this way [they do] worship. Without a woman, the practitioner cannot perfect [the *mantra*] at all. He should mentally evoke [the *mantra*] together with a woman and together with her, he should offer into the sacrificial fire as well. Without her the practitioner cannot perfect [the *mantra*] at all. Women are Gods; women are the life-breath."[46]

Again we see in the *Secret Practice Tantra* (GST): "Together with the woman, one should recite the *mantra.* One should not recite the *mantra* alone."[47] That the practitioner performs the practice with women—and here it appears women are doing the same things men are doing, contemplating the deity, saying the *mantra,* making offerings into the fire—shifts the role women take in the practice.

Also, one more point of interest, as the Māyā Tantra (MT) notes, the rite of sexual union that the "Kālī Practice" prescribes is different from the infamous *cakra pūjā,* the rite that is probably best known in the West as the "depraved" Tantric "orgy," where a group of men and women perform a ritual that includes feasting and orgiastic rites. The MT first describes the rite of sexual union connected with the "Kālī Practice."[48] After the MT's author finishes this description, this author continues on to say, "Now, I am going to tell you a different practice. Pay close attention. Having worshipped a woman who is the wife of another (*parakīyā*) in the circle (*cakra*), [he should worship] his own beloved deity."[49] The *cakra* or circle worship involves the wife of someone else chosen among the partners in the circle. This "circle" rite, which was simultaneously sensationalized and presented as a scandal, informed much of what was imagined in the West about Tantra.[50] For our purposes here, the scandal attached to the *cakra pūjā* is not important, but rather that the spatial organization of these two rites differs fundamentally and as a result, the rhetorical effects of the rites, the "messages" they give, also differ.

In the *cakra pūjā* the participants are arranged in a circle and a centrally located altar instantiates the goddess. The goddess is invoked for the rite, usually into a pot of water, which is worshiped as temporarily housing her. So she is present in the rite, but present as separate from the participants, including the women participants. In the version of the *cakra pūjā* that we find in the earlier KuT, in a carnivalesque fashion, the women are made to drink as the men pour liquor into their mouths (KuT 8.70); general drunkenness ensues. The "yogis dance, carrying pots of liquor on their heads" (KuT 8.71b).[51] Then "the yogis, drunk with wine fall down intoxicated on their chests; and the yoginīs of the group, intoxicated, fall on top of the men. They mutually engage in the happy fulfilment of pleasure" (KuT 8.73–8.74).[52]

In contrast, in the "Kālī Practice," there is not a group of women. Moreover, in the "Kālī Practice" the woman is at the center of the rite, both spatially and ideologically. In this case, the living woman *is* the goddess, not considered separate from the goddess. She herself is considered and worshiped as the goddess instantiated. And aside from the woman, only the person worshiping her is present.[53] Spatially, she, not the image of the Goddess, takes the center, the place of importance, and ideologically she is the center because she is the goddess. The ritual and spatial encoding of the two rites send different messages with respect to the status of ordinary women. In the *cakra pūjā,* the woman is not particularly venerable and one can see how, for such a rite, it would be easy to view women as necessary tools during the course of the rite, who would then be unimportant after its conclusion. The rite described in the BT (6.20ff.), on the other hand, inculcates a more psychologically durable reverence for the living woman who is worshiped.[54]

What is also important to recognize with this is that the practice of the rite of sexual union was by no means monolithic in its performance or function. It is also interesting to notice that even one of our medieval sources points out that the rite had more than one version.

How Is She a Goddess?

Now a question arises: if the woman is worshiped as the goddess, exactly how is she the goddess? Does she get possessed by the goddess in the course of the rite? We might venture this, and elsewhere, apart from this particular "Kālī Practice" this is likely the case. Interestingly, however, here the texts are explicit about precisely not viewing the woman as a medium for the goddess. "And there [in this rite] one does *not* do the invocation of the Goddess."[55] This suggests that it is as a woman in her ordinary nonaltered state, not when she is speaking in tongues, nor when some special external divinity empowers her, but that as herself, that she is divine. The difference between a rite that features the woman as a medium, possessed by the goddess, and a rite that considers an ordinary woman herself as divine is salient. If she is possessed, then this state is temporary and, ultimately, not hers, not her own subjectivity. Here however, the point is to see a normal, nonpossessed woman as divine.

In this context, the practice of constantly viewing women as goddesses starts to make sense. If a woman is the goddess only at a specific time, if only during the rite is she a medium for the goddess, then only at that time would it be necessary to treat her with the reverence due to a deity. There would be no need to maintain this attitude beyond the confines of the rite. On the other hand, if the divinity, which is the goddess, is intrinsic to her being, something she carries around with her all the time, something she *is*, then her status in general shifts. Then one would need to be vigilant, constantly maintaining an attitude of listening to her to make sure that the goddess standing before one will be pleased and therefore benevolent. It is precisely the act of looking to her, as ordinary woman, which affords a shift in the normative discourse between the genders and that allows for a recognition of her as a subject, as a person to whom one *should* listen.

In an interesting way this parallels to some degree what we find in some twentieth-century cases of women being possessed by the goddess. These women were often viewed as keeping some of the power of the goddess even when not possessed, which, one could argue, effectively arrived at a similar situation where the woman was revered all the time.[56] The example of the well-known contemporary "Hugging Saint" Ammachi comes to mind, whose "Devi Bhava," "mood/trance of the Goddess" was originally presented as an instance of trance possession by the goddess, but which over time was clarified to indicate that the saint did not experience any change of her essential awareness or consciousness during the "Devi Bhava." One difference we may note here between our textual versions and what we find in contemporary reports is that in contemporary reports women who are possessed are special, to some degree extraordinary women. The rite described here, however, tends to suggest that all women, and even ordinary women, are divine.

Apart from a recognition that this manifests as not harming women and not doing things that upset them, as we saw above, we also see an attentiveness to fulfilling her desires. "Whatever she may desire, that one should give her" (BT 6.30b). Keep in mind here that this goddess is a living woman. As such, she can talk back. So it's not just a matter of making an offering to an image in a temple and receiving much of it back[57] as *prasāda*, the blessed offering. Here the woman keeps it, uses it, and can also ask for what she wishes.

This practice of listening to her is key. It doesn't matter how much other spiritual practice one does, because, as the MT says, "one's worship is in vain, one's *mantra* recitation is useless, placing the *mantra* on the body is useless, the hymns one recites are in vain, the fire ceremonies with gifts to priests; all these are in vain if one does that which is offensive to a woman."[58]

In addition the texts direct the practitioner to respect the rights of the bodies and minds of women. So as we saw earlier with the BT we also see elsewhere in other texts that the practitioner "should not hit women or criticize women or lie to women or do that which women find offensive."[59] The GT and NST advise: "never should one strike a woman, with an attitude of arrogance, not even with a flower."[60] Even further, the BT tells us, "not even mentally, should one harm a woman."[61]

Even if the practitioner feels that a woman has hurt him, or has violated his rights, the response should never be to harm her. "Even if she has committed an extreme offense, one should not have hatred for her. One should never hate women; rather one should worship women."[62]

Now, this is not done out of a sense of superiority, in the sense of a chivalrous behavior toward women that accepts their offenses without striking back because women are the "weaker" sex. We might expect this because we are familiar with this attitude in the West. However, here it is exactly the opposite. One doesn't harm a woman, not because she's weak, but rather more like the reason one doesn't harm a powerful yogī or a sage like the cranky

Durvāsas. She has power, and she might get offended and then one had better be wary of her curse. So the NST tells us "when a woman gets angry, then I [Śiva], who am the leader of the clan, always get angry. When she [a woman] is upset or afflicted, then that Goddess who gives curses is always upset."[63] So if a woman is offended, she brings the ire of both the god Śiva and the curse-giving goddess onto the offender.

This shift in attitude is crucial, precisely because it sees women not as weaker but as stronger. She has power, which, in itself, entails the prerogatives both of subjectivity and social clout. The disempowered may not have a voice, and the refinement of civilization commends the strong for taking pity upon the disempowered. And a chivalric discourse, especially one easily recognized in the West, recommends treating women mildly for just this reason. On the other hand, here we have a different matter. In this case it is a different emotion than pity; it is fear that drives one to accept the offenses she may give.

Women and Their *Mantras*

Perhaps what's most important here, however, is the way that this power is coded. The MT tells us, "A woman who is engaged in practicing the Durgā *mantra* is able to increase well-being and prosperity, however if she gets angry at a man then she can destroy his wealth and life."[64] What is key here is that the source of her power is her spiritual practice, the fact of her repetition of the Durgā *mantra* (*durgāmantraratā*). Like the yogī, and like the Brahmin, she has a power in her due to her spiritual attainment and her anger carries an edge. Just as the curse of the peevish Brahmin sage Durvāsas sticks, so her anger will stick, whether one deserves the curse or not.

Now this is incredibly important because we see here an instance where women have power and it is not connected to their sexuality or to their capacity to be faithful to their husbands. These two types of feminine power are ubiquitous in South Asia, and one can see these two as part of a continuum. That is, a woman has a dangerous power in her sexuality, which, if tamed into a faithfulness toward her husband, as in the case of Kannagi,[65] and notably also for the *satī*,[66] can become a potent force for cursing, even for burning down a whole city—but here we have something different. That is, contrary to the normative coding of a woman as a sexual being and dangerous because of her sexuality—or because she's managed to effectively channel and bottle up her sexuality—here we have a perilous leap into a world where a woman is dangerous because, like the Brahmin priest, like the guru and like the yogī, she knows how to wield a *mantra*.

We also find that women as a class have a special ability to master *mantras* effortlessly. The BT tells us, "The restrictions which men contend with [in the practice of] *mantras* are not at all there for women. Anything whatsoever, by whichever [means], and moreover in all ways [is attained], for women magical attainment (*siddhi*) occurs, without any doubt . . . for a woman, by merely contemplating [on the *mantra*] she in this way becomes a giver of boons. Therefore one should make every effort to initiate a woman in one's own family."[67]

The GT iterates this as well, "she doesn't have to do worship (*pūjā*), or meditate, or purify herself with a bath, or establish the *mantra* in the body; just by merely thinking of a *mantra* women quickly get the power to give boons."[68] I discuss this more below in the context of women's initiation; here we can note that it is her gender, her status as a woman that entails this power, yet not her sexuality. Rather more like the Brahmin, who simply because he is born into the Brahmin caste, has a tendency to tell the truth, as we see in the Upaniṣadic story of Satyakāma Jābala, so a woman, because of her status as woman, naturally can perfect a *mantra*. In the well-known story of Satyakāma Jābala from the Upaniṣads, the young boy Satyakāma Jābala does not know whom his father is. His prospective teacher concludes that he must be none other than Brahmin caste because the boy instinctively tells the truth.[69] Similarly, persons by fate born into the caste of warriors have the capacity to endure pain, as we see in the well-known story of Karṇa with his guru Paraśurāma, who realizes that he is of the warrior caste despite his claim otherwise, because he can endure pain. Similarly, simply being born a woman, that is, woman as a species, affords this facility with *mantras*.[70]

We may note here as well a coherent connection the texts make with this power that women have with *mantras* and with the fruits that come from the practice of worshiping and focusing on women that is the "Kālī Practice." That is, interestingly, the main reward that comes from the "Kālī Practice" is not magic powers such as the power to fly, or to spot treasures buried in the earth, or to kill one's enemies, which we see so commonly elsewhere in the lists of rewards of Tantric practice, but is rather a facility with language.

Women as Practitioners, as Gurus

We also find women in an uncommon role in these texts: as gurus and as practitioners. With this, women are accorded subjectivity through a recognition of their spiritual competence. Now, we do find evidence in contemporary Western scholarship that women play key roles in Tantra today, even taking the esteemed role of guru. The data is readily available and clear in modern and contemporary anthropological studies,[71] especially in anthropological evidence focusing on modern saints like Anandamayi Ma. We find evidence for this also from the nineteenth century, in the case of Ramakrishna's Tantric guru, the Bhairavi and Gauri Ma,[72] also from the sixteenth century in the case of Sītā Devī.[73] We also see this in Assam in the sixteenth century where we find two women, Kanaklata and Bhubaneshwari, who become leaders of Vaiṣṇava groups, in the role of gurus for the groups.[74] Here we find this also in our Sanskrit Tantric texts associated with the "Kālī Practice," even as it is something we tend not to find elsewhere in Hindu Sanskrit texts.

We will look first at the *Blue Goddess of Speech Tantra* (NST). The NST presents women as gurus in a casual way, which suggests that something is ubiquitous and taken for granted. The NST tells us the appropriate honorific endings to tag onto the name of one's guru and gives the endings for a male guru and for a female guru "The male gurus who give all magical attainments have 'lord of bliss' attached to end of their names. If the guru is a woman, then 'mother' is attached to the end of her name."[75] Without any fanfare, this text assumes that women function in that most esteemed of roles, as guru, and the text's reader ought to be aware of the proper ending for the guru's name.

In the *Secret Practice Tantra* (GST), more is made of the notion of a female guru. After the God Śiva gives the visualization of the male guru, the goddess Pārvatī responds, "The initiation given by a woman is proclaimed to be auspicious and capable of giving the results of everything one wishes for, if, from the merit accumulated in many lives and by dint of much good luck, a person can acquire a woman as guru. O lord, what is the visualization of the woman guru? Now I want to hear the visualization one uses in the case of a woman guru. If I am your beloved, then tell me."[76] Śiva gives the visualization,

> Listen, o Pārvatī, overflowing with love for you, I will tell you this secret, which is the visualization of a woman guru, where she is to be meditated upon as the guru. In the great lotus in the crown of the head on a host of shining filaments is the female guru, who is auspicious (*śivā*). Her eyes are like the blossoming petals of a lotus. She has firm thick breasts, a thousand faces,[77] a thin waist. She is eternal. Shining like a ruby, wearing beautiful red clothing, wearing a red ring on her hand and beautiful jeweled anklets, her face shines like the autumn moon adorned with bright shining earrings. Having her lord seated on her left side, her lotus hands make the gestures of giving boons and removing fear. Thus I have told you, o Goddess, this supreme meditation on the

> female guru. It should be guarded strenuously. It should not be revealed at all.[78]

A number of elements are similar in both the visualizations of the male and female gurus. For instance, both their faces shine like the autumn moon, and they both have eyes like lotuses. They both have the same hand gestures, of giving boons and the gesture of removing fear, and they both have on their left side their partner. Also, the practitioner meditates in both cases on the guru as being located in the crown of the practitioner's head.[79] The visualization of the female guru takes an extra verse, and this extra verse includes the description of her red clothing and ruby ring.

This visualization of the female guru and its source text, the GST, was also well known enough for Rāmatoṣaṇa Bhaṭṭācārya to cite this visualization in his well-known Sanskrit compendium on Tantra, the *Prāṇatoṣiṇī* in 1820. In this context he also cites a hymn from the *Mātṛkābhedatantra*, which gives the "armor" of protection (*kavaca*), sung to the female guru as well as a hymn that is the "Song of the Female Guru" (*Strīguru Gītā*) from the *Kaṅkālamālinī Tantra*.[80] Interestingly, the hymn to the female guru apostrophizes the female guru as the goddess Tāriṇī, a goddess strongly associated with the "Kālī Practice" and the hymn is mythically sung by Śiva to Tāriṇī.

That this female guru is *not* simply the wife of the male guru, who, because she is his wife, also receives worship, Rāmatoṣaṇa makes clear by including a few pages later the specific form of worship that one offers to the wife of the guru.[81] This separate praise of the female guru who is precisely not the guru's wife is important because it indicates a female authority not dependent upon or derived from a male relative.

Interestingly, here, just as in the visualization of the male guru,[82] we find the consort of the guru to the left of the guru, and this goes for both the male and female gurus. That is, the consort of the male guru is on the inferior side, his left, and the consort for the female is also on the inferior side, her left (GST 2.25), suggesting that there is not a spatial indication of a gendered hierarchy in the visual arrangement of the sexes when one visualizes the guru as a woman. One may read this as an acceptance of the woman guru as being as much of an absolute authority as we find in the case of the male guru here and elsewhere. Given the importance of the guru in general in the Tantric tradition, this is saying quite a lot.[83]

Moreover, that it is the goddess Pārvatī who takes the time to frame the insertion of the visualization of a female guru also deserves attention on our part. It suggests a reflexive self-consciousness on the part of this section's author. The author is aware of the relative rarity of the female guru, and yet chooses to gloss the fact that we do not frequently see female gurus as a sign of the general lack of attainment of the practitioners. It takes many lives of good deeds, as Pārvatī says, "the merit acquired from many lives"[84] and most people simply do not have this "right stuff." We may read this as a species of historical revisioning, but in any case it highlights a vision of women that does not denigrate them but rather elevates them.

In this context it is a woman, the goddess Pārvatī, who asks for the visualization of a female guru, suggesting that it might be women who would articulate the need for this type of representation, and, further, that women are able to speak for women.

Even considering that Pārvatī is a goddess, nevertheless, two other things need to be taken into account. First, in the Indian context the line between gods and humans is not so rigid, and certainly not rigid to the degree that it is in the West. Second, since in this context women are goddesses embodied, and vice versa, it makes sense to read this preeminently as a woman speaking in this context—and especially so since, of all the goddesses, Pārvatī tends to be one of the most docile and domesticated, a *saumya* (benevolent) goddess, not noted for her independence from a dominating male spouse. In this sense she stands as a good representational figure for the role that the majority of ordinary women in the Indian context play, that is, not independent from their husbands.

Furthermore, that we see a woman speaking up for women—indeed a woman praising the power and efficacy of a woman guru—hints at a sense of solidarity among women. Women can exist in relation to other women, not in competition for male favor. They are capable of promoting the status of women in general.

Apart from these texts specifically promoting the "Kālī Practice," we find the notion that women are teachers and initiate others in *mantras* elsewhere also, though perhaps less emphatically than in the texts associated with the "Kālī Practice." For instance, we see a passage in that most elusive and ubiquitous of texts, the *Rudrayāmala* that talks about purifying the *mantra* given by a woman. Here a woman is the initiating guru: "in the initiations gotten in a dream, however, there is no rule or procedure for the guru or the disciple. When obtained in a dream and when given by a woman [the *mantra* initiation] should be purified through a consecration ceremony."[85] The *Rudrayāmala* then immediately continues on to describe the qualities that make a woman qualified to be a guru, praising such a woman and extolling her capacity to be a guru:

> The woman practitioner (*sādhvī*) who has conquered her senses, has devotion for the teacher and engages in good conduct, who knows the essence of all the cosmic building blocks (*tattva*) and the meaning

> of all *mantras*, who is skillful and always engaged in worship; she who has all the auspicious marks, who practices silent *mantra* repetition, and who has eyes as beautiful as the lotus flower; she who wears jewels and is adorned with the [knowledge of] letters of the alphabet and the various worlds; she who is peaceful, of a good clan, born from the clan; who has a face beautiful as the moon, and gives prosperity; she who has infinite good qualities; this beloved woman who bestows the state of being like the God Rudra, she is the form of the Guru. She gives liberation and she explains the knowledge pertaining to Śiva—this woman indeed is fit to be a guru. This characterization excludes the widow. The initiation given by a woman is declared to be auspicious, and the *mantras* are known to be eight times more powerful [than that given by a man]. Except that taken from a widow or a woman with children, which only brings debts and obligations.[86]

This text not only assumes a female guru, it praises such a guru and describes her qualities. Also, the power of the *mantra* the woman gives has to do with her own practice and devotion to her guru and not her sexuality per se. This description may be read as part of a pattern commonly found where the qualities of the guru are described, often as a prescriptive tool to alert the seeker reading the text to know what to look for in a guru. Here the description of the female guru is similar to what we typically find in prescriptions for male gurus. On the other hand, the widow and the woman with children are excluded,[87] though we should note that exclusions also apply to male gurus, such as the common exclusion of bald men from the role of guru that we frequently find in discussions of the ideal male guru.

It is also not surprising that Goudriaan and Gupta date this text of the *Rudrayāmala*[88] to the same late date and same region as the texts associated with the "Kālī Practice." This mention of women as gurus in the *Rudrayāmala* may be attributable to this connection. Moreover, Tantric digests of this time and region, such as the nineteenth-century Rāmatoṣaṇa Bhaṭṭācārya's long digest, the *Prāṇatoṣiṇī*[89] and the sixteenth-century Bengali writer, Brahmānanda Giri's *Śāktānandataraṅgiṇī*, cite women as gurus. When Rāmatoṣaṇa gives the visualization of a woman guru, he cites the *Secret Practice Tantra* (GST), the text associated with the "Kālī Practice" analyzed above. Parts of this passage from the *Rudrayāmala* are also quoted in Brahmānanda Giri's *Śāktānandataraṅgiṇī* and in Rāmatoṣaṇa Bhaṭṭācārya's *Prāṇatoṣiṇī*. Brahmānanda Giri's *Śāktānandataraṅgiṇī* also extols the initiation given by a woman, with that given by one's mother to be eight times as potent, something we also find mentioned in the *Rudrayāmala*.[90] In a passage reminiscent of the *Rudrayāmala* text cited above, Brahmānanda Giri praises a woman who is devoted to her guru. On the other hand he excludes widows and also makes a woman's initiation contingent upon her appropriate male guardian, that is, father, husband, and son, for women of youth, married life, and old age, respectively.[91]

Now, what does it mean for women to be gurus? In this society the guru represents spiritual authority as well as authority in the social and public sphere. The guru also represents a moral authority, a voice in the lives of his or her followers, which is construed as looking to the interests of the followers. The inclusion of women into this space of public authority, I propose, is part of the same configuration that enjoins the worship of women. That is, it is not an accident that the same texts that propose the "Kālī Practice" also take for granted the presence of women as gurus. The fact of women in this position both signals a marker of an increase in status on public and social levels for women, at least for these writers, and further catalyzes a process that acknowledges the competence that women possess, and by dint of their intrinsic nature, ought to possess.

Again, we should note that we do not find women as gurus in earlier Tantras from before the thirteenth century, such as the KCT or the KuT, even as we find that several of these texts otherwise borrow from the KCT and the KuT.

Women Should Be Initiated

It is not just that women figure as gurus, they also figure all the way down, suggesting that not just exceptional women were accorded this respect, but ordinary women as well. We find references to the process of initiating women, to women as practitioners, and to the exceptional facility with *mantras* that women as a class possess. So, we find that "one should make every effort possible to initiate the women of one's clan, one's family (*kula*)."[92] Indeed, this act of initiating women is a great blessing for the family, and it will affect future generations. "Whoever does this auspicious act [of initiating women]—in this lineage are born men equal to Bṛhaspati. There is no doubt about this. This is the truth, this is the truth, o Goddess."[93] Bṛhaspati is the guru of the gods and noted for his learning and eloquence. So it is interesting that initiating a woman will not bring sons who will become emperors or great warriors but rather sons who will be learned.

The *Celestial Musician Tantra* (GT) as well supplies the verse the guru speaks to the woman as he or she initiates her, which carries with it a somewhat domesticated impulse toward marital fidelity. As we saw earlier, men repeat *mantras* alongside their women. "Together with the woman, one should recite the *mantra*. One should not recite the *mantra* alone."[94] By way of example, the *Secret Practice Tantra* (GST) informs us that the wives of the mythic figures Kṛṣṇa and Brahmā attained perfection of *mantras* along with their husbands. The GST even goes so far as to assert that these male figures themselves only attained perfection of the *mantras* because they had the advantage of having wives who also practiced the *mantra*. "O beloved of the mountain, Brahmā attained perfection [of the *mantra*] together with Sāvitrī and in the city of Dvārāvatī, the God Kṛṣṇa attained perfection together with his wife Satyā."[95]

However, as I note above, what's especially interesting about women's practice is the special facility women appear to have with *mantras*. We noted earlier the dangerous power a woman who repeats the Durgā *mantra* has (MT 11.33). We also noted—"just by merely thinking of a *mantra* a woman quickly gets the power to give boons."[96] The power to give boons is usually only something a very experienced yogī or a guru can acquire. Yet women have a special ability to acquire this power effortlessly: "She doesn't have to do worship (*pūjā*), or meditate, or purify herself with a bath" (GT 36.5b). As we saw earlier, just by thinking of a *mantra* she has this power. Her attainment of this power is likened to a series of other astonishing, yet well-known events. For example, "just as by merely remembering the holy Gaṅgā river, one becomes free of sin"[97] and "just as by merely seeing a flower, a celestial musician becomes happy"[98] and "just as by drinking milk a person oppressed with hunger conquers his desire for food"[99] and "just as by merely contemplating the Goddess Tripurā, liberation and enjoyments both arise."[100] In the same way, we find that "by mere contemplation women would acquire magical powers, without a doubt."[101]

This spiritual power that a woman has is iterated elsewhere in the *Blue Goddess of Speech Tantra* (NST) and the *Celestial Musician Tantra* (GT), with some of the same analogies; for instance, we find the analogy to the sin-destroying power of the Gaṅgā and the power of contemplation on the goddess Tripurā as well as the analogy to a hungry person being satiated by drinking milk.[102] Here also in the BT, as we saw earlier, we find that the rules for *mantras*, which apply for male practitioners, do not apply to women. "The restrictions which men contend with [in the practice of] *mantras* are not at all there for women. Anything whatsoever, by whichever [means], and moreover in all ways [is attained], for women magical attainment (*siddhi*) occurs, without any doubt . . . for a woman, by merely contemplating [on the *mantra*] she in this way becomes a giver of boons. Therefore one should make every effort to initiate a woman in one's own family."[103]

These three texts in this context extol women's spiritual competence, offering these analogies as comparative cases to present the argument as to why one should initiate women in *mantra* practice. These three texts conclude this argument with the advice to initiate women.[104]

The BT and the KCT

It may be useful to compare what we find in our group of texts, particularly the BT, with the *Kulacūḍāmaṇi Tantra* (KCT). The KCT presents a good point of comparison for several reasons. First, both texts deal with the left-handed rite of sexual union. Second, both focus on and emphasize Kāmākhyā as an especially sacrosanct site. Third, it is likely that the author(s) of the BT read the much earlier KCT since the later seventeenth through eighteenth-century BT borrows a number of verses from this much earlier tenth-century text.[105] At the same time, however, even though the BT borrows from the KCT, it nevertheless tends to frame what it borrows differently from the KCT.

So, for instance, the BT borrows a short hymn of ten verses from the KCT.[106] In the KCT the hymn is recited into the left ear of women who have not yet been initiated into the joint male-female worship circles (likely similar to the *cakra pūjā* mentioned earlier). These women who are not initiated are being asked to participate in the group rite, something that should not happen. Only initiated women should participate.[107] The KCT offers the hymn as a quick and easy makeshift mechanism for incorporating an uninitiated woman into the rite. The hymn substitutes for the initiation of women, since, as the KCT notes, "if the woman is not initiated, how can there be the *kula* worship?"[108] In the KCT, singing the hymn into a woman's ear guarantees her the same level of purity, necessary for her ritual participation, which she would have if she had, in fact, been initiated. We should note here that the KuT as well suggests that for the rite, the practitioner should quickly perform the initiation for the woman who is not already initiated. "If the woman is not initiated, he should quickly perform the initiation, o Goddess."[109]

In contrast, the BT does not use the hymn in this context at all, but rather enjoins the hymn to be sung into the left ear of the mother of a young boy who is about to be initiated with a *mantra* to increase the boy's eloquence. The hymn also differs slightly, perhaps relevantly, in the two versions. Where the KCT version says to the woman, "you are mother and father," the BT philosophizes the image of the mother, singing to the woman standing with her son, "O Goddess, you are subject and object of perception, and you make both subject and object manifest externally [in the world]," in this context apostrophizing the human mother of the boy as the highest absolute deity.[110] As a minor point, here also, the hymn plays upon a pun, where the word for "mother" also always means the "subject" as opposed to the "object." By highlighting this homonym, the hymn articulates an inherent homology between mothers and subjectivity, perhaps hinting toward an inherent subjectivity for the mother. This is, of course, a minor point, yet if this ritual was performed as the text prescribes, perhaps it may have been awkward for this ordinary mother to hear such expansive praise, but it could have also possibly established for her a level of status and respect from the other male and female observers, including her son, watching the rite's performance. And even without a knowledge of Sanskrit, this obvious pun would have likely been caught by the listeners.

And despite the fact that these and other Tantric texts in general contain within a single corpus a medley of various and sometimes mutually contradictory positions and prescriptions, nevertheless one can note a difference in the general tone of the BT in contrast to the KCT, and especially in its attitude toward women, despite the fact that both texts essentially address a path that involves the use of sexuality. So, for instance, the KCT generally follows the portrait of the Tantric male as depicted by much contemporary scholarship on Tantra—that is, mostly interested in the instrumental value of women for the success of the rite,[111] along with emphasis on the use of her sexual fluids[112] and tinged with the desire to have women unaccountably sexually attracted to the practitioner (in a James Bond sort of way).[113] At times the KCT almost reads like the *Kāma Sūtra*, and was likely influenced by it, with its descriptions of the tortured states of desire that the KCT aspirant induces into the women he wishes to attract. For instance, we find in the KCT: "gazing at him with a sideways glance, the composure of her mind is broken by her longing," and "flustered, she reveals her body by adjusting the end of her garment," and "she goes here and there, unable to bear the sexual desire."[114] These elements are absent from the BT. In contrast, the BT enjoins the practice of treating women with respect—something missing from the KCT—and stresses an innate divinity all women possess, even in their ordinary nonritual activities and states, whether they participate in the rite of sexual union or not, and beyond the spatial and temporal confines of the rite.[115]

With respect to the initiation of women, the BT offers no quick substitutes for initiation. Like the KCT, the BT adheres to the same dictum—that the *kula* rite cannot be performed with a woman who is not initiated.[116] However, instead of a loophole hymn, the BT, on the contrary, strongly advocates the initiation of women. Women, the BT's author(s) argues, ought to be initiated because it is very easy for them to perfect a *mantra* (7.189), and, as we saw earlier, the text presents a further enticement for the spiritual education of women, declaring the initiation of women an act of great merit, which also ensures that one will have a descendant equal to the guru of the gods, Bṛhaspati (7.199).

No Purity Rules

One more key feature of the "Kālī Practice" is that there are no rules to follow for worship or recitation of the *mantra*. Always accompanying the verses given earlier that proscribe against having hatred for women or treating women badly, we find also the lack of rules. "There are no rules for time or place and no rules for one's situation. There are no rules for the times for mantra recitation and no rules for worship or for making animal sacrifices."[117] Further, in a striking contrast to nearly all ritual performance elsewhere on the subcontinent, no concern or need for purity. "Here there is no regard for purity and no fault in being filthy or impure."[118] And, contrary to normative ritual expectations, without having bathed, the practitioner can worship, and the practitioner can worship after having already eaten food.[119] We should note here in particular that this lack of rules is not exactly the same as the typical Tantric reversal of rules, where one purposely inverts rules in order to transgress. Rather, in this case it involves a neglect of common rules–rules, which, by the way, often still hold good even in transgressive practices that are designed to "break" the rules.

Now, one of the most remarkable and pervasive features of Tantra in general is its excessive attention to ritual regulations. Alexis Sanderson points out how, more than rejecting earlier Vedic ritual, the Tantric becomes a "superritualist."[120] The result is something like a hypertrophied obsession with ritual. Indeed, a quick perusal of almost any Tantric text makes this readily apparent, and apart from this special "Kālī Practice," the texts consulted here also supply no dearth of ritual regulations.[121] The eschewal of ritual regulations for this particular practice then is striking.

Why the rejection of rules? How might this operate in the context of this practice? I'm going to suggest a possible function. On the one hand, much of the ritual regulation we find in these Tantric texts—for example, the rule to not eat before the worship is complete—operates to generate a sense of purity. Now, as Louis Dumont pointed out,[122] the notion of purity can be seen as being at the root of status and hierarchy in India (even taking into account modifications suggested by an astute thinker like Veena Das,[123] to focus on auspiciousness as a key ingredient in the equation). So on one level, upsetting the ritual edifice shakes up the order of things. It undermines the underlying template that divides and sets aside certain things, times, and people as being more pure than others.

This function of Tantra we find elsewhere also. For instance, it may be possible to see a particular practice that Abhinavagupta discusses in the *Tantrāloka* as a precursor to this practice.[124] He describes a path that lacks the regulations for purity and impurity, which he then continues on to explicate in terms of what we might see as an acknowledgment of the linguistic mutual imbrication that opposites share, that is, how it is the case that the positing of a particular thing always implies its absence.[125] The differences from the rite we address here have to do with the fact that (1) Abhinava does not connect this with women; and (2) Abhinava's explanation is a more sophisticated linguistic argument. What these differences do share, however, is that both operate upon an assumption that the destruction of the categories of pure and impure leaves open the possibilities for reconstructing identity. It's as though this destruction of the idea of order clears the way to reconstitute the fabric of hierarchy, and in this case, we might add, the menstrual rules limiting women's ritual capacities, which also contribute to the hierarchical relation of the genders.

Rules, after all, in general function to create parameters for social identity. Rules shape us, define who we are, and how we relate to society. Remove the rules and the sense of self is left in an aporia; a void of identity ensues. It may not be too far off to suggest that this neglect of rules functions to wipe the slate clean, to undermine the normatively socially constructed and socially imbricated identity the participant has. One can see this encoded in the Hindu practice of the *saṃskāra*. The *saṃskāra* is a ritual enactment, usually encoded into the body, which distinguishes the recipient, often to establish a hierarchy that makes him or her superior to those who have not undergone the rite and that must be maintained usually through ritual regulation. In this case the rules are erased and with it the distinguishing marks for the practitioner. It may be possible to understand this rejection of regulation in these terms, as a way of reconstituting the social template, which implicitly orders relations into a structured hierarchy in order to create a space for something different, in this case to restructure the relation between the genders.

The Key Again: Women Are Gods

Earlier I mentioned a particular signature half-verse that is repeated across several texts and that signals a rescripting of the view of women. "Women are Gods; women are the life-breath" the verse proclaims.[126] Since women are gods, it makes sense to both honor women and to construct an ethic in relation to them whereby one does not offend them; in other words, to treat a woman as one treats a god. And indeed we find that this innate and divine power that women have is profound. Women are, after all, like gods, since, as the *Secret Practice Tantra* (GST) tells us, "Women are the source of the world, women are the source of everything, O Goddess."[127] With this statement the GST assimilates women as a class to the level of creator deity, which may partially help to explain their apotheosis into divinity. The innate and divine power women possess is so great, in fact, that in the *Blue Goddess of Speech Tantra* (NST) and the *Māyā Tantra* (MT) women head the list of gods and godlike figures to whom one owes allegiance, even displacing the great gods Śiva and Viṣṇu.

In an interesting expansion upon this idea of the ordinary woman as important, as even akin to the divine, we see that the NST advises the practitioner to give priority to this ordinary woman. The NST urges one to rather abandon one's mother and father and even one's Guru than to insult one's female partner. "Better to abandon one's mother and father and one's guru . . . than that one should insult one's beloved (fem.)."[128] This, in fact, precisely inverts the common Hindi proverb that Gloria Raheja gives us: "Whoever kicks [i.e., offends] his mother and father to strengthen his relationship with his wife, his sin will not go away even if he wanders through all the pilgrimage places [where sins are said to be removed]."[129]

In contrast to Raheja's proverb, in the *Blue Goddess of Speech Tantra* (NST), the Great God Śiva says, "Better to abandon Brahmā, Śambhu and Hari, better that I (Bhairava) myself be abandoned, than that one should insult one's beloved (fem.)." "One's worship is in vain, one's *mantra* recitation is useless, the hymns one recites are in vain, the fire ceremonies with gifts to priests; all these are in vain if one does that which is offensive to a woman."[130]

If one insults a woman, then all one's spiritual endeavors are useless. In this instance one can imagine this playing out on the domestic front—a husband all wrapped up in his spiritual quest, worshiping the gods while his wife tries to get him to take care of her and the family's needs. (The husband protagonist in Deepa Mehta's *Fire* [1998] comes to mind.) In our scenario here, this wife would have a scriptural injunction to back her case. Śiva, however, goes further than this; he continues, "Better to die than to do that which is offensive to a woman."[131]

The MT offers the same advice as the NST, and then goes even further. Here, not only are the male gods playing second fiddle, and one should give up one's life rather than insult a woman, but more than this, even the goddess is relegated to a secondary position. "Better even that one should abandon the Goddess (*devī*); but one should not in any way abandon one's own beloved female partner."[132] This is especially key in that the ordinary woman is given more importance than the goddess. Usually we find that the ordinary woman has importance only because she is understood as the goddess temporarily incarnate. However, here, this author contrasts the two and declares the ordinary woman more important. The MT also supplies the rationale for prioritizing one's female partner: "Not the creator, not Viṣṇu, not Śiva, not the beautiful Goddess, not the primeval eternal Goddess—none of these [gods or goddesses] will be able to protect the person who does that which is offensive to women."[133] That is, this ordinary woman has a power intrinsic to her being and deserves respect as a result. So women are accorded this respect because intrinsically they are gods, "*striyo devaḥ*." However, it is rather curious that the texts all use the masculine word *god* (*deva*). That is, women are gods and not goddesses. Elsewhere in these texts in profusion, women are assimilated to goddesses. For instance, Śiva says to the goddess, women are "in their essence, you,"[134] using the feminine form. Why are they here in the "Kālī Practice" indicated by the masculine term *god*?[135]

I'm going to suggest that the use of the masculine here is a linguistic marker referencing another class of gods, and that as a class of gods, women resemble this other class of living breathing gods. That is, the status that we find for women in these texts in many respects parallels the *bhū-deva*, the "earth-gods," that is, Brahmins, that class of humans who are like gods, but walk the face of the earth.

This is corroborated in other ways; for instance, the GST applies the same procedure of feeding Brahmins for the attainment of religious merit to women. "Earlier the rules were given that one should feed a Brahmin according to one's ability. In the same way one should feed a woman" (GST 5.9bf.). Women are like Brahmins, and just as feeding a Brahmin brings merit, so does feeding a woman. Similarly, the BT also tells us that worshiping a woman brings results equal to that which one gains by giving a learned Brahmin a field rich with grain (BT 6.7f.). Elsewhere, in a list where we might expect to find Brahmins listed, women take their place. The CT says, "One should make great efforts and with devotion worship the guru, goddess, *sādhus* (itinerant practitioners), woman, and the immortal self."[136] It would not have been at all against normative expectations to find Brahmins in this fourth position slot; instead here we find the category "women." Again, the GST describes for each of the four castes the state of beatitude one can expect from the repetition of the *mantra* associated with the Five Ms.[137] Here, the Brahmin is absorbed into the supreme self; the warrior caste (*kṣatriya*) gets to dwell with the supreme goddess eternally; the merchant attains the same form as the supreme goddess (*svarūpa*); and the servant caste (*śūdra*) gets to live in the same general world as the goddess (*saloka*). The text then includes women as a fifth caste, who get absorbed into the body of the goddess.[138]

The point of interest for us here is that women are marked as a class, like Brahmins, like the other three castes. They function as a category, just as Brahmins function as a category. One should not harm women as a class, because women are a class. Like Brahmins, who should also not be harmed because they are earth-walking gods (*bhū-devaḥ*), women are also a class of gods who happen to be walking on earth. And again, just as we find in normative Hinduism that serving Brahmins, these earth-walking gods, leads a person to salvation, so similarly, all "beings reach salvation by serving women."[139] Earlier I noted a verse from the GST that assimilates women as a class to the creator god. In fact, this is precisely what we find with Brahmins who get linguistically and otherwise assimilated to the creator god Brahmā.

This class action reverence is not at all like the respect accorded to the guru or the yogī. In the case of the guru especially, most Tantric texts, including these, are eminently cognizant of the existence of both good and false gurus, and take no pains to supply us with lists of the qualities we might expect to see in both. Gurus are individuals and individually merit worship and respect. Not so the case with Brahmins, and here with women. Just as Brahmins as a class are categorically offered respect, so these texts enjoin this sort of class-based respect toward women. We should keep in mind here how radically this diverges from normative Hindu tradition where women as a caste are mostly lumped in with, or placed on a par with, the lowest of the four castes, the *śūdras*.[140] Likewise, women's facility with *mantras* extends to members of the class as a whole and not specifically to particular women.

What does this class action reverence mean for women? It affords a way for shifting the status women have in the social sphere. For our own purposes, what's interesting about this is precisely that it does not rely especially upon a version of gender founded on a duality. This nonbinary model, I suspect, is part of what's key in the reconfiguring of women's roles. A dualistic model, one could argue, implicitly structures itself around a notion of self and other that inevitably encodes an agonistic model, which by its very form as duality resists reconciliation. It may be that, as Kristeva and Lacan argue, insofar as we construct our sense of self out of an element that must be extruded outside and alienated as "other" to our selves—and as an other that has historically taken the form of woman, as both Lacan and Kristeva note[141]—this "other," as a perpetually alienated "other," then becomes and remains intrinsic to the stability of self. That is, we can't get rid of the "other" without destabilizing our sense of self. This indeed presents a formidable psychological barrier to seeing women as equal, to releasing them from the category of "other." On the other hand, the model that these texts present offers one possible way out of the impasse we find with the binary self/other (echoed in the binary of man/woman). The very multiplicity of the terms destabilizes the system. This may offer possibilities for rethinking gender outside a dualist hierarchy.

2

Sex Talk and Gender Rites

Women and the Tantric Rite of Sexual Union

If having sex with women could give enlightenment, then all the creatures in the world ought to be enlightened.

—Vasiṣṭha, in dialogue with the Buddha
(Cīnācāra Tantra 4.23)[1]

Tantra has become an orientalist wet dream, a transgressive, weird, sexy, dangerous world.

—Wendy Doniger

Representations of Sex/Sex as Representation

The "Kālī Practice" that we saw in chapter 2 includes the Tantric rite of sexual union. One, of course, wonders, "Did anyone ever really do this?" That is, were these practices of Tantric ritual sex ever enacted? And, further, what might it mean for a woman to participate in the rite of sexual union in the first place?

This chapter looks at the Tantric rite of sexual union as we find it in this particular group of Tantric texts from the fifteenth through eighteenth centuries located in northeast India. With this, I want to counter the notion that sex in Tantra universally functions to construct women as objects for male gains.[2] I suggest rather that the Tantric rite of sexual union is a more varied phenomenon. At times, as here in this version found in texts associated with the "Kālī Practice,"[3] we find a picture of the Tantric rite that reimagines its Tantric attitude toward women, and we should note that here we deal with living ordinary women and not goddesses inside the male body. This is not, I should emphasize, how I see the Tantric rite of sexual union to typically function, nor how much other fine scholarship has depicted it.[4] In fact, I was surprised to note the differences this portrayal of the rite presented. The differences we find here, on the one hand, remind us that Tantra is by no means monolithic. Its practices varied and its attitudes toward women varied. On the other hand, the differences here offer us other models for understanding both women and ways of imagining the relationship between the body and the "spirit."

Key in the portrait of the rite here is that it moves away from a notion of ascetic mastery over the body and women. This is coded in the rite gesturally, in the ways that bodies act in relation to one another. It is also iterated conceptually. The God Śiva tells us in the *Great Blue Tantra* (BT) that there is a particular secret behind the Tantric rite of sexual union. This secret has to do with the understanding that the *feminine* principle is not matter, but spirit. We may remind ourselves that almost universally in India (and the West) the feminine is otherwise coded as *matter*. The idea that the feminine is matter and the masculine is spirit, which is a legacy of early Sāṁkhya theory, pervades throughout in Indian thought, and, we might add, also in the West. In this Tantric view, however, the masculine principle is coded as matter, the insentient "dead" body. This secret that the BT reveals is an unusual representation of the feminine, and the author of this text is no doubt aware of the deviance from the norm that he makes.

Yet on further reflection, we realize that with this image of the feminine as spirit, this author actually simply carries to its logical conclusion the ramifications of a pervasive Tantric maxim. That is, one finds everywhere the Tantric saying that the god Śiva—who usually is conceived as supreme spirit—is actually a mere corpse (*śava*), a dead body, mere matter, without the feminine principle (*śakti*). The male god is the "dead body" while the female is the enlivening "spirit." Iconographically, this appears in the well-known image of the goddess Kālī astride the corpse Śiva. What might this mean in the context of the revelation from the BT's author of the secret that women are "spirit"? For the god Śiva to declare that the feminine, which is typically "body," is in fact "spirit"—and with this the intention is that the female is not object, not matter—entails a rejection of the notion that one should "master" the feminine. Thus, the rejection of a model of male asceticism is conceptually coherent with the rewriting of the feminine as "spirit."

What we see in this depiction of the rite is essentially a discourse around women's bodies, bodies in general, the practice of sex, and how identity gets configured. This discourse contributes to our understanding of the ways that "talk" about women and about sex sets the terms for how we understand women and their bodies.

In this chapter as well, however, we take up the problem of the relation between sex represented in a text and the question of whether "anyone ever really did this." That is, what does it mean to portray a rite involving sex in a textual source? In this sense, this chapter is also about how we enact identity, and especially about how sex and language—and language about sex—get employed in this process. We have to keep in mind that texts that talk about the rite of sexual union are doing just that—"talking" about sex. We do not directly document ritual practices involving sex from the fifteenth through eighteenth centuries, but rather we see how these practices are represented. That is, here we confine ourselves to looking at "talk" about sex in the fifteenth through eighteenth centuries and how this discourse might be interpreted. Especially, here it is important to place this "talk" about sex in relation to the ways that we in the twenty-first century employ talk about sex. How does our "talk" about sex differ from theirs?

Moreover, what does it mean to "talk" about sex? For our contemporary world, "talk" of sex is often construed to degrade women, such as that we find in a popular understanding of pornography (as if the *speaking* of sex, the very act of representing it, somehow inevitably entails an element of the pornographic). Here I am thinking specifically of Catharine Mackinnon's legal arguments against pornography, but her view is not an uncommon one.[5] What this rite may help us to discover is that "talk" of sex need not necessarily be scripted in only this way.

Against the grain of a pervasive objectification of woman *as* bodies and the consequent silencing of women's voices that "talk" of sex often engenders, we find a creative reappropriation of sexuality here. The rite of sexual union here teaches us that women are "spirit" rather than body, and it offers a model to shift away from an idea of male mastery over women and over the body. With a prescience that, from our position in the twenty-first century, we cannot help marveling at, these authors appear to recognize the links between an ideology of ascetic mastery (especially mastery over the body) and the denigration of women.

I focus in chapter 1 on the "Kālī Practice," a specific practice that gets rid of all rules except one: treating women with respect. We may note that when the texts describe the "Kālī Practice" in this group of texts from the fifteenth through eighteenth centuries, one always finds the rite of sexual union associated with it. What is interesting in this association is that what the "Kālī Practice" encodes prescriptively, in letting go of rules except the rule of treating women with respect, gets reiterated on the level of gesture in the rite of sexual union through its ritual incorporation of physical gestures of respect toward the woman. This idea of respect toward women is further encoded metaphorically through narrative in the story of Vasiṣṭha learning this rite. For the discussion here I draw mostly from two texts in this group of eight texts associated with northeast India, the *Bṛhannīla Tantra "Great Blue Tantra"* (BT) and the *Cīnācāra Tantra* (CT).

We should note that Tantric texts vary in their representation of this rite, and earlier texts such as the *Kulārṇava Tantra* (KuT) or the *Kulacūḍāmaṇi Tantra* (KCT) offer a different version of the rite, even as the later BT borrows in numerous places from the tenth-century KCT. So, for instance, the BT enjoins that the practitioner bow to the woman with whom he performs the rite, something we do not see in earlier "left-handed" Tantras such as the *Kulārṇava Tantra* (KuT) or the *Kulacūḍāmaṇi Tantra* (KCT).

Rather, the much earlier KCT offers a flamboyant image of the male Tantric hero, an ultimate womanizer, virile, attractive to women, and yet himself "cool," unmoved; he just "uses" women, albeit for their bodily fluids. To illustrate briefly some of the difference, we can look at a passage in the much earlier (ca. tenth-century) *Kulacūḍāmaṇi Tantra* (KCT), "when he has finished repetition of the *kūlākula mantra*, instantly he attracts the woman whose name he has written in the ritual diagram. Even if she is a hundred leagues away, on a mountain or in the middle of a river, guarded with chains in the middle of a thousand islands, her eyes rolling with desire, her waist trembling from the weight of her breasts . . . she comes, her heart desiring the practitioner."[6]

We find a kind of machismo in this image of the suave magical seducer and the passion of the woman he magically controls, a machismo nowhere present in the BT. On the other hand, we find in the BT an advocacy of reverence toward women outside the context of the rite, and even toward women whom he never participates with in the rite—something we do not find in earlier "left-handed" Tantras like the KCT or the KuT.[7]

Similarly, in the KuT the image of woman differs from what we find in the BT. For the earlier KuT the woman as *yoginī*, female counterpart to the yogī, predominates. She appears fierce, and we are not dealing with merely a fierce deity, but an image of woman as akin to a fury, a mad devouring creature, ready to eat the practitioner who makes a mistake. So we find in the KuT, "the fool who makes distinctions based on caste while in the middle of the *cakra* [rite], the *yoginīs* devour him."[8] We do not find this or a similar depiction of a female in the BT. The psychological implications of a devouring female are potent. They signal an image of woman as as enemy, encoding an agonistic attitude toward women. Especially it signals the category of the female as the projection of male fears. The differences we find may be read as a shift in attitudes toward women for the later text, acknowledging women in the place of the subject, and, that in a way that does not project images of women as inhuman, uncontrollable devouring creatures. In appendix 1 I examine in greater detail the differences we find between the BT's configuration of the rite of sexual union and what we find in other Tantric texts elsewhere.

Also, I suggest that this—what we might call "reappropriation" of the rite of sexual union—is deliberate and consciously crafted by these authors through the details and shifts these authors add. Beyond this, we should also note that through this "talk" of the rite, the BT's coding of the rite of sexual union offers another language in addition, encoding its message in the gestures of the otherwise mute body. In this sense we find two kinds of "talk," language that describes and the performative silent speech of the body's gestures.

In what follows we first explore the myth of Vasiṣṭha learning the rite of sexual union and how this teaching moves away from a model of ascetic male domination over women and over the body. Following this we address some methodological considerations for how we can use texts, apart from other forms of evidence, to discuss images of women in Tantra. After this, we then briefly address representations of Tantric sex for the West, and then how we may use contemporary feminist discussions of sex as representation to help us situate the representation of Tantra for the West. This discussion takes up a thread of looking at different forms of speech, particularly speech that documents or records events in contrast to speech that is performative, "doing" what it says.

In the final part of this chapter we look at the Tantric text itself, in this case the BT, in terms of its own status as a representation that also functions to enact identity, just as our current discussions about Tantra do. Here we explore the relationship between the text as speech and the rite of sexual union as gesture, which gives a "message" enacted on the body. Finally we conclude by addressing how the particular version of the rite of sexual union in the BT contributes to enact a particular identity for women. With this we examine the details of the rite of sexual union in the BT.

The Education of Vasiṣṭha

The myth we look at here revolves around a particular man, a sage named Vasiṣṭha. Vasiṣṭha is well known in the Hindu landscape as a role model of piety. Soft-spoken, calm, with the divine docile cow at his side, Vasiṣṭha embodies the Brahmin ascetic. He stands for the values of orthodox Hinduism.[9] On the other hand, his Tantric persona is less well known. In Kāmākhyā, his piety undergoes a sea change. Rather than the mirror-perfect image of pious Brahmin perfection, he presents a hard-headed and fastidious adherence to empty and inhibited rules of purity. He conquers the senses, but his is a fanatical ascetic excess, a denial of the sensual, the body, and all that is associated with, in his mind, the tainted world of desires (*Cīnācāra Tantra* [CT] 1.34).

In Vasiṣṭha's story the *Cīnācāra Tantra* (CT) tells us, "Worshipping the Great Goddess of Illusion, Vasiṣṭha conquered his senses excessively; indeed, his worship lasted a thousand years."[10] Elsewhere in this text his worship on the Blue Hill in Kāmākhyā lasts even longer, ten thousand years.[11] Despite the fervor of his worship, however, the text tells us, "the Goddess Tārā, the savior who carries one across the cycle of birth and death, did not bestow her grace on him."[12] He prays to Tārā, who is here also called "Mahāmāyā," the Great Goddess of Illusion, and she just ignores him. Why is she ignoring him? Vasiṣṭha, who cannot bear being ignored by her, is blazing with anger (*kopena jvalito*), and he seeks out the creator god Brahmā for answers. Brahmā responds: "And that Brahmā said to the sage, 'listen to my words, son. Tārā, who is a *vidyā* [Goddess as magical speech], contains within herself the knowledge of all the elements of the cosmos (*tattva*). She carries one across the worlds. With your mind linked to perfection, worship her auspicious feet. Really, because of her grace I create the fourteen worlds and I produce the four Vedas."[13] Vasiṣṭha's interview with the male creator god Brahmā provides no good answers as to why she keeps ignoring his intense worship, but rather sends him back to asceticism. Even after still more long but fruitless efforts, Tārā still ignores Vasiṣṭha. At this point Vasiṣṭha has had enough. The text tells us, "Then, that lord of sages blazing with great anger, then having taken water, he proceeded to curse her."[14] Only then, at this point does she appear to him. However, she does not succumb to his anger and does not grant him a boon. Rather she rebukes him for his harshness, politely informing him that his method is wrong, and all his many sensory restraints completely useless. Even as Tārā rebukes Vasiṣṭha, she maintains a polite demeanor, addressing him as "bhavān," a term of respect.[15] We see here,

> Then the Goddess of Great Illusion, the Saviour who gives all magical attainments, spoke to Vasiṣṭha, the best of sages and highest among the practitioners. "Sir, how is it that you with your mind full of harshness have cursed me? There is one person who knows the procedure for worshipping me, no one else. That is Viṣṇu, who has

> taken the form of the Buddha. Your intense ascetical restraints and the time you have spent are completely useless, wasted. Without knowing the essence of me you have with this practice created obstacles. Now go to where Viṣṇu is, who has taken the form of the Buddha."[16]

Thus she sends him off to the Buddha. Vasiṣṭha's methods are all wrong, but he has no clue about what exactly is not right in his method of bull-headed mastery over the body, in his ten thousand years of asceticism. What then does the Buddha teach him? The Buddha teaches him the rite of sexual union.

When Vasiṣṭha fails after the first round of ten thousand years of asceticism, he initially seeks out Brahmā, desperate for answers on his failed worship. Brahmā responds against Vasiṣṭha's expectations. Brahmā refuses to commiserate with Vasiṣṭha and refuses to act as intermediary for him with the goddess. Instead, Brahmā praises the greatness of Tārā. He even subordinates his own position as creator to Tārā's, telling Vasiṣṭha that his own creation of the four Vedas, the preeminent holy books of India, came by the grace of the goddess Tārā. After Vasiṣṭha recounts his fruitless efforts, Brahmā again urges him to go back to Kāmākhyā and continue his efforts. Vasiṣṭha, who has anyway conquered his sensual desires, gives it another try, and fails, and finally curses the goddess Tārā in his frustration.

She, however, also thwarts his expectations. Tārā does not give in to his outburst of temper. She responds to his curse, pointing out his unsagelike anger, "How is it that you with anger and such a harsh attitude curse me?" The politeness she displays, using the honorific forms to address him, throughout her rejection especially makes a point here. Even as Tārā rebukes Vasiṣṭha, her politeness in the process highlights her superiority to him. He, purportedly a self-controlled sage, loses his cool, becoming emotionally distraught and uncontrolled. With his emotional outburst, he rather acts out a frequent charge leveled toward women, that is, an "emotional irrationality," while she, the "woman," the one typically culturally coded to be the "emotional irrational" one, on the other hand, maintains a sense of self-control. She is polite and calm, offering a cool, deliberate refusal of his curse. In the end she controls the interaction and ends it, sending him off to the Buddha, who is here an incarnation of the Hindu god Viṣṇu, for proper teaching. In this sense also, her initial silence ought not to be read as the silence of the woman as subaltern, but rather as a sign of her power. While her "talk" here eventually clarifies their relative power, the silence behind it is one that suggests her choice rather than his.

What strikes one especially in this tale of Vasiṣṭha's education is first, how this goddess Tārā upsets the normative cycle of events—typically, austerities *must* confer results from the gods worshiped. The innumerable uncouth demons who gain powers that they then use to harass the gods are the most salient example of this mostly incontrovertible law of austerity. Even when the practitioner is otherwise unworthy and impure of heart, and the deity knows it, she or he is still constrained to offer a boon, albeit frequently with a tricky loophole. Some especially well-known examples would include the demons Rāvaṇa, Tāraka, Hiraṇyakaśipu, Mahiṣāsura, but also numerous others.

Second, we note how she upsets typical representations of the feminine, as well, especially in that she manages to elude both poles of a pervasive bifurcation of woman as either nurturing, a motherlike figure, or a temptress, what Tracy Pintchman describes as an ambiguity that make women either "instruments of salvation" or "temptresses."[17] The goddess Tārā, in contrast, presents an image of a woman that is neither a nurturing mother, nor a temptress. If anything, we might analogize her to a demanding and meticulous connoisseur of fine food or art who just knows when it's all wrong.[18] She matter-of-factly points out his ignorance, how he "with this practice which is all wrong" (CT 1.43a) needs proper instruction. Her ability to upset typical gendered expectations establishes for her in this case an autonomy and subjective agency; she is emphatically not at the whim of this conquering ascetical Brahmin.

The Buddha's Teaching: The "Kālī Practice"

When Vasiṣṭha first sees the Buddha, like the good Brahmin that he is (and also like a number of good nineteenth-century orientalists), Vasiṣṭha is appalled by the Tantric Buddha's profligate behavior with women and wine.[19] Vasiṣṭha sees the Buddha drinking wine, "his eyes red and rolling with intoxication,"[20] and "excited with love play."[21] The CT tells us "from afar, in this way, Vasiṣṭha spied the Buddha. He became filled with confusion. Remembering the Goddess who carries one across birth and death, he [thought], 'What is this karma that Viṣṇu is doing in the form of the Buddha! This crazy, intoxicated behavior goes against my [understanding] of the doctrine of the Veda.' "[22]

Vasiṣṭha is surprised and initially skeptical about the value of the rite of sexual union. He says, "If having sex with women could give enlightenment, then all the creatures in the world ought to be enlightened from relations with women."[23] However, after Vasiṣṭha hears a mysterious voice from the sky urging him onward (CT 2.8–11), he decides to take teachings from the Buddha. "Thus the great-souled Vasiṣṭha was thinking [about the Buddha's crazy behavior], and then a voice in the sky announced, 'Do not worry like this, o man of a good vow. O sage, this behavior is the highest truth in the worship of the Goddess Tāriṇī, the Saviour.' "[24]

Vasiṣṭha's hair stands on end when he hears this voice. Then we see, "Vasiṣṭha, thrilled [by the sound of the voice in the sky], fell flat on the ground like a stick as it were. Then, rising up, the sage brought his palms together in obeisance and said 'I bow.' He went to Viṣṇu, who was in the form of the Buddha, o Pārvatī. Now, that Buddha, who was staggering happily from the wine, when he saw him, the Buddha, happy in himself, said, 'what brings you here?' "[25]

The Buddha then teaches him the "Kālī Practice,"[26] the special practice discussed in chapter 1, which emphasizes a complete absence of rules except one. Here, as we see also in the BT, there are no rules regarding time, or place, or food, and so on.: "Everything is pure; there is never any time that is not auspicious" and "he can worship the Goddess in any way at all, [even] without having taken a bath, [even] having already eaten."[27] This stands in stark contrast to typical Tantra, where rules permeate every activity in abundance. Especially the rules about bathing and not having eaten before worship are normally important. Yet here what is important, the text continues on, is that "one should not ever have hatred towards women, even more so of the worship of a woman. He should not ever criticize women or abuse them; and moreover, he should not ever lie to women or do that which they do not like."[28]

That the text tells the practitioner to be honest with women is interesting and not found in earlier texts like the KuT.[29] I do not think it is suggesting too much to say that for this text to prescribe that men be honest with women signals a shift in attitudes toward women. It suggests treating women, this otherwise typical "other," as men would like to be treated, and in this way suggests that women, too, occupy the subjective place that men assume. We find here also the statement "Women are Gods, women are the life breath."[30] Further, in this lesson Vasiṣṭha discovers that "all beings reach salvation by serving women,"[31] a reversal of the more typical well-known dictum whereby women reach salvation by serving their husbands, or low-caste persons reach salvation by serving Brahmins.

Specifically, this "talk" about how women should be viewed, a talk directed specifically against asceticism, enacts a different attitude toward women. With this practice centered on women, the Buddha advocates to Vasiṣṭha a recognition of a subjective autonomy for women, in their bodies, which he advocates should not be physically abused, and in their subjective sense of self, in his advice to speak truthfully to women and not to criticize women.[32]

Bodies and Mastery

In terms of the specifics of the rite of sexual union, what exactly does the Buddha teach Vasiṣṭha? What the Buddha teaches him is not a better technique for mastery, one that here utilizes the female body and the act of sex. Sometimes one gets this image from descriptions of the Tantric rite of sexual union—that what Tantric sex is really about is a technique used for employing bodies, especially female bodies, and in this context the use and abuse of female bodies as objects, simply manipulated for male gains, most often in order to obtain some particular supernatural mastery of the world, for instance, the power to fly through the air. I am not suggesting that these representations of the Tantric rite of sexual union are incorrect. In fact, we do find just this attitude in a number of texts, and I discuss this in greater detail in appendix 1.[33] Rather, I suggest that we should be hesitant in applying a monolithic and unitary view of the motive for Tantric practice. If we look closely at the various texts available, we find that the practice of the Tantric rite of sexual union reveals a variety of different agendas and motivations. Indeed, as indigenous sources imply by their use of varied nomenclature, searching for unitary motives within a complex history, all aligned under the single vague and slippery rubric "Tantra," may in fact work to muddle key differences.

What, then, does the Buddha teach Vasiṣṭha? Vasiṣṭha's initial attempts are driven by an ideology of mastery. If he just practices long enough, ten thousand years, he will force the goddess to yield to his prayers, or so he thinks. He hangs onto an ascetic purity that represents not only a wrongheaded clinging to outward forms, but, with this, the CT points to the deeper underlying problem in his attitude, that it clings to a model of domination. For Vasiṣṭha, ascetic practice entails a mechanical application of laws.[34] In the same way that he masters and subdues his body and senses, Vasiṣṭha also attempts to master, rather than listen to, the goddess Tārā. Vasiṣṭha's vain attempts at domination result rather in her criticism of his harshness. In one sense, her neglect of him, ignoring his continued worship, is only simply mirroring to him that his apparent worship is at its core an attempt to actually "ignore" her, by construing her as object rather than subject. She is not a subject in relation to him; he sees her as object, mechanically forced to confer boons for his long asceticism.

The Buddha teaches him to let go of his force-laden asceticism, to instead embrace a model that involves a recognition of the other, in this case, the "other" as women. If asceticism is a denial of a need for help from another, the goddess Tārā, through the teachings of the Buddha about how to worship her, appears to be deconstructing this model of isolation, especially through a teaching that reincorporates the body rather than denying it. It is the body especially that Vasiṣṭha conquers through his long asceticism, and it is precisely the body that is reenlivened, and allowed to register a variety of needs, desires, and states of pleasure through the rite of sexual union.

The body in many ways stands as quintessential other; the body is often associated with the feminine in precisely this context. To get Vasiṣṭha to recognize rather than deny the body is to revoke a rule of dominance that subjugates nature and its representative in the body and, by extension, women. These three—nature, the body, and woman—are connected as secondary members of a pervasive binary pattern (mind/body, man/woman, subject/object, spirit/nature, and so on) that we find not only in medieval India but also in the West as well. Here the secondary member is relegated to a marginal and inferior status in relation to the first. Yet, even as the second member of this binary is extruded from the proper domain of subjecthood, it nevertheless functions to constitute the idea of a subject, by standing outside and apart from it. For Vasiṣṭha's education, the more normative typical coding, where the first member of these binaries is master of the second, is unlearned.

What Vasiṣṭha learns (or unlearns) from the Buddha is to shift away from an attitude of rejection and subjugation of the body, the feminine, this second element in the binary. In allowing a slippery incursion into Vasiṣṭha's world of this habitually excluded other, he experiences a greater displacement of solipsistic, egoic identity than any amount of self/(body)-denying austerity could have ever afforded. He shifts from his initial, world-denying abstraction of his self as a self that excludes anything that might taint it with the smell of contingency. The Buddha's lesson leads him instead to a recognition of his own embeddedness within a world where he must efface not the trace of his body through austerity, but the impulse to make that which is other to him, both the goddess and his body, into mere objects. What is key here is that the enlightenment the Buddha offers presents a shift in paradigms; it is a move away from a notion of attaining a transcendental self. The Buddha offers a model that relationally incorporates the body and others as existentially legitimate.

What is more, he shifts his attitude toward women and the body through a practice of sex. For Western ears, where talk of sex is more frequently associated with the pornographic,[35] this may initially sound like an odd depiction of the function of sex. I suggest that it may be helpful to work against our Western presumptions regarding "sex" if we stress the first term in the phrase "rite of sexual union" rather than the second. As rite, this depiction of this act involves an enactment (reenactment?) of the social order. In this sense the rite serves to construct identities.

In the final analysis, what he teaches with this special "Kālī Practice" is more about an attitude than a technique—about listening to women, not forcing them to mechanically fulfill his own desires. As we see in teachings of the "Kālī Practice" in the BT, "women should not ever be coerced (*haṭhād*) . . . not even mentally" (6.343f.).

Methodological Caveats

What does it mean for a seventeenth-century Indian author to suggest in the voice of the Buddha that women maintain a sovereign right over their bodies and that women should be esteemed? Is it some unexpected form of a proto-feminism that takes its own contours, one, perhaps to our view, oddly connected with sex? We should keep in mind, however, that this is discourse, a kind of "talk." The articulation of this special "Kālī Practice," especially across several texts, suggests both its possible implementation, and the obverse, a world where this understanding did not figure as normative, hence the desire to say it in texts.

With this, I do not attempt to make claims regarding the historical behavior of actual women or male Tantric practitioners. This is clearly a desideratum, however; recovering the "what really happened" of seventeenth-century northeast India is a project that from all sides and methodologies is fraught with the inevitable contortions of representation. What we address here is especially how we might go about making sense of all these representations, all this "talk" about how one should view women and the relationship between women and sex. Part of what this chapter does, then, is to explore how we in the twenty-first century also bring to our discussions of Tantric sex in the seventeenth century our own embedded presumptions about women and sex, so that we may not merely naively read into the images of women and sex that we find in these textual representations of women and sex. Keeping in mind the refractory lens we employ, we can glean a strand of seventeenth-century life, an attitude toward women that at least some people in this late medieval period were "talking" about.

More than this, however, I suggest that what is really valuable about the rite depicted here is not so much how well it portrays seventeenth-century practices. Rather it is significant because we see the historical propagation of a discourse about women. These texts reflect the emergence of a discourse, "talk," addressing social relations between the genders. I suggest that its importance lies in the challenge, as discourse, that it presents to normative classifications.

I should repeat that I use the terms *subject* and *subjective* here not so much as a designation of some sort of "real" or existentially autonomous entity—certainly there are considerable philosophical and cultural problems entailed in assigning this notion to a nonmodern non-Western context. So, instead of discussing real or historical subjects, I rather point to a designation that signifies a slippery but rhetorically and grammatically effective and prevalent category, even without our being able to precisely demarcate the locus or limits of this being as representation.

I should also emphasize that this rite associated with the "Kālī Practice" does not homologize women to goddesses, and then venerate only the abstract goddess, recognizing the woman only coincidentally and temporarily as her channel during the few hours while the rite lasts. It is also not about worshiping goddesses who are stone images, or far away, or intangible goddesses (those typically more amenable to pronouncing precisely what the aspirant wishes to hear). Rather, this practice is about venerating ordinary, living women.

So, in the Tantric rite of sexual union as the CT lays it out, the goddess is explicitly *not* invoked for the rite. The CT is explicit on this point, "And there the Goddess is not invoked,"[36] precisely because this ordinary human woman, in her prosaic everyday state, is already, without any necessary transformations, the deity to be worshiped. She is explicitly here not a temporary channel for the goddess, but divine in her usual, normal, nonexotic and nonextraordinary self.[37] And, as we saw in chapter 1, the "Kālī Practice" goes against the more typical rule of only treating the woman as a goddess during the short span of the rite, where she afterward reverts again to her ordinary status as second-class citizen.[38]

Tantric Sex in the West

To help contextualize what may appear as a reading against the grain of the way sex is typically understood to function, including its perceived function within Tantra, in what follows below we look at a particularly pervasive view of Tantra, the notion in the West of Tantra as sexually titillating.

For the West, even the idea of the Tantric rite of sexual union in general has more typically been portrayed as a titillating display of the exotic and lascivious East, especially for the early European interpreters of Tantra. The well-known Indologist and author of a Sanskrit dictionary, Monier Monier-Williams, in the early twentieth century, for example, would write how Tantra represented a "degenerate" "licentiousness."[39] In fact, Tantra's prurience is for

Monier-Williams so excessive that he cannot quite bring himself to even designate these practices with a religious terminology—as rites. Instead, they can only be named as "orgies"; so he writes, "the rites, or rather orgies of the left-hand worshippers. . . ."[40]

Encoded within his critique is also a gendered element to the disdain he professes. So, when Tantric worshipers follow the method that favors male gods over goddesses, we find them in his view as being there "not with any undue preference for the female divinity, and not with any implication of impure ideas,"[41] suggesting in his categorization, and even in his syntax, an equation of the female and the impure. In his view there is a natural correlation between female divinities and "impure" "licentiousness." And in keeping with this, in his view it is the worship of the goddess that merits the negatively connotated language of "orgies," implying, as he does elsewhere in this passage, that the inclusion of the feminine as deity could somehow only result in a perverse sexual licentiousness. So he notes regarding the doctrine whereby the feminine is incorporated into absolute godhead in Śiva as Ardhanārīśvara, "the God who is half woman," the half male and half female form of the god Śiva: "it may easily be imagined that a creed like this was likely to degenerate into impure doctrines."[42] Further, in an incorrect but telling reflection of his biases, he asserts that the female goddess Durgā presides over two operations, sexual intercourse and the acquisition of magical powers.[43] Today, in the twenty-first century, the degree to which Tantra is still popularly conflated with a *Kāma Sūtra*–style enhancement of sexual pleasure is all too readily apparent from even a cursory glance at the World Wide Web.[44]

Even though this appraisal of Tantra as a topic of titillation has been mostly discounted in recent scholarship—(and I will here, as one example among many, cite Paul Muller-Ortega's fine scholarship,[45] which focuses on deciphering the metaphorical understanding of physical practices as a "phenomenology of consciousness"[46] particularly in the schools of Trika Śaivism associated with Abhinavagupta)—and despite this palpable shift away from sex in contemporary scholars, nevertheless, this attitude lingers.[47] Biswasnarayan Shastri in his introduction to the *Yoginī Tantra* says that secrecy in Tantra has to do with "repulsive" practices that likely devolve into a drunken orgy, and the use of sex and liquor.[48] Similarly, S. C. Banerji writes of a popular Tantric attitude that resulted in "Tantric practices of incredible indecency" and a "license and lasciviousness that corrupted the society."[49] Given his generally sympathetic introduction to the text, it would be hard to argue that Shastri, an Indian scholar, evinces an especially orientalist disdain for the *Yoginī Tantra*; and similarly with Banerji's work on Tantra. Rather, one might read this language as a symptom of a lingering association, where the word choice of "repulsive" and "lascivious" reflects the obverse and politically correct side of a repressed titillation.[50]

More recently, Wendy Doniger's review of David White's recent *The Kiss of the Yoginī* elicited a critique from a segment of the Indian immigrant community, accusing her of misreading sexuality into Tantra.[51] Doniger's review is both far more circumspect and subtle than her critics suggest; more exact would be to conclude that it is not that her review reads sexuality into these texts, as that she is noting how sexuality has, in the past, been read into these texts. That is, she describes and documents an element already embedded in the history of a Western understanding of Tantra.

She delineates just this element of titillation as a component of the Western study and representation of Tantra, using phraseologies borrowed from pornography: "soft-core" and "hard-core."[52] This language referencing well-known categories for levels of pornographic exposure accurately references the *Western* historical reception of Tantra, even as it also implicitly links by extension with the discourse it references: pornography.

"Talk" and Titillation

I present here mere snapshots, which at best only allude to a complex history of Tantra's representation for the West. My purpose in this chapter is not to flesh out this history, but merely to suggest the possibility of shifting our lens to incorporate other possibilities for how we might understand sex in Tantra. So it is important to throw a spotlight onto this lingering connotative element where Tantra is associated with titillation and the pornographic in order to clear a space for reexamining the ways that "talk" about sex can function, and how it does function in our context with the BT. With this in mind, to highlight by comparison some of the problems associated with talking about sex in Tantra, we may briefly address an example taken from talk about sex in the West.

In a discussion on how pornographic language operates, Rae Langton suggests that trying to talk about sex disinterestedly does not work, even when that talk is explicitly designed to expose and condemn the element of titillation in such talk.[53] What happens instead, for Langton, is that the woman as object of sexual titillation is silenced in the process. Her talk cannot be heard. That is, it is difficult to "talk" about sex without simultaneously enacting a sexualization of the woman in the process of talking. Judith Butler extends Langton's philosophical arguments to examine the case of Anita Hill's sexualization in the Thomas hearings. In the case of Hill, her speech, her testimony against

Thomas does not function properly as testimony, but rather her speech as a woman is sexualized; it is read pornographically, where every "no" she gives is read as a "yes."[54] In this case, when Hill tried to speak to document, to "tell" what happened, her speech in effect was silenced, read as performative, as reenacting a sexualization of her as woman.

Langton offers also a more striking example in the case of the autobiography of Linda Lovelace, whose real name was Linda Marchiano. Marchiano presented evidence for court describing her abuse in the making of the pornographic film *Deep Throat*, detailing and protesting this abuse in her autobiography. While her words were intended to document what happened, Langton notes the painful irony implicated in this book's sale within a mail-order catalog for "adult only" pornography.[55] This use for Langton illustrates how when it comes to sex, there is no way for women to speak or be heard without their words being read as a performative speech enacting the sexuality they speak of, no matter what their intention is in speaking of it.

I should make it clear here that while I appreciate the points that Langton makes, I do not entirely agree that the conclusion we should take away from these two examples is that speaking of sex necessarily silences women. Following Judith Butler's assessment of the Hill case, I see talk about sex as more polyvalent, as capable of constructing identity in a variety of ways.[56] In other words I do not mean to suggest that talk about sex is bad, or good, rather I want to point out how a particular use of speech affords the construction of identities (in ways that can be *both* positive and/or negative for those affected).

In any case, in terms of reception, Langton's example demonstrates how speech about sex intended to merely document it becomes itself viewed as enacting, "performing" through the titillation what it only seeks to describe. The apparently simple documentation inadvertently repeats a feeling of abuse attached to the idea of the sexual as pornographic and recirculates it. And, while I do not think this necessarily must be so, viewing the idea of talk about sex in Langton's terms may help us to understand aggrieved Indian immigrant responses to the documentation of a historic association of Tantra with sexuality. Here this community sees a documentation of a sexualized history of Tantra as a sexualization of its own identity. Even when White forcefully and eloquently argues against contemporary popular representations of "Tantric sex" as an abusive commercial packaging of what were originally complex practices involving a system for understanding the relation between the body, especially its fluids, and the powers entailed in enlightenment,[57] the misheard effect of "talk" of sex is lost in the din by both supporters and detractors of the "New Age" commercial appropriation of "Tantric sex." In other words, if we think of the pornographic as "talk" of sex designed with the fundamentɛ of titillation, then it would be very hard to read White's work as moving i direction. Rather, he suggests that sex acquires a different function: a t‹ cal means for acquiring supernatural powers. While the texts I deal with here suggest a different use of sex than White's sources, in both cases the emphasis is away from sex merely functioning as titillation. And in this context, the work of scholars like Jeffrey Kripal also comes to mind.[58]

With this in mind, even if Linda Marchiano's story told to expose the evils of the porn industry is then nevertheless itself sold as pornography, it does not seem appropriate to respond to this violence of perversion and appropriation of her words by either a silencing of her words, since they may be appropriated, or by the apparently impossible legislation against reading her words as pornography. As Toni Morrison suggests in her 1993 Nobel Prize–winning speech, we cannot control into what hands our writing will fall or how it will be read and used. Perhaps at best we can try to "talk" conscientiously about difficult subjects.

And just as the silence of the goddess Tārā to Vasiṣṭha is also, in one sense, her attempt to avoid his violent appropriation of her words, at a certain point she also refrains from a mere silence. She speaks to indict his motive, and to offer him a way out of his inability to "read" her correctly.

The Powers of Speech to Enact Identity—The Text

With this discussion of the ways speech operates, I hope to locate the painful effects of a contemporary politicized academic difficulty, where one minority community sees a documentation of a sexualized history of Tantra as a sexualization of its own identity. Given that I too here talk about the rite of sexual union, I wish as loudly as possible to frame this speech precisely so that it does not reinforce a misconstrued "licentiousness," to cite Monier-William's phrase, or a "repulsive" image of Tantra.

Now, a question arises; how does the BT itself represent and document the Tantric rite of sexual union? I want to point out here that the texts that document and prescribe the rite of sexual union may also themselves be understood in terms of their representational force. After all, what we find here in the description of the rite of sexual union in the BT, or the CT, is not sex, not even a depiction of sex, but a representation of how a particular imagined depiction of sex *should* occur. Here this representation refers to a distanced deed, which, as deed, expressly incorporates language in a way that describes and prescribes what should be done. As descriptions of how a rite should be performed the text's speech offers itself as performative, and blurs the boundaries between the deed, the language recording it, and the identity it formulates vis á vis a formal gestural incorporation of the body and its postures.

As I suggest below, the use of the body and speech ritually acts to rescript identity, but a rescripting of identity also occurs through the ways the text "records" or documents the rite within a history of gods and their deeds. It would be a mistake to suppose these writers of Tantric texts did not have their own strategies for reenacting new identities, even as they, as writers, purport merely to record the already true and existing state of things. Like our own academic speech that aims to document, the speech of these texts purports to simply document the history of who practiced the rite, even, however, as these late medieval authors at times clearly evince an awareness of how their speech reverses normative understanding. In the process these medieval authors reconstruct new identities and new norms. That is, just like us, these authors write about sex in ways that appear to attempt to avoid prurience and, like us, they use a variety of strategies to represent what they have to say in ways that work to shift preconceived notions about their topic.

So, for example, in the BT we find a story similar to the story of Vasiṣṭha's encounter with the Buddha. In the BT, right after verses that prescribe the rite of sexual union, in an apparent bid to justify this seemingly antinomian behavior, the author narrates a story that the god Śiva relates to the goddess Pārvatī:

> Now o Goddess, listen to this highest secret. A long time ago in the lovely Dāru forest, [a group of] intoxicated [sages] were deluded by attachment and desires. They were fooling around with other men's wives and constantly sipping liquor. Viṣṇu came upon them there and having seen their innappropriate actions, Viṣṇu said [to the God Śiva], "o God of Gods, Great God, God of all, who is a treasure house of compassion, o God, those sages in the Dāru forest are afflicted with sins, constantly enjoying liquor. They are fooling around with other men's wives and are deluded with attachment and desires. They are naked and these fools are truly exerting themselves. What kind of a path is this?" Having listened to his words, I, however, said to him, "the great feminine *mantra* that is the Goddess Kālikā, who is none other than the Unstoppable Goddess of Speech is said to be the queen of feminine *mantras*. These [sages] are practicing that *mantra*. And by reciting her Gāyatrī formula they will become

> completely liberated. By her influence all the Gods have become liberated. Even Paraśurāma was liberated from [the sin] of killing his own mother. Dattātreya, the son of Atri was liberated from [the sin] of drinking wine. The God Indra was liberated from [the sin] of an affair with the sage Gotama's wife. And Vaśiṣṭha was earlier liberated from [the sin of] having relations with an outcaste woman. The moon was liberated from [the sin of] an affair with the wife of the planet Jupiter. I, myself, Śiva, was liberated from the sin of chopping off the head of Brahmā. Even Rāmacandra was liberated from [the sin of] killing Rāvaṇa. I will tell you a secret. The wise, having heard this, always keep it secret.[59]

The secret he goes on to tell Viṣṇu is the Gāyatrī *mantra* for the goddess Kālī. In this passage in the BT, which functions as a rationalization for the rite of sexual union by offering mythic precedents of transgression, the god Śiva tells Viṣṇu that behind this transgressive practice is the recitation of the feminine *mantra* (*vidyā*) of the Unstoppable Goddess of Speech, who is here also Kālī. The *mantra* has the power to liberate one from any kind of heinous sin, though one implication is also that a part of the practice involves just these transgressive behaviors.[60] The Moon sleeping with the wife of the planet Jupiter, the sage Paraśurāma killing his own mother, the king, Rāma, killing the demon, Rāvaṇa, along with others; all these are rescripted as elements of an otherwise secret and efficacious practice for attaining enlightenment, or that, in any case, this practice of the *mantra* makes it so that none of one's sins stick. Now, it's fair to say that normatively, probably few of the examples cited are elsewhere understood in the terms that this writer portrays them, as underwritten by the recitation of the *vidyā*, feminine *mantra* of the Unstoppable Goddess of Speech, who is Kālī.

Rather, the author(s) enacts new identities for these gods and their deeds, even as they frame this speech as merely a reiteration of "what happened." A different but structurally similar example of revisioning the gods and their deeds occurs also in the YT, which claims that various gods, including Śiva and Kṛṣṇa, attained their powers through the practice of the rite of sexual union.[61] Apart from this, that certain elements do not seem to fit—that is, Rāma's slaying of the demon Rāvaṇa in battle is really nowhere considered a transgressive act—also clues us in to a precise self-awareness of an author who consciously rescripts "histories" of the gods to lend authority to the practice he advocates. This example illustrates medieval reappropriations through "talk" about sex to shift perceptions about the rite of sexual union.

How Does the Rite Work?

Apart from the revisioning embedded in the discursive recording of the "history" of the rite that the text offers, the gestural codes of the rite itself also serve to reappropriate the rite to enact new identity. Specifically we examine how the elements of the rite serve precisely to shift away from conventional attitudes toward women that make them into objects.

How does the rite work? To begin with, it's a ritual performance of sex—a scripted performance of that which in the West we mostly think should be spontaneous. Further, this scripted performance takes a few dramatic left turns in comparison with its more usual "spontaneous" performances, specifically in employing this preconceived scripting to recode the relations of hierarchy between the genders.

We should also keep in mind here that as ritual performance, the recoding it enacts takes place on the level of the body. As Elaine Scarry[62] points out, the use of the body is especially effective in making and unmaking identities, even as she dwells on a decidedly negative employment of this power, through the damage inflicted upon bodies as a means for unmaking the self-identities of those tortured. Scarry argues for the centrality of the body in the making and unmaking of identity. I suggest that the process of the Tantric rites implicitly operates with this insight in mind, using it to remake identity through the manipulation of bodies in a ritual context. This aspect of Tantric ritual is not only found in the texts I examine here, it appears more generally, for instance in the common practice found across Tantric traditions called the "purification of the elements" (*bhūta śuddhi*). In this widespread practice the practitioner imagines the body being dried up, burned, and washed, and then replaced with a new, divine body made of the syllables of sacred *mantras*. The body is in this sense reconstructed through the use of Tantric ritual.

This, of course, also suggests the implicit assumption by practicing Tantrics that the body itself influences the identity of the "person" and that the body is not already given. It can be remade ritually, through habitual ritual practice. Here, the very practice of Tantric rites, the "ritual purification of the five elements," earth, water, and so on, known as "*bhūta śuddhi*," for instance, works against a notion of Tantra as aiming toward a transcendence of the body. Now, if we understand, as Scarry suggests, that the shifts in identity that occur through the body have an especially indelible effect on identity, then the Buddha's response to Vasiṣṭha's question is one that takes into account a need to include the body in any project of enlightenment—both in that the body itself takes on importance as the representative of materiality (and by extension, women) and in that the effects imprinted on the body have a peculiar staying power.

In another way also, the body as the medium of a powerful emotionally cathecting experience through sex also plays a role in the rescripting of identity. Sex is key because it emphasizes the contingency that is the body, and at the same time affords a space where the solipsistic subject loses itself, even becoming the object of another's pleasure, or situated outside the subjective experience of pleasure that one sees the other experiencing. In this sense, as Joan Copjec notes, the act of sex functions to "shatter the ego's boundaries,"[63] opening a space for a new construction of identity.

While sexuality may function to enact a variety of identities, for instance, in torture, in the degradation of identity enacted with rape, in the titillation that accompanies making women into objects in pornography,[64] I suggest that the particular formulation of bodies in the grammar of this rite deliberately works to a different end. Functioning obliquely, most palpably outside the medium of words, these texts suggest that the rules of hierarchy encoded in the syntax of bodies might possibly be rewritten. Through a rescripting of the body's gestures—especially as these gestures unfold in an act as self-shattering and volatile as sex—the script is purposely altered away from the ordinary habitual gestural patterns that perform a social hierarchy of gender.[65] Instead these rescripted gestures work to enact a recognition of the subjectivity of women. (And just the possibility of this uncommon use of sexuality I hope may help us in the West to rethink the ways that we presume sex functions, especially to rethink an unreflective assumption of sex as invariably merely titillating.)[66]

The Rite of Sexual Union

What exactly is the rite of sexual union? The rite of sexual union is a ritual mostly lacking in Western religious contexts. It involves a ritual performance of sexual union incorporated within a series of ritual actions focused on worshiping women. Considering differences we find in different texts' presentations of the rite—for instance, differences between the BT, on the one hand, and the KuT and the KCT, on the other—I suggest that we ought to recognize that the rite itself was variously enacted and with a variety of agendas.

The rite depicted in the KuT, for instance, is the notorious *cakra pūjā*. The *cakra pūjā* rite involves not just two people, but a group of men and women. In this carnivalesque rite, "having filled the mouth with wine, the beloved women are made to drink,"[67] as the men pour liquor into their mouths. General drunkenness ensues. Then the "yogīs dance, carrying pots of liquor on their heads."[68] Following this, "the yogīs, drunk with wine fall down intoxicated on their chests; and the yoginīs of the group, intoxicated, fall on top of the men. They mutually engage in the happy fulfilment of pleasure."[69]

After this rite is concluded, however, the participants go their own ways and the usual hierarchies resume.

The BT, on the other hand, describes the rite as involving two people, not a group. Also, as we saw earlier in chapter 1, the BT prescribes reverence toward women outside the context of the rite. Again, what I think is key in the BT, what prevents this gesture from slipping back into a simple temporary reversal such as we find in other examples of liminal rites, the carnival, for instance—and in earlier Tantric texts—is that the "Kālī Practice" advocates a shift in attitudes toward women on a constant, permanent basis.

The basic outlines of the ritual involve (1) seeking out the woman, (2) worshiping her as one would worship a deity, (3) the performance of the sexual act, (4) discussion of the attainments acquired via the worship of the woman, as well as usually (5) a panegyric of women. We may also profitably compare the KCT's depiction of the rite with the BT, especially since the KCT as a text also focuses on the rite of sexual union, also upon the site of Kāmākhyā, and also since the BT borrows from it at a number of places. The circa tenth-century KCT is, however, much earlier than the BT, which likely dates to the seventeenth–eighteenth centuries.

For the KCT, the first step outlined above is intricately more elaborate than the BT's version, in ways that might be characterized as being akin to a James Bond syndrome. So, in this tenth-century text, in seeking out the woman, the male practitioner employs a variety of state-of-the-art gadgets, *yantras*, copper or hand-drawn plates that the seeker uses magically to effect events in the world and to control persons. Of course, the *yantra*, which elsewhere in Sanskrit has the connotations of a mechanical device, is a gadget only in the sense that it is designed for mechanically manipulable effects on the invisible spiritual plane. Yet, in an important, functional, way it is analogous to James Bond's use of gadgets. Like James Bond, the practitioner employs a technology here, albeit a magical rather than physical technology, but one that nevertheless operates mechanically on the persons it targets. Further, like Bond, the practitioner is irresistible to women. Not only does the woman he wants come from miles away desiring him as we saw earlier, we also find, "looking and gazing at him with a sideways glance, the composure of her mind is broken with longing . . . as carnivorous beasts and thirsty men feel at the sight of meat and water . . . so she is shaken. Her mind is troubled, and raising her shoulder, her garment falls down . . . she goes far and then stands near, with her heart unable to bear the sexual desire."[70]

The irresistible attraction women feel for the practitioner also faithfully parallels the operational male fantasy in a James Bond film, especially with the images of her "rolling eyes" and "waist trembling from the weight of her breasts" (KCT 3.7), after which the male practitioner, like Bond, subdues her with his attractive virility (KCT 3.10).

On the other hand, this sort of depiction does not occur anywhere in the 2,804 verses and 24 chapters of the much later BT, even though the BT borrows at numerous places from the KCT. Instead, the BT assumes that attracting women will not be a problem and begins with and focuses extensively upon the second step, how one goes about worshiping the woman, a step comparatively neglected by the KCT. So we see the rite depicted in the BT:

> Having led her near at the beginning [of the rite], whether his own wife or the wife of another, and first having offered her a seat, following that he gives water for her feet. He should give her the water offering as enjoined in the prescribed rules. And with a good mental disposition he should also give water for sipping. He should have [water] given to her for her to take a bath saying "*vauṣaṭ*"[71] at the end [when he hands her the water]. He should give fragrant scents, and also the eight types of scents. He should give delightful flowers with scent, frankincense incense, a light made with ghee, in a copper dish beautifully decorated. He should give [her] a supreme feast, tasty and pleasing to the mind. Together with several different items, he should give a coconut. He should give banana, śrīphala fruit, a lotus flower. He should give honey, O Goddess, measured with two straws.[72] He should give freshly clarified butter and meat for honor's sake. Together with a variety of substances he should give yogurt mixed with milk and the best betel nut which is very tasty and well-dressed. He should give camphor and so on, arranged with betel nut. He should give that which can be chewed, sucked, licked and drunk, o Goddess. He should give water well-dressed with camphor. Indeed whatever she desires, he should give her that, by which the beautiful woman will become especially pleased.[73]

The rite here details quite a lot of things; the woman gets the royal, or, in this case, divine treatment. That the text goes out of its way to list so much detail, something we do not find in earlier depictions of the rite, suggests that the author wants the reader to take this part of the rite seriously. The focus on the woman in front of him and giving her things that she will appreciate shifts the relationship the practitioner has with the living woman before him. The ritual effort entailed here encodes an attitude of attention to the woman, who is here, not an abstract goddess, but a living woman. He seeks to please her by offering her the ritual implements offered to gods, offerings of a seat, water for washing her feet, water offering, water for sipping, offerings of flowers and scents, a light, different fruits, and so on. We should also keep in mind that the attitude of respect is also enjoined outside of the performance of the rite. Further, we do not see in earlier texts like the KuT or the KCT this elaborate attention to giving things and honoring the woman in the rite.

Beyond this the text prescribes also a personal attention to the physical body of the woman: for instance "arranging her hair with a variety of pleasing objects."[74] The aesthetic impulse here perhaps plays upon stereotypes of women as bodily/appearance oriented, and at the same time privileges rather than denigrates the representation of woman as physical presence, concerned with the body. This gesture may be read as reinforcing that the body should be *his* concern as well. Even throughout, many of the items he gives her operate to create bodily pleasure, such as the tasty meal and the water for her bath. Indeed a key element of this discourse is the attention it gives to the body.

Following this the practitioner writes potent magical syllables on the different parts of the woman's body. "On the two breasts he [writes] the syllable 'ram,' on each side of her jaw [he writes] the syllable for good fortune, below the armpits he should write the two syllables of the one who carries the Ganges river, o Goddess."[75] The writing on her body functions as a type of *nyāsa*, a pervasive element in Tantric practice whereby magical syllables, which are deities, are magically inserted and enlivened in the physical body.[76] He continues with this and then in the ceremony he bows to her. After this the rite concludes with procedures leading up to union.

The details of the worship of the woman, even the final portions where union occurs, center on seeing her as a subject with her own desires. The verses describing this suggest attention to the woman's experience in the act of union.[77] I suspect that a calculated effect of worshiping the live woman before him as goddess is that it becomes more difficult for the male practitioner to construct woman as a distant idealized abstraction, more difficult to bifurcate woman into two categories, the denigrated woman he lives with and the distant idealized goddess on a pedestal. (And, this effect would also no doubt be heightened if the woman worshiped was the practitioner's wife.)

We should pay attention here to the construction of subjectivity through the idea of desire. Foucault articulated a notion of subjectivity constructed in terms of desire, no doubt taking his cue from Freud's formulation of the *id*.[78] For our purposes, we see that the rite here offers her the space to articulate her own desires. "Whatever she desires, he should give her that, by which she will become especially pleased."[79] This seemingly innocent textual prescription contains the seeds of resistance to the frequent suggestion that female desires should be channeled into fulfilling male ends. That is, her desire here is not predefined by his needs, but left open to her articulation. In effect, she partakes of that pervasive signifier of subjectivity, her own capacity for desire and pleasure. Prioritizing her desires effects a shift in the relations between the sexes. It overthrows that order so visibly exemplified in the ubiquitous rule that the wife should treat her husband as a god (*devavat*) (*Manu Smṛti* 5.154). Visibly, literally, the rite reverses this dictum. Here the woman becomes the god, offered flowers and incense, and fed.

For the Lawgiver Manu, of course, a reciprocity in the relations between men and women like this was never intended. The male as the "god on earth" (*bhūdeva*) expected and was accorded absolute veneration. Even on such a basic level as food—typically in this culture males have the first right to food and whatever is left over is what women get. Food is a basic support for the body and self, and rescripting this priority of who eats first recognizes an existential right, and consequent subjectivity in the woman. The rite in the BT ritually scripts this reversal, so that the woman has the first right to food. In this context we should also remember that the BT emphasizes practicing this attitude toward women all the time, 24/7, and not just as a temporary reversal of status, though in a text like the KCT, the elements of the rite do function as a temporary reversal.

Again, we have to keep in mind that the shifts here exist on the level of textual discourse; I do not make claims regarding a historical recognition of women's subjectivity through this rite, but rather that this text articulates a challenge through language to normative constructions of women's identities.

The rite, then, purports to reconstruct both male and female identity, and their relations to each other. This man performing the worship of the living woman seated before him engages in a rearticulation of his normative understanding of the relations of the genders. The fact that the woman in front of him is a living woman is important, since it prevents him from constructing female divinity as an abstract form.

Further, in another register, this text affords agency to the woman by giving her a say, a choice in her participation. The text urges against overpowering her, even against emotional abuse, and techniques for emotional or mental control. She may be invited but not ever coerced into the ritual. The BT's author(s) tells us: "Blaming, censuring a woman, humiliating, injuring her and attracting her by force [to the ritual] should not be done, not even mentally" (BT 6.343b).[80]

The KCT, on the other hand, presents a different view. Women are, there, objects to be gotten, by whatever means, and *mantras* and *yantras* happen to be the most effective. What does it mean, in contrast, for the BT to articulate this different view? On the one hand, even to recognize that the woman might have a preference in whether or not to participate has already granted her a modicum of subjectivity. But further than this, stipulating this attention to the means of bringing her to the rite suggests a discursive attempt to shift the status of women, particularly since this includes "fuzzy" forms of manipulation, such as blaming or criticizing her.

"Flat on the Ground Like a Stick"

So far we see he worships her, feeds her, pleases her. In culmination the text prescribes that he should commit a profound gesture of reverence. The male practitioner should bow to the woman in front of him in the most obsequious manner: "he should bow to her, flat on the ground like a stick."[81] With this explicit physical gesture, he does something a male in this medieval Hindu society typically never does, bowing down to a woman with whom he has sexual relations. Particularly, this full prostration is reserved for the guru, or perhaps a powerful temple deity, not usually a woman. Rather, typically the woman bows to the male, and universally the wife bows to the husband. When the reversal occurs, where he bows to the woman, the consequence is a restructuring of the order of things. The BT allows both for bowing to one's own wife as well as women of other castes, both higher and lower who are not his wife (BT 6.21) and also outside the context of the rite.[82] When the Tantrika bows, he accomplishes what Collins sees as the male allowing himself to be a "supportive self-object," that is, to subordinate his own sense of self to her, a feat that Collins does not see happening in Sāṃkhya.[83]

Of course, different versions of the rite vary on this point. The male practitioner bowing to a woman in the course of the rite of sexual union does not occur in the much earlier KuT or the KCT. In the KCT, during the rite of sexual union the male practitioner bows to the guru (here a full prostration—*daṇḍavadbhuvi*), but not at all to the woman he has sex with (KCT 2.37ff.). Further, unlike the Kālī Practice, which, as we noted earlier, does not invoke the goddess into the woman or women to be worshiped, the KCT explicitly requires that the goddess be invoked (KCT 3.32), that is, to "possess" the woman, this in a different context than the rite of sexual union, and only in this "possessed" state does the practitioner bow to her. Immediately after this, the goddess is ritually made to depart (KCT 3.48 *namaskṛtya visṛjyaiva*).[84]

Normally, the Brahmin male, who has the prerogative to function as the guru, this "god walking on earth,"—is bowed to and he is the subject experiencing the world.[85] As we see in the KCT's version, the practitioner subordinates himself to the guru and thus bows to the likely male, likely Brahmin guru. In the context of the BT's rite it is the woman's desires that become the focus of attention.

The Secret

What is secretly most seditious in this reversal is a heady philosophical shift: desire transferred to the woman affords a *subjectivity* to that which is elsewhere construed as *object*. This gets iterated elsewhere in the BT when the god Śiva says: "O Goddess I am the body (*deha*) and you are the conscious spirit within the body (*dehin*)" (BT 7.86). That is, here the *feminine* principle, normally associated with matter and body becomes the locus of consciousness—subjectivity, while the male principle, usually associated with the conscious subject, here becomes the object.

To flesh this out—the pervasive classical conception of cosmology for medieval Hindu India encodes gender in an essentialist binary structure.[86] The feminine is "nature," *Prakṛti*. In this world she is object, absolutely inert dead matter. In contrast, the male is encoded as spirit, *Puruṣa*, who is consciousness, sentiency. This binary opposition is repeated in various permutations, as a mostly unquestioned structure. The male is therefore classically the proper subject; the female "nature" is object, profoundly denigrated as that which lacks real sentiency. To shift the subjectivity of these categories, against the weight of Sāṃkhya and nearly all of classical India—to make the feminine the subject is to enact a rewriting of male and female identity. Now, it is precisely this secret knowledge of the essential subjectivity and consciousness of the feminine that the god Śiva reveals as the secret essence of the rite of sexual union. "Now O Goddess, fix your mind, the 'Kālī Practice'[87] O Goddess, is about to be revealed: I am the body; o Goddess, you as the form of all, are the conscious spirit within the body. Just as a fish is thrown in water, so in the same way, you, o great Goddess, are the true Self. There is nothing that cannot be told to you, o beautiful one."[88]

Apart from other functions of this secret, one element to consider is the impetus for secrecy deriving from an imbedded social insubordination present here, one that calls to mind Butler's notion of recontextualizing labels as a way of resisting hegemonic structures.[89] We should keep in mind also that the Sanskrit word *spirit* (*dehin*) affords a host of images—of an integral self, a soul, an idea of the essence, which animates and affords the identity of selfhood. Further, this word (*dehin*) also suggests the concomitant presence of the inhabited body (*deha*). Especially key here is the incorporation of the body—even as the typical relegation of women to body is deconstructed by this author's rescripting of who is body and who is soul. While an image of women as mere vessels precludes the possibility of agency on the part of women, this reversal of creative agency acknowledges an inherent agency to women. Further, this occurs explicitly within the context of recognizing that this female creative power, the goddess, is everywhere present in the bodies of living, breathing, instantiated females.[90]

Who's on Top?

The rewriting of gender hierarchy is again repeated spatially in the ritual. The BT announces the revelation of a highly potent "secret" (BT 6.76): the sex act performed where the woman is on top of the man (*viparītarata*), a specific Tantric practice found also in earlier Tantras such as the KCT.[91] The use of the word *viparīta*, "reverse," is revealing. Monier–Williams's Sanskrit dictionary, in addition to defining it as "reverse" also glosses the word as "perverse," "wrong," "inauspicious," "contrary to rule," "false," and so forth. Typically, it connotes a sense of transgression, that which opposes normative behavior and hierarchies. The extra merit attached to the inversion of the sexual position in this case probably does not correspond with some supposed increase in physical pleasure for the male practitioner, instead it represents graphically and ritually, in the spaces and contortions of physical bodies, a recoding of hierarchies. Who's "on top" reverberates through to encode the lessons of privilege onto the body.[92]

To get a sense of the cultural significance of this, we should note that the text of the *Kāma Sūtra*, which lists such an incredible profusion of postures for making love, does not include this very simple position of "perverse love-making" where the woman is on top and the male penetrates from below. For the text of this infamous *ars erotica*, the only time that the woman is on "top" is when she is no longer "woman." If the woman is on top, acting out the "perverse love-making" (*viparītarata*), for the *Kāma Sūtra*, she acts like a man (*puruṣāyita*), and she takes some instrument, a rod (*sahayya*), which she then uses as a phallus to penetrate her partner, who is thus designated as the female (*Kāma Sūtra* 8.1). The woman on "top" in the Tantric rite, however, is *still* a woman, and the male is just as male as he was before, only he penetrates from below.

What does it mean to place the woman (or man) "on top"? Certainly this "perverse" form and the fact that it is encoded as "perverse" refers more to orthodox discourse about the relations between the genders than it does to what would probably be actual sexual practices. That is, we come back to the notion that this text constructs a discourse that it uses to shift or enact identity. Could one read this "perverse" reversal as an abrogation of a male impetus to dominate? A mute sign, it could, of course, be read in a variety of ways.[93] Yet, however one reads it, a certain political implication is unavoidable. Putting the woman on top, according this normatively marginalized "other" the superior place, suggests a rescripting of women's role, a move away from a dominating gestural posture toward them.

The inverted posture pervades through "left-handed" Tantra. One finds it mentioned in a variety of Tantric texts, not just the texts used here. It is also implicated in some iconography that places Kālī above Śiva. I suspect that in earlier depictions it may have functioned as we saw above in the KuT as a temporary reversal. We can recall here the rite as given in the KuT where the men fall down drunk and the women fall on top of them. In this case the ensuing union would also be of the inverted (*viparīta*) type, though after the completion of the rite the castes go their separate ways and the gendered hierarchy between men and women is reestablished. The BT's injunction that the practitioner should bow to women outside of the rite as well suggests it may have functioned differently in this context.

The rite of sexual union in its representation in the BT uses the body to suggest moving away from a model of male mastery over women and over the body. It promises and presupposes a different kind of world; as we see shortly, the revelation of the rite itself is framed in a vision of a world without domination and fighting. The structure of the rite also counters the notion of male ascetic mastery and especially mastery over the body. This has broad implications because mastery of the body is mastery of women, and vice versa, since women are traditionally, historically coded as "the body,"[94] so if one eschews mastery over the body, this entails also a shift in attitudes toward women. Especially in the bodily gestures it encodes, the BT's rite proposes a shift in attitudes toward women. Finally, even in the rewards it promises, it moves away from ideas of mastery over nature. Throughout the BT, we keep coming back to the reward the text promises for the rite, and rather than powers over nature and the body—the power to fly, for instance—the text simply promises eloquence, a facility with language.

The Rite of Sexual Union and an Ethic against War and Fighting

In the seventh chapter of the BT, the goddess Pārvatī asks her husband Śiva to tell her about the practice for the rite of sexual union, "O God of Gods, o great

God, you, who cause the world to be maintained and to dissolve, I have one question here for you, o man of a good vow. Having left aside [our] dice games, the [answer] should be revealed, o god who destroys the suffering of existence. The great 'Kālī Practice'[95] has not been revealed. If you love me, then tell me about it right now."[96]

The god Śiva declares that it is a secret and then agrees to tell her: "This is not to be spoken of, in the three worlds. With a pure intention in the mind and senses, O ruler of Gods (fem.), I will tell you. There is no one more loved by me than you; who indeed other than you? Now O Goddess, fix your mind, the 'Kālī Practice,' O Goddess, is about to be revealed: I am the body; o Goddess, you as the form of all, are the conscious spirit within the body."[97]

He reveals to her that the secret teaching of the rite of sexual union is a rescripting of feminine identity, one that rejects a denigration of the feminine as unconscious inert matter. Rather, the secret that the rite of sexual union teaches is an understanding of feminine identity as pure spirit, the principle that animates all life (*dehin, ātman* BT 7.86–87). Here this "talk" especially recodes female identity to incorporate a notion of female subjectivity. Spirit, the marker of self as subjectivity, is accorded to woman.

Right after this Śiva appears to think better of his agreement to reveal the details of the practice, since he would not only be revealing this to her but also to the rest of creation. Presumably, she would pass this knowledge on to humans as well as other beings, gods, demons, and the Indian equivalent of fairies, among others. The god's objection to the revelation of this powerful truth is that most of the world's inhabitants—whether human, divine, or semi-divine, animal or demonic—are "engaged in bad deeds." He says to his wife, Pārvatī,

> You are the true self, O Goddess. There is nothing that cannot be told to you. However, these [others,] some Gods and humans, some demons, tree spirits, and malevolent spirits, those dwelling in the nether worlds of snakes, and horse-men, and the hosts of celestial musicians and river nymphs, whether domestic beasts or wild beasts, birds, these which move on the earth—these are all very stupid. The nature of all these is such that all are mutually fighting in battle. All are constantly doing bad deeds, eagerly subscribing to the views of bad paths. None of these know the bliss of the wisdom of the absolute, or the happiness of the absolute. O, Goddess, how can I tell you that [secret rite]?[98]

Thus, human nature is such that "these are very stupid; the nature of all these is such that all are mutually fighting in battle." In a manner resembling the hagiographical Buddha's initial hesitation at teaching the dharma to uncomprehending humans, it is the inadequacy of these stupidly competitive beings, constantly fighting among themselves, that causes the god to hold his tongue.

The goddess then cajoles him with a hymn praising his compassion (7.92ff.), that causes him to relent. This dramatic device serves to psychologically frame the author's agenda—the textually necessary revelation of the procedure for the rite. At the same time it insinuates both a cosmology—that the goddess in essence occupies the place of the subject; she is pure consciousness, spirit—and it also offers as well a psychological profile of the goddess, as a fount of compassion. In this sense the teaching of the rite of sexual union is framed as both a reconfiguration of gender relations, and a shift to a better kind of ethic, a move away from a senseless competitive "mutual fighting." At least in the mind of this author(s) from the fifteenth through eighteenth centuries, the worship of the goddess, through the use of the rite of sexual union, entails a vision of both a recognition of women's subjectivity and a vision of a better world, where warfare is not the norm. To come back to Monier-Williams's early Western representations of Tantra, the disjunction between these two worlds' understanding of women is profound. Monier-Williams's early twentieth-century assertion that any sort of worship that might be connected with goddesses or the feminine could only inevitably result in the worst of possible worlds, an inevitable "degenerate" "licentiousness," stands in poignant contrast to the suggestion made by the BT's author(s) that this worship of the goddess as living woman offers hope as a radical ethical counterpoint to a world of senseless violence.

3

The Other/Woman

The Role of Wives and Goddesses in a Tantric Rite of Kāmākhyā

The forbidden "other" woman, exotic, outcaste, and dark skinned, is the common image of the female partner for the Tantric rite of sexual union, and one not unsupported by scholarship on Tantra.[1] This socially "other" woman belonging to another man (*parakīyā*) is imagined especially as unfettered, unattainable, and exotic—everything the male practitioner's wife is not.

But what about wives? What role, if any, do they play in the Tantric rite of sexual union? This chapter focuses on a neglected counterview within Tantric praxis: the participation of the wife as the male practitioner's partner in the Tantric rite.[2] Given the constraints of a serious Tantric praxis, this practice likely may have been not as uncommon as either Sanskrit textual sources or scholarship on Tantra would lead us to believe, yet it has not been given much attention.[3] Admittedly, the texts, which enjoin the wife as partner to the exclusion of an outside woman, are a minority. Nevertheless, that it occurs at all suggests we need to expand our images of Tantric practice. The alternative it offers is also useful in making it apparent that dominant representations did not exist uncontested.

For this chapter we draw from the "*Celestial Musician Tantra*" (*Gandharva Tantra*, GT) and the "*Great Blue Tantra*" (*Bṛhannīla Tantra*, BT), which both offer passages proposing the wife as the preferred ritual partner for the Tantric rite of sexual union. Among the group of eight texts used for this study, only these two offer a passage suggesting that the "other" woman is not suitable, and that, rather, the wife should be the partner for the rite of sexual union. Thus I am not suggesting that this is a common representation. Elsewhere among this group of texts (and even in these two texts) we most frequently find that either the wife or an "other" woman is suitable for the rite.[4]

Why the lack of attention for the wife as partner? No doubt, the unexotic wife as partner adds little to a notion of male machismo that we sometimes find in Tantric texts. That is, embedded in the mythology of the male Tantric hero is the image of an ultimate womanizer, who is virile and attractive to women, and yet himself "cool," unemotional; he just "uses" women, albeit for their bodily fluids. Here, by way of example, we can note again the passage I cited in chapter 2, on what we find in the much earlier (ca. tenth-century) *Kulacūḍāmaṇi Tantra* (KCT), "When he has finished repetition of the *kūlākula mantra,* instantly he attracts the woman whose name he has written in the ritual diagram. Even if she is a hundred leagues away, on a mountain or in the middle of a river, guarded with chains in the middle of a thousand islands, her eyes rolling with desire, her waist trembling from the weight of her breasts . . . she comes, her heart desiring the practitioner."[5]

This much earlier text written for the male practitioner may to our eyes seem droll, perhaps a little like a Harlequin romance, with its images of the woman uncontrollably attracted to the male practitioner, who, for his part, takes the role of suave seducer. It is hard, in any case, to miss the exotic and tantalizing impetus of this much earlier description and the male role as magical seducer of this woman from afar. We will look at one more passage from the earlier KCT: "The Kula practioners however should make much effort to ascertain the attitudes of household [residents]. Then by some or other strategem the female fluids are willingly [given]. Having taken it, he should put it in the gold or copper vessel called the *kula* [vessel]."[6]

Thus, we see in this much earlier tenth-century text why the practitioner woos the woman—to obtain her bodily fluids, a point that David White has also made elsewhere.[7] The portrait we find of the rite for this earlier text leaves little space for the domestic wife, and the KCT does not take the position we find in the BT, that the wife should be the partner (even if *we* might imagine that the wife's bodily fluids would be more accessible). One cannot help suspecting that the very lack of the wife's exoticism makes her a not especially interesting topic for discussion, apart from whatever experiences may or may not have ensued in practice (the wife as partner is not "sexy"—the word used by one of my male colleagues—and clearly the machismo imputed to the Tantric practitioner applies to the Western world as well).[8]

Nevertheless, the very fact that we find an instance that *does* prefer the wife as the partner suggests we ought to expand our images of Tantric practice.

While I am not suggesting that this is a common representation, I am suggesting that even one occurrence of it merits attention. The wife as partner tends to mitigate against the typical representation of women in Tantra and, for this reason alone, ought to be explored.

This chapter addresses and attempts to understand the preference for the wife as partner in the Tantric rite of sexual union that we find in these two texts. This, at least textually, otherwise uncommon practice that advocates the wife offers us one alternative view on what the Tantric rite of sexual union may have meant in some cases for its practitioners. If we reflect upon the implications of this practice we find that the participation of the wife as the partner offers a view that disrupts normative relations between the genders.

This disruption operates through recoding transgression in terms of gender rather than in terms of the notion of sex as illicit act—especially since, after all, there is nothing *illicit* about sex with one's wife for the male practitioner. In other words, the social transgression here derives from the sign of difference that the woman (as a nonmale human)—presents, particularly when the female does not get assimilated into an object for the male. Related to this, and a consequence of it, is that the advocacy of the wife as partner in the Tantric rite of sexual union undoes the more typical coding of women as male property.

The Function(s) of Tantric Transgression

Reflecting on the presence and absence of wives in the Tantric context allows us to see an otherwise obscured element of transgression as a religious phenomenon: that it may here, in part, derive from the anxiety of difference that woman presents. For Western scholarship so far, the presence of a religiously sanctioned transgressive element in Tantra has presented a somewhat baffling problem; the very variety of explanations put forth alone attests to a bewilderment that mostly still prevails (as I discuss in the notes).[9]

In this context I suggest that the notion of woman presents an inassimilable difference. Typically the difference that woman presents is socially contained through subsuming the identity of the woman into the male family. She is exchanged between families and as wife is contained under the rubric of male property. In this more normative context, the woman is politically disenfranchised, without a public voice, and relegated to the dominion of the husband and his family. On the other hand, the transgression coded in the rite of sexual union that involves the wife as partner involves an underlying disruption of the coding of woman as property and, with this, an alternative response to the anxiety that woman presents.

I also suggest that part of the problem in understanding the transgressive elements of Tantra is the assumption that the transgressive must function monolithically across the wide range of Tantric texts and practices and traditions. I suggest that it is a fundamentally misguided appeal to an ahistorical structuralism that assumes that it may be possible to think of Tantra in general, or the transgressive element in Tantric ritual in particular, as a uniform praxis or as having a uniform function. Accordingly, the presence of transgressive practices must be explicated with respect to specific historical contexts, with an eye to the possibility that Tantric writers in different times and regions may appropriate notions of transgression for entirely different agendas.

Particularly here, if we reflect upon the context of Assam in the seventeenth through eighteenth centuries, we realize that the notion of transgression differs very much from what, for instance, Alexis Sanderson notes for the ninth through twelfth centuries in Kashmir. For this period and place, Sanderson describes how Tantric transgressive praxis violated caste-defined rules of purity, with a goal of upsetting caste identities.[10] On the other hand, the classical transgressions of Tantra, specifically, for instance, dietary transgressions, as we will note below, held little force in Assam, leading us to suspect that the transgression of the Tantric rite likely functioned in a very different way in the Assam of the seventeenth century.

In what follows below we first address the notion of the transgressive in Tantra. After this, we explore the idea of the wife in Tantra and of the wife more generally. We then address the notion of woman as transgressive when she presents an inassimilable difference, especially when her identity is not subsumed under the rubric of male property. Finally, we address a curious redefinition of the Tantric transgressive in the BT, which explicitly identifies the woman, apart from sex—that is, the idea of woman—as one of the transgressive elements of Tantric practice.

What Exactly Are the Five Ms and Why Are They a Problem?

What do we mean when we talk about the "transgressive" in Tantra? The idea of the transgressive gets neatly encapsulated within the Tantric tradition in a simple and pervasive list of words all beginning with the letter *m*.[11] The "Five Ms," a list of five substances, including, for instance, liquor and sex, become incorporated within ritual worship of the goddess. The five elements are meat (*māṃsa*), fish (*matsya*), alcohol (*madya*), parched grain (*mudrā*), and illicit sexual relations (*maithunam*).[12] The transgressive ritual that incorporates these substances is designated as "left-handed," following a nomenclature also prevalent in the West where the right hand is the auspicious and normatively socially acceptable hand and the left represents that which must be repressed and expelled.[13]

The "Five Ms" have elicited a concatenation of emotional Western and Indian appraisals of Tantra ranging from a Victorian repulsion and embarrassed dismissal to ecstatic embrace by contemporary popular culture in the West.[14] Aside from the emotional charge and challenge a ritual incorporation of sex presents, what do we make of the antinomian elements, especially sex, in Tantra? Western scholars are by no means in agreement over the function of the transgressive elements of Tantra. Are its functions political? social? spiritual (if this word itself is not problematic)? Or does it function in a combination of ways?[15]

On the surface the "Five Ms" are all the things a good Brahmin should not have. By the medieval period most Brahmins were theoretically supposed to be vegetarian, so meat and fish fit easily in this list of the transgressive as substances one ought to shun. Similarly, drinking wine is prohibited for the upper castes as one of the five great sins (*mahāpātaka*) one should avoid.

Now, we should note here that Tantra in Assam offers a different scenario from this classical model. While Brahmins elsewhere were vegetarian, in Assam of the seventeenth through eighteenth centuries, they were not at all vegetarian and neither was anyone else, for the most part.[16] This should begin to lead us to suspect that the idea of the Five Ms for Assam may have had a different import than it had in other regions of India.

Mudrā is more puzzling. Usually translated as "parched grain," it is difficult to see how something similar to Rice Krispies could be considered so transgressive as to merit a veil of secrecy. *Mudrā* may refer to a form of meditative trance or possession state as Sanderson notes or the woman as producer of menstrual and sexual fluids as White reads it.[17] Either of these could be construed as socially transgressive for different reasons—trance or possession as a state that disrupts normative behavior and menstrual blood as a substance fraught with the danger of impurity in a normative Hindu view.

Again, if we understand *mudrā* as a state of trance or possession, the transgressive element may not have had the same social force for an Assamese context in the seventeenth through eighteenth centuries, particularly when we keep in mind that the Ahom rulers patronized a state cult of possession with the *deodhai/deodhanis*, persons who would get possessed and then act as oracles.[18] With official state sanction, the illicit element of this "M" tends to be mitigated.[19] One sees this also, for example, in the Tibetan Buddhist context where the "M" signifying *mudrā* is kept in the list of transgressions, but where it does not signify a state of possession in a society which regularly patronizes state-controlled possessions and other forms as well. In this case, the word *mudrā* is defined differently to mean the partner.

Maithuna, illicit sexual relations, is also more problematic than it appears on the surface, and its varied depictions also indicate that despite an apparent conceptual unity implied by the single term *maithuna*, the antinomian use of ritualized sex may have fulfilled widely diverging purposes in different Tantric rites and for different Tantric practitioners. In the context of eleventh-century Kashmir, when Abhinavagupta enjoins ritualized sex with one's mother, the rite functions to shatter a sense of social identity based upon purity[20] and perhaps also to address a deeply rooted psychological dynamic. However, elsewhere the ideal partner is an attractive young dark-skinned woman, as we see in the *Kulārṇava Tantra*: "He should worship a dark-skinned young girl, who is enchanting to the mind, wearing black, thin and in her youth, mentally perceiving her as the deity."[21] This is not a choice likely to shatter a sense of normative social identity for the male Tantric practitioner who chooses this. Elsewhere in another text, however, the practitioner should not even look at a young girl: "The sex organ of a young girl, animals playing, and the breasts of a naked woman . . . he should not in any way look at these."[22] Instead what's key for this text is that the woman should belong to someone else: "They constantly engage in caressing the wife of someone else (*parastrī*) and in drinking wine; by the grace of the Goddess these [practitioners] attain liberation."[23] And in another context still, what's crucial in the *maithuna*, the rite of sexual union, is that it affords the potent female sexual fluids one offers to Devī, the goddess (*Kāmākhyā Tantra* 2.45).[24]

Now it is easy to see how ritualized sex enacted with one's mother could function to break through socially constructed and confining images of self-identity. But it's not so clear that the pervasive trope of sex with someone else's wife (*parakīyā, parastrī*) would have the same effect. Rather, the thrill of seduction, the fear of getting caught—one can imagine all sorts of psychologically different effects arising from this different use of ritualized sex, even if some of the emotional and psychological effects might overlap.

In contrast, we find at places in the BT and the GT the suggestion that the male practitioner should not engage in relations with the "other" woman (*parastrī*). I should make it clear that these texts are not entirely consistent. So we do find in the BT also the suggestion that both the wife and the "other" woman, the wife of someone else, may participate as the partner: "Beginning [the rite], O Goddess, his own wife or the wife of someone else should be led there, and first having given a seat he should then give her water to wash her feet."[25] In this instance both categories of women are possible partners. Elsewhere, the BT, however, condemns practicing the rite of sexual union with the wife of another. The context here is that Pārvatī asks the god Śiva to explain the proper conduct regarding the wives of other men, since she has heard that the practitioner can acquire magical perfection of the *mantra* if done in the context of relations with the "other" woman. Śiva responds by rejecting the practice of going to the wife of another man. "O Goddess who lifts one out of adversity, listen; out of love for you, that which should not be revealed [I] will reveal. The Vedas condemn the practice of going to the wife of another. O Great Goddess, by consorting with those [women who belong to another] he [the practitioner] becomes engulfed in the hell of murky darkness. Having ascertained the meaning of the Veda, how could the practitioner do this? He should not at all go to the wives of other men."[26]

Thus, while elsewhere in this text we find both categories of women, one's own wife (*svastrī, svakāntā, svakīyā*) and the "other" woman (*parastrī, parakīyā*), here the latter category is rejected. The GT also offers a passage that prefers the wife. "When one's own wife who travels the path with one is a practitioner (*sādhvī*) and a good wife, then why go to other women? Just so am I [Śiva], only with you, [Pārvatī]."[27] The text continues to praise the wife for several stanzas, making the comparison with the gods, who each have a single wife, and finally concluding with, "O Goddess, the one who goes to the wife of another, that is the lowest path."[28]

Frederique Apfel-Marglin hints at a similar situation with the Kaula *cakra pūjā*, a group event involving ritualized sex in Orissa, where the wife is the chosen partner.[29] One can see how, practically speaking, practicing the sexual rite with one's spouse might be far easier in terms of sustaining an ongoing praxis and maintaining a relatively calm family life to support the time and resources needed for the elaborate ritual preparations the sexual rite requires. [30]

In any case, this clearly doesn't sound like the same sort of Tantric experience we hear about elsewhere, where the male Tantric seeks out the low-caste washerwoman or barber's daughter, or the wild wandering female Tantric ascetic (*Bhairavī*).[31] What I'm suggesting here is that, in fact, they aren't the same experience and that there was more than one Tantric use of ritualized sex.

To return to the issue of the partner, what's at stake in the choice of one's own wife or the "other" woman? If a man's ritual partner is the "other" woman, then one can imagine a particular type of social transgression that occurs with an extramarital sexual relationship, with all its concomitant excitement. As Dimock notes, it's hard to take the elusive "other" woman for granted.[32]

On the other hand, if the preferred partner is one's spouse, then it is likely not the idea of sex per se that is transgresssive. After all, most men and women have sex with their spouses and there's nothing at all societally transgressive in this. In an oblique way Vasiṣṭha raises just this issue in his dialogue with the Buddha when he's learning the secret *kula* practice involving the Tantric rite of sexual union from him: "If having intercourse with women could give enlightenment, then all the creatures in the world ought to be enlightened" (CT 4.23).[33] What then would it mean for the rite to have the wife as the partner?[34] We should note also that we find a curious listing of the Five Ms in the BT, one that includes both the rite of sexual union (*maithuna*) *and* woman (*mahilā*), suggesting that this author conceived of these two as separate elements in this secret rite. While we will explore this in greater detail below, it may be useful to suggest here that perhaps the woman in the rite, in her own right, apart from the practice of ritual sexual union, also presents a transgression, a social transgression, that tends to destabilize normative hierarchical relations between the genders, particularly one that works against the notion of the wife as male property. At this point we will explore the idea of the wife.

A Good Wife

What is a good wife? A woman who supports her husband and feels her first loyalty to him, over her own familial relatives? A woman who treats her husband as a god? If we follow Manu's prescription (*Manu Smṛti* 5.154), it is especially this—a good wife understands her husband as her god.[35] This equation enacts itself in an ultimate display of devotion with a final sacrifice of self for this god. In the death of the husband the good wife abandons her own life, by herself entering the flames that consume his corpse, dying on top of his burning corpse. Complete self-sacrifice of a nonreciprocal sort is one public articulation of her ultimate fidelity and chastity for a "good" Hindu wife.

The role model for this wifely fidelity derives from the myth of that first and best of faithful wives, Satī, the wife of the god Śiva, who sacrificed herself at her father's sacrificial fire in order to protest the insult her husband received at his hands. Following this *illo tempore* establishment of good wifely behavior, human women who make the ultimate sacrifice for their husbands, following them to the grave, are said to commit *satī*, after the name of this first female sacrifice, the goddess Satī, for her husband Śiva. In the case of ordinary humans, when the relatives burn the husband's dead body, the model wife, the human *satī*, climbs on top of the burning pyre, her own body burned with his. With the advent of the British, the practice was made illegal (though the political etiology and implications of the British prohibition were complicated and not entirely made only in the interest of women, to say the least).[36]

Nevertheless, even as recently as 1987 a celebrated case of *satī* made the newspapers, when the young Rajasthani bride, Roop Kanwar, committed *satī*.

In the myth, the goddess Satī generally does not immolate herself (though she does in the *Mahābhāgavata Purāṇa*[37]), but rather dies by entering a yogic trance. After she dies, her bereaved husband Śiva, grief-stricken over the death of his wife Satī, carries her corpse over the terrain of India while the god Viṣṇu trails behind him surreptitiously hacking away at her lifeless body. Each site where a body part falls becomes holy, a historical place for pilgrimage for the devotees of the goddess.

One notices here a disjuncture between the myth and the historical practice based on the myth in that the original Satī does not burn, and unlike the human husband, the god Śiva is not dead. Ostensibly, the gesture of loyalty the human *satī* performs by immolating herself with her husband's corpse is her refusal to exist apart from him. On the contrary, when the goddess Satī sacrifices herself, she enacts precisely a separation from her husband. The two are not one; the difference is expressed in her separation from him and his grief. She moves to the world beyond while he remains grief stricken and, for some time, alone here in this world.

In this context, one other important and frequently articulated function of the wife's immolation becomes apparent: it ensures her continued chastity. A dead woman cannot find a new man to replace her husband.[38] This fact articulates a deep-seated anxiety that human women pose for men, in the possibility that a woman's sexual desire may extend beyond the man who legally possesses her, even from his grave. The wife is his property, in a way that a goddess never is, a commodity that he exclusively enjoys and what makes her properly his is his exclusive privilege to her body. The power that a woman has, evidenced especially in her power to make new life, is contained and controlled by her husband; her chastity is the legal sign of his possession of her as object.

The word *satī* itself doubles as the feminine form of the present participle, that is, "being" in the feminine gender. As a minor point to reflect upon, the insidious implication of this homonym is that for a woman, the process of "being" entails that she choose to not be, that she sacrifices her being to her husband's honor. She is a shadow, contingent on her husband. As we might expect, this gesture is not reciprocally observed by her husband, who does not climb on her pyre, but instead is encouraged to remarry after her death.

In the myth, the god Viṣṇu hacks away at Satī's dead body; in the dispersal of body parts, the sex organ—that organ that more than any other codifies the gendered identity of woman, woman as the other of male—falls on the hill of Kāmākhyā. Where it lands the earth becomes dark blue (*nīla*) and the body part turns into stone. The hill where this body part falls becomes known as the Blue Hill (*nīla parvata*) and this site becomes a temple to the goddess Kāmākhyā. What does it mean for the sex organ of the ideal wife, Satī, to land here? Does Kāmākhyā become the prototype of a place for faithful and chaste human wives to congregate?

Not exactly. Rather, in an ironic, but, as I will argue, psychologically coherent subversion of the notion of the chaste wife as commodified property of the husband, the city of Kāmākhyā becomes linked with a deviant and excessive sexuality, with a subversion of the normal gendered economy of sexuality. Kāmākhyā is for a literary Tantric tradition the place where a secret and deviant sexuality is practiced, where secret rites, which worship the goddess through sex, take place. And nearly all of the eight texts consulted for this study reference Kāmākhyā.

So when the upright and conservative Hindu ascetic sage Vasiṣṭha takes up the left-handed path and seeks out the Buddha to learn about the secret and transgressive rite of sexual union (CT 2.1ff.), Kāmākhyā is the place where it happens. We should also recall here that for a late medieval Hindu tradition, the Buddha is frequently depicted as both a Hindu turned apostate, and a particularly tricky incarnation of Viṣṇu destined to lead the masses astray from the true dharma. Kāmākhyā wears its reputation for the transgressive like an emblazoned scarlet letter.

In fact, Kāmākhyā's Tantric potency makes it a notorious haven for black magic. One Tibetan writer in the seventeenth century would report that "there are so many witches (*ḍākinīs*) and various kinds of demons and devils that even a person who has fully mastered the Tantras can hardly stay there."[39] Who are these witches, the *ḍākinīs* who, along with devils and demons, make life intolerable for our Tibetan Tantric author in Kāmākhyā? Ostensibly an evil sorceress, the witch has magical powers that supercede those of even a skilled practitioner of Tantra.

Now, why would this site commemorating the sexed being of wifely fidelity and chastity incarnate, of that most faithful and chaste of Hindu wives, Satī, become linked with an apparently unconnected representation of woman in the form of the highly sexed witch? Exactly why is Kāmākhyā connected with transgression, especially transgressive sexuality? That is, what is a good girl like Satī doing in a place like this?

Of course, it is not Satī herself, just this one bodily organ of hers: a free-floating organ without a body, a dismemberment of self that is memoralized, remembered, and enacted in myth and pilgrimage. One other interesting disjuncture between the myth and the historical practice of *satī* is that the "good wife" in the historical practice leaves no bodily organs to be revisited. Both the goddess and the human woman are sacrificed, but while the former emerges dead but whole, the body of the human woman is transfigured into a disidentifiable mass of ash, mingled with her husband's, and the river into which they are thrown. On the contrary, Satī of the myth has all her bodily organs intact, even if she is spread out over the subcontinent of India, her limbs never acting in unison. A disparate cacophony of limbs dissected, and yet each bodily organ reconstructs or recathects itself into a whole goddess, whose particular bodily part becomes her symbolic identity.[40]

Women and Transgression: Difference and the Same

What is the difference between a mass of ashes that was once a woman, and petrified and dispersed body parts that are worshiped as the remnants of the ideal wife? The disintegrated ash of the human maintains the image of the chaste woman while the petrified body part of the goddess becomes the locus of the transgressive, a place where witches and black magic proliferate. Both, I suggest, are elements of a single representation of the feminine. It is, rather, the mode of their disposal that differentiates them. That is, in the case of the human woman her identity, as different, sexually different from her husband, is reduced to a nonexistence. Her ashen remains signify a process of assimilation of her identity, her differentiation from him into a palpable amorphous unity with him. Her difference is erased by her transformation into a unified gray mass. In Hegelian terms, both identity (the husband) and nonidentity (the wife) are assimilated into the Same. The disintegration of her body, the erasure of her bodily difference, especially facilitates the process of erasing the difference that woman as the other of the man offers.

On the contrary, the goddess maintains the existence of difference from her male husband, albeit in a fragmented, fetishized way. Her difference as woman is fragmented, particularized into the far-flung dispersal of her dissected body parts. By an act of metonymy each body part then comes to stand for the whole of the goddess as woman. Here difference survives, at the price of a fragmentation of being.[41]

To come back to the question of Satī's presence in the land of black magic, we can read the Tibetan's condemnation of this black land as what happens when a "good" wife goes "bad." That is, insofar as her difference as woman survives—that is, so long as one can see the sign of her difference, her intact sex organ—then this difference must be extruded from the boundaries of social order, relegated to an existence in the margins, made into a no-man's-land of witches and devils. What cannot be made into the Same must be pushed outside the order of normative power.

The Feminine as Transgression

Not only does this city of the chaste goddess's sex organ carry the import of transgressive sexuality. Goddesses in general evoke this response whenever they are elevated above a male consort, and even more so when a goddess is worshiped independently from a male consort. Alexis Sanderson, in a well-documented research article, succinctly maps the historical evolution of the antinomian elements of Tantra from an incipient presence in the Pāśupata, a tricksterlike figure hanging around the cremation grounds in the early centuries of this millennium, through the medieval emphasis on ritualized sex.[42] Here he makes the very important observation that there is a connection between the "left-hand," that is, the transgressive, and goddesses. That is, the more transgressive the practice, the more goddesses figure in the ritual.[43] Additionally, the more antinomian the ritual, the more we find goddesses ranking at the very top in the pantheon of deities, independent of, and towering above, their male consorts. What is it about goddesses, particularly the independent, insubordinate goddesses, that links them to the transgressive? I suggest that the idea of woman, as the site of difference, is what links them.

Insofar as she sustains the idea of difference—especially codified in that quintessential emblem of difference, the sex organ—she presents a rupture in a system of assimilation that subordinates what is other by making it into an object or absorbing its identity within an absolute unity of self.

The human woman herself is an emblem of the transgressive; not her sex as object of desire or mastery, nor sex as activity per se, but her gender, sex as the place where difference is articulated. Woman in her difference from males, as a being who is other and who resists assimilation, must be elided from discourse; she is pushed to the outside beyond the borders of normative social and political power.

That is, the difference that woman is—woman not degraded to the status of object or property—is itself transgressive. This difference is transgressive because it disrupts a deep structural assumption of male privilege and possession of women endemic to Indian culture (and to patriarchal culture in the West, for that matter).

The Difference between Witches and Chaste Wives

The danger Kāmākhyā presents derives ostensibly from all those witches living there. What exactly is the difference between a witch and a chaste wife? Here the dichotomy of the witch and the chaste wife is two poles of a single continuum. The one is the inversion of the other.

The chaste wife dutifully acquiesces to the status of being property of the husband, an object subjected and subordinated to his being and desire. Especially her sexuality, her desire, is subordinate to his. The containment of her desire signifies his mastery and her status as object. The witch, on the other hand, represents the specter of the independent woman who is master of her own sexual desire. She maintains her own subjectivity and with this she subverts the legal code, which makes women property exchanged between males. This is dangerous because when independent, she becomes linked to the practice of magic, especially black magic.

The witch and the chaste woman probably both function more as representations of psychological categories than as living individuals. Not ever what we might think of as actual women, both exist in a realm of representation, imaginary categories. As categories they are two sides of the same figure, two poles of a single continuum reflecting the degree to which the difference a woman presents is assimilated or not into the "sameness" that is the object, that is, the degree to which she is made into male property. Both probably cater more to male psychological need and male anxiety than female reality; both are constructed out of a male gaze, or mis-seeing of women.

These two poles of the chaste wife and the witch converge in the image of Satī who is at once the image of the chaste wife *and*, in Kāmākhyā, the iconic formula for profligate sexuality and black magic. That both these representations arise out of the single figure of Satī points to a fundamental identity between these two images of woman, two sides of a single coin.

Goddesses Again

On the surface it might appear more radical to engage in ritualized sex with someone outside, someone not one's normatively assigned spouse/sexual partner. However, I suspect that the reverse is actually true. To outline the logic here, in the BT and the GT (and among a diverse set of other Tantric and Purāṇic texts, associated with different historical time periods and regions), the goddess sits at the top of the pantheon of deities. This position already represents a break with normative social order. That is, normatively, male deities take the top seats in the pantheon of gods, just as, normatively, in this particular society, males hold the seats of power in the public and social arena. To place a goddess in the position of the supreme deity, creator, and savior reconfigures the divine hierarchy. In terms of the normative gender arrangement, this placement is, in itself, a societal transgression.[44]

Now as Cynthia Humes points out, lots of *Śāktas*, worshipers of the goddess, see the goddess as supreme and yet they are not transferring this veneration or power to ordinary women. What is the difference? What I suspect is the operative difference is precisely what gets reflected in the debate on *parakīyā* and *svakīyā*, the "other" woman and one's own wife.[45]

The wife is typically and normatively construed as male property. This wife is normatively expected to assimilate her identity to that of her husband, in effect, to erase her difference, which constitutes her identity by becoming an object, that is, male property. The goddess, on the other hand, is more like an "other" woman, elusive and distant.

As Hegel notes in his famous discussion of the slave and the bondsman, when the slave becomes entirely object, entirely subordinated to the master, then he no longer offers a possibility of recognition for the master. It is the *process* of conquering the slave as other that ensures the psychological coherence of identity for the master. After the process is completed, the slave loses his worth and subjectivity, which are what guarantee the value he has for the master.

In this sense, written into the dynamic of the relations between the genders is a doublespeak. On the one hand, the voice of male authority denounces the witch, whose gendered difference as other cannot be mastered, and on the other hand, this denunciation is the trace, which reveals precisely an internalization and repression of just this desire for the unassimilable difference that this witch presents, and that the docile wife, who does not have her own independent voice, cannot fulfill. At this point we can adumbrate more precisely Satī's two poles around the middle term between them, which is the goddess as other who walks a fine line, in her many representations, between docile consort, and independent woman who, on occasion, degenerates into uncontrollable female fury. What we should note is how the amnesia that opposes these images, instead of recognizing their fundamental unity, is what fuels the need for conquest.

The process of assimilating and conquering the "other" offers the possibility, in Hegel's terms, for the master to be recognized. This is the impetus of the transgression involving the "other" woman. On the one hand, the other woman, unlike the wife, but like the goddess, initially maintains the sign of difference that woman presents. However, the process of assimilating her and erasing the difference she presents begins to be put into play with the excitement of the conquest of the "other" woman. She is transgressive precisely because her difference has not yet been, but will be, in the future, assimilated. That is, so long as the "other" woman dwells in the nebulous interior of the continuum, not clearly placed onto one pole or the other, so long as she is not conquered, not transformed into the status of object/property, she is transgressive. And so long as she offers the incipient possibility of assimilation, the transgression she presents is "sexy" because it affords the possibility of recognition, so at this point she is not denounced, not relegated to the marginal existence of the irredeemable witch.

To go outside to the "other" woman is to affirm the power of the goddess, the sign of woman as difference, but yet still to distance it, not let it reach the core of quotidian life. The goddess is all-powerful, but she is, after all, an "other" woman, someone one can get excited about, but not someone one has to actually shift one's identity for. A person can worship a goddess in all sorts of elaborate ways and never have to really listen to what she might say. In this sense, the goddess also remains a mute object. Even as she is being worshiped, the icon does not talk back.[46] Rarely does she visibly make demands on a person the way a live embodied woman does, especially in the way that a live embodied woman with whom one resides 24/7 would make demands.[47]

On the other hand, the practice involving the wife as Tantric partner ingeniously circumvents the psychological distraction that asserts the bipolar fabrication of the docile wife and independent witch as two really distinct representations. This practice with the wife reintegrates these two images into a single form of woman, reintegrating her fragmented being into a whole, that is, re-membering her, undoing the amnesia that split her identity.

To have to acknowledge one's own wife as the goddess shifts things considerably. It entails taking seriously the desires and demands that another living being voices, and not simply in a calculated maneuvering of one's own interests—that would be precisely not to see her as a goddess and could work only with a woman/partner one would meet with only infrequently—or with a disembodied goddess, who remains a mute icon. What it requires is actually listening to her speech. The shift suggested by the BT and GT and other texts, which involves the wife as the Tantric partner, affords a deconstruction of the male egoic identity as master of his property as wife. The wife's claims to subjectivity are recognized.

Now how is this transgressive? It entails a subversion, which strikes at a much deeper core of our social fabric than any sort of sex with an "other" woman could, than any type of pornography could. It cuts at the root of the sexual order as an order of power. It allows us in our own society to see how much sex functions as a way of constructing identity and especially constructing identity in relations of hierarchy and dominance. In recognizing the claims to subjectivity that this other presents, an other who is irrevocably other by the mark of her sex, the otherwise unalterable pattern of hierarchy and dominance loses its absolute claim to being the "natural order." It begins to unravel possibilities for her claims to the specific privileges that subjectivity entails.

Woman and the Fifth M

Earlier I noted that Tantric traditions are multiple and that their use of the Five Ms reflects diverse agendas. The choice of wife as partner in the rite of sexual union in the GT and the BT points to the idea of woman herself as the sign of the transgressive rather than an idea of illicit or forbidden sex. One more important element in the BT suggests a conscious appreciation of the transgressive as connected to the idea of woman. The list of "Five Ms" is altered to explicitly propose woman, not woman as object of sexuality, but woman as gendered difference as the fifth M.

As a list, the Five Ms have one characteristic that makes them a little unusual: that the list typically does not vary across texts. Most lists we find in Tantric texts—whether a list of gods or goddesses or pilgrimage sites or practices—present varying degrees of fluidity. The members of the list vary from one text to another, with repetition across lists but with a degree of flux in the items mentioned. On the other hand, the number of items in the list usually is often invariable, despite the fact that the elements can vary from text to text.[48]

In striking contrast to the normal pattern of lists, the list of Five Ms rarely varies.[49] The BT, however, in its citation of the "Five Ms" makes a significant and interesting departure from this nearly invariable collection of transgressive items. The fifth *M* for the BT is woman (*mahilā*). The usual list, again, is presented as wine (*madya*), meat (*māṃsa*), fish (*matsya*), parched grain (*mudrā*), and sexual intercourse (*maithuna*). It is also significant that the list always concludes with sexual intercourse as the final item.

By contrast, the list in the BT excludes parched grain and offers a different final *M* as woman (*mahilā*), using the highly respectful form of the Sanskrit word, *mahilā* which is best translated as "lady" (BT 6.329). Now, the BT's list includes both sexual practice *and* women, suggesting with this list that sexual practice is a different transgression than the transgression involving women. This means that at least for this author the worship of women is not essentially equated with women as simply objects to fulfill the rite of sexual union (whether the rite involved simply fulfilling lust as some critics understand, or whether the rite involved a technology of sex as a means for spiritual enlightenment). This inclusion of woman as the fifth *M* suggests that a woman is transgressive in her very being. The BT's list implicitly suggests that apart from any utilitarian function she performs as sexual partner,[50] she also entails in the very fact of her being the sign of transgression. This transgression is fundamentally the sign of difference, which her bodily form as woman instantiates. In this context also, the god Śiva declares to Pārvatī, "the fifth [*M*= *mahilā*] is your true form."[51] That is, all women are the goddess; all women are both divine and irrevocably other.

We should note here also what we saw earlier, that in the context of the BT's revelation of the rite of sexual union, Śiva reveals a very potent secret: that the secret essence of the rite of sexual union is a rescripting of feminine identity. That is, woman is not, as we usually see in the subcontinent, coded simply as unconscious inert matter as *prakṛti*, a notion that would tend toward an easy assimilation of her as property. Rather, the secret that the rite of sexual union teaches is an understanding of feminine identity as conscious spirit (*dehin, ātman*; BT 7.86–87), according her inherently the status of subject, as opposed to object or property.

Conclusion

So what is transgressive in the practice of this secret Tantra is the gesture not to elide the difference that women present. What does this mean? That women represent not merely objects, property, or the possibility of sexual gratification, but an opening up into the possibility of difference as the subjectivity of the other. This suggests a valuing of women: not to value as in to evaluate, which would be to ask again the question, "what is a good wife?" but to value in the sense of according an esteem not connected with the market equivalence of the labor women supply, or with the exchange value of the beauty they possess, or with the semiotic capital accruing to the husband in the sons they mother. That is, to see woman as transgressive is precisely not to reinsert women into an economy of exchange where their identity remains contingent upon a commodification of their worth. Rather, a recognition of the difference women present offers the possibility of a choice not to objectify women. This recognition recodes gendered relations inscribing woman discursively in the place of the subject.

4

To Speak Like a Woman

The Feminine Mantra and Bodied Speech

Words too, like women, once had the value of (magical) objects; and to the extent that words have become common property, "la chose de tous," losing their character as values, language "has helped to impoverish perception and to strip it of its affective, aesthetic and magical implications."

—Teresa De Lauretis, quoting Lévi-Strauss's *Elementary Structures of Kinship*[1]

This chapter addresses representations of women's speech. I propose here a link between "female" speech and the female body. In this chapter I will give three different examples representing women's speech, a myth in the BT that tells the story of the birth of the feminine word, and by way of comparison, two other examples as stereotypes of women's speech; representations of the *satī*, the "good wife," who burns herself on her husband's pyre, and a recent representation in the United States of woman's speech.

To begin with the story told in the BT, the distressed gods pray to the Blue Goddess of Speech to help them win back their kingdom from demons who have taken over. She answers their prayers by appearing before them and producing out of her body twelve goddesses who are speech embodied. These goddesses are feminine magical words of power (*vidyā*). *Vidyā*-s in general are magical words; they are feminine *mantras,* secret formulas several syllables long that a Tantric practitioner mutters softly over and over with a *japa mālā*, an Indian rosary, in hand, to help count the number of repetitions. A powerful magical speech, the practitioner softly or silently recites these formulas in order to acquire powers—the power to fly, or to conquer enemies, or, in the case of the "Kālī Practice" discussed in chapter 2, to gain the gift of eloquence. Effectively, this magical speech helps to manifest one's wishes, to make things happen in the world.

In this case this myth literally represents this magical speech as female and as bodies. These *vidyā*-s are speech. At the same time, they are also female beings—goddesses—and in this tale graphically so. They emerge from the body of the Blue Goddess of Speech in bodied feminine form, the word as goddess, joyfully dancing on the toes of the Blue Goddess's feet (BT 12.83).

This chapter looks at this feminine speech, the *vidyā*, through this story. The *vidyā* in general is a *mantra* with a female deity, though even generally, we should note, Tantric magical speech, the *mantra*, aligns with the feminine, even when its deity is male. As the eminent Tantric scholar P. C. Bagchi notes, "The *mantras* of the Tantras differed according to the deities, though they are all supposed to be different forms of Śakti."[2] That is, as a form of *śakti*, the feminine, the *mantra* ultimately exists as female, even when this female is configured as a male deity. The myth we address below explicitly portrays the *vidyā* as feminine *mantra*, as speech that is explicitly female, envisioned as female beings, dancing goddesses.

Thus, the BT makes the link between "female" speech and the female body explicit with its story of these bodied dancing goddesses as words. Further, we find this link connecting female speech to the female body elsewhere as well, in other stereotypes of women's speech. In making the connection between female speech and the female body I would like to draw attention to one more element in the equation. Bodied feminine speech is a performative speech. In the BT's story explicitly we see this, since as *mantra*, that is, as "magical" speech, this feminine speech enacts events in the world. Indeed, as potent ritual speech, it performs what it "says" simply through the saying of it. The practitioner recites the *mantra*, and the mere recitation magically manifests what the *mantra* says. We explore the function of feminine speech as performative in the myth in the BT, and also with reference to the two other examples that I give of stereotypes of women's speech, the case of the *satī*, the "good wife," who burns herself on her husband's pyre, and a recent representation in the United States of woman's speech in the case of Anita Hill, both of which also incorporate elements of the body and of performativity in the stereotype of woman's speech.

No doubt, we need to emphasize that this stereotype functions more as part of a symbolic order than as an actual description of women's speech. As stereotype, it points to the ways women are "represented" in the larger culture, not to anything that could be construed as an accurate picture of women's actual speech. What is interesting for our purposes here is that the BT's myth turns around the valuation of the stereotype of "woman's speech." It presents the idea of woman's speech, that is, speech that is feminine, bodied, and performative, in a more positive light than these other two examples I give.

One more element is salient in this chain of associations: as bodied, feminine, performative speech, this magical speech disrupts the normative order of language. It disrupts the idea of language as logocentric. Andre Padoux, as well, notes for the Tantric *mantra* more generally its nonlogocentric character, its fundamental dissimilarity from the Western notion of the word as logos.[3] In the West the dominant paradigm has been a binary that asserts the priority of transcendent meaning over the physical sign of the word (along with the host of binaries that align with this, such as spirit/matter, male/female). One element of the binary implicit in logocentricity prevails in India as well, where spirit takes precedence over matter. While it may be fair to say that the word as a physical form or sign has probably also been more important in Hinduism than in the West, nevertheless, we still find that most schools of thought tend to incorporate the dualism of body and spirit, referenced most archetypally in the Sāṃkhyan legacy of *puruṣa* and *prakṛti*.[4] What happens then, when we find a use of the word, as we do with the BT's use of the Tantric *vidyā*, that upsets this binary? In other words, what happens when we find a bodied language?

Bodied feminine speech, these dancing goddess-words, offers us a word that acts like a body rather than a sign. With this we find a recoding of the value attached to the body, matter and materiality. I also suggest that a consequence of this is a notion of identity that is multiple. Not constructed upon the exclusion of that which is "other" to the self, this model does not reject the body and matter and offers an image of the feminine self conceived multiply.

In what follows below, first we look at what a *mantra* is. After this, we examine the story from the BT that tells the story of the birth of the feminine *mantra*. We then address other images of woman's speech including the *satī* and the Anita Hill case in the United States. Following this, we look at what happens when the fusion of word and body takes place in the case of the *vidyā*. With this I suggest that the stereotypes of women's speech, visually analogued in the goddesses as words of the BT, as it fleshes out, literally and conceptually, a bodied, performative, female speech, offer a conceptual understanding that prioritizes the body and matter, and nature.

The *Mantra*

What exactly is a *mantra*? The *mantra* is the Indian version of the magical charm, words used ritually as a sacred formula. The Tantric *mantra*, a ubiquitous presence in Hindu and Buddhist medieval texts, presents us often with a mere string of meaningless sounds—for instance "*Om hūm śrīm*," an untranslatable semantic void, "non-sense."[5] What does it mean to use a language that doesn't *mean* at all in the ways we normally construct meaning?

By way of definition, and simultaneously to illustrate graphically something of the conceptual impasse one encounters in the attempt to decipher for the West the meaning of the *mantra*, I will cite Agehananda Bharati's classic pioneering work on Tantra, where he gives a definition for the *mantra*. Bharati tells us: "A *mantra* is a quasi-morpheme or a series of quasi-morphemes, or a series of mixed genuine and quasi-morphemes arranged in conventional patterns, based on codified esoteric traditions, and passed on from one preceptor to one disciple in the course of a prescribed initiation."[6]

We should not be too dismayed if there appears to be in this definition a willful obscurantism. Rather we may consider that the opaqueness of his definition arises perhaps because the very idea of a definition,[7] using language—words, signs—to convey what a thing means, is fundamentally at odds with what it means to encounter language as *mantra*, as a collection of "quasi-morphemes." Bharati tells us not so much what a *mantra is*, but rather what it looks like, how its form appears, physically and audibly, *as* form. Rather than define the *mantra*, he lets us know it has a bodily form. *Morpheme*, after all, derives from *morphe*, shape or form. And, after telling us it has a form, he tells us that it is *per*-formed, passed on through lineage initiations.

The obscurity of his definition, in this case I think, highlights the fact that the *mantra* does not lend itself to discursive space. The *mantra* does not *mean* in the way that words usually mean something, so its definition appears impenetrable. We do not quite "get" what Bharati means by his definition. The *mantra*, these unintelligible "quasi-morphemes," offers a linguistic sedition.

The *mantra* functions as an alternative form of language. This shadowy counterpart to language traces its steps obliquely; a fissure in the order of language. The Tantric *mantra* presents something like a deliberate excess, a stammer that jams the system. Literally, actually, the use of the Tantric *mantra* enacts a stammer in the semantic order; one repeats it over and over and over, far beyond a point where meaning could have been conveyed.

I noted Bharati's pioneering definition of *mantra*,[8] and alluded to Staal's assertion of the Vedic *mantra* as "nonsense."[9] A number of other scholars have also noted the performative aspect of the *mantra*,[10] as well as the generative and transforming quality of the *mantra*. I discuss these in the notes.[11] However, I will here mention one other aspect of the *mantra*. In a recent article of hers, Laurie Patton discusses the priestly appropriation, via *mantra*, of a woman's power to give birth. In her analysis the priests employ *mantra* as a substitute for the woman's fecundity to ensure the life of the embryo. Patton discusses how the *mantra* was used as means for displacing the power of female body and consequently to appropriate its function and control it.[12] Salient for our purposes is both the creative power of the *mantra* as language, and the fact that even in this earlier Vedic context, in the realm of language it is precisely the *mantra* that functions as a linguistic homologue for the image of woman, in this case for the functional identity of the woman in her power to give birth. In this context I should suggest that the *mantra* can co-opt this feminine power because it analogously is "feminine," generatively creative.

Elsewhere in the BT we also find the generative power of *mantra* explicitly linked to the generative power of woman. The hand gesture called "the vagina gesture" ("*yoni mudrā*") where the two hands entangle together in a pose that visibly resembles the female sex organ, is, the text informs us, "the enlivening power of the *mantra*": "whoever does not know the *yoni* gesture which is the enlivening power of the *mantra*, how can he perfect the *mantra*, even with a hundred thousand repetitions?"[13]

This recalls Laurie Patton's point, though in a sense from the opposite side of the coin. Whereas the Brahmins she describes appropriate the feminine power to give birth by their own control of the *mantra*, here the author(s) of the BT explicitly recognizes the feminine as the ultimate source of the power of even the *mantra*. So a *mantra* is like a woman in that both have the power to make new life. While the Brahmins Patton describes get at this power through the *mantra*, in contrast, however, for the BT's author(s), the feminine is the power that enlivens the *mantra* to begin with.

The Story of the Birth of the Feminine Word

At this point we address the myth we find in the BT, which describes the genesis of the feminine *mantra*. Two elements are especially relevant for our discussion here. First, the feminine *mantra* is bodied. We see this literally as the *mantras* are born out of the Blue Goddess of Speech, and take anthropomorphic forms as goddesses with bodies. Second, the *mantra* is feminine speech. Again this is figured quite literally as the *mantras* are born and take bodies of feminine gender. These literalized depictions offer a technique for spelling out philosophical concepts that reconfigure the notion of materiality through a visual analogue.

The basic plot of the story is that the besieged gods are waging a war with the demons and the demons are winning. The gods seek out the help of the great gods Viṣṇu and Śiva. The BT in the voice of the god Śiva telling the tale, says, "Brahmā went gladly to Goloka [where Viṣṇu lives] accompanied by Indra. O Goddess, with a variety of speeches [praising] the supreme Lord [Viṣṇu], [he said], 'be pleased and happily lift us up out of our work we have to do.' Having heard the speech of the great Brahmā, Viṣṇu said with great respect to Brahmā, 'Sir, it is not possible for me to do this.' O great Goddess, Brahmā and Viṣṇu then came to my abode. With various types of divine praise they pleased [me]. O Goddess, I [Śiva] said, 'I am not able to kill [the demons].' "[14]

Both Viṣṇu and Śiva explain that they cannot help the gods in this war and that they should instead seek out the Blue Goddess of Speech. When they meet the goddess she agrees to help them and she consoles them, saying, " 'You go; where the demons are, I will come there. In every way [I will] be near the Gods.' Having said this, that Great Goddess Tāriṇī who moves about freely, just as she likes, according to her own desire, the supreme Goddess who bears the form of illusion vanished."[15]

She wraps up her consoling speech to them with a sudden disappearing act. Then they return to their exiled stronghold on the mountain where they must wait for five years. "The Gods who were born from the light went there for five years. Dead, as it were, their kingdom lost, weak with suffering, they [stayed] in the hills,"[16] distressed without their kingdom. This element of the myth appears to echo the short retelling of the gods' encounter with the Great Goddess of Illusion, Mahāmāyā, in the *Kālikā Purāṇa*, when she kills the demon Mahiṣa (KP 62.63ff.). However, the BT differs first in that the goddess is not formed out of the energies emitted from the gods, and, second, in that she emits forth from *her* body the goddesses who will bring victory for the gods, as *vidyās*.

Also, here the hills connote a primordial exostructure. That the gods have to go to the hills signals their loss of political power. They go there because they are exiled and because the hills are outside of the circle of power. They can hide there from their demon enemies. Typically, in the medieval period when powerful invaders conquered Assam, such as, for instance, the muslim Mir Jumla in the seventeenth century, the defending Assamese would flee to the hills, hiding out and waiting for a better time to strike back. In this sense, reflecting a historical political strategy, it also suggests the notion of being outside the circle of political power, especially to not have a voice politically.

Even today the idea of the hill tribes connotes groups considered to be uncivilized and politically without a voice.

Their prayer to the Blue Goddess of Speech is metaphorically apt in these circumstances. What the text appears to suggest with this is that only when they assimilate and understand what it is like to be marginalized, to not have a voice, are they able to connect with the Blue Goddess of Speech.[17] The goddess does not help them immediately. Instead, they wait for five long years on the outside, without a voice. In other words, before the Goddess of Speech helps them, they must first experience being silenced.

Now, this Blue Goddess of Speech who deludes the whole universe[18] appears to be not entirely predictable. At this time she promises a presence, but the gods do not actually experience this presence until later in the story when she appears suddenly (*pratyakṣa*), *ex nihilo*. By her behavior she plays with the ideas of presence and absence, suddenly disappearing, and suddenly reappearing. "Moving about according to her own desire" (*kāmacāriṇī*), her entrances and exits are not predictable. This stands in contrast to the more normal mundane appearances of the gods Śiva and Viṣṇu, whom the gods also seek out for help. There is nothing sudden or remarkable about their entrances and exits. One goes to where they reside and there they are.

The Blue Goddess of Speech, on the other hand, appears and disappears suddenly. When she disappears, they wait and they worship her; however, waiting and remembering her, without any real power, seems to be the best the gods can do to impose a scheme of causality on her presence and absence. Eventually, she does come to their aid, and gives birth to the feminine words who then win the war for the gods.

Meanwhile, on the mountain the gods do the prescribed worship, offering to the Blue Goddess of Speech a conventional prescribed list of substances.

> O, Goddess, [they offered] a seat, a welcome, water for washing her feet, the ritual water offering, and water for sipping, a milk and honey bath, and for sipping, clothes, and ornaments, scented flowers, incense and a lamp, food, and they bowed. With sixteen different substances [they worshiped] the Blue Goddess of Speech. Having worshipped her and having given the animal sacrifice to the Goddess [or the wild jackal] with various auspicious substances, o ruler of Gods, the group of the best among the Gods did *japa*. Having first said the great mantra, o Goddess, having done 100,000 repetitions of the *mantra*, with this they offered clarified butter with lotus flowers pleasing to the mind. They did a fire ceremony with sesame seeds mixed with sugar also. In this way having offered a fire ceremony,

> o great Goddess, they did one tenth that number [of offerings] again as offerings with sprinkling [milk]. They did one tenth that number of offerings with everything as a water offering, o Goddess. And, when that was finished they worshipped the Goddess at midnight. And after that, having given an animal sacrifice to that great Goddess, they had divine food. In this way they completed this pleasing karma.[19]

With all of this repetition of the *mantra* and ritual extravagance, she still does not show up. Finally then, after all this is concluded, the gods remember her, and only then, when they finally *remember* her, does she suddenly appear. "Then, o Goddess, when the Gods remembered that Goddess, that Great Goddess with the Blue form and a big belly, that Goddess became pleased, and she appeared visibly in front of the Gods. 'What can I do for you? Where shall I go, o Gods; tell me why you have called me?' "[20]

The notion of remembering her is important. Just as Vasiṣṭha's intense asceticism cannot compel the goddess to appear, so here as well, only when the gods relate to her by remembering her, rather than operating on the assumption of a mechanical model of the efficacy of ritual performance, does she actually appear. When they remember her, in effect they move away from an understanding of the rite as being mechanically effective. This certainly references the idea of devotion (*bhakti*). It also entails a recognition of her as a person, that is, as a subject rather than object. Her unpredictability, no doubt, enhances this effect; the gods cannot take this goddess for granted. They need her help and they must relate *to* her in order to gain her help, because she will not show up until they do. We see this elsewhere in the BT, where the author tells us that *bhāva*, that is, one's attitude and especially an attitude that internalizes an understanding of the practice one performs, is key in this practice. So we see, "[Even doing] much *mantra* recitation, fire ceremonies and many ways of afflicting the body etc. through austerities, without *bhāva*, o Goddess, the *mantra* gives no results."[21] Further, we see, "by *bhāva* one attains enlightenment and strenthens the clan. By *bhāva* the lineage (*gotra*) is strengthened; by *bhāva* one does the spiritual practice for the clan; [if one doesn't have *bhāva*] why do the various *nyāsa* (ritual placement of the alphabet on the body), why the various bodily purifications; why do worship if *bhāva* doesn't arise?"[22]

In other words all spiritual practice is useless without the proper attitude.

By *remembering* the Blue Goddess of Speech, in one sense, they reintegrate into their own sense of self-as-subject the idea of this female as also subject, rather than object that they can compel. Recognizing her subjectivity may be read to entail some degree of "othering" of their own selves; we see this narratively encoded in their position of marginalization, as political, social "other" during their time on the mountain. Yet, recognizing her subjectivity is what enables the gods to connect with the power she affords.[23]

Bodied Language

When she does appear, the gods seem stunned, perhaps because they were not expecting her to appear. Perhaps one might read their inability to articulate their desires in her presence as a sign that they have not quite transitioned from a mechanical model of the rite's efficacy. The Blue Goddess offers them a boon, and this is when they should ask for her help in the battle with the demons, yet they can only say

> "Be pleased, o Ruler (fem.)." Then the Goddess with the Blue form, who delights the mind, seeing the Gods collected there, that Goddess Tāriṇī, who fulfills all desires, out of her own body created twelve supreme Vidyās, feminine magical words. [These were] Kālī, Mahādevī and Mahāvidyā and also Ṣoḍaśī and Bhuvaneśānī, Bhairavī, Chinnamastakā, Dhūmāvatī, Bagalā and Mātaṅgī, Kamalā and Ātmika. These Vidyās, O great Goddess are famous as the Perfection Vidyās (*siddhividyā*). These great Goddesses arose from the body of the Goddess of Speech. And other Mothers were born from her, o beautiful one. [Then] in supreme joy, all these Goddesses danced on the tips of her toes.[24]

The Goddess of Speech herself, this savioress (*Tāriṇī*), summing up the situation, produces out of her own body (*svadehataḥ*) bodied language. Twelve words, which are simultaneously bodied goddesses, arise out of her body. They are not just goddesses; they are words. Not just words, they are the bodying of sound into female forms. This feminine anthropomorphized speech fuses the notion of sign and thing, giving us a word that is presence rather than the sign of absence. As words, they do not point to a being beyond themselves. They do not function the way words usually do, standing in as a sign for some *thing*—the thing as presence, while the word itself is the mere sign, an absence of the real as *thing*. These words do not point to a being located elsewhere; they are the presence of being, the goddesses themselves: the dark Kālī; the great Mahādevī; Bhuvaneśānī, ruler of worlds; the fierce Bhairavī; Chinnamastakā, who holds her severed head in her hand, and so on.[25] They are the bodied representatives of a language that has lost its semantic bearings. And after the goddesses are born from the body of the Blue Goddess of Speech, the text tells us, with a barely circumspect glee that these Words that are simultaneously goddesses, exuberantly dance on the tips of the goddess's feet.[26]

The text's use of the very explicit "out of her own body" (*svadehataḥ*), "arising from her body" (*dehodbhūtā*), and "born from her body" (*dehājjātā*) emphasize that the *mantras* are emitted out of her body, not formed and spoken by her mouth. This is a language that is not so much spoken as it is simply born. These feminine *mantras* arise spontaneously, emitted from her body as whole beings. The image is more similar to that of a woman giving birth to a child than of the way one speaks language.

These *mantras* arise out of her body as substance, as a materiality of thought. They are not bound by the usual temporal structure of language that ordains a successive concatenation of words, each following on the heels of what went before. The feminine *mantra* is nonlinear and ruptures the a priori tempo that places words in time. No wonder the gods in the tale are spellbound.[27] Because this Goddess of Speech does not move through time as language normally does, but instead is presence, referenced as the visual image of the dancing goddess-words, so in her presence the gods also find it hard to speak. Her production of a language that is not sign, which is presence more than meaning, defies even time. It is a language without referent, which stands as the outside of language's power to denote.

Words that are also goddesses dancing on the toes of the Blue Goddess of Speech evoke also a sense of the performative. They are dancing words. As magical speech, they are also words that perform what they say. By saying these words things happen. These words win battles for the gods by their presence. Thus these words as bodies, as perfomative speech, dance outside of a logocentric view of language.

Mantra as Bodied

We should note that, apart from this tale, the *mantra* is also explicitly coded as a body elsewhere in the BT. In fact, in a section of the BT that outlines various methods for making *mantras* potent, conspicuously, most of these methods depend upon treating the *mantra* as if it were a physical body. So, one method for increasing the potency of the *mantra* involves "nourishing" it (*āpyāyana*), that is, sprinkling water on it with a leaf of *kuśa* grass. "He should sprinkle each letter of the *mantra* with the *japa* done with the water of *kuśa* grass with that mantra. This is known as 'nourishing' [the *mantra*]."[28]

Similarly, one can make the *mantra* efficacious by "striking" the *mantra* with sacred leaves covered in fragrant sandal paste water. "Having written out [each of] the letters of the mantra, he should strike them with water mixed with sandal wood powder."[29] In both these instances the physical "body" of the *mantra* is highlighted; in fact, the *mantra* is, if anything, a "body" in these contexts. This is how the *mantra* becomes potent, that is, capable of "doing things." Treating the words as bodily form effects the power of these words.

Curiously, in the second example, the BT employs the same word, *striking*, in "striking" the *mantra* with leaves, as it uses to describe the act of intercourse during the rite of sexual union: *tāḍayet*.[30] In terms of gender, this also aligns the *mantra* with the feminine since in the BT and elsewhere, men "*tāḍayet*" ("strike") women and here one "*tāḍayet*" ("strikes") the *mantra*, placing the woman and the *mantra* in the same place in the equation. The word *tāḍayet* itself has a complex connotation. Often translated as "strike," the (ostensibly) male practitioner "strikes" a woman in ritual sexual intercourse; one "strikes" a musical instrument; one can "strike" an enemy, and the word is also especially associated with lightning and the brilliant splendor that occurs with lightning. Monier Monier-Williams's Sanskrit dictionary also notes that it means to "speak" or to "shine," suggesting a curious association between speaking and acting upon the body.[31] Apart from the suggestion that a *mantra* is like a woman in this use, we should note that the *mantra* is treated as though it were a physical body. In this sense the *mantra* is ritually understood to be bodied language.

Also, the idea of the goddess and the *mantra* as a seamless boundless unity of being is not unique or isolated to this text. It forms a motif surfacing elsewhere in the Indian landscape. A popular hymn to the goddess Lakṣmī, for instance, tells us "O Goddess, whose form is always the *mantra*, homage to you."[32] In this popular hymn as well, the goddess is embodied language.

Woman's Speech

At this point we will look at two other instances that link woman's speech with the body and performativity. Above we noted that the feminine *vidyā* in this Tantric view is bodied, performative, and outside the order of logocentricity. Here we see that in other representations outside of the BT's Tantric view, much of this characterization persists, although it is offered in a less positive light. Especially, we find still the notion that woman's speech is outside of a notion of language as logocentric and that woman's speech is performative.

We take these two representations given below from an example of the speech of the *satī*, the "good wife" who burns herself on her husband's pyre, and a recent representation of woman's speech as performative in the United States.

To begin with the *satī*, I have suggested in chapter 3 that the key to the equation of the *satī* as the "good wife" who immolates herself upon her husband's pyre, is that her death by fire erases the body. The sign of difference that the female body encodes, the female sex organ, is forgotten, while her formless ash remains mingled with that of her husband. Her difference as woman is erased; she is mute, and insofar as she does not exist apart from her husband, the difference, which constitutes her own identity, is un*re*membered.

In this sense she is a "good wife" because in both death and life, her voice and identity remain submerged in the will of her husband. The "good wife" (*pativratā*) is entirely subservient to her husband; she has no needs of her own. This might also be read to explain why her difference as woman must be erased. Subsumed in the identity of her husband, this erasure facilitates that the question of her own needs or desires does not arise.

So, demure in life, she has no separate voice; in death also she has no separate voice. Here, however, I want to point out a peculiar feature of the *satī*. In the short interim between her husband's death and her own death, for a brief span she acquires a voice. Lindsey Harlan points out this feature in her discussion of the *satī* in general, and especially of the Satī Godāvarī.[33] In the brief period during which Godāvarī enacts her will to die on her husband's pyre, as Harlan points out, she acquires a voice and agency.[34] What does this voice look like? It is an instance of performative speech.

During this ritually charged span of time, everything the *satī* says happens, magically, instantaneously. Her speech is a potent performative speech. So when Godāvarī's friend Dhāpū tries to talk her out of her death by fire, Godāvarī curses Dhāpū with leprosy and instantly Dhāpū's body manifests the advanced stages of the disease.[35] Similarly, several other instances of Godāvarī's potent performative speech are demonstrated in the story Harlan presents. The words of this ideal woman are performative speech, effecting what they say by their mere pronouncement. In the case of the *satī*, this gets expressed negatively, as the Satī Godāvarī goes on a cursing rampage.[36] Here the power of her speech to instantly "do" what it says wreaks havoc on her fellow villagers.[37]

In deciphering this story for our purposes here, we need to keep in mind the relational identity of the *satī*. The *satī* attains power not through her own individual identity, but through her role as the "good woman," the ideal wife in relation to her husband. She is the sign of woman as representation (or stereotype) acting out an ideal relation to the male who governs her. The power she acquires—she who is otherwise throughout her life and death silent in the face of her husband—is the power of a particular and peculiar form of speech, performative speech, which enacts what it says in the utterance. The story elucidates exactly what kind of speech we might expect when the "good woman" finally speaks. For the brief period where this ideal and typically silenced woman actually acquires her own voice, her speech steps outside of the normative logocentric patterns of speech, to a speech that fuses what it says with what it does. The picture we have of this ideal woman's speech suggests that woman's speech *is* performative speech.

We should note that often one "sign" remains to mark the *satī*'s death—the signature of a handprint on a wall. Curiously, this very emblem suggests through a linguistic homology that this writing on the wall, her sole identifying "textual" remains, are a piece of performative language. That is, the cognate Sanskrit/Hindi word for hand, "*kara*"[38] derives from the root *kṛ*, which means to do or perform an act. This, of course, is not a mere coincidence; the hand is, after all, the emblematic organ for "doing," something we find throughout philosophical literature, especially evinced in the Sāṃkhya categories for the organs of action (*karmendriya*). What this suggests is that even in her death, the text the *satī* speaks alludes to a notion of this speech as performative speech, a speech that enacts through its utterance.

In her discussion of women's voices Rajeshwari Sunder Rajan points out a "valorization of silence as a desired 'feminine' attribute."[39] Further, she suggests that the *satī* presents a silencing of the woman as subaltern. Explicitly, Sunder Rajan deals with what she notes are representations of women, and in a move that tends toward a rejection of an essentialism inherent to Lacan's notion of the woman as outside of language and a rejection of Gayatri Spivak's assimilation of an incapacity to speak as defining the subaltern *satī*,[40] Sunder Rajan instead attempts to reconstruct the notion of women's speech. For her, the silence of the *satī* is not intrinsic to the category of woman. She suggests: "Women's speech, in the first place, is often confined to the space of the home. . . . But when women *are* allowed access to public forums, the very exceptionality of this entry may produce various kinds of linguistic excess: confession, curse, polemic, diatribe, profession of faith, revelation and prophecy proliferate notoriously in existing accounts of, for instance, women's court trials."[41]

Sunder Rajan notes on a general level what we see specifically in the case of Godāvarī Satī: that the woman's speech "fails as statement, testimony or communication."[42] In other words, a woman's speech stands outside of normative speech. It does not operate in the bounds of the logocentric order of language. Sunder Rajan construes this nonlogocentric speech as a type of "linguistic excess." More precisely, however, the types of speech she lists tend toward speech as performative, speech especially connected to ritual behavior. The curse, the confession, and the profession of faith all fall under the rubric of performative speech, but also the prophecy, the polemic, and the diatribe also cohere as performative speech.

Now, lest we conclude that a stereotype of women's speech as performative is exclusively confined to India, we can note here as well one recent instance from the United States that also tends to support Sunder Rajan's characterization of women's speech. In a recent discussion of the Anita Hill case, Judith Butler notes that Anita Hill's testimony against Clarence Thomas, which, as speech, ought to have been read *as* testimony, that is, as speech that cites or records a sequence of events, was instead read as a type of pornography, precisely because her speech was heard as performative speech.[43] In the debate following the hearings, Catherine Mackinnon points out that Anita Hill's inability to be heard, her exclusion from the order of proper speech as testimony, indicates how the pornographic representation of women, women as objects of sexualization, effectively silences them, depriving women of a proper voice.[44] In analyzing this case, what Butler notes is that Anita Hill's speech functioned as a type of performative speech. Butler argues that when Hill talks *about* her sexual injury, recording and citing it, this woman's speech is read as *confessional* speech, speech that reenacts and *performs* the original sexualization of the injury.[45] That is, just as Sunder Rajan notes for the Indian context, in the United States as well, Hill's speech functions as a performative speech. What this suggests is that on the level of representation, of stereotype, when a woman, especially *as* woman, that is, as a gendered human, speaks, her speech is often construed as performative.

In her discussion of Anita Hill's case Butler also stresses other elements as well, namely, that the model for performative speech is located in the image of the sovereign[46] and with this that Anita Hill's subjectivity in the act of her speaking is one that cannot be located in the intentionality imputed to a subject "speaking," since the content of Hill's speech is displaced from her status as witness to what "happened." Hill's speech instead reenacts the sexualization of the female body precisely because her speech is gendered (and in this case racialized as well). Her speech is heard as a performative speech reenacting the sexualization of her body.[47]

I would suggest in this case that the speech as performative derives from an endemic pervasive stereotype that locates normative speech as speech distinct from the body and from actions, speech as a transcendent mode. Performative speech, on the other hand, deviates from the normative because of its association with the body and especially with the female body.

The Binary and the Multiple: The Two versus the Many

What we see in the two examples above is that there is a link between women's speech, the female body, and speech that functions performatively. Now the question is, how do these links between body, speech as performative, and the feminine work in the context of the feminine *mantra*? Are the stereotypes we noted in the examples above reinforced? The *vidyās* are also feminine performative speech. That is, they *do* something as speech. In the story they win a war for the gods, and generally the *vidyā* and the *mantra* function performatively as speech enacting events in the world by their utterance.

I suggest that one way the *vidyā*, this female magical speech, differs from the two examples above may be seen in that the *vidyā* in the story tends to undermine the foundations of logocentricity as a binary of word and referent. In the two examples of the *satī* and Anita Hill, the binary remains in place; women's speech is outside of the normative speech—it is construed as "excess," that is, external to the order of speech. This speech as "excess" does not disrupt the authority of normative logocentric speech. Rather, it circles on the fringes, at the outside; we might say, following the metaphor of the BT's myth, that it stays marginalized on the mountain. In the center, normal logocentric speech dominates, and in doing so, asserts that this speech of "excess" that is "woman's" speech be dismissed as incoherent, as outside the proper boundaries of language, as not "logical."

How does the *vidyā* undermine the authority of normal logocentric speech? Normatively, language functions to separate, to create categories, that is, to construct the world by separating the world and self in terms of subject and object and so on, that is, into a binary that echoes the binary of the word and its referent. Language seemingly describes the world; in doing so it constructs a distance, a barrier between the world and the self. In fact, to suggest that language "describes" the world is to be beguiled into internalizing the notion of logocentricity, that is, into a notion that the world "out there" is referenced by language. This logocentric model masks the creative contribution that language as a structure makes to what we perceive as existing "out there." In contrast, when the *vidyā* fuses being and word into sheer presence, the order that divides self and world/other begins to falter. The unexpected takes place. Because this feminine magical speech is not a word *denoting*, pointing to some absent "other," it possesses the power to give birth, to make real that which one desires. It is a dizzy presence, which makes things happen. As we saw earlier in the image of the goddess emitting the *vidyās* that then dance in joy on her toes, they bring the promise of victory for the gods.

However, more than this, they make things happen because they are a language not one place removed from being. Even within the text of the story, the *vidyā* exists as a presence apart from the story, and apart from the moral encoded within this story as narrative. The *vidyā* acts upon the reader, inciting the reader to also act, to engage this nonlogocentric speech through a performance. That is, the point of the story—that the *vidyā* helps the gods win a war with demons, that it fulfills one's desires—incites the reader to *act*, to engage this speech in a manner that moves beyond a logocentric relationship to language, in other words, to also recite the feminine *mantra* ritually over and over. By recognizing the alternative power and authority that this feminine speech possesses—that it is a speech that is efficacious in addressing life's needs, the BT's author(s) suggests that the reader also take the time to step outside of a normative logocentric approach to language to ritually repeat the *vidyā* over and over, far past any point where meaning is conveyed, that is, to *perform* it.

Now, the fusion of being and sign, which in normative language presents an incompatible dichotomy, is literalized in the goddess's capacity to emit from her body a multiplicity of goddesses. Where this fusion occurs, we find a multiplicity ensues. Moreover, the notion of a singular goddess and a multiplicity of goddesses is in this context interchangeable. The twelve goddesses that arise from the body of the Goddess of Speech are both not different and at the same time different from the Goddess of Speech. Similarly, in the *Devī Māhātmya*, the demon fighting the goddess in battle complains he has to fight an army of goddesses. If the goddess were not a coward, she would fight him single-handedly, alone, and not rely on the strength of others. As the goddess points out with her response, he clearly does not understand her relationship to these other goddesses. The goddess responds, "What other one is here? All are forms of me" as she then withdraws all the multitude of goddesses back into her body.[48]

In the economy of Plato's Forms the feminine is deprived of *morphe*, of a shape, thus designating it as a nonliving, shapeless thing, a nameless materiality.[49] The view of the feminine in these Indian texts stands in contrast. The feminine presents a multiplicity of forms, a host of goddesses, all varying, shifting, and precisely delineated. Here the materiality of the feminine "bodied" word multiplies profusely; a multiplicity is the hallmark of the feminine logos incarnate. That is, when the word fuses with the thing, the body, we see a fecund multiplicity ensuing. The goddess in the BT, as in the *Devī Māhātmya*, contains and emits a multitude of varying forms, which are all still her own.

With this, even the category of "other" is undermined because the multiplicity of shifting forms explodes the binary logic that founds the idea of an "other." In one sense there is no "other." There is both unity and multiplicity, but nothing stands as "other." There is no other because the other arises precisely out of a subject formed within the symbolic construction of the world; that is, language divides the world into self and other. The multiplicity of the goddess's forms as bodied language offers a way out of the dilemma of the ultimately frangible if apparently determined construction of self that is created by excluding that which is "other."[50] The goddess's "self" is not clearly demarcated. She is both a single goddess as the Blue Goddess of Speech and a multiplicity of goddesses, that is, Kālī, Bhuvaneśānī, the fierce Bhairavī, and so on. She is bodied visible form, and (as we see especially in the next chapter) she is the collection of all the words. She takes form as the female jackal who prowls around boundaries where the Tantrika performs secret rites; she also, as we saw in chapter 2, is the form of all women. She also takes the form of rock—as we see in a popular contemporary story in Kāmākhyā where about sixty years ago she became upset with the engineer trying to build the road to the top of the Blue Hill at Kāmākhyā because his dynamite blasting for the road blasted a part of her body as rock. In this popular story, the goddess was offended and afflicted the workers with cholera. In the end, the chief engineer had a dream where the goddess at Kāmākhyā appeared to him and asked him why he was blowing up her body. The engineer shifted his road plans and as expiation an annual buffalo sacrifice was enacted to commemorate the event.[51]

In this context the very ease in which the pieces are disbursed and reintegrated—both the image of a host of goddesses dancing on the toes of the Blue Goddess of Speech in the BT and in the *Devī Māhātmya*, the multitude of goddesses who both emerge and are reabsorbed into Devī—structurally reconceives the idea of self away from an idea of self as a fixed (if finally fictional) entity. In this sense the goddess's response to the demon in the *Devī Māhātmya* who asks her to fight alone, without the help of others, appears equally to be a response to the linguistic postulation of identity as determinate image—as it is to the demon's demands for a "fair" fight.

Śaṅkara and the Classical Tradition—One Body or Many Bodies?

One is reminded of the *Śaṅkaradigvijaya*'s dilemma as the celibate Śaṅkara, who advocates transcending the body, must debate upon a topic of which he cannot possibly have knowledge: the art of love. Now, according to the BT, it is really only insentient matter (*prakṛti*) that can offer knowledge. As the BT tells us, "That which is not manifest, and that which is manifest, both are known by

'Nature,' *prakṛti*. Consequently, without being linked with *prakṛti* that is not known at all whatsoever, just as a pot is not visible (*pratyakṣa*) unless it is connected with 'potness' i.e., the state of being a "pot'."[52]

Nature as materiality is what offers us categories and with this, knowledge. Now, the pot as an example in itself connotes materiality—at its most embodied level. A common image used in philosophical texts, the pot (*ghaṭa*) comes to represent matter as the product of the creator, where the god who makes the world is likened to the potter who makes pots. So the pot is a metonymical image of the world and especially of all the "matter" that makes up the world. Apart from this, the pot also ritually represents the feminine. The goddess is worshiped in a pot of water for the nine-day festival to the goddess in the fall, and as Stephanie Jamison notes, the pot in general is assimilated to the womb.[53]

So playing upon this idea of the pot as the feminine and as the world, this author(s) extends the function of the feminine nature (*prakṛti*); she brings into being the visibility (*pratyakṣa*) of objects. The embodiment she causes becomes the condition for knowledge. Matter functions as the substratum for the very possibility of knowledge. Indeed, even further, in order for things to be *present*, that is, visible (*pratyakṣa*), things must be connected with this feminine nature/ matter. To put this another way, existence is contingent upon bodily instantiation. There is no body-free transcendence.

Interestingly, the classical, non-Tantric text of the *Śaṅkaradigvijaya*—despite the fact that Śaṅkara was a strict monist specifically interested in transcending nature and matter—appears to also reference the perspective of the BT since in Śaṅkara's case, he must make use of the unwieldy heap of the body to gain the knowledge of the art of love he needs to win the debate with his rival, Mandana Miśra.

Śaṅkara thus embarks upon an adventure into the body of a dead king, temporarily reviving it in order to gain carnal knowledge to use in his debate, so that he can avoid implicating his own celibate body in the messiness of the art of love. In this case, the transcendent ascetic's solution works an impossible fantasy, in what one might see as the reassertion of the male prerogative to both be free of the messiness, the excess that is the body, and to still co-opt, that is, to master the knowledge that only the body conveys. The only real danger in this fantastic exercise of the skills of mastery acquired by the ascetic yogī is the fear of ultimately being trapped in the very body that affords him knowledge.

Interestingly, in this case, when the dead king's men come to burn the inert corpse of Śaṅkara, whose "spirit" is habitating elsewhere in the body of the king, to save his (original) skin, Śaṅkara must invoke with a hymn of praise what we might construe a beastly embodiment, the animalistic—half lion, half man fusion (*naramṛgarūpa*), the Narasiṃha incarnation (*avatāra*) of Viṣṇu.[54] Perhaps we should consider his salvation via the animal as a reemergence of the displaced equation "body = mute beast."

On the other hand, upon closer inspection this episode reveals an apparent structural flaw in the notion of the one. Concomitant with the structure of unity, the idea of the one, which the transcendent monism of Śaṅkara's Advaita uses to encompass all of life, there appears to be an ineluctable repetition of this structure of one. Insofar as "spirit" represents a unifying structure, a metaphysical oneness, it lacks the power of its antithesis, the body, to multiply. So in this case there can inevitably be only ever one "spirit," one "real" Śaṅkara, which according to the logic of the hierarchy of spirit/body, then occupies the place of the center, in the face of the multiple bodies proliferating the periphery. The unity that is the "person" cannot conceivably inhabit both the dead king and his own body at the same time. Instead he faces the dilemma of which body to choose. In the context of this metaphysical dynamic, the very structure of the power of the center logically, inextricably depends upon there ever only being *one* center, and some other bodies, the amorous king's, for instance, which must be excluded.

On the other hand, the goddess, in contrast, resides fundamentally in the proliferation of bodies.[55] Her being is inextricably linked with form (*rūpa*), with bodies. She is both a single goddess and multitude of goddesses simultaneously. Consequently, only she has that capacity to proliferate spirit and form simultaneously, inhabiting a multiplicity of bodies—that of a multiplicity of goddesses, of living women, even a corpse, a stone, and a jackal—all at once. This suggests a notion of female identity not constructed upon the exclusion of that which is "other" to the self. It also proposes a notion of identity that conceptually integrates the body and matter as crucial elements of self.

Conclusion

In this chapter on the birth of feminine magical speech, the myth the BT gives begins with a gender binary, where we see a linkage between the female, the body, the performative and magical speech. In this case, the feminine is not excluded from speech, rather it is connected with a particular kind of speech, the magical performative speech of the *vidyā*. We also see that this stereotype is not entirely absent elsewhere, in representations of the *satī* and in the West, and thus that it points to a pervasive representation of women's relationship to language. What the BT adds to this stereotype is first of all to make the linkages graphic, to literalize them through visual analogues in the image of dancing-bodied goddess-words. More than this, though, the BT's myth implodes the function of the stereotype to create a binary. By reversing the hierarchy normatively encoded in the opposition between female "performative" speech and normative (read: male) speech the BT creates an image of the feminine that does not remain on the margins of logocentricity. Rather, it offers an alternative model that moves away from a notion of language as positing determinate, fixed identity as the norm. Like the reversal that we saw in chapter 3, where women are encoded as spirit rather than body, this view offers a philosophical rewriting of women's relationship to language.

In the quote of Teresa De Lauretis we saw at the beginning of this chapter, she critiques Lévi-Strauss's structuralist model because it presumes a binary structure in which woman always already has assumed the role of objects to be exchanged. De Lauretis's method of critique is to expose and deconstruct the underlying philosophical binary that powers the system that leaves women both absent as subject and the object of male proprietary drives. The system of language enacts the binaries of subject and object, of word and thing and curiously it parallels the system of kinship relations. In other words, the way we employ language—the very system of the use of language—is connected to the way women are viewed and is implicated in the objectification of women, in making women objects of exchange for male owners. By critiquing the underlying premises of the binary that bolsters language, she makes apparent its contingent status. We may also read as critique of this system of language the BT's move to reconstruct feminine language as bodied speech. Through an implicit coding in myth, in its own way, it offers also a contesting model to the binary, reconfiguring the value and relation of women's speech and of women to language.

5

How the Blue Goddess of Speech Turns Blue

In chapters 3 and 4 we saw how woman's speech, in the case of the *satī*, in the case of Anita Hill, and in the case of Linda Marchiano, is effectively silenced through a discourse that reads her speech in terms of her body. In this chapter we look at a myth that literally enacts the silencing of woman's speech—in this case by silencing the Goddess of Speech herself—through male violence.

In this myth from the BT, Nīlasarasvatī, the Blue Goddess of Speech, is abducted by two male assailants, Horse-neck and Moony (Hayagrīva and Somaka), and a symbolic if not literally articulated rape occurs, with the final result that she becomes both silenced and "defiled." In this case, her defilement is registered bodily, since the poison they use to keep her prisoner eventually transforms her from a white-skinned goddess to a dark blue one. If we read this tale through a symbolic lens, one that homologizes this female goddess as victim of male violence to the plight of women more generally, what does it tell us about women's susceptibility to male violence and male responses to this violence? That it is the Goddess of Speech who loses her voice in the face of violence records a psychological acuity on the part of this text's author. This myth narratively makes transparent the links between violence and the loss of speech. One might also read the myth's suggestive representation of the goddess as defiled and dark-skinned as presciently anticipating Gayatri Spivak's question, "can the subaltern speak?"[1] In this case in its calm compassionate response it offers a refiguring of the ability and strategies for speech for the defiled woman.[2]

However, two things are especially salient about the myth the BT presents; first, that it metaphorically recognizes violence toward women as a problem that affects all of society and, second, that it offers a humane response to violence toward women, one that does not stigmatize women as somehow being at fault for this violence. This chapter addresses discourse on violence toward women from a voice not usually registered: this Tantric view of the BT's author(s). In what follows below, I suggest that this precolonial discourse around violence offers what we might construe from our position in the twenty-first century as a prescient and enlightened contrast to British colonialist discourse around this same subject, of violence toward women, a century or so later, in the nineteenth century.

One of the markers of civilization is precisely the capacity for speech; speech marks the human.[3] Along parallel lines, we find also that to be civilized also means to understand that violence perpetrated against women is especially heinous. In India also, after the 1857 mutiny, when the Indian soldiers revolted against British rule, the British rulers of India cited just this particular crime of violence against women—the rape of English women—perpetrated by Indians, as a reason for imposing the superior, "civilized" British rule (even though it was quickly established that this charge of the wanton rape of English women was nearly entirely fabricated by the British).[4] We should keep in mind that British discourse employed also the *satī* as one other example of violence toward women; the British abolition of the practice of *satī* functioned polemically as the sign of superior British "civilization."

Jenny Sharpe writes about this period of British rule in India, through the nineteenth and twentieth centuries, suggesting that the rape of women, and the threat of it, was part of a British masculinist chivalraic discourse that was in the end less about women and more about men gaining power over other men, both through enacting the violence of rape on women's bodies, and promising to save women from this threat of rape.[5]

One might also suggest that encoded within the discourse of a chivalric protection of women is that very element that perpetuates this violence against them, a notion of male mastery over women. This mastery protects women because they are weaker, but since they are weaker views them as objects, ultimately property. Consequently as object and property, the woman easily becomes a pawn in men's agonistic struggles with one another. And, it may be possible to also read the critique of male ascetic mastery, which we find in the CT discussed in chapter 2, as encoding also a psychological awareness of this connection between ascetic rejection of the female—which rejects her because she is object—and the easy shift to violence toward this insentient object/woman.

We can recall in this context what we learned from chapter 2 regarding the reversal of the subject/object binary in the scripting of the sex rite. That is, right before he reveals the secret sex rite, the god Śiva tells us its secret essence: that woman is pure spirit, the subject—not in any way object.[6] Likewise, the hesitation that the god displays around revealing the secret rite stems from his awareness of the generally agonistic relations between men. He tells us that most of the world's inhabitants—whether men (*narāḥ*), divine, or semidivine, animal or demonic—are "engaged in bad deeds." "These are very stupid; the nature of all these is such that all are mutually fighting in battle; . . . Thus, how can I tell you that [secret rite]?"[7] That is, these agonistic relations between men are, in this god's view, connected with their noncomprehension of woman as subject rather than object, and their bad deeds perpetuate the cycle. Śiva's reason for not wanting to reveal the secret is that the endeavor is nearly hopeless, given these stupid, fighting beings.

Of course, the caveat I brought up earlier applies here as well; we need to keep in mind that we deal with textual sources, which do not necessarily reflect actual historical behaviors toward women in Tantric circles in the fifteenth through eighteenth centuries. Nevertheless, at least someone articulated the particular point of view toward women that these stories encode. As discourse these stories offer an indigenous perspective, which helps to reframe our historical understanding of pre-British Indian attitudes toward women, particularly for the nonorthodox Tantric perspectives.

The Myth

The tale begins when the gods oust the demons in a battle and the chagrined and flailing demons seek revenge with the aid of two especially powerful male demons, Horse-neck and Moony (Hayagrīva and Somaka). This tale also incorporates the motive Sharpe notes above in her discussion of British discourse about violence toward women, with males enacting violence upon women as a way of attacking other males. Here, the two demon abductors of the Blue Goddess of Speech are really trying to get back at other males, the gods who defeated them in battle. In any case, that the text's author(s) glosses the bad guys as "the earlier gods" (*pūrvadevāḥ*[8]) rather than other more common words for demons, such as *rākṣasa* or *asura* may perhaps be read to suggest a cognizance on the part of our author of a lack of any intrinsic difference between these two groups of males. It again recalls the statement we see the god Śiva make right before he reveals the secret sex rite, that most of the world's inhabitants—whether human, divine, or semidivine, animal or demonic—are very stupid (*jaḍatara*); "the nature of all these is such that all are mutually fighting in battle."[9]

In any case, these two demons do fierce austerities in order to gain a particular boon from the goddess Sarasvatī, the Goddess of Speech, this goddess who, as the text tells us here, is "the Goddess who attracts words."[10] "Those two bad brothers, Horse-neck and Moony did austerities directed towards the Goddess who attracts all words. Pleased with their intense austerity, the Goddess who attracts words said, 'you two choose a boon that you desire.' The Goddess said this to those two, in order to answer their prayer for a boon. 'Let us two be given the boon of attracting all the words,' [they said]. 'Let it be so' she said to those two arrogant demons."[11]

When the Goddess of Speech appears before them and asks them to choose a boon, they ask her to give them the power to attract to themselves all the words. Without hesitation she acquiesces in what will be her own calamitous downfall, with the usual reply that a god or goddess utters when giving a boon: "let it be so." The law of austerity is fairly universal for Hindu texts: austerity brings its rewards regardless of the moral capacities of the person performing the austerity. This inexorable law functions theodically; it explains why seemingly "bad" people, demons in this context, can attain positions of power, and why "bad things can happen to good people." This is especially poignant here because, in the final analysis, this goddess loses her power over words simply because she gives it away. The art of fulfilling boons is a tricky business; a careful god like Viṣṇu always manages to leave a loophole. If a demon gets a boon making him invulnerable to death during day or night, Viṣṇu manages to kill him at twilight.

The Goddess of Speech is, however, "true to her word." That is, the goddess who controls words, "she who attracts words," the goddess who *is* the word, rather uncharacteristically lacks the ability to use words deceptively, even for the sake of her own skin. This tragic generosity results in her own kidnapping and seems to point to a moral of not trusting and to a moral of nondisclosure.

In this case the goddess grants the two demons their request and they become immediately exceedingly arrogant. They use the boon to draw to themselves all the words in the world. As they make good on their boon, the world becomes mute. "That Goddess Sarasvatī, with her shining form, who is the form of all the words, manifesting in her divine body, she abandoned the mouths of all the sages. She was forced to come to the awful house of those two powerful demons. Crying and helpless, they led her to an enclosure underwater in the hell called Pātāla. Having made a pit with the poison called halāhala, mixed with dark water, there they tied her up with ropes made from snakes and submerged her."[12]

When the demons exercise their boon, all the words leave the mouths of the sages and become bodily manifest in their original divine body as the shining goddess Sarasvatī. She is the bodily and primordial signifier, the bodily life constituting words, their very form (*śabdarūpiṇī*).[13] As they attract the words, it is she who, as the text tells us, "abandons the mouths of all the sages." With this the world is left mute. This works to the advantage of the demons, since the gods are strengthened when humans recite the Vedas, and if humans are mute, then the gods get weak, without their word-nourishment.

At this point the metaphor of rape is enacted. This goddess, as the bodied form of words, crying, is led by force into her prison in the hell realm of Pātāla, submerged in a poisonous watery abode. She is tied up with ropes made of snakes. We can note here that the visualization that the BT gives for the Blue Goddess of Speech that we will see in appendix 2 also depicts her adorned with a variety of different-colored snakes.[14] Here, in the meantime, the curious boon missile leaves a void of meaning in its wake. "With the arrow of the demons attracting all the words on the surface of the earth, with this arrow, the twice-born ones (upper castes), became speechless. They forgot the Vedas. In this way by forgetting the *mantras,* the feminine magical speech (*vidyā*) in the sacrifices were banished. With the sacrifice destroyed, deprived of their share [of the rites], the strength [of the Gods] waned."[15]

With this, the sages become speechless. Brahmins cannot remember the Vedas any longer. They forget the *mantras,* and female magical speech (*vidyā*) also no longer has a place to dwell. The gods are then deprived of the nourishment they gain from the sacrifices of humans and they lose their strength. Through a metaphoric capture and rape of the woman, Horse-neck and Moony are able to strike their greatest blow against their male foes, the gods. In this sense, the demons deprive the gods of a voice, and political power, by literally abducting the woman who is the source of all speech.

It may be jarring for Westerners to imagine this odd shift where the temporal becomes spatial, where language as a phenomenon through time is presented visually, physically anthropomorphized as this shining goddess. This, of course, recalls the bodied feminine word (*vidyā*) as goddesses dancing on the toes of the Blue Goddess of Speech, in the myth presented in chapter 4. The myth here seamlessly and visually underscores this identity of goddess as word. The goddess *is* language; she is not a goddess *of* language. She is not an abstract principle, but the very words uttered in human mouths.

The irony of silencing the very source of speech manifests a profoundly rich web of meaning. On the one hand, the literalness of imagining words as a body recalls our discussion of "bodied" speech in chapter 4, with its implications of feminine bodied language as a potent and primordial performative speech—speech that makes things happen in the world. On the other hand, it also evokes the image of woman as being subject to a male violence that can only leave her mute, without language, a silencing of women, which is both effect and source of the violence given to them. The moral here is loudly pronounced, since the abuse given to the woman here results in the whole world becoming mute. That the world itself becomes speechless in the face of this abuse evokes both the idea that the natural response to violence is speechlessness for those who witness it, and also that the people in the world—all of life—are interconnected. This roundabout way of disempowering the gods by depriving humans of speech highlights the interdependence of humans and gods, with the contractual nature of speech as the conduit. Hence violence given to the woman cannot help being felt also as the loss of speech everywhere.

Meanwhile the two demon brothers sitting tight in their underwater house do not yet realize they are marked men and that the great god Viṣṇu decides to take his incarnation as a thousand-toothed fish to disrupt their word-abduction scheme. "In this way, having put to flight all the wise persons, Hayagrīva and Somaka remain in their house inside the ocean. [Meanwhile] they are marked by Viṣṇu's discus [as demons to be destroyed]. Then Viṣṇu, the eternal lord, takes the form of a great fish."[16]

This would sound like prime material for an action film, if the metaphorical and metaphysical implications of tying up language were not so boldly transgressive of our notions of categories. The images we see move fluidly across linguistic registers; the demons "tie up" words as though they were material objects—which, in this case, as an embodied goddess, words are material. The image of using arrows to draw away words from mouths functions similarly. Tying up words and using arrows to draw away words from human mouths fluidly moves across linguistic registers. In itself it offers a type of categorical wildness not familiar to the West.[17]

In any case, the text appears clearly Vaiṣṇava here, reminding us with an echo from the *Bhagavad Gītā*, that age after age Viṣṇu incarnates for the sake of uplifting the world. "Just as with the boar incarnation, submerged in the ocean, eon after eon he saves the world. In the same way the lotus eyed lord in the form of a fish, moving to and fro, stirred up and flooded the city under the ocean."[18]

Viṣṇu dives into the ocean, splashing water into the underwater prison and then morphs into a more battle-ready form, sprouting four arms and his accustomed retinue of weapons, especially including the discus, and then engages in a battle that lasts one thousand years.[19]

The Dark Defiled Body: A Tantric Response to Being Blue

In the battle that ensues, the chivalraic Viṣṇu saves the Blue Goddess of Speech. On the one hand, she appears not so distressed by her ordeal; she is smiling (*smitā*). "Hari spoke to Sarasvatī, who was smiling. She[20] sang first the magical feminine words of the three Tārās which are the root of all procedures with mantras. The Goddess with this obtained for us that knowledge. . . . [Viṣṇu said,] 'You have become blue in the middle of the pit of poison, [but] your limbs are complete and full, and your lotus face is smiling.' "[21]

Her bondage in the midst of the pit of poison has turned her blue, and in her own eyes, marred her physical beauty. Whereas before she was white, she has after this ordeal become blue (*nīla*), that is, dark skinned. Order is indeed restored, however, with irremediable loss. This is what she regrets and laments to Viṣṇu. "By means of your incarnation as a fish, I am well-protected. There is no fear whatsoever, and a good outcome has been obtained. However, my shining form, which was otherwise fair-skinned, has become blue. This causes me some regret."[22]

Here, her defilement, the humiliation she undergoes, is referenced in the body. Her blue color signifies the loss of her purity, and it is psychologically appropriate that she both loses her voice and becomes blue. Here her dark skin is poignant also because it signals the literal defilement of a rape. She is deprived of speech—which is, as her name suggests, her own inherent power, of which she is the original master, she who is the giver of eloquence. On another level, she becomes also, in this sense, imaged as the dark other. Dark skin is also a perennial marker for the low caste, the voiceless subaltern. It is no accident that when she loses her voice, when her language is silenced, she is figured as the dark skinned, figured as the speechless would be. Metamorphosed into the dark-skinned aboriginal, without rights, she is literally gagged and deprived of speech.

Typically in the Indian context, if a woman is held captive in the house of another man, it signifies her sexual defilement. The case of Sītā in the *Rāmāyaṇa* is exemplary. She is kidnapped by the demon Rāvaṇa and held forcibly in his home until her husband Rāma finally comes to her rescue. In this context, even though it was public knowledge that the demon Rāvaṇa could have in no way defiled her, since he had a curse put on him where his head would shatter if he raped any woman, nevertheless Rāma, her husband, rejects her because of this rule that a woman who lives under another man's roof would inevitably be defiled by him. This, of course, assumes that Sītā does not willingly give in to Rāvaṇa's advances, which is perhaps, precisely, what Rāma suspects. Rāma makes her endure an ordeal with fire, where she must prove her purity by immolating herself, and even when she emerges unscathed by the flames, he still questions her purity. In this well-known episode from the *Rāmāyaṇa*, Rāma, whose character exemplifies the paradigmatic and virtuous man, is more concerned with his own honor and status in relation to other men than with the plight of his wife who has been forcibly kidnapped by the enemy. In this sense, Sītā functions as his property, an object that he can consign to flames if she does not add to his own sense of status. At times one hears an apologetic for Rāma's behavior here, which runs, "Rāma himself knew she was pure, he simply had to prove it to the people around him, to the citizens of his kingdom." This response actually, however, all the more highlights that Sītā is merely an object for Rāma, that what is key for Rāma in this situation is his own honor in relation to other men, and not the welfare of his wife.

The story we find in the BT offers a striking contrast. Rather than reject her, instead Viṣṇu gives an uncommonly down to earth reply to her distress. "You're alive! Your ordeal in the pit of poison is ended!"[23] he says, with joy and relief. He tells her, "Do not grieve . . . you were dragged by force into this pit of poison, and so you became blue-skinned. How is it your fault?"[24] He consoles her loss of fair skin poetically, citing a host of reversals where what is dark is actually the sign of the good. "The color blue makes things prosper."[25] He tells her:

> The color blue makes things prosper; the color blue is indeed a God. The soft, kind Goddess Sāvitrī, the light of the world, [Kālī], is blue and the ancient teachings in the throat of [the God Śiva] are blue. The great Indra, emperor of the Gods is blue and the rain clouds which give life to the world are blue. The vault of the sky that gives space to all living things is blue. The moon which is the source of light has a blue stain. Even I myself, the abode of virtue [Viṣṇu], am blue. What's wrong with the color blue?[26]

To shift her out of her dismay, Viṣṇu offers a litany of positive images of the color blue. The goddess Kālī is blue, Śiva's dark throat, which became dark from the stain of the poison he swallowed to save the world, is blue; the king of heaven, Indra, is blue; the rain clouds that give life to the world are blue; and he points out that he himself is blue.[27] Further, his eulogy on the color blue skillfully rescripts the responses one might have to her imputed sexual defilement, registered in her dark skin. With a kindness that overturns a common social reaction toward the "raped" or abused woman, he adroitly emphasizes that a (sexually) abused woman is not a "fallen" woman, he tells her, "You were dragged by force into this pit of poison, and so you became blue-skinned. How is it your fault?" The notion that her dark skin is an imperfection reflects the socially normative conception of beauty for this time and place—where fair skin is the norm of beauty. Precisely what this story attempts to reread is the trope that the fair is beautiful and the dark is not.

And as if to emphasize that this is the proper ethical treatment of women, Viṣṇu at one point in the text addresses her as Lakṣmī (BT 11.84), the name of his own wife, suggesting in this case the contrast to the similar motif of the captured wife Sītā in the Rāmāyaṇa, who was in that tale an incarnation of the goddess Lakṣmī.[28] In contrast, in this incarnation, however, he is more concerned about the welfare of the goddess than about either the loss of his honor or the loss of her unsullied white skin.

The British Response to Being Blue

In the context of this violence toward women, Viṣṇu's response is exactly what the British response was not. Sharpe notes that British discourse around the rape of women could not countenance a life after rape. The woman must choose death over defilement and those who did not were not readily admitted back into British society.[29]

Much of the reporting of the Indian mutiny focused upon the rape and mutilation of English women's bodies. The atrocity against English womanhood circulated as the sign of superior British civilization, that is, as the rhetorical establishment of British power in the agonistic encounter with Indian soldiers. In this struggle, women, and as Sharpe notes, especially women's bodies—and, we may add here, women *as* bodies, that is, women as objects—functioned to displace the fear of violence against men onto women as the property of men, in effect distancing the anxiety by transferring it to the woman as object. A consequence of this was that the woman-as-object could no longer have a life after she was no longer the proper property of the English male. Thus, after rape (or before rape to prevent it), the woman (at least in discourse, that is, textually) had to commit suicide.[30]

Sharpe cites in particular the case of the daughter of a general, Miss Wheeler, who was captured with several of her companions in the battle at Cawnpore during the 1857 mutiny. In this story, which was reported throughout the press in a variety of versions at the time, and even enacted in playhouses across England, this young woman exhibited exemplary bravery as she slew several of her attackers, but in the end, she could not live with defilement. In each of the several versions she commits suicide in order to avoid defilement.

That this sensational story was disproved some years later—Miss Wheeler had instead gone off and cohabited with her Muslim captors—emphasizes the notion of woman as image, a rhetorical fiction bandied about in the contemporary discourse for political effects. However, as discursive image, the contrasts Viṣṇu's response to the defiled woman in the BT's myth provides are profound.

Alterity: The Color Purple and the Color Blue

The BT's story proposes an alternative response to a woman who is defiled, apart from her banishment or her death. This I suggest derives from a subtle scripting of woman in this text, which does not see her as male property. As property, the logical outcome of her defilement is death. However, in this tale, she is a subject in her own right, not merely property to be discarded when it no longer carries social value, and Viṣṇu is really simply happy to see her alive. On the one hand, Viṣṇu does not compound her chagrin by laying the blame at her feet (something our society frequently does—"her clothes were too suggestive"); on the other hand, as we saw, he consoles her with examples of virtuous representations of dark skin, including his own dark form. Indeed, "the clouds which give life to the world (as water) are blue. The vault of the sky which opens up space for all living beings is blue," and so on.[31]

A nice analogy from a Western context might be Alice Walker's *The Color Purple*.[32] Purple reflects the dark skin of the African American reflected through the prism of the beauty of purple in all of nature. In both these stories a woman is defiled and in both she passes through the ordeal with a sense of self as subject. And, in both, this passage through violence rescripts a normative social coding of values, to reclaim the dark as profound beauty, and as a beauty that is bigger than social codifications of beauty. The beauty of blue and purple pervade everywhere in the vistas of natural life, in flowers, in the sky, in the clouds, and this darkness, which is life itself, and can in no way be really ever defiled.

What's salient in these two panegyrics of dark things is the rescripting of the dark, the defiled self into a perspective that recognizes its inherent beauty, despite defilement. Form signals the trace of defilement and violation, and this eloquent and vast rescripting of darkness should alert us to the recognition of the pain of defilement. But especially here it references a way of accepting that which is fallible or defiled, the marginalized, the not entirely powerful or not powerful enough, and the imperfect and stained body.

Viṣṇu ends with a moving "You are alive!" The loss of her fair skin is
all, only skin deep. It does not touch the core of her being. The narrato
concludes, "So since that time, she has been known throughout the wo
the 'Blue Goddess of Speech,' She who gives liberation."[33]

Her speech revives, with this the world can start speaking again. The Brahmins remember their *mantras* for the sacred rites and the gods receive their offerings. The world comes back to order. The story of her ordeal, however, makes graphic the point that without her speech, no one can, in fact, speak.

On another level however, the story's conclusion suggests that her ordeal is not simply all loss. When her speech revives, it does so upon a new and deeper level, etched upon her body with the experience of an irremediable loss. Her beautiful fair form is gone forever, but she herself becomes a more powerful goddess, capable of giving liberation. Evocatively, the text suggests that she can give liberation perhaps precisely because she herself has lost the illusory hold onto a static, mirror-perfect identity. Her own identity has been irreparably fractured. With the loss of her fair, beautiful skin color, she can no longer maintain the fiction of outward perfection and this knowledge is in a profound sense freeing, liberating. Perhaps it is this enlightenment, her own newfound liberating awareness of her identity, which moves beyond a notion of a "skin-deep beauty"—the limited identity of herself tied to her beautiful fair skin—that makes her a goddess capable of giving liberation to others, that is, passing on this knowledge and freedom of identity to others.

In this case the text offers its own answer to the question of whether the defiled, violated woman[34] can speak. It proposes an image of woman that counters both the *satī* and the Miss Wheelers of the British Empire. It offers a vision of woman who regains her voice.

Conclusion

We began this book with two alternative visions of a woman dancing. While the Sāṃkhya portrait of nature as woman dances for the sake of the male as spirit, in contrast, the Renowned Goddess of Desire, the Goddess Kāmākhyā on the Blue Hill dances for her own pleasure. This Goddess at Kāmākhyā is called *Mahā-Māyā*; literally, she is the master of this illusion we call the world. The image she offers allows us to imagine an idea of woman as her own master, master of her body and her dance. With this book, I bring to the forefront alternative representations of women in Tantra, representations that upset business as usual and offer a greater diversity of possibilities for the ways we can imagine women.

I present images of women that contest the dominant and more normative portraits of women that we find in Tantra. I look at attitudes toward women and I look at representations of goddesses. I have drawn from ritual prescriptions, from philosophical statements, and from myth to offer these alternative images. We have progressed through women as gurus, to the woman on top, to the wife as the ritual partner in the rite of sexual union, to the Blue Goddess giving birth to bodied magical speech, to the abduction and silencing of the Blue Goddess of Speech. These varied representations, like a prism, reflect a multiplicity of facets, each in their partial refractions offering a multidimensional proliferation of windows into the idea of woman.

What I have done through this study especially is to shift focus so that we understand that the portrait(s) of women we encounter in

Tantric texts is indeed multifaceted. These alternative images of women are useful because they expand our horizons. Especially the uncommon inflections that we find in these representations of women offer other possibilities for the ways we can imagine women.

Thus, one of the obvious points my reader may take away from this study is that Tantra is by no means monolithic. More than this, though, my purpose here has been twofold. On the one hand, I have pointed to the places where we might find challenges contesting women's images and rescripting women's identities. Representations that move away from construing women as objects for male gain particularly work in this way to reconfigure women's roles, to present women in the role of subject, and these images come to the fore in chapter 1. On the other hand, I hope to offer with this study a way of thinking about images of women that will allow us to reflect upon the very categories that direct us and limit us in our discussions of women.

With this second purpose in view, throughout this study my overarching hermeneutic framework has been to locate these alternative images of women within the parameters of speech and representation. What does it mean to read talk about women in books written by men several centuries ago, and what does it mean for *us* to talk about women who lived centuries ago, when these women are themselves silent? In each of the chapters I reflect upon the issues involved in representing women, how representation of women is intertwined with women's ability, or not, to speak and how women's bodies are represented in their speech. Thus throughout this book the theme that has guided our journey has been a return to the question of speech, speech about women, and the implication of women's bodies in this speech.

With this I should make it clear again that the images of women I focus on here present only one element within the texts consulted. Typical of much Tantric literature, we find here a bricolage of ritual prescriptions, encoded *mantras*, and stories. These texts tell us, for instance, how to worship at the crossroads, or how to read the omens when the wild jackals eat the meat offering of the sacrificial animal. We find the revelation of secret *mantras*, frequently in code language, and all of this intermixed with stories of the gods and goddesses. Topics shift abruptly, at times without even a sentence introducing the new topic. One mostly finds neither a clear narrative nor a clear progression of thought through most of these texts. In my readings of these texts, however, I have especially brought to the forefront elements offering alternative images of women because their very presence gives us pause, and causes us to reconsider the dominant portraits of Hinduism. These alternative voices allow us to expand our understanding, both in terms of the complex variety that Tantra offers, and in terms of the complexity of images of women.

Perhaps we may best approach this complexity of diverse refracted images of women in this Tantric milieu, this prism of images, by looking with a sideways glance, what Slavoj Zizek calls "looking awry." Drawing from Shakespeare's *Richard II*, he presents the metaphor of the eye, with its tears as a faceted glass offering a multiplicity of images. This eye "divides one thing entire to many objects; | Like perspectives, which rightly gaz'd upon | show nothing but confusion; ey'd awry distinguish form." In his analysis of this passage, Zizek suggests that looking straightforwardly at an object often misleads us. "If we look at a thing straight on, i.e., matter-of-factly, disinterestedly, objectively, we see nothing but a formless spot; the object assumes clear and distinctive features only if we look at it 'at an angle.'"[1] He continues in a different direction than ours, but for our purposes here, I would suggest that by "eyeing awry," that is by looking at the complexity of perspectives these texts offer through bringing to the fore elements that disturb our habitual portrait of women in Tantra, we can see more than a mere formless spot. (And here if we follow the analogy to our context of the study of Tantra, it may not be too far off to suggest that a view where women serve primarily as objects for male gains indeed renders them as a mere "formless spot.") In other words, through allowing our gaze to fall upon these alternative views of women, we can begin to reconceptualize the category of "woman."

This reconceptualization of women begins with Pārvatī's question to her husband Śiva, on whether a woman also worships in the Tantric rite. She asks him whether women, like men, also act as agents and subjects, and like men, act to gain the goal of liberation. The question itself insinuates women in the place of subjectivity, as agents in Tantric rites. The "Kālī Practice," a particular practice centered on women, works also to this end in shifting attitudes toward women, enjoining its practitioners to respect the wishes of women and their sovereignty over their bodies. With this, we saw how the texts that present this practice also exhibit images of women in roles where we usually do not find them, as guru and as skilled practitioner. In this light, Pārvatī's question also offers us the image of a woman *speaking* and claiming a subjectivity for women as a group, through pointing to their role in Tantric praxis with her question.

In the construction of women as practitioners of Tantra, the idea that women have a connection with language plays a focal role. Key in the image of women as venerable is their special facility with the magical speech of *mantras*; women can perfect magical speech, effortlessly. This skill is a crucial ingredient in the shift in attitudes toward women. I suspect that it is precisely this representation of women—as having a facility with magical speech—that makes them more akin to Brahmins, the traditional wielders of magical speech, than to the Śūdra servant caste, where women have otherwise been traditionally classed.

Thus, women are linked to speech, though not ordinary speech, but rather speech in its more powerful, primordial form as *mantra*. In this sense, women are not located outside of speech, but have a special skill with a particular form of language; they are intimately connected with its secret magical form. It is also suggestive, and likely not mere coincidence, that the chief result that comes from the "Kālī Practice," this practice centered on women, is that it gives the gift of eloquence in speech.

Chapter 4 as well takes up this theme of the connection between women and magical speech. Women's connections with magical speech follow a homology connecting their speech both with the body and with the notion of speech as performative. Women's speech is performative and bodied, and in this sense it operates like the magical speech of *mantras*, which is also performative, and as we saw here, bodied. In this chapter we also stepped outside the purview of the texts studied here to draw from other examples of women's speech similarly classed as connected with the body and with ideas of performativity. Thus in these texts' representations of women and the feminine, their bodies are intertwined with their abilities to speak.

The representation of women's bodies also plays a part in the depictions of Tantric rites, and attitudes toward the body at times reflect attitudes toward women as well, as we saw in the linkage between a rejection of asceticism and Vasiṣṭha's espousal of the "Kālī Practice." What the textual sources depicting the "Kālī Practice," a practice associated with Kāmākhyā, also show us are alternative attitudes toward women, including a discourse enjoining respect for ordinary women, including recognition of women's bodies as their own and a postulation of women's subjectivity. Just as the goddess at Kāmākhyā, the Renowned Goddess of Desire displays her subjectivity and mastery over her own body, so the "Kālī Practice" suggests a discourse offering respect toward women and their bodies.

We saw also that representations of women shift in different depictions of Tantric rites, especially in the rite of sexual union, which has become a notorious element of Tantric practice. The topic of the Tantric rite of sexual union is a politically charged one, on many different fronts, and I think it important to locate this discussion of this rite within a context of what it means to talk about these issues. Both for us today and for our late medieval writers as well, the ways we talk about sexuality and women's bodies frame and anticipate the very possibilities that then function to determine women's identities. For this reason chapter 2 especially takes time to frame the problems and issues involved in representing, in "talking," about women's bodies and the sexuality associated with women's bodies. What we take from this is that there is more than one version of the rite and thus, more than one template for understanding how the *representation* of women's bodies may function.

The final myth we address, on how the Blue Goddess of Speech turns blue, brings to light the interconnections between violence and the loss of speech. Literally, the abduction of the Goddess of Speech takes away her power—as woman—to speak. In this portrait we might read her as narratively enacting woman as voiceless subaltern, and, yet, a further repercussion of her abduction emphasizes that the loss of her speech is not just her problem, but a problem that affects the entire community. When she is abducted, the whole world becomes mute as well in the face of this violence. What we saw with this loss of speech especially is that this loss becomes indelibly imprinted upon her body, literally turning her permanently blue. With this we find again the link between women's speech and their bodies.

This fifth chapter focuses explicitly on the Blue Goddess's loss of speech, though this goddess appears throughout our exploration of speech about women and by women. The Blue Goddess of Speech both bodily literalizes women's relationship to speech and exemplifies these alternative and complex images of women that we saw in these textual representations. This Blue Goddess, who is assimilated to the fierce and independent goddesses Tārā and Kālī, is also frail and unfortunate enough to be abducted and held captive in a demonic underwater prison. This Blue Goddess is the source of human power to represent; she is the goddess within whom all language resides, so that when she is kidnapped, the world becomes mute. She creates the world through language, and bodily so, she gives birth to female magical speech (*vidyā*) out of her own body. She is also the tutelary deity, along with Kālī and Tārā, of the special "Kālī Practice" centered around women, which, as we saw, is a practice that gives eloquence in speech. She is an independent goddess, and yet apart from her assimilation to Kālī, she is not so fierce, even as one visualizes her wrapped with a variety of multicolored snakes. Who then is the Blue Goddess of Speech? She is, as the *Great Blue Tantra* (BT) frequently glosses her name, "Mahā-Māyā," the Renowned Goddess of Desire, assimilated to Kāmākhyā, the Goddess on the Blue Hill, the "Goddess who is the Master of this Illusion we call the world," who, through her capacity to proliferate language, allows us to refashion our world.

Appendix 1

Sources, Other Tantras, and Historical Context

With this book, I have presented a case study of women and goddesses in Tantra. Throughout I have argued for a more nuanced assessment of the complexity of Tantric attitudes toward women. With this appendix I offer background information on a variety of Tantric texts to help flesh out a more comprehensive picture of the texts used for this study as well as for other Tantric texts I did not use. With this I give detailed information on the sources used for this study and I compare these sources with other Tantric texts. I discuss some of the differences we find among particular Tantric texts, specifically as they pertain to representations of women.

Also, looking at the history of Assam in particular and the wider cultural images of women for medieval Assam may help to explain some of the particular attitudes toward women we find in this group of texts. Thus, after addressing the sources, in the second part of this appendix I address the historical context, particularly with a view to women and attitudes toward women.

As it may become apparent from the discussion below, my survey of the literature guided me to an observation that helped to shape the contours of the sources eventually used. That is, the group of texts used cohered in terms of regional affiliation and dating, and, importantly, in a particular message about women that they offer. Not all texts from this region and this period espoused the attitudes toward women found in this group. And while the group of texts here would all probably merit the designation "left-handed," not all "left-handed" texts from this region and period, nor "left-handed" texts from other regions and periods, provided the attitudes toward women found in the group used here. Also, we tend to find the attitudes I discuss here in later texts, after the sixteenth century. And while it is not the case that all later texts reflect the attitudes I have pointed out in this study, nevertheless, it is the case that one does not find these attitudes in earlier texts. Moreover, my survey revealed that texts that enjoined the use of women as a consort for the rite of sexual union were not uniform and that the presence of women as partners in the rite of sexual union did not necessarily coincide with an attitude toward women that offered respect for women, nor preclude simply using women for male gains.

The texts I did use offered evidence in this other direction. Especially important in my estimation was evidence of a shift to revering women as a category, and separate from the rite of ritual union, along with a systematization of this practice to the degree that it merits a special name. Consequently, this study is a case study; it does not make broad general claims about attitudes toward women in Tantra as a whole. It deals only with a group of texts, which are valuable in the very striking images they offer of women and attitudes toward women.

Since much of the detail here may be of interest to the specialist, but perhaps not to the general reader, I have included this as an appendix rather than as a chapter within the book.

Dating and Placing the Sources and Their Relation to Other Tantric Texts

I am presenting here again the list of primary texts I draw from, which are also listed in the introduction. All these texts are published; none are manuscripts. The main source I draw from for this study is: (1) *Bṛhannīla Tantra* (BT)—"*Great Blue Tantra,*" a 256-page text based in part on an earlier and shorter published version entitled the *Nīla Tantra* (NT), "*Blue Tantra.*"[1] I draw most of the myths I discuss from this text. The other texts I draw from are:

2. *Cīnācāra Tantra* (CT)
3. *Gandharva Tantra* (GT)
4. *Gupta Sādhana Tantra* (GST)
5. *Māyā Tantra* (MT)
6. *Nīlasarasvatī Tantra* (NST)
7. *Phetkāriṇī Tantra* (PhT)
8. *Yoni Tantra* (YT)[2]

Sources for the BT

The primary text used for this study, the *Bṛhannīla Tantra* (BT) has not yet been the object of much scholarly attention. In appendix 2 I supply a synopsis of its contents. The text I work with is an edition published by Butala and Co. in Delhi in 1984, which is a reprint of a 1941 edition, which, in turn, was published in Srinagar and edited in Kashmir by the Kashmiri scholar, Madhusudan Kaul. This published 1984 reprint of the 1941 edition, coming to 256 pages of Sanskrit, is based on one manuscript and a Bengali-published edition of the *Kāmākhyā and Other Tantras* in Bengali script published by Rasikmohan Chattopadhyaya in 1877–84, which includes the *Nīlā Tantra* (NT) mentioned by Goudriaan.[3] The text is titled the *Bṛhannnīla Tantra, "Great Blue Tantra,"* however the text itself in the colophon refers to itself simply as the *Nīla Tantra, "Blue Tantra."* The BT appears to be an expanded edition of an earlier NT, however the extant published version of the NT (published in 1965–66, in *saṃvat* 2022 by Kalyan Mandir in Prayag/Allahabad with the Sanskrit text edited and with a Hindi introduction by Bhadrasheel Sharma) appears to have also derived from an earlier, different version of the NT. This published version of the NT is not only much shorter than the published version of the BT (approximately one-fifth the size of the BT) it also has some material not in the BT. Both texts, however, contain a common core element that includes the discourse on treating women with respect. For instance, both relate the special "Kālī Practice" described in chapter 2, where there are no rules of time or place and where women are venerated and should never be harmed or lied to (NT, p. 28, lines 14–16; BT 8.90f.). Numerous verses with minor variations occur in both; some examples, for instance, BT 6.80 corresponds to NT p. 28, lines 21–22; and similarly, BT 6.88 corresponds to NT p. 28, lines 26–27; BT 7.88–89b corresponds, with minor variations, to NT p. 36, lines 6–9. And both contain the signature verse "women are Gods, women are the life-breath" (BT 6.75b; 8.90; NT p. 28, lines 15–16). On the other hand, there are some differences. For instance, with regards to the "Kālī Practice" the BT offers an attitude not commonly found when it says, "And here in this great Kālī Practice, in fact, there is no need even to think about the guru."[4] Near absolute reverence for the guru is a core, fundamental element of nearly all Tantric paths, and the extant NT does not step outside this boundary. The BT, on the other hand, even as it also includes a great deal of praise for the guru in other parts of the text, is remarkable in this one line.

S. C. Banerji also mentions a version of the NT that appears to be different from both of these published versions. The version he mentions contains twenty-two chapters rather than the twelve chapters of the published version of the NT or the twenty-four chapters of the published version of the BT. He does not list this NT in his bibliography, though he does list the published version of the BT that I use, which, however, does not correspond to the contents of the NT that Banerji outlines. He unfortunately only gives a very brief sketch of each of the chapters in his version of the NT, which makes it not entirely possible to ascertain the contents of his version of the NT. Nevertheless, he mentions some elements that can also be found in the BT, though his version of the NT does not correspond to the published version of the BT, since his descriptions of the contents, chapter by chapter, differ substantially. As a precise instance of a divergence, Banerji notes NT 19.2–5 and NT 21.20–22 as citing a list of other Tantras; these verses are not present in the BT version.[5]

I would suggest that the BT, in any case, was likely modified to some degree from earlier recensions titled the NT, even as much was also retained. This is evidenced in part, as I discuss below, by the fact that Brahmānanda Giri in the sixteenth century quotes only from the NT, whereas the Sanskrit writer, Rāmatoṣaṇa Bhaṭṭācārya, writing his *Prāṇatoṣiṇī* in 1820, mentions the BT, the NT, and another text called the *Mahānīla Tantra*.[6]

The major Western libraries that own a copy of the BT (for instance, the University of Pennsylvania and the University of Chicago) own the 1984 reprint. Only the Niedersachsische Staats-und Universitatsbibliothek owns a copy of the 1941 edition.[7] Interestingly, the catalog documentation for the 1941 version of the BT lists the *Mahānirvāṇa Tantra* as an alternate title for the BT, apparently confusing the two texts. This confusion is interesting because the BT takes a decidedly different position than the *Mahānirvāṇa Tantra*, which, on the whole, tends to be conservative. And further, the conservatism of the *Mahānirvāṇa Tantra* may be traced to the political agenda of its likely author, Hariharānandanātha. Considering his capacity as an associate and guru of the extremely influential Bengali Ram Mohun Roy, one may read his text as at least in part a response to British presence in northeast India.[8] The confusion, in conjunction with the evidence given below, may suggest also a late date for BT and a likely northeastern Indian provenance. Including the 1984 reprint and the 1941 publication of the BT, recensions of this text have been published five times. For a list of editions before the volume used here, see Teun Goudriaan and Sanjukta Gupta's excellent bibliographic study of the Tantras.[9]

Where Are These Texts From?

Keeping in mind that very few Tantric texts give irrefutable evidence of place and, further, that many Tantric texts are compilations that might in fact span a variety of authors and places, nevertheless, several factors suggest a northeastern Indian locale for these texts. One primary factor, which I took as external evidence of a northeastern presence, was the existence of manuscripts and published editions of nearly all of these texts in Bengali script, and along with this, a Calcutta publication venue. A good number of the texts consulted here were published earlier, in Bengali script, by Rasikmohan Chattopadhyaya between 1877 and 1884[10] in Calcutta. S. C. Banerji also suggests a northeastern provenance, and specifically Bengal for the NT, though his version of the NT seems to differ from the BT consulted here. I have also relied upon Goudriaan and Gupta's survey of Tantric literature, particularly in terms of the school groupings he makes, as an indication of regional affiliation. All but one of the texts used in this study are at least briefly mentioned in Goudriaan and Gupta's study.[11]

Internally, the recurring mention of Kāmākhyā in Assam as a preeminent site for worship and pilgrimage suggests a northeastern Indian location (i.e., BT 14.1–2; BT 5.69–73). This mention of Kāmākhyā (or alternatively Kāmarūpa) is often not in conjunction with the famous list of four sacred goddess sites, Oḍḍiyāna, Jālandhara, Pūrṇagiri, and Kāmarūpa, which is characteristic of early Tantras. While this is not conclusive evidence—it is possible that Kāmākhyā could be venerated from afar—nevertheless, it more likely indicates this region than elsewhere.

And of course, two of the three primary forms of the goddess the text dwells on, Tāriṇī and Kālī, are also particularly well known to be associated historically with northeastern India. Gudrun Buhnemann also cites the assimilation and equation of the goddess Nīlasarasvatī with Tārā, noting Tibetan Buddhist influence for the iconography of these two deities.[12] David Kinsley also notes Tibetan influence for Hindu forms of the goddess Tārā.[13] In this context we might also appropriately mention that the preeminence assigned to Tārā in these texts, especially in the BT, the NST, and the CT likely suggests some degree of influence from Tibetan Buddhism.

The BT, the NST, and the CT, like the YT, appear to favor Viṣṇu over the god Śiva in their narratives.[14] This offers additional support for a northeastern Indian provenance. For example, the BT (5.57ff.) gives instructions for worshiping the goddess with sandalwood paste and then concludes by enjoining offerings to the goddess and Hari (Viṣṇu). The text here employs a pervasive Vaiṣṇavite terminology in explaining the results of this worship: that is, attainment of proximity to Viṣṇu (*Harisāyujyatāṃ*). Particularly compelling also is the fact that in the tale in the eleventh chapter of the BT, which tells the story of how the Goddess of Speech, Sarasvatī, came to have a dark skin, it is the god Viṣṇu who plays the primary role in rescuing the goddess and defeating the demons.

The connection of the goddess with Viṣṇu is frequently associated with northeastern India and the Bengal region. Schoterman notes this coupling in his discussion of the YT, and, like the YT, which has a marked affiliation with Kāmākhyā, the BT also follows this pattern with both a priority given to Kāmākhyā and greater attention and importance accorded to Viṣṇu. The BT is, on the other hand, a much larger text than the YT, roughly fifteen times the size of the YT, and deals with a greater variety of material; however, the consistency with which it deals with (1) the three goddesses, Nīlasarasvatī, Kālī, and Tāriṇī, and (2) "left-handed" transgressive rites suggests a similar regional affiliation and dating.[15] A minor phonological point that may be evidence as well suggesting the northeast of India is the spelling of the demon Niśumbha as Nisumbha, shifting the "sh" into a "s," and vice versa, spelling Vasiṣṭha as Vaśiṣṭha, replacing the "s" with a "sh." This reversal is a commonplace phonological shift that occurs in the Northeast.

Internally, some elements in the BT particularly suggest an origin in Assam. The myth I discuss in chapter 4, found in chapter 12 of the BT, where the gods flee to the mountains in response to the invasion and takeover by demons was the usual response of Assamese kings to invasions of their kingdoms. This occurred especially in response to Muslim invaders, such as the invasion of Mir Jumla in the mid seventeenth century, who did not know the landscape so well as the indigenous Assamese. However, it also occurred with even indigenous kings such as the Ahom king Khora Rāja, who in the 1560s fled from the Koch king Naranarayan to the Naga hills.[16]

Similarly, the imprisonment of the Blue Goddess of Speech in a watery prison, discussed in chapter 5 above, is another element that would be familiar to an Assamese writer and reader, given its frequent flooding during the long monsoon season. Also, the *śol* fish, which Sarma describes in his discussion of medieval Assamese food, may correspond to the *śāla* fish mentioned in BT 5.53.[17] Similarly, the fifteenth chapter of the BT describes a variety of holy places in a mountainous and hilly region, which is not the Himalayas (15.4), with reference to Kāmākhyā throughout, again suggesting Assam.

Additionally, we might note that the BT appears to know about a myth we find in the tenth chapter of the YogT, where the goddess orders the three gods, Brahmā, Viṣṇu, and Rudra to work out the scheme of creation. A version of this myth appears in BT 12.16–29a. This also may suggest that both works derive from a similar locale, and since we know for certain that the YogT comes from Assam, it supports the suggestion of Assam for the BT.

The GT, on the other hand, likely derives from a slightly different provenance than the other texts used here, though most of the early published versions come from the Bengal region.[18] I suggest this because it incorporates a number of elements from the Śrī Vidyā tradition, which may suggest a provenance further west, perhaps Varanasi, which it mentions. The fact that it also incorporates elements of the practices we find in the other texts used for this study tends to make a south Indian provenance for the GT less conceivable, though it does not rule it out.

Regarding the YT, Schoterman presents compelling evidence for Kāmākhyā as the provenance of the YT,[19] along with connections between the YT and the *Yoginī Tantra* (YogT),[20] a text that, in its second half, comprises a geographical panegyric of shrines associated with the landscape of this region.

We also find that the YT is also explicitly mentioned in the NT[21] and the YogT mentions both the PhT and the Nīlā Tantra (NT) (in YogT 3:30). The NST contains several sections identical to those in the BT, as does the GST; the BT gives a version of a myth similar to that of the YogT. The YogT does not offer the same attitudes toward women as the texts consulted here, as I discuss below; however, its fairly definitive dating and placement in sixteenth-century Assam can help us to place these other texts in terms of dating and location. The network of references, which the texts analyzed for this study present with one another, along with content reproduced from text to text, suggests a historical affinity among these texts, along with a reproduction of common ideas across these texts. Here, again, we should note that these texts, especially the BT, which is quite long, offer a variety of practices and that the elements I emphasize do not occur in every chapter of the BT, only in some. In addition, that the texts diverge on specific points, such as the observance of caste regulations, while maintaining a common stance on women, suggests various authors and a generally accepted notion among them of the particular attitudes toward women associated with the "Kālī Practice."

When Were They Written?

Dating Tantric texts is a notoriously difficult enterprise, not the least so because most Tantric texts are likely compilations spanning an extended period of time and with multiple authors. In this case, nearly all of the texts used here have been assigned relatively late dates in Goudriaan and Gupta's comprehensive survey of Tantric texs, *History of Indian Literature: Hindu Tantric and Śākta Literature.* The PhT appears to be somewhat earlier and one of the texts consulted here, the Nīlasarasvatī Tantra (NST), is not mentioned in Goudriaan and Gupta's work.

The version of the NST that I have was published in 1999 by Chaukamba Surbharati Press in Varanasi, and I first became aware of it when I discovered it in the library at the temple in Kāmākhyā. This text contains the Sanskrit text of the NST with a Hindi translation and introduction. The Hindi introduction to the text provides an interesting discussion of the goddesses Tārā and Nīlasarasvatī, equating them, as does the BT. It also provides information for the spiritual aspirant interested in pursuing the *sādhana* outlined in the NST, but little information regarding the textual sources for the published volume of the NST, except to mention help from other scholars in the preparation of this text for publication. S. N. Khandelwal, the text's translator, also mentions in the introduction that some pages of the text were found in Bengali script (7), suggesting some affinity to the northeast region. I also very briefly, in chapter 2, mention a rite in found in the *Sarvavijayi Tantra*, which is explicitly a rite that a woman performs. This tantra almost exclusively focuses on the use of herbs in spells, and is also not mentioned by Goudriaan and Gupta.

My reasons for concurring with Goudriaan and Gupta's dating are as follows. To begin with, stylistic similarities between these several texts, along with verses and similar content reproduced across texts suggest that many of the texts were produced in somewhat similar environments and are likely chronologically relatively close to one another. Further, based upon dates given for the YT and the YogT,[22] and based upon stylistic considerations, a later date is more likely for this group of texts, probably between the fifteenth and eighteenth centuries. Goudriaan and Gupta give the date for the YogT as the latter part of the sixteenth century and as the YogT mentions by name the NT and the PhT, it makes sense to expand the time period to only as early as the fifteenth century, at least perhaps for some of the early recensions of the NT (which are likely later incorporated into the BT), though much of the BT likely dates later than this.

The sixteenth-century author Brahmānanda Giri also cites twice the NT, which likely refers to one of the early recensions of the text. That the sixteenth-century Brahmānanda Giri cites the NT, but not the BT, suggests that the BT was compiled after the NT, though we should keep in mind that the BT in its own colophon calls itself the NT. And, we should also keep in mind, as I mention below, that the later nineteenth-century Rāmatoṣaṇa cites both the BT and the NT.

Narasiṃha's *Tārābhaktisudhārṇava* (TBS) written approximately in the third quarter of the seventeenth century, quotes from the NT, again, which is likely the shorter version that forms the source for the BT. The TBS cites its source as the NT, and we find the verses that the TBS quotes in the BT, however, the TBS quotes directly from the BT only partially, and the rest of the quote only loosely approximates BT 7.135ff., again suggesting that the BT derives from an earlier source text that was also titled the NT.[23] A number of other authors, including the fifteenth- or sixteenth-century Sarvānanda in his Sarvollāsa Tantra, also cite the NT, which suggests that at least some version of the NT existed as early as the fifteenth or sixteenth century.[24]

Rāmatoṣaṇa Bhaṭṭācārya mentions by name both the BT and the NT in several places, for instance, when he discusses the worship of the guru and the lineage, when he discusses the incorporation of both Vedic and Tantric forms of the *sandhyā* rites, and similarly when he discusses the *kumārī pūjā*.[25] He cites these two texts separately in different places and the fact that he distinguishes between the two texts suggests that by the early nineteenth century they formed two separate works. While he does not give specific citations for his quotes from various texts, several of the quotes he gives appear in the BT. He also occasionally cites a *Mahānīla Tantra*, which is not referenced elsewhere.

This dating is corroborated also by textual references within the BT, the CT, the YT, and the NST to Vaiṣṇavism, especially as a code of social behavior, which would have likely become more in evidence after the sixteenth-century revival of Vaiṣṇavism in Assam by Śaṅkaradeva and Caitanya in the Bengal region. Goudriaan and Gupta note the phenomenon of Kālī-Viṣṇu Tantras that takes place in the sixteenth century as a result of a Vaiṣṇava revival, which he relates to the figure of the sixteenth-century Bengali Caitanya.[26] In this case, however, we could also equally look to the Vaiṣṇava revival in Assam with Śaṅkaradeva's movement.

While the BT tends mostly to not reference other texts, it does, in fact, in its first chapter and in chapter 14 refer to the Kālī Tantra,[27] to which Goudriaan and Gupta attest a later date, again placing the date of the BT as later.[28] Banerji notes that the NT lists several other Tantras including the *Bhairava*, YT, *Guru*, *Kulācāra*, GST, *Nirvāṇa*, *Ḍāmara*, and numerous others, however, the citation he offers is not found in the extant, published BT.[29]

The BT as well recounts a myth that may refer to the short period of Muslim rule in Assam in the third quarter of the seventeenth century (BT 12.35ff.). This myth tells of the abduction of the Goddess of Speech, and a subsequent takeover by demons that causes an abrogation of brahminical sacrificial rites. The myth suggests an invasion and it may be possible to relate this to the first successful Muslim invasion of Assam by Nawab Mir Jumla in 1662, during which Mir Jumla's stated intentions, according to his secretary, Shihabuddin Talish, were for "rooting out idolatry and spreading Islam."[30] This would then give a later date for the BT, after the end of Assamese-Moghul conflicts in 1682, thus dating this part of the text to the late seventeenth or early eighteenth century. Although this evidence could also apply to other areas in the northeast region, the scenario fits well with the Assamese situation, even to the extent that the gods in the myth are compelled to flee to the mountains, which is precisely the recurrent pattern we find with the Assamese Hindu kings in the case of invasions. Further, when Mir Jumla conquered Assam, he exhumed graves in order to pilfer them of gold, which might easily have been construed by Assamese Brahmins as a "demonic" practice, especially if we consider that by the late seventeenth century Brahmins were employed by and held in esteem in greater numbers by the Ahom court and would have likely seen Mir Jumla's invasion as affecting their interests more personally than they might have earlier when they had less power in the state machinery. This would again be also accentuated by Mir Jumla's stated intentions, as I noted above, for "rooting out idolatry and spreading Islam."[31]

Interestingly also, and perhaps useful in terms of dating this group of texts as a movement, the *Kālikāpurāṇa* is both clearly associated with Kāmākhyā and contains numerous references to the transgressive "left-handed" rites. However, it differs from the texts I used for this study in two important respects: (1) it has been fairly definitively dated to a much earlier time period than that of the group of texts used here, to not later than the eleventh century,[32] and (2) it does not contain the view of women promulgated by the texts I use for this study, nor to the "Kālī Practice," again suggesting a later date for the group of texts I reference. I discuss the *Kālikāpurāṇa* in more detail below.

Thus, to summarize, we could likely date the BT, the NST, the YT, and the CT after Caitanya, or Śaṅkaradeva who died in 1568. This might help explain the prominence of Viṣṇu rather than Śiva in these texts. Similarly, if we interpret the incident in the myth where Brahmins flee the land, unable to perform rites (because the words have been kidnapped) as an analog for an invasion of a king who stifled brahminical rites, it may be possible to attribute this to the period after the successful recovery of Kāmarūpa by the Ahoms after 1682. The GST is stylistically very similar to the BT and the NST and likely comes from the same region and period. Further, Goudriaan and Gupta also note that the inclusion of Tārā as a goddess tends to locate a text in Bengal and the northeastern region and with a relatively late date.[33] While the MT tends to reference Durgā especially, and Bhuvaneśwarī, unlike the other texts, it nevertheless, like the other texts, appears quite similar to the GST, BT, and NST, stylistically and in content.

The PhT appears to be one of the older Tantras among this group, and likely would require an earlier date, since the sixteenth-century YogT names it (3.30), along with the NT. Also, Buhnemann points out that the description of Ugratārā in the PhT derives from an early source, Śāśvatavajra's eleventh-century Buddhist *sādhana* text, and subsequently becomes the source for later Hindu Tantric compendiums.[34] The GT's incorporation of elements that we find in this group of texts, despite its major focus on the Śrī Vidyā, suggests that at least portions of it were written down in the same period as the other texts in the group.

Thus the general similarities we find between these texts and the network of cross-references they exhibit also suggest that they may historically and geographically locate similarly, with a northeastern provenance, and with a relatively late date, from approximately the fifteenth century to the eighteenth century.

Possible Authors for the BT

It is possible that later layers of the BT were written by a Śākta who may have been a beneficiary of the queen Prathameśvarī's liberal literary patronage in the early eighteenth century.[35] I discuss her rule below. This later date would explain the prominent position of Viṣṇu in the BT and this might also help to explain the respectful attitudes toward women. A powerful queen supporting Śākta practices may have given some impetus or perhaps inspiration toward a Śākta practice involving reverence toward women. However, we should also keep in mind that most of these texts are layered compilations, with various sections added at different times.

The BT's author, and also possibly those authors of several of the texts used here, likely resided near Kāmākhyā, since we find it mentioned prominently, but he likely did not reside *in* Kāmākhyā proper. My reasons for suggesting this are that one would suspect that a Śākta devotee of the goddess residing in Kāmākhyā would have made the goddess at Kāmākhyā central rather than making either the Blue Goddess of Speech or Tāriṇī central. It would still, I think, be possible to find a text devoted to Kālī penned by a resident of Kāmākhyā, but the BT includes all three of these goddesses, and the Blue Goddess of Speech takes a central role. Further there are no temples to the Blue Goddess of Speech in the near vicinity of Kāmākhyā. Neither does the history/story of Naranarayan's rebuilding of the temple at Kāmākhyā find its way into the BT, even as we find a variety of stories told in the BT. Also in the myth where Viṣṇu saves Sarasvatī, discussed in chapter 5, he takes his fish incarnation. If the author were in Kāmākhyā one might expect more reference to the boar incarnation, since the boar incarnation plays a key role in the dynasties associated with Kāmākhyā, although the fact that the only other mention of Viṣṇu's ten incarnations in this passage is a reference to the boar incarnation might be read to suggest the author's familiarity with Kāmākhyā's dynasties. Schoterman suggests Koch Behar as the regional affiliation for the

Yoni Tantra.[36] The BT, on the other hand, offers no compelling evidence for direct affiliation with Koch Behar. It may be that the BT was written a little farther east in Assam.

The caste affiliation of the authors would have likely been one of the groups who were literate, namely, Brahmins, Kayasthas, Kalitas, and Ganaks. Throughout these texts we find references to specific astrological terms, especially the *nakṣatras*, a way of calculating auspicious times based upon which of the twenty-seven asterisms the moon is transiting. This, of course, requires only a very basic level of astrological expertise, yet it does suggest that the Ganaks, a caste of professional astrologers, ought not to be ruled out as authors.

In terms of a general psychological profile of the authors of some of these texts, especially the BT, based on some of the themes we find, one might conjecture that the author had some experience with the brutality of war and did not see this as an especially desirable way of living. One can see throughout, especially in the BT, a sense of an author who felt a need to limit violence, to the extent that this author repeatedly emphasizes the importance of not harming others. There is a Vaiṣṇava thread to most of these texts, but not to the exclusion of other sects, such as Śaivas, and these texts are explicitly Śākta; that is, they advocate the worship of the goddess. Interestingly, we find the emphasis against violence nearly always in proximity to descriptions of the rite of sexual union.

One more point needs to be stressed here. The BT and other texts used for this study, as I discuss below, are considerably later than the texts David White draws from in his study on Tantra, where he utilizes especially texts several centuries earlier than the BT.[37] Similarly, Ronald Davidson's study of Buddhist Tantra also deals with texts that are several centuries earlier than the BT and other texts used here.[38] Likewise, Alexis Sanderson's wonderfully cogent descriptions of Tantric practice also do not focus on the texts used for this study. Rather, they especially focus on a much earlier period, that associated with the time periods preceding and extending through the eleventh-century writer, Abhinavagupta. Hugh Urban also, in his article on Assamese kingship, as I discuss, draws primarily from the much earlier *Kālikā Purāṇa* from the ninth through eleventh centuries, which presents different attitudes toward a variety of issues from the texts used here. I will discuss below in greater detail differences we find among various Tantric texts, especially as they relate to women.

These texts would likely have been circulated in manuscript form, limiting their readership to people who were literate—likely Brahmins, Kayasthas, Kalitas, and Ganaks—but taking the form of secret Tantric texts. I suspect that these texts were also circulated among other non-Brahmin caste groups, because, at least textually, we find lower caste participation in the rites. Nor is it too far-fetched to conjecture that these texts may have been read aloud among small groups of persons who were interested or initiated in certain Tantric traditions. This may have given a greater number of women oral access to these texts. And educated women, again as I discussed in chapter 1, may have also been able to read them. Further, given especially the emphasis on women's initiation that we find in these texts, one could imagine women being included in the small Tantric circles where these texts may have been discussed.[39]

We find references to some of these texts, in Brahmānanda Giri's *Śāktānandataraṅgiṇī*,[40] for instance, suggesting some readership, but not an extensive commentarial tradition on this group of texts, and certainly not a tradition that provides a running commentary to individual texts. Also, as I note above, the Sanskrit is not the best; we find grammatical mistakes, suggesting that the texts were likely not especially popular among the best, most literate Sanskritists, who would have been, one surmises, perhaps more orthodox. One very interesting example of challenged grammatical usage can be seen in YT 2.25 where we find the odd compound "parapuruṣīm." Could one read this as perhaps the "supreme person in the form of a woman"? or as the "wife of another man"? In any case, the grammar suggests an oxymoron, since puruṣa, the primordial male is here given a feminine ending. Curiously, we find this also in Jayaratha's commentary on the Vāmakeśvarīmatam.[41] In Louise Finn's edition with translation, we do not find it; she has emended the reading to "pañcapuruṣam." We also find this odd word in the YT, 2.25. Moreover, only occasionally do we see anything like an attempt at fine poetry, and one suspects that these sections were lifted out of texts elsewhere. These small details help to give us an inkling of a portrait of our copyists/authors—people who were not the most educated, but had a passable grasp of Sanskrit.

Other Texts

I want to address here the issue of why I chose the Tantric texts I did, and not others. I examined a number of other Tantric texts in the course of this research and found that Tantric texts are by no means uniform in their attitudes toward women. A variety of views may be found and some of the differences may be attributable to when and where the texts were written. Not all texts present the attitudes toward women that I illustrate in the BT. In this section below I delineate some of the differences, what some other Tantric texts say about women, and how they differ from the BT in their attitudes toward women. These texts we can group heuristically for the purposes of this study into three categories: (1) earlier Tantric texts, especially dealing with "left-handed" rites; (2) texts belonging to the region and time period of the texts I consulted, but that nevertheless differed in their attitudes toward women; and (3) other texts from other regions and traditions.

The first category discussed here includes some well-known "left-handed" Tantric texts from earlier periods, usually several centuries earlier. The differences we find in these texts as compared to the texts I use for this study, which date to several centuries later, helped make it clear to me that there are differences among Tantric texts, and that some of the differences may have to do with when they were written. I should emphasize that some key elements I found in the texts I used for this study were not found in earlier texts. Thus, the BT, even as it derives elements from earlier Tantric texts, nevertheless presents a different view of women in Tantra than the view that White presents in his fine study of Tantra, and these differences have everything to do with which Tantric texts one consults. I include below a discussion of several of the texts White uses. These are texts in this first category, that is "left-handed" texts, dating in most cases to several centuries earlier than the BT. These earlier texts present important differences from a later text like the BT. The images of women in the earlier texts appear more tangibly ambivalent; this element is especially striking, with women as powerful and as dangerous, as devouring females.

I use a couple of these texts on occasion, namely the *Kulacūḍāmaṇi Tantra* (KCT) and the *Kulārṇava Tantra* (KuT) to highlight the contrasts between earlier Tantric texts and the group of texts used here, particularly because they are earlier examples of "left-handed" texts that nevertheless differ in their attitudes toward women, even as the texts I use borrow from these early texts.

Especially below I focus on some of the differences that the KuT presents since this early and paradigmatic Tantra has been one of the main sources used in studies on Tantra. I have also incorporated discussion of the KCT within the other chapters of this book. Because the BT seems to borrow especially from the KCT, more than it borrows from other texts, I have for this reason included it in the discussion within the chapters and do not discuss it separately here.

I should also mention that some of the later texts that I do use, such as the YT, for instance, present a mix, retaining some of the elements that White discusses, such as the use of sexual fluids, and other elements found in the BT, such as a defined practice of treating all women with respect—not found in the earlier texts White references. I use a later text like the YT because of the shifts it does offer in ritual prescriptions and in myths presented, even as I recognize that the YT is a historically layered text, as are most of these texts. Hence, one sees something like a developmental process occurring in the history of these texts.

The second category includes Tantric texts I initially thought or conjectured might be similar to the group of texts actually used for this study, based upon their regional affiliation and dating, but which presented different attitudes toward women than those found in the group used here. Among this category were a number of "left-handed" texts from the late medieval period and the northeast region, which nevertheless did not concur with the texts used in their attitudes toward women.

The third category, as a catchall category, includes texts that did not offer the perspectives on women that we find in the group of texts used, and that were clearly aligned with other schools and especially associated with other regions. I did not expect these texts to offer similar attitudes toward women, and they do not, nevertheless I reference a number of texts from this group here in order to show the relationship and position that the texts consulted have within the larger context of Tantric literature.

For the first category, foremost among this group of earlier Tantras is the *Kulārṇava Tantra* (KuT) from the tenth through thirteenth centuries.[42] This text is frequently cited in Indian Tantric digests and also cited in Western scholarship on Tantra, such as White's study of the use of Tantric fluids.[43] Also, another indice of the KuT's importance and its paradigmatic status for Western studies of Tantra may be noted in the fact that in the index of Goudriaan and Gupta's comprehensive study of Tantric literature, the KuT is cited more frequently than any other Tantric text.[44] We will briefly examine elements of this text here precisely because this well-known text, with its fairly well-circulated ideas on what Tantra is, for the West especially, offers an interesting contrast regarding attitudes toward women with what we find in the BT and the later texts used for this study. Especially, looking at the KuT helps us to delineate differences among various Tantras in their attitudes toward women.

To begin with, one important difference we find between the KuT and the BT is the importance and attention given to the *Yoginī*, the female version of the *yogī*, who, in these early texts appear to be at times semidivine beings, and entities that the practitioner attempts to establish in his body. For instance, the practioner in the "Śānti Stotram" in the KuT 8.52 prays "may the Yoginīs and the guardians of this site be established in my body."[45] One can find references to the *Yoginī* scattered throughout the KuT. Chapters 7 and 8, which refer to Kaula rites, especially reference the *Yoginī*. In this context one finds *yoginīs* listed with other divine and semidivine beings such as spirits of a place (*kṣetrādhipa*), *bhairavas, baṭukas,* tree spirits (*yakṣa*), ancestral spirits (*pitaraḥ*), and ghosts (*bhūta*).[46] A cult of *Yoginīs* develops with various temples in India dedicated to the sixty-four *Yoginīs* in the earlier medieval period, and this importance is also reflected in an earlier Tantric text like the KuT. Thus, for instance, we see a prayer offering homage to the group of sixty-four *yoginīs* at KuT 8.31. This cult becomes less important in later centuries, a shift that is reflected in the BT's comparative neglect of the *Yoginī*. The relative absence or presence of the *Yoginī* may sometimes help to date a text, though this certainly does not work in all cases, specifically not in the case of texts dedicated to this tradition, including the *Yoginī Tantra* and the *Kaulāvalīnirṇaya*, both texts dating to about the sixteenth century.

The *Yoginī* of an early text like the KuT is at times a fierce figure, and not merely a representation of a fierce deity, but an image of woman as akin to a fury, a mad fierce devouring creature. So we find in the KuT, "The fool who makes distinctions based on caste while in the middle of the *cakra* [rite], the *Yoginīs* devour him."[47] This or a similar depiction of a female we find nowhere in the BT. The psychological implications of a devouring female are potent. They signal a representation of woman as "other," as enemy, encoding an agonistic relationship rather than one based on mutuality. Especially, it signals the category of the female as the projection of male fears.

We also find in the KuT numerous references to a phenomenon that White points out, the use of fluids (*dravya*) in the ritual, which may be read as sexual fluids (for instance, KuT 5.66ff.; 5.75), though in some cases this fluid (*dravya*) appears to be wine (KuT 5.28).

Also, we do not find the KuT advocating treating all women—that is to say, women as a class—with respect, as we see in the BT. In the BT, the practitioner, "having bowed down to a little girl, to an intoxicated young woman, or to an old woman, to a beautiful woman of the clan (*kula*), or to a contemptible, vile woman (*kutsitā*), or to a greatly wicked woman, should contemplate on the fact that these [women] do not appreciate being criticized or hit; they do not appreciate dishonesty or that which is disagreeable or disliked (*apriyam*)" (BT 6.73–74; NT p. 28, line 14).

This sentiment, toward both good and "vile" women, does not appear in the KuT, or the KCT, or the KJN, texts dating several centuries earlier than the BT.

The KuT, rather, takes pains to enlighten the practitioner upon the differences between women, especially on the differences between a good partner (*śakti*) for the rite of sexual union and the partners that one should avoid (*varjyā*). So after enumerating the eight types of women, a common typology of women used for the rite of sexual union found in numerous Tantras, which refers especially to caste, including the outcaste *caṇḍālī*, the outcaste leather worker (*carmakāṛī*), the dog-eater (*śvapacī*), and the prostitute (*viśvayoṣit*) (KuT

7.42–43), the KuT also outlines the characteristics of a "good" partner for the rite of sexual union. A good partner is "good looking" (*surūpā*), "bright" (*śuciḥ*), without doubts or hesitation (*śaṅkāhīnā*), full of devotion (*bhaktiyuktā*), has a smiling face (*smitāsyā*), speaks sweetly (*priyavādinī*), is eager to worship the deities (*devatārādhanotsukā*), and enchanting (*manoharā*), to list several of her characteristics (KuT 7.46–48). The list's idealized version of woman reads like what we might expect to find in the application portfolio for a medieval Kaulika Miss World, that is, the woman here embodies male desires and projections. The women one should avoid are "cruel" (*krūrā*), "of bad conduct" (*durācārā*), "lazy" (*alasā*), "greedy" (*lubdhā*), "full of fear" (*bhītā*), "lacking a limb" (*hīnāṅgī*), "afflicted by illness" (*vyādhipīḍitā*), "bad-smelling" (*durgandhā*) "vile" (*kutsitā*), "ugly" (*virūpā*), "lame" (*paṅgū*), and "with an ugly face" (*vikṛtānanā*), to list several of the qualities of these women (KuT 7.49–51). We do not find this distinction made between the various types of women in the BT.

While the KuT recommends avoiding the "vile" woman, the BT, on the other hand, enjoins the practitioner to bow to the "vile" woman (*kutsitā*) and to contemplate on the fact that such a woman does not appreciate being lied to or hit or criticized. The internal reflection upon women reflects a shift, a difference, in the attitude toward women that these two texts display. The KuT, the KCT, and the KJN never offer this sense of reflection upon the women as subjects, as real people who might not like the very types of treatment that men do not like—being lied to, being hit, or criticized.

Where we might expect this injunction not to lie to women to occur, at KuT 11.62, the text offers instead this injunction with relation to the *male* kula *yogī*, the male practitioner, "He should not say what is disagreeable nor what is not truthful whatsoever to a male practitioner of the group."[48]

At its best, most sensitive toward women, the KuT offers advice that we as readers cannot help interpreting as being motivated by a self-interest on the part of the man who needs the woman for the rite of sexual union and her fluids. Immediately following the injunction to speak the truth, and say it nicely, to other *male yogīs*, the KuT tells the practitioner, "He should not say to a woman of the group (*kula*), 'you're ugly' or 'you're black'" (KuT 11.62).[49] There is an important, if apparently subtle difference between the internal reflection of the practitioner in the BT and the practical advice of the KuT on what one should say to the woman one wishes to engage with in the rite. In the KuT one should be honest with other male practitioners, but not necessarily with women practitioners. This is in contrast to the BT's injunction to speak the truth to women.

Further, we find no mention in the KuT of women being able to master *mantras*, nor the general attention to women that we find in the BT and other texts used for this study. We do find, however, one precursor to the notion of a woman as being capable with *mantras*: we see that the *mantra* given by a woman (as well as the *mantra* one receives in a dream), unlike that given by a man, is always good, not subject to being an "enemy" (*ari*) and so on, which could destroy the practitioner who uses it (KuT 15.98). This, of course, may be interpreted as presuming that women acted the role of gurus giving *mantras*, even though the KuT does not elaborate upon this statement, and even though it is thrown together with the dream-given *mantra*.

We find another element in the KuT that appears to be a precursor to what we find in the BT, and which is interpreted slightly differently in the KuT compared to the BT. This is the notion of a practice with no rules. I mentioned earlier the "Kali Practice," which I discuss in chapter 2, where there are no rules except treating women well. We find also a Kaulika practice in the KuT that, on the surface, appears to be similar to or a precursor of this Kālī Practice; however, there are important and interesting differences between the two.

In the KuT this practice is not called by the names we find in the BT and in the texts I have cited above, that is, as the Kālī Practice, the Chinese/Tibetan Way, or the Great *Mantra* Practice, but rather it is designated as the Kaulika practice. In the KuT's Kaulika practice the Kaulika "acts according to his own desire."[50] We see further that for the Kaulika, "what is not to be drunk is to be drunk; what is not to be eaten is to be eaten" (KuT 9.57a).[51] Further, "there are no rules and no restrictions, no merit and no sin. There is no heaven and no hell for the Kaulikas, o Goddess of the Kula" (KuT 9.58).[52] This description continues for a number of verses, and especially what repeats throughout are, first, a listing of apparent contradictions and, second, the idea of the Kaulika as having transcended the pairs of opposites that characterize ordinary life in the world. So again, the Kaulika is poor, and yet gives away great wealth (9.59), and so on. The notion of the transcendence of opposites characterizes the path of the Kaulika.

Now, in contrast to the BT, there is not here in the KuT the one rule of treating women well. Women do not figure into this practice at all. Essentially, the lack of rules here is not so much a special practice, and one centered around women, as it is an indication of the state of transcendence of rules for the Kaulika because the Kaulika has attained a state of perfection beyond the necessity of rules. In this sense the Kaulika is like the yogī that the KuT describes throughout the earlier sections of this chapter (9.2ff.). He is the sage who has gone beyond the strictures of society. Citing this passage describing the Kaulika right after the description of the "*brahma-jñā*," the knower of Brahman, appears to be a strategy for assimilating the image of the Kaulika to the more classical representation of the state of the yogī who has transcended the world. It may be possible to understand the BT and other texts that are used for this study as appropriating the element of this earlier definition and transforming it into a different practice centered around women, or it may be that the "Kālī Practice" of the BT and these other texts derives from a different source altogether. In any case, we can especially note how Tantric ideas shift and move to contextually offer very different meanings in different texts, even as core verses and core bits of ritual injunctions are reiterated and reused along the way.

We may also note here the differences in the portrayal of the rite of sexual union between the KuT and the BT. Since I discuss the BT version in chapter 2, I will not go into detail here, except to emphasize that the rite for the BT involves two people, the man and the woman. The BT in a different description from the one I discuss in chapter 2 also gives a version of a rite that appears to be a group worship or *cakra pūjā*, where the men and women dance (BT 6.339a). This *pūjā* however does not end with the rite of sexual union, but rather the seeker "should worship the woman with lotus flowers, red powder and scents, with ornaments and garlands, however only with the attitude towards a mother."[53] Where the BT does describe the rite of sexual union, it describes it in explicit detail making it apparent that the rite is one of sexual union.

On the other hand, in the KuT version we find the well-known and notorious *cakra pūjā*. The *cakra pūjā* rite involves not just two people, but a group of men and women. In this carnivalesque rite, the women are made to drink as the men pour liquor into their mouths (KuT 8.70); general drunkenness ensues. The "yogis dance, carrying pots of liquor on their heads" (KuT 8.71b).[54] Then, "the yogis, drunk with wine fall down intoxicated on their chests; and the *yoginīs* of the group, intoxicated, fall on top of the men. They mutually engage in the happy fulfilment of pleasure" (KuT 8.73–74).[55] In this context we should also note that Jñānānanda Paramahaṃsa's description of the rite of sexual union in the eighth chapter of his *Kaulāvalīnirṇaya* is also a *cakra pūjā*, following along the KuT's version.[56] As we saw in the discussion of the rite of sexual union in the BT, the two versions of the rite differ.

We should also note that although there are numerous differences between the early KuT and the later BT, there are, nevertheless, elements that suggest a continuity. These elements include borrowed verses, even as the verses borrowed are set in new contexts with new meanings. We also find an incipient presentation of some ideas that are later expanded and shift to some degree in the later BT. For instance, we find also in the KuT a verse that is repeated in the later texts used here, which enjoins the practitioner not to hit a woman: "One should not hit a woman even with flower, even if she has committed a hundred offenses. One should not count the faults of women; one should rather announce their virtues" (KuT 11.65).[57] This verse, which is not elaborated upon here in the KuT, nevertheless presents a precursor that is elaborated and associated with a name and a specific practice in later texts such as the BT. I address many of the differences that the KCT presents from the BT in chapters 2 and 4 and so will not repeat that here.

Another important early text referencing Kāmākhyā is the *Kaulajñānanirṇaya* (KJN), an early Tantra from the ninth through eleventh centuries, apparently penned by the Siddha Matsyendranātha and possibly located in the Northeast, though not all scholars agree upon a northeastern provenance for the KJN.[58] This text as a whole is quite dissimilar to the BT, particularly in the elements that I focus upon for this study, even though Kāmarūpa is mentioned (KJN 22.10). For instance, this text does not refer to the "Kālī Practice" or the "Tibetan Way" or the "Great *Mantra* Practice," which we find in the texts used. And though one may infer a reference to the rite of sexual union, it does not delineate the rite of sexual union, or explicitly address it, as we find in the BT, CT, or YT. In fact, the text apparently penned by Matsyendranātha focuses instead on internal worship throughout. For instance, Bagchi notes regarding the KJN (3.14–15) that the worship of "*liṅgas* made of stone, earth and metal should be abandoned. Devotion to the *liṅga* which is seated in the body—the *mānasa* [mental] *liṅga* is conducive to *siddhi* [attainment]. Such a *liṅga* only is to be worshipped and not with external but with mental flowers and incense."[59] He goes on to affirm that "external modes of worship, we have seen, are not approved of in the [KJN]."[60] A further difference is that the KJN as a text focuses a good deal of attention on bodily immortality and youthfulness, something also not emphasized in the BT. And the means to youth for the KJN is also through a mental visualization. So the KJN says, "The yogī should continuously practice, visualizing sprinkling himself with poisons (*viṣais*). He becomes released from aging and free from all disease" (KJN 5.20).[61]

Further, the KJN does not contain the signature verse noted above and, generally, throughout, this text rarely talks about women, but instead focuses on mystical practices of the inner feminine power (*śakti*) and the inner *cakras* or subtle wheels within the body (for instance, chapter 3, chapter 5, chapter 6, chapter 10, chapter 17, chapter 19, chapter 20). The eighteenth chapter refers to a *pūjā* offering blood (*rakta*) and semen (*śukra*), but the rite is not described nor are women mentioned here; rather, the closest we come to women here appears to be mental or spiritual beings with their male counterparts. That is, *yoginīs, siddhas,* and heroes are mentioned and the goddess is mentioned as appearing apparently magically, or perhaps mentally (*bhavate*) as a result of offering a number of substances, including rice and so on. In this context one worships the guru (*gurupūjā*) and one worships the hero (*vīrapūjā*), but not the female *yoginī* (18.21) (nor is there mention of worshiping *siddhas* here). This is unlike the BT, which expressly advocates worship of women.[62]

And where the KJN prescribes the *pūjā* in the eighteenth chapter, where blood (*rakta*) and semen (*śukra*) are offered, the rite of sexual union itself is not mentioned. Again, curiously, where the "left-handed" worship is prescribed in the twenty-first chapter, with meat, wine, and fish, sexual intercourse again is not mentioned: "On the full moon night, on the new moon night, on the eighth day and the fourteenth day of the moon, one should offer a sacrifice (*baliṃ*) of oneself, of fish, wine and meat, and in this way the teaching should be done. The teacher should be free from doubts" (21.8–9).[63]

This exclusion should not be taken necessarily to mean that the rite of sexual union was not practiced, as we see below in the list of types of women involved in the "external rites" (*bahisthā*), however this generally ancillary depiction of women in the KJN does indicate a different attitude toward the rite and women than the attitudes we find in the BT.

In two places the KJN refers to women. We see one when it mentions the three types of women for the external rites: "When [practice] is performed with one's wife, that is *sahajā*, The prostitute they call *kulajā*; an outcaste woman is called *antyajā*. The outward forms are told to you, o Goddess. Now listen to the inward forms" (KJN 8.7–8a).[64]

In this case nothing is said about these embodied women. The other place we see women does appear to be an earlier precursor to attitudes toward women that we do find in the BT. The KJN, in the last lines of the text (which may suggest a later addition), says, "One should never show anger in one's speech to the [sixty-four *yoginīs*], o ruler of Gods, nor at all to women or young girls" (KJN 23.11).[65] This one line evokes what we find later but is not elaborated or explained and if it is not a later addition, which its placement at the end of this text might suggest, then it may be read as an early, though inchoate precursor to what we find more fully developed later. It is interesting here that the sixty-four *yoginīs* are seen as a different category from women and girls.[66]

Another important early text, the *Kālikā Purāṇa* (KP), dating to likely the ninth through eleventh centuries is clearly based in Assam and the Kāmarūpa area since portions of it detail the geography of the Kāmarūpa region, especially chapters 51, 62–66, and 77–80.[67] The first portion of this text, a little more than half, deals with myths of the gods, especially the myth of Satīs death. After this the text engages in extensive discussion of Tantric rituals and *mantras*. Thus one might suspect that this text would be similar to the texts I use for this study; however, this turns out not to be the case, with differences perhaps attributable to the difference of some six to seven centuries.

Specifically, this text also does not outline the rite of sexual union. K. R. Van Kooij also notes this element of the KP: "The intoxicating liquor, the women, the red colour, the corpse, etc. is likely to play a part in the *Vāma* cult, which includes orgiastic practices and abhorrent rites, about which, in contrast with the Tantras, the KP remains practically silent."[68] Nor does the special "Kālī Practice" I describe in chapter 2 figure in the KP. Attitudes toward women in this text are, on the whole, much more conventional. So, for instance, we find Viṣṇu telling the god Śiva "my body has become contaminated" (kāyaḥ pāpakaro; KP 30.34b) "because of having sex with a woman on her period" (rajasvalāyāḥ saṃsargād; KP 30.34a). The context here is the author of the KP telling of a myth in which Viṣṇu in his boar incarnation has sex with the goddess earth, who happens to be on her monthly period. For this text with its more conventional attitudes toward women, the result of this union with a menstruating woman can only be demonic offspring, three sons named Suvṛtta, Kanaka, and Ghora.

Similarly, we find in the KP advice to a king that is reminiscent of Manu's attitudes toward women: "Women, however, should be made constantly dependent on the king. Women who are independent in fact, always cause harm" (KP 84.127b–28a).[69] Finally, we should note that unlike the later Tantras we reference, in this earlier text from Kāmākhyā, Vasiṣṭha performs austerities in Kāmākhyā not to please the goddess, but rather to please the male god Śiva (KP 51.104ff.). This text is, however, a good specimen for comparison precisely because we know that it comes from the earlier date of the ninth through eleventh centuries and the contrasts it offers to the texts we use for this study help to highlight the tangible differences we find between earlier and later Tantric texts. Especially notable is the emphasis on the god Śiva rather than either the goddess or Viṣṇu.

This text, the KuT, and the KJN, for instance, make more apparent both the variations we find in Tantric texts—that is, not all Tantric texts are alike—and that some of the differences we find may be attributable to different historical periods. We should also note here that, as with the other texts discussed in this group, nowhere do we find the verses suggesting that women should be treated with respect, not hit and not lied to, as we find in the BT and other texts used for this study.

More generally, an early Tantric text such as the *Ṣaṭsāhasra Saṃhitā* (SS), which dates to likely the twelfth century,[70] also offers a point of comparison with the group of texts used. This early text, which comes out of the Kubjikā tradition and styles itself as Kaula, focuses especially on mantric formulations and the mystical linguistic mapping of the human body, especially with the powerful sites of the goddess (*piṭha*), and does not include the "Kālī Practice" or the attitudes toward women that we find in the BT. This text, for instance, mentions Kāmarūpa, but here Kāmarūpa is within the human body (SS 1.47). Also, the SS describes invoking the "*yoginīs*" and honoring them with "beautiful garments, blossoms, incense and with all kinds of nourishment including liquor and meat" (SS 3.25–26); however, the rite of sexual union is not mentioned. Simply the practitioner asks the *yoginī*'s permission to explain the teaching to the student, similar to what we saw above in the KJN. It is not entirely clear that the *yoginīs* here are actual women. Nor do we find the signature verse mentioned above. Similarly, the *Toḍala Tantra*, an earlier text mentioned in some old lists,[71] does not contain the practices centered on women, even as it does focus on Kālī, Tārā, and refers to the Blue Goddess of Speech.[72]

Among the second category of texts—texts that I initially thought might be similar to the group of texts actually used for this study, based upon their regional affiliation and dating, but which presented different attitudes toward women—are included preeminently the *Mahānirvāṇa Tantra*. As I mentioned earlier, this late text shows traces of British influence, which are evidenced in its attitudes toward women. While the *Mahānirvāṇa Tantra* deals extensively with the "left-handed" rites, it does not present the same attitudes toward women found in the group of texts used. Rather, we find that this text repeats Manu's dictum that a woman "should remain under the control of her father in childhood, when she reaches her youth by her husband, in her old age [controlled] by her husband's relatives. She should not ever be free or independent" (*Mahānirvāṇa Tantra* 8.106).[73] This text diverges from Manu in that a woman in her old age should be controlled by her relatives rather than by her son, as we find in Manu. As we might expect, we find neither the "Kālī Practice" I outline in chapter 2, nor the signature verse regarding women.

Apart from this text, also included in this category is, more surprisingly, the *Yoginī Tantra* (YogT), a sixteenth-century text clearly associated with Kāmākhyā as is evidenced by the second half of the text devoted to a geographic panegyric of the region.[74] I had initially supposed that this text from Kāmākhyā would be similar to the BT in its representations of women, and, in fact, the YogT actually cites the *Nīla Tantra* and another text I use, the PhT (YogT 3.30). Further, the YogT references Kāmākhyā throughout.

On the other hand, in describing the Kaula path, the practice for this text that involves the use of the Five Ms, including liquor and the rite of sexual union, the YogT cites the *Kulārṇava Tantra* as its authority (YogT 6.18), which, as I discuss above, offers different attitudes toward women than we find in the BT. The YogT also, as we might expect from its title, makes numerous references to the *Yoginīs*, something that we find especially in the *Kulārṇava Tantra*, which, as we saw earlier, often refers to semidivine beings rather than ordinary women.

In general, the contents of the YogT reveal an author(s) who was very much concerned with matters of state. This author(s) focuses on the history of the kings of Assam, their wars, and state politics for several chapters from chapter 11 through chapter 15.[75] In fact, the editor, Biswanarayan Shastri uses the historical matter of dynasties and wars located in the eleventh through fifteenth chapters to help date the text. It would not be surprising if further research into this text revealed that the author was a Brahmin who performed the duty of *Kakati*, a high post of envoy or ambassador for the Ahom king, a position that began eventually, with Sanskritization, to be given to Brahmins rather than Ahom nobility. Such a position would explain his conservatism and also his intimate knowledge of the geography of the country.

As we might expect with a writer as keenly connected to matters of the state as this writer is, the YogT is more conservative regarding issues of caste. So the author in delineating partners for the rite of sexual union prescribes same-caste partners for the rite: "The brahmin takes a brahmin woman, the warrior takes a warrior woman and the merchant takes a merchant woman. This is the rule prescribed in the rite of sexual union" (YogT 6.37b–38a).[76] Of course, this is not the rule that we most commonly find elsewhere. In the event that a suitable partner is not available, the YogT allows for the traditional practice of *anuloma*, where men partner with women who are a caste below, but not the reverse where the woman is of a higher caste. This pattern is one that the law book author Manu allows for marriage, and this Tantric writer's appropriation of it suggests a mainstream or conservative attitude toward the Tantric rite. It curiously goes against the frequent and popular presentation of the woman for the rite of sexual union as belonging to a very low caste, such as the barber, or the washerwoman, which is what we find in the KuT. The YogT also makes an allowance for the times when the proper woman is not available, "in case women of the upper three castes are not available, the *śūdrā* (fem.) woman [is acceptable]" (YogT 6.39b).[77] Here again, though, usually the washerwoman is of the *antyajā* caste, that is, outcaste. In other words, for the KuT and the KJN the prescribed partner is an outcaste woman and not a woman of the *śūdra* caste, which is as low as the YogT will go for a woman's caste.

The YogT also allows different rules for the ascetic (*yati*), for whom the rite of sexual union refers to the inner goddess of the *Kuṇḍalinī* as she merges in the thousand-petaled lotus in the head of the practitioner (YogT 6.41). The *avadhūta*, or wandering mad sage, also has different rules, and he is allowed to engage in the rite of sexual union with any woman except a (his?) mother and a virgin: "He [the *avadhūta*] can practice the rite of sexual union with any woman [lit., in all *yonis*]; except the *yoni* of (his? a?) mother. He should have intercourse with a non-virgin. He should never have intercourse with a virgin [lit., "never beat an unbroken *yoni*]" (YogT 6.44).[78]

With the use of the word *tāḍayet*, "he should beat" or "strike," one is also reminded in this context of Tulsidas's infamous misogynistic statement where he declares that women, drums, and dogs should be beaten, where he uses a form of this word. It may be that perhaps in Tulsidas's case, he was punning on a generally accepted sexual connotation implied in the word *tāḍayet*.

Also important for our purposes here, we find elsewhere in the YogT an unusual classification of women for the rite of sexual union, not found elsewhere. Rather than the classification of women based upon caste, which is what we frequently find in Tantric texts, for instance in the KuT, instead we find a classification based upon how women look. This unusual depiction focuses centrally on how a woman looks, and women are chosen based upon which of the six acts in Tantric ritual (*ṣaṭkarmāṇi*)—most of which are rites designed to effect nefarious deeds such as killing other people and creating enmity, and so on—a woman's looks makes her suitable for.

This classification, which accompanies a description of the six acts, tells the practitioner which type of woman is best used in the rite of sexual union depending upon which of the six acts, that is, rites of killing, rites of controlling others, and so on, the practitioner wishes to perform. We find, "The Padminī [type] is declared [suitable] for giving peace, the Śaṅkhinī [type] is considered [good] in rites for controlling others; the Nāginī [type] is well-known for rites of driving people out and paralysing people. And in killing, Ḍākinī is extolled for bringing death to the enemy" (YogT 4.30–31a).[79]

The YogT also describes how these women look, so, "the Padminī [type] has fair limbs, long hair; her speech is always full of nectar. She has reddish eyes and she has an amiable disposition. She is auspicious for practice" (YogT 4.31b–32a).[80] In contrast, the Ḍākinī type of woman, whom the practitioner employs for rites of killing, looks like this: "The Ḍākinī type has short hair and a long nose. She has harsh speech. She is always irritated and has a long body and she likes to make loud shouts" (YogT 4.35).[81] This classification of women based on how they look differs from the more common caste-based classification. It also differs from the BT's practice of not focusing on differences among women.

In general, the YogT does not present the attitudes toward women that we find in the BT, although apart from the rite of sexual union, the YogT in particular places a relatively greater importance upon the rite of worshiping a young girl (*kumārī pūjā*).[82] Nevertheless, it also does not include the practice of treating all women with reverence found in the texts I relied upon, nor does it contain the signature verse. Thus, even though it is affiliated with the region and time period of the texts I do use, it presents a different type of tradition and a different attitude toward women.

Similarly, the *Kāmākhyā Tantra*, despite its name, which might lead us to associate it with the group of texts used here, in fact, does not present the same attitude toward women that we find in the group of texts used. This is a "left-handed" text and it does extol the "*yoni*," that is, the female partner.[83] It contains some elements that are similar to what we find in the texts, such as, for instance, *not* invoking the goddess: "There the acts of calling down [the goddess] are not done in any way" (KāmT 2.68).[84] On the whole, however, it is hard not to read the praise of the *yoni* in this text as dissociated from the woman as a person outside of the rite of sexual union. This text describes ritual actions toward women only within the rite of sexual union, not outside the rite of sexual union. This text also only advocates the "other" woman: "The wise man should especially worship after having obtained the *yoni* of a woman belonging to someone else (*parastrīyonim*)" (KāmT 2.72).[85] This text continues in the next line to advocate the prostitute (*veśyā*) as the woman of choice. "The *yoni* of a prostitute is supreme (or is the "other" woman); O Goddess, there he should do the practice" (KāmT 2.73a).[86] Further, it does not include the verses we find in the group of texts used that prohibit harming women, nor does it recognize women as skilled in *mantras*, or as gurus. Texts such as the *Gāyatrī Tantra, the Muṇḍamālā Tantra*, and the *Bhūtaśuddhi Tantra*, though found in the same collection as several of the texts used here, do not incorporate the elements of the group used.[87] Nor did I use the Kashmiri-based *Devīrahasya*.[88]

Some texts present a mix, and were not used because of the balance of elements not presenting enough or clearly enough the features addressing women found in the group of texts used. One example here is the *Niruttara Tantra* (NUT).[89] This text cannot be easily dated, and Goudriaan and Gupta do not offer a date for it. Like the BT and several of the texts used, it connects the goddess Kālī with the Blue Goddess of Speech and with Tārā, and makes this connection in the context of the rite of sexual union (*latāyāṃ pūjayet*, NUT 1.9) It also suggests that the practitioner should worship one's own partner (*svaśakti*, NUT 10.41), a term that may suggest one's wife as the partner. However, the NUT also contains a number of elements associated with earlier texts such as the KuT, including a focus on *yoginīs* (e.g., NUT 10.48) and menstrual blood (e.g., 10.40), and does not contain the signature verse on women.

Some of the texts used, such as the *Yoni Tantra* (YT), also emphasize the use of menstrual blood, however the story of Vasiṣṭha in the YT, which offers a stance against asceticism, makes the YT important for the ideas of women presented in this study. In this case, while the YT is similar to the NUT in a number of respects, I did not draw from the NUT because the elements supporting its inclusion, that is, references to the goddess Tārā and the suggestion of one's wife as partner for the rite of union, were outweighed by the inclusion of other elements not reflective of the texts used, and the NUT does not offer any substantial insights into the attitudes toward women found in the group of texts referenced for this study. One more factor mitigating against the selection of the NUT is an odd nomenclature for the rite of sexual union, *kalā pūjā*, which is repeated too much to suspect this to be merely a scribal error (NUT 1.25, 29, 30, 31, 32, 33, 34).

Similarly, the Kaṅkālamālinī Tantra (KMT) is, for the purpose of this study, a mixed text. As a text that especially extols the use of insignia related to the god Śiva, such as ash (*bhasma*) and *rudrākṣa* beads (KMT 5.32–86), it also, like the YT, focuses a great deal upon the *yoni* and the hand gesture called the *yoni mudrā* (especially in chapter 2). Furthermore, this text also gives one key feature of the "Kālī Practice," namely the absence of rules: "And here there is no regard for purity nor are there prohibitions. There are no rules for time or place etc. here" (KMT 5.7).[90] Rāmatoṣaṇa cites this text when he gives the "Song to a woman guru,"[91] however, in the KMT itself, the hymn there it is not presented as a hymn to a female guru. Rather, the hymn is here the hymn to the goddess Pārvatī as the guru, and the KMT in no way suggests that this hymn should be sung to ordinary women. In itself it is suggestive, especially in light of Rāmatoṣaṇa's understanding of it, however, in general the KMT does not offer the elements I used in selecting the group of texts. For instance, this text does not contain the signature verse on women. Further, it relegates women to an inferior status, lumping them in with the lowest caste of śūdras, and allowing neither of them the use of the sacred syllable "OM" (KMT 5.119–21) or the ability to perform the standard prerequisites to perfecting a *mantra* called *puraścaraṇa* (KMT 5.287). For these reasons, this text has not been included.

The *Rudrayāmala* presents a special case. Generally considered quite old, Goudriaan and Gupta nevertheless date the extant *Uttara Tantra* version to a much later date, in alignment with the group of texts used here, and to the Bengal region. We find in this *Uttara Tantra* text a version of the story of Vasiṣṭha's journey to acquire teachings from the Buddha, related in chapter 3 above, and perhaps, not surprisingly, we find also in this text mention of women as gurus, which I cite below in the discussion of Brahmānanda Giri's *Śāktānandataraṅgiṇī* (2.107ff.).[92] Sections of this text may be partially relevant or comparable to some of what we find in the group of texts used, however I have not used it because as a whole this text contains much that does not entirely cohere with the group of texts used and, further, elements of this text appear to be older or from a different provenance than the group used and thus, not entirely in keeping with the coherence of the group of texts used. For instance, in one place in this text, but in none of the texts in the group used, the "Chinese/Tibetan Conduct" (*cīnācāra*) is glossed as the practice belonging to the "female demons" (*rākṣasī*),[93] and further, the description of it varies to a large degree from what we find regarding the "Chinese Way" or special "Kālī Practice" in the group of texts used.

I have also consulted a few Sanskrit digests by particular and well-known authors to get a sense of the brahminical representation of women for the northeast region in the period I look at, the fifteenth through eighteenth centuries. Of foremost importance among these texts is Brahmānanda Giri's works, including here the *Śāktānandataraṅgiṇī*.[94] In the *Śāktānandataraṅgiṇī* Brahmānanda Giri quotes twice from the NT and cites the NT by name, so he was familiar with this text, which contains passages describing the "Kālī Practice." However, he does not cite this practice; the verses he quotes from the NT have to do with ritual instructions for the bath and the seat for the deity in the obligatory and occasional rites.[95] He mentions also the "sacred tree" (*kula vṛkṣa*), an element of the practice often found in proximity to descriptions of the rite of sexual union, but he does not, however, talk about the rite of sexual union.[96]

Brahmānanda Giri, in fact, talks very little about women; however, he does mention that women and *śūdras*, the lowest of the four castes, have the right to initiation, though only for some *mantras* and not for the "Om" *mantra*.[97] Women are also, unlike *śūdras*, praised in the *Śāktānandataraṅgiṇī* for their power to give *mantra* initiation. Quoting from an unnamed source Brahmānanda Giri says, "The initiation given by a woman is proclaimed to be auspicious; that given by one's mother is eight times more auspicious. And, regarding the initiation obtained in a dream, [the same holds]. There is no need for further consideration here" (2.31).[98] In a further quote, again unnamed, but which can be found in the extant version of the *Rudrayāmala Uttara Tantra*, he describes the qualities of a woman who is fit to be a guru. In this same context, as we find also in the *Rudrayāmala*, the widow is excluded from being a guru. He says, "The woman practitioner (*sādhvī*) who has conquered her senses, has devotion for the teacher and engages in good conduct, who knows the essence of all the Tantras, is accomplished, always engaged in worship—this woman is fit to be a guru. This characterization excludes the widow" (2.32).[99]

We find these lines taken and slightly changed from *Rudrayāmala*, 2.108, and the third line from 2.11b. The *Rudrayāmala* in this context also mentions the dream initiation. While there is not space to explore this further in this book, it may be worthwhile to note that the connection of women and dreams may be read as part of a larger pattern of the representation of women, which

I discuss in chapter 4 where I talk about women's speech being seen as irrational.

I do think it notable that this sixteenth-century brahminical writer maintains the idea of the woman as guru, which is found in the texts I use for this study. It suggests that in Brahmānanda Giri's world a woman guru was not considered a complete anomaly, and that some of the ideas of these texts found acceptance among very respectable persons. Brahmānanda Giri, on the other hand, takes no note of the other elements of the practice centered on women and respect for women.

In another of his writings, the *Tārā Rahasya* (TR), Brahmānanda Giri offers alternate versions of the *śākta* practice, that is, the worship of the goddess. One of these does not include liquor or women in the rite, while the other version does include meat, liquor, and the rite of sexual union.[100] The first version ends with a verse describing this practice as the "Great Chinese/ Tibetan Practice" (*mahācīnākrama*), which, however, does not look like any other versions of this practice, since it does not contain the use of the Five Ms, including liquor and women. The second version, called the *śakti sādhana*, "Practice with the Woman, or Feminine Power," does include the use of women, liquor, and meat. This practice describes the rite of sexual union as the *cakra pūjā* involving a group of men and women.[101] This is the version we saw described in the KuT above, which differs from what we see in the BT. One difference we see between the TR's version and the version described in the KuT is that in the TR the practioner "bows to the [other] male practioners and to the female practioner again and again" (3.63b).[102] We might read this as an added element of formality introduced in this later text (or practice) to shift away from the seeming pandemonium of drunken bodies in the earlier KuT version.

That this brahminical writer does not mention the elements of the practice centering on women or reverence toward women, even as he mentions texts where we find the advocacy of treating women with respect, I think indicates that official and mainstream attitudes tended not to recognize these practices. However, his acceptance of women as gurus suggests that these practices nevertheless may have impacted mainstream opinion on some issues regarding women, in this case that women could perform the role of gurus.

All this may suggest that this practice centered on women, and treating women with respect was perhaps not a practice advocated by writers of some authority, and not likely by kings or state powers (we are reminded here of the KP's suggestion to the king to not let women be independent), but rather that this was a practice that circulated more popularly and with grassroots affiliations. In the case of the brahminical writer Brahmānanda Giri, we do find that even as he simply quotes other sources as his method for explaining Tantric practice, he also quotes selectively, and in this process he also nods toward state powers, for instance, when he declares that human sacrifice is a prerogative only for the king (*Śāktānandataraṅgiṇī*, 13.58).

We find a similar response from another important brahminical writer of a later period, Rāmatoṣaṇa Bhaṭṭācārya. Rāmatoṣaṇa Bhaṭṭācārya's long digest, the *Prāṇatoṣiṇī* (PT),[103] pulls together quotes from a variety of sources following a framework guided by subject matter. Rāmatoṣaṇa Bhaṭṭācārya cites short sections of the NT and the BT throughout, some thirty-four times.[104] He also cites the verse we found in Brahmānanda Giri, which I quoted above, "the initiation given by a woman is proclaimed to be auspicious" (PT, p. 288), and verses that describe a woman who is qualified to be a guru (PT, p. 288). The verses in the PT are similar to those in the *Śāktānandataraṅgiṇī*, 2.32ff. They differ in a particular emphasis on the "woman of the clan" (*Kulajā*). So we find that Rāmatoṣaṇa Bhaṭṭācārya also subscribes to the view that women functioned as gurus. He in fact does cite the GST's visualization of the female guru, which I discuss in chapter 2.[105] Immediately following this he gives also the "Armour Hymn of the Woman Guru" taken from the *Mātṛkābhedatantra*, another text that Goudriaan and Gupta's *History of Indian Literature* assigns a late date and that belongs to the northeast region.

Rāmatoṣaṇa Bhaṭṭācārya, in his *Prāṇatoṣiṇī*, also gives the hymn of "armor" of a woman guru and the song sung to the woman as a guru (*strīgurugītā*). Interestingly, the hymn to the female guru apostrophizes the female guru as the goddess Tāriṇī, and the hymn is sung by Śiva to Tāriṇī. Separate from these he also gives the hymn for the worship of the wife of the guru.[106]

However, like Brahmānanda Giri, Rāmatoṣaṇa Bhaṭṭācārya does not cite the sections of the BT pertaining to women or the special "Kālī Practice," or the signature verse we find in most of the texts used for this study. Again, like Brahmānanda Giri, this brahminical authority, even though he is familiar with the texts that present this practice, and even as he draws elements from this practice, such as the figure of the woman as guru, nevertheless does not discuss women's roles beyond these citations. Nor does he draw from the myths in a text like the BT.

I also consulted Narasiṃha's *Tārābhaktisudhārṇava*, which I had initially supposed would be likely a similar text, especially because its title refers to Tārā, an important goddess for most of these texts; however, this text's position is in general much more conservative in terms of its attitudes toward women, and does not contain the attitudes toward women found in the BT or the signature verse.[107] I also did not use writers such as Nīlāmbācārya and others belonging to the Kāmarūpa school of dharma śāstra, since they do not offer the perspectives on women found in the texts I use and they clearly predate them.

Most of these texts, excluding, of course, the *Mahānirvāṇa Tantra,* have not been translated into English, though three, namely, the NST, KMT, and Niruttara Tantra, have Hindi commentaries by S. N. Khandelwal.

The third category includes texts from farther afield, such as, for instance, texts from the highly philosophical Kashmiri nondual Śaiva tradition, including those from the Pratyabhijñā school of Utpaladeva, Abhinavagupta, and Kṣemarāja, as well as some of the early Tantric texts affiliated with this region and the commentaries on some of these texts by members of this school, including here, for instance, the *Netra Tantra,* and the *Svacchanda Tantra* both with Kṣemarāja's commentaries, or Abhinavagupta's *Tantrāloka* or *Tantrasāra,* or texts such as the *Kramasadbhāva,* the *Spanda Kārikās,* or the *Śiva Sūtras,* along with their commentaries. Apart from the distance in time and place that texts such as these present, they also do not offer the attitudes toward women that we find in the group used.

Similarly, I do not draw from texts associated with the Śrī Vidyā tradition, such as the *Yoginīhṛdaya* with Amṛtānanda's *Dīpikā,* the *Nityāṣoḍaśikārṇava, Saundarya Laharī,* and *Ānandalaharī,* the *Tantrarāja Tantra,* and including also Bhāskararāya's *Setubandha* and the commentary on the *Lalitā Sahasranāma,* to mention a few. I did not, as I mentioned earlier, use Bhāskararāya's commentaries, since the Śrī Vidyā tradition forms a separate and distinctive tradition, not aligned with the practices, such as the "Kālī Practice" discussed in this project. In this group of texts we do on occasion come across statements that reflect a sense of treating women well, such as, for instance, this verse in the *Tantrarāja Tantra*: "One should not harm or have anger towards women, even if they are bad" (5.80b).[108] In this particular instance we should note that this rule given by the *Tantrarāja Tantra* applies specifically to the aspirant practicing *puraścaraṇa,* the lengthy prerequisites to gaining perfection of a *mantra,* and not to a general practice. For the most part, this group of texts tends to favor an internalization of the feminine as the goddess within, and especially as the goddess that rises through the six cakras in the human body, along with a mapping of mantric sound as cosmos.

Nor do I include broad reference digests by individual authors such as Lakṣmaṇadeśika's *Śāradātilaka,* with its commentaries, or the *Prapañcasāra,* the *Mantramahodadhi* of Mahīdhara, which, again, do not present the types of attitudes toward women that we find in the fifteenth to eighteenth century texts from the northeast that I address in this project. These lists are not intended to be comprehensive, but merely to generally locate the project engaged in here.

Thus, to conclude, the available textual sources themselves shaped the contours of this study and guided my selection of sources. Again, the group of texts used coheres in terms of regional affiliation and dating, and, importantly, in a particular message about women that they offer.

That not all texts from this region and this period and not all "left-handed" Tantras espouse the attitudes toward women that we find in the group of texts used alerts us to the necessity of recognizing the complexity of Tantra as a historical phenomenon. Tantric traditions are diverse, and perhaps part of the problem that scholars have encountered in trying to define Tantra derives from the diversity of its traditions.

Further, for my purposes here, my survey revealed that women's roles as textually represented were not by any means uniform. The texts I have drawn from offered evidence in a particular direction, and I hope that this study has made it apparent that views of women within various Tantric texts are diverse and complex. Consequently, this study is essentially a case study; it does not make claims about attitudes toward women in Tantra as a whole. It deals with a group of texts that presents a coherent affiliation with a place and time and that offer valuable insights and images of women and attitudes toward women.

Historical Context

Throughout the medieval period Assam was under a fairly unified kingdom. The Ahoms ruled most of eastern Assam from the thirteenth century to the nineteenth century, and, at various periods, parts of western Assam as well. This likely contributed to a sense of stability for the region. Throughout this period other smaller kingdoms existed, such as the Koch kingdom in the sixteenth and seventeenth centuries in western Assam, including the district of Kāmarūpa, where Kāmākhyā was situated, and westward into Bengal. We find also other smaller kingdoms, such as that of the Jayantias, the Kacharis, and Bhuyan landlords, simultaneously with the Ahoms, who offered some form of tribute to the Ahoms. A brief exception to Ahom rule occurred under the Hinduized Koch king Naranarayan, who managed to subjugate the Ahoms for a short period during the sixteenth century.

The Ahom kings initially came from Burma and brought with them their own separate traditions of religious practice. They slowly assimilated Hindu practices and ideas, and eventually adopted Assamese as the state language, as did many of the other tribal groups, such as the Chutiyas and the Kacharis, which also helped to create a sense of a unified state.[109] In general, most state offices and positions of power were reserved for the Ahom nobility, and not given to Brahmins or other non-Ahoms.

By the seventeenth century, however, the Ahom kings and Ahom nobility began to actively patronize Hindu practices, temples, and Brahmins. The Ahom king, Pratapa Simha, who ruled from 1603–41, attributed the exorcism of a demon that had possessed him to Brahmins, and he established a temple to the god Śiva at Deorgaon.[110] He also built a temple to Śiva at Bishnath. Shortly before this time, Brahmins had begun to fill some state offices, especially that of the *kakati*, an envoy or messenger to other governments. Pratapa Simha made it a more general practice to employ Brahmins in this position, rather than the Ahom nobility, because he felt that Brahmins were less servile and would represent him better when interacting with other rulers.[111] Pratapa Simha's rule marked a decided shift toward Hinduization.

In general, throughout their rule, however, the Ahom kings tended to tolerate religious diversity, offering patronage to a variety of groups.[112] There was very little religious persecution, even though the ethnic Ahom aristocracy held most positions of power.[113] Neither was there much in the way of caste restrictions.[114] This held true also even for western Assam, which was mostly not under Ahom rule, but rather had a history of Hindu kings from the fourth through twelfth centuries in the Varman, Śalasthamba, and Pāla dynasties, and later under the Koch kings in the sixteenth and seventeenth centuries. Further, in an interesting deviation from much of the rest of the subcontinent, even the dharmaśāstra writers for the Kāmarūpa area in Assam tended to be more lenient in rules of caste and food, allowing Brahmins to eat meat.[115]

So, Assam was generally a fairly liberal place regarding caste and diet. Further, even though the Ahoms were not initially patrons of Hinduism, they nevertheless did not oppose the practice of Hinduism, and their position as rulers made Assam a generally favorable place for Hindus. Also, unlike what we find though much of north India during the medieval period, the Ahoms, with their allies, managed to keep out Muslim invaders, with the exception of a short period in the seventeenth century. The state tolerance of a variety of groups and the absence of Muslim rulers generated a favorable climate for the gradual expansion of Hinduization among the different groups in the region. Additionally, only rarely did Assam suffer widespread famine as a result of droughts, and the abundant rains and river silt tended to keep the soil fertile with little need for the use of composting fertilizers.[116] Consequently, food production was a generally easy task and this likely also helped contribute to the stability of the region.

The effect of the political climate and policy for the writers of Sanskrit texts—and this is important to dwell upon because our source texts for this study were likely penned by upper-caste writers—I think, tended to place Brahmins and other upper-caste Hindu groups for the early part of the Ahom rule through the seventeenth century on the outside of the major power structures in Assam, especially in eastern Assam. This started to shift in the sixteenth through seventeenth centuries as Ahom rulers started to patronize Brahmins and employ their services for the court.

On the other hand, patronage of Brahmins in western Assam began as early as the fourth century and continued through the twelfth century, as I mentioned, under the Varman, Śalasthamba, and Pāla dynasties. For the period we are examining here, the Koch kings ruled over western Assam including Kāmākhyā, beginning in the early sixteenth century. Here, patronage of Brahmins began earlier and more vigorously than in the Ahom kingdom, with the rule of Viśva Simha in the early sixteenth century. Encouraged both by the Koch kings and the regional Bhuyan landlords in the area around Kāmākhyā, Brahmins from Bihar, Uttar Pradesh, and Bengal migrated into western Assam during the Koch rule.[117] Throughout this time period Brahmins had a much more substantial position in state government in the Koch kingdom than in the Ahom kingdom. Even some of the most well-known Hindu preachers, such as the sixteenth-century Śaṅkaradeva, the well-known Vaiṣṇava preacher, moved from the Ahom kingdom to the Koch kingdom because the political climate was especially favorable to a Hindu preacher.[118]

The Koch kings, though they also patronized Vaiṣṇavas and Śaivites, were primarily Śāktas, worshipers of the goddess, and particularly, worshipers of the goddess at Kāmākhyā. Indeed, the Koch king, Naranarayan, and his brother Śukladev/Chilārāya rebuilt the temple at Kāmākhyā in 1565 after the Muslim general Kalapahar sacked it. This is the same Naranarayan/Naranārāyaṇa we saw earlier in the story where the priest Kendukalai betrays the goddess at Kāmākhyā in order to let the king, Naranarayan, watch her dance. The Ahom kings also eventually became Śāktas as well, but they only shifted decidedly toward Śākta Tantrism later in the seventeenth century.

Śākta Tantra

While we find in Assam from the fifteenth century onward the propagation of Vaiṣṇavism, the worship of forms of the god Viṣṇu, which I will discuss in more detail below, and which was certainly an important social movement from the beginning of the sixteenth century onward, nevertheless Assam has a reputation as a pre-eminent site for Śāktism, that is, for worship of the goddess. Especially, we find worship of the goddess in its Tantric forms, which involves elaborate ritual and the praxis of the "six acts" (*ṣaṭkarmāṇi*), rites designed with a specific end including rites of pacification as well as rites of destruction and of harming. Certain forms of Tantra, and in particular Śākta Tantra, are characterized by a transgressive ritual praxis, that is, the use of illicit substances such as meat and alcohol as ritual implements, along with ritualized sexual union. This use of illicit substances is generally designated as the "left-handed path" (*vāmamārga, vāmācāra*).

As Edward Gait notes, throughout Assam Śāktism was prevalent, and we find there especially the practice of "left-handed" rites, involving transgression.[119] In literature as well, Kāmākhyā in Assam gains the reputation as the exemplary site for "left-handed" praxis. Gait also tells us that Śākta Tantra is a "religion of bloody sacrifices, from which even human beings were not exempt. . . .When the new temple of Kāmākhya [*sic*] was opened, the occasion was celebrated by the immolation of no less than a hundred forty men, whose heads were offered to the goddess on salvers made of copper."[120] M. M. Sharma convincingly construes this as Gait's misreading of the word *paik*, which refers to the system of laborers for the state being assigned to the temple and not to human sacrifice.[121] On the other hand, Chutiya kings in eastern Assam likely *did* practice human sacrifice to the goddess Tāmreśvarī.[122] Also, the *Tungkhungia Buranji* records an incident in the seventeenth century where the Ahom king asks one of his ministers to supply a sacrificial victim for the Chutiya city Sadiya. The minister chooses a strong young man named Bhotai who had killed a bear that entered into the minister's house. The Buranji tells us, "Having seen such courage and pluck on the part of Bhotai, the [minister] thought of sacrificing him at the Deoghar [temple] of Sadiya."[123] Examples like these, mixing Ahom and tribal practices along with Śākta practices, may help explain Assam's notorious reputation.

One interesting incident we find in the *Ahom Buranji* records that in a battle with Muslims in 1616 C.E., the Ahom king defeated the Muslims and then made a garland (*muṇḍamālā*) of the decapitated heads of the defeated Muslim soldiers.[124] This image, of course, strikingly reflects portraits of the goddess Kālī with a garland of severed heads around her neck. It also suggests either the influence of Tantric images of Kālī on practices in Assam, or an influence of Ahom war practices incorporated into Tantric literature, or possibly both.

While Tantric rites to the goddess, the Śākta Tantric practice, especially of the "left-handed" variety, typically employs the otherwise illicit substances such as meat and liquor, in considering this practice in Assam, however, we should keep in mind that Assamese food and drink practices were much more liberal than elsewhere in India. Most of the population was nonvegetarian, and even Brahmins in the medieval period in Assam mostly consumed a nonvegetarian diet.[125] As I noted above, even the generally orthodox *dharmaśāstra* writers for the Kāmarūpa school allowed for Brahmins to follow a nonvegetarian diet in Assam.[126] This liberal attitude regarding food and drink in Assam, as well as the general attenuation of caste distinctions in Assam,[127] lends itself to an easy incorporation of the transgressions of food and caste that we find throughout Śākta Tantrism. One might argue, thus, that in this case the use of apparently transgressive items in the Tantric ritual, such as meat, may not have functioned particularly as an instance of transgressive ritual—which we find as an important feature of Tantric praxis elsewhere and in other time periods. After all, in the Assamese region the people generally ate meat, the Ahom kings ate meat, and Brahmins in Assam also conformed to local customs and ate meat. In this case, the transgressive element in using meat for the rites would be minimal.

Considering this, one wonders to what degree and in what ways the goal of Tantric practice in Assam had to do with transgression, particularly in terms of transgression as a defiance of codes of purity, and associated with dietary restrictions. Rather, we might conjecture that the goal would be likely less about transgression, and not especially a practice designed to uproot a brahminical sense of limited caste-bound identity such as we find in Abhinavagupta.[128] Instead, the practice would serve other more magically oriented functions. We do, in fact, particularly in the texts used for this study, find very little attention to transcending caste identities. On the other hand, the general attitudes of the Assamese would make Tantric practices involving meat and liquor more socially acceptable and thus make it easier for such practices to actually be practiced and to spread.

For my own use here I understand transgression to operate for these later texts associated with Kāmākhyā less along the models that Sanderson finds in his study of Brahmins in the earlier period, before and during Abhinavagupta's time,[129] and that Urban uses in his study where he focuses on the *Kālikā Purāṇa* from the tenth through eleventh centuries.[130] Rather, I understand the word *transgression* with regard to the five transgressive substances—meat, liquor, fish, hand gestures, and the rite of sexual union—also known as the "Five Ms," especially in the context of the texts from, approximately, the seventeenth through eighteenth centuries, studied here to suggest shifts in social awareness that do not radically transform identity, so much as to offer alternative ways of interacting with women. In this respect, the difference can be especially seen in that, as Sanderson points out, Abhinavagupta and his commentator,

Jayaratha, especially exclude the wife from the rite of sexual union.[131] In contrast, in the *Gandharva Tantra* (GT) we find a passage that prescribes only the wife for the rite. The GT concludes with: "When one's own wife who travels the path with one is a practitioner (*sādhvī*) and a good wife, then why go to other women? Just so am I, [Śiva] only with you, [Pārvatī]."[132] Further, most of the texts from the fifteenth through eighteenth centuries drawn from for this study do not present the exclusion of the wife from this rite, but rather the option of either the wife (*svaśakti, svastrī*) or another woman (*paraśakti, parastrī*). So we see in the *Yoni Tantra*: "Having placed in the center of the ritual circle one's own beloved, or a well-dressed woman who is married to someone else, and having first given marijuana, he should worship with an attitude of devotion."[133] We find also in the BT: "Beginning [the rite], O Goddess, his own wife or the wife of someone else should be led there, and first having given a seat he should then give her water to wash her feet."[134]

Also, in terms of caste and authorship, in Assam not only Brahmins were literate in Sanskrit. Castes that would be classified as *śūdra* elsewhere in India, such as the Kayastha caste, were also proficient in Sanskrit. The Kayasthas are elsewhere in Bengal scribes and bookkeepers who are impure in part because of their association with Muslim rulers, which again may reflect elements of dietary considerations of purity—which probably were less important in Assam. So, for instance, the great Vaiṣṇava reformer Śaṅkaradeva was a Kayastha who was well trained in Sanskrit.[135] The castes that received an education in Sanskrit, and who could have therefore possibly been authors of the Sanskrit texts used for this study include several: Brahmins, of course, and also Kayasthas, Kalitas, and Ganaks or Daivajaās.[136] Even women, according to Satyendranath Sarma, of the upper classes were taught at home to read and write.[137] This will be addressed in more detail below.

Vaiṣṇava Reform

In the late fifteenth century a *Kayastha* named Śaṅkaradeva/Śankardeb began preaching a new form of Vaiṣṇava devotion, which involved exclusive devotion to Viṣṇu. The form of *bhakti* he preached differed from the earlier devotion to Viṣṇu in the Assam region, which was a form of *Vāsudevism* connected to the *Pañcarātra* cult,[138] and was a form that Śaṅkaradeva had picked up and synthesized through an earlier pilgrimage he made throughout India. One aspect of the new movement involved the translation into Assamese of several important Vaiṣṇava texts, including the *Śrīmad Bhāgavatam*. He predates Caitanya, however, and began preaching his form of Vaiṣṇavism before

Caitanya began preaching around 1510, though Śankaradeva's biographies state that he met Kabir on his first pilgrimage through India.[139]

Several elements of Śaṅkaradeva's new bhakti are key. First, Śaṅkaradeva propagated a creed that directly opposed the practice of animal sacrifice, which was otherwise, in practice, quite common in Assam, especially in Śākta Tantrism. This element of Śaṅkaradeva's creed seems to have had some effect. The Englishman, Ralph Fitch, writing during the reign of Naranarayan in Koch Behar in the last part of the sixteenth century describes the compassion for animal life he found among the people in Naranarayan's kingdom: "They kill nothing. They have hospitals for sheep, goats, dogs, cats, birds and all living creatures."[140] It also occurred in an environment where animal sacrifice was more generally the norm. So, for instance, Śaṅkaradeva's biography tells us that in his first meeting with his eventual successor, Mādhavadeva, the latter was on his way to sacrifice a goat to the goddess, and Śaṅkaradeva argued with him and talked him out of it.[141]

We see what may be the reflections of this Vaiṣṇava practice in the BT, where it explicitly condemns any violence, even to animals—this of course, outside the context of the ritual propitiation of the goddess, "He should not harm creatures, especially not domestic animals (*paśu*). Unless he is giving a sacrificed animal (*bali dāna*) to the goddess, he should everywhere avoid harm or violence (*hiṃsa*). It's well known that there is no fault (*doṣa*) in the violence which is for the sake of *bali dāna*" (BT 6.80–81).[142]

This emphasis on the problems of violence to animals, which is not so common in earlier Tantras (and we find this injunction against harm more than once in the BT),[143] suggests that the author(s) of the BT was aware of the Vaiṣṇava impact in this regard on the cultural awareness of the people, and it appears that this author agreed with this Vaiṣṇava perspective in general, even as the BT's author exempts the Śākta practice of sacrifice from the general rule.

That the BT's author feels a need to justify this Śākta practice may be seen from the fact that the author continues for four verses justifying this point of view. On the other hand, that the author readily criticizes harming animals in all other cases may possibly suggest a later date for this portion of the BT, since one might expect a response more like disdain to a novel practice introduced by a newcomer. Though one might also suggest Buddhist influence in this practice of nonharm, this may be harder to trace or prove in the generally Tantric Buddhist environment of the region and time period.

In any case, the attitude of the BT in this context does not support Hugh Urban's argument for Tantric practices, that "as in the case of other animal sacrifices, the focal point of the human sacrifice is the dangerous, frightening power that lies in the severed head. Indeed the sacrificer must carefully observe just how and where the severed head falls."[144] In the BT, of the thirteen times that the animal sacrifice (*bali*) is discussed (humans are nowhere in this text recommended for sacrifice), by far the majority of cases specifies the animal sacrifice as meat that is then to be enjoyed as food by the practitioner or practitioners, or others. So we find that BT 6.337 includes the sacrificed animal as part of a community feast for the male and female practitioners (which, in this case, appears not to involve the rite of sexual union)[145] and the sacrificed animal becomes dinner.

Another discussion of the sacrificial animal revolves around the meat of the animal as food for the wild jackals roaming about deserted places, which were understood to be embodied representatives of the goddess. In this case, one should "worship the Goddess Śivā (i.e., the Goddess as a jackal) who has the form of an animal (*paśu rūpā*) in a place where there are no people" (BT 6.54a). The text continues, "Where one jackal is fed, there all the gods are pleased, which is a difficult thing to obtain."[146] This standard element of Tantric ritual appears to be a food offering to the wild jackals roaming about in a lonely place, which, practically speaking, might also otherwise harass a lone practitioner.

Another instance involves feeding women with the sacrificed animal the morning after the late night ritual. "After having worshipped the [goddess], after having bowed down, after having done the mantra repetition with good concentration, and in the morning having given the sacrificed animal to women, perfection of the mantra will occur."[147] In all the discussion of the animal sacrifice in the BT, no attention is given to the head of the animal. Instead we find repeated references to the meat. Given the mostly nonvegetarian diet of the Assamese, the meat from this animal sacrifice would likely have been a welcome gift. This use of animal sacrifice as part of one's diet is in line with the nonvegetarian habits of the Assamese, including Assamese Brahmins.[148]

Śaṅkaradeva also stressed exclusive devotion to Viṣṇu. No other deities could be worshiped.[149] Illustrating this point, we find that one of Śaṅkaradeva's disciples, a Brahmin named Vyāsa Kālia, whose son had died from smallpox, tried secretly to sacrifice to the goddess Śītalā Devī to protect his other ill son. When Śaṅkaradeva found out, he kicked the Brahmin out of the movement.[150] His successor, Mādhavadeva, intensified this aspect of Śankaradeva's movement, with the result that the movement split into several factions on the death of Śaṅkaradeva. This element of Mādhavadeva's influence on the movement gets exemplified in a story told where Mādhavadeva secretly removes the *ghar deuti*, the household goddess kept in the kitchen, before he agrees to eat at his teacher Śaṅkaradeva's house.[151] In this story he trumps even Śaṅkaradeva in his zeal to allow only the worship of Viṣṇu. What this story also suggests is that this new movement was paying attention to what women were doing, and what they were doing in what were considered traditionally women's spaces. As we see below, this also entailed offering initiation to women.

One more key element of Śaṅkaradeva's movement that helped it to spread rapidly throughout Assam was the message of equality. Śaṅkaradeva's Vaiṣṇava movement made no distinctions in caste or clan in giving initation,[152] and the practices of the group greatly facilitated social mobility and equality.[153]

Śaṅkaradeva also initiated women into the movement, and some women became leaders in the movement. Two women, in fact, became heads of different subgroups of the movement after his death; one was his granddaughter, Kanaklata, and another was Bhubaneśwarī, the daughter of one of his disciples.[154] This acceptance of women in roles of leadership in this popular Vaiṣṇava movement in Assam likely contributed to the esteem for women we find in the texts used for this study. Or, at least, it may have reflected larger social patterns of esteem for women in Assam in this period.

In any case, we see that some elements in the movement were drawn from Śākta Tantrism, and perhaps some also came from Buddhism. Śākta influence in particular surfaces in that initiation was required by all followers. Even women who were merely cooking for a festival were not allowed to cook unless they had been initiated.[155] The idea that women should be initiated is also something we find in the texts used for this study. The move to require the initiation of women among both Vaiṣṇavas and Śāktas reflects a shift in attitudes toward women, though it may be difficult to judge whether the Śākta tradition influenced the Vaiṣṇava tradition, or vice versa in this case.

We also find a sect of "night-worshiping" (*ratikhowa*) Vaiṣṇavas who apparently claim to have derived from early leaders of the sect, including Mādhavadeva, and who appear to have synthesized Śākta practices with Śaṅkaradeva's Vaiṣṇava movement, even though they appear to have been rejected by more mainstream Vaiṣṇava groups. This suggests that a current of Śākta practices was incorporated in a Vaiṣṇava milieu,[156] and that even after Vaiṣṇavism became the tradition of the masses, elements of Śāktism remained.[157]

In a very short period of time, Śaṅkaradeva's Vaiṣṇava movement gained a widespread popular appeal. Its growth was also no doubt enhanced by a couple of highly effective organizing techniques. One was the *sattra* system, which set up communities of Vaiṣṇavas all over Assam. Another was the implementation of *namghars*, building structures found in most villages that were used as community halls and places of public prayer for Vaiṣṇavas affiliated with the new movement. These buildings were not like temples, in that they were funded by the communities and they functioned as community gathering places, not as abodes for deities.

Eventually, the group with its various branches became very powerful and was patronized by kings, who offered large tracts of land with servants attached to various *sattras*. The *Tungkhungia Buranji* tells us that before he became king, the Ahom king Gadadhar, on the run from his enemies, had sought shelter in one of the *sattras*. He was not especially well treated and he noticed the extensive wealth the *sattras* had acquired.[158] The initial tendency to exclusively worship Viṣṇu became more pronounced, especially in the branch deriving from Mādhavadeva, and also at times their call to exclusive devotion to Viṣṇu put them at odds with the Ahom monarchy, as in the reign of Gadadhar Simha, who tried to curb the power of the *sattras*. Ostensibly, his reason for limiting the power of the *sattras* had to do with the fact that numerous males were joining the *sattras* in order to get out of having to do the yearly three-month service to the government that was required of citizens (*paiks*).

One ramification of the Vaiṣṇava reform movement was that its popularity, combined with its creed of exclusive devotion to Viṣṇu, tended to eclipse Śākta Tantrism and force it to go underground as a practice.[159] The earlier ascendency of Śāktism gave way to Śaṅkaradeva's Vaiṣṇavism. So, for instance, Śaṅkardeva's grandfather Caṇḍivara was a well-known Śākta, while the tide shifted toward Vaiṣṇavism after Śaṅkaradeva. The central role of Śaṅkaradeva's Vaiṣṇavism, however, also started to shift back when some of the Ahom kings became Śāktas, especially when Prathameśvarī, who ruled in place of her husband, Śiva Simha, became the monarch. This I will discuss further below. In any case, it is clear that while certainly some of the authors of the texts used for this study, and especially the BT, were influenced by the Vaiṣṇava movement, they were clearly not aligned with it, and not the least because of the Vaiṣṇava prohibition against worshiping any god other than Viṣṇu.

Women

Women's roles in Assam present an interesting case and we can expect that aspects of contemporary socially prevalent attitudes toward women likely affected the authors of the texts used in this study. On the darker side, we find that slavery existed in Assam throughout the period we examine here, and women were often sold as mere property. Even as late as the 1685, we find a record of a woman being sold, though we should keep in mind that men were bought and sold as well.[160] Often, aspiring men offered their sisters and daughters in marriage alliances to other more powerful rulers in order to keep peace or to strengthen their political position, and with these women female slaves also were thrown into the bargain.[161] We also find in the *Ahom Buranji* a passage that explains and justifies why the Ahom god Lengdon sent the Ahom rulers down to earth. One of the reasons given has to do with women. The god Lengdon says, "There is no ruler on the earth. I think, there, the wife of one is forcibly taken by another."[162] Ostensibly, the function of rulers is to prevent men from forcibly taking other men's wives. The implicit assumption is that women are property, liable to theft.

On the other hand, we also find in the *Ahom Buranji* an incident recorded where an Ahom noblewoman defies the order of the king to send her son as a surety to a foreign country as part of a peace treaty. Nāngbakla Gābharu refuses the king, criticizes him, and proposes to fight the enemy in place of the men.[163] The king gives in to her and sends his own brother instead. This is an image of a woman who is warlike and not cowed by any authority, especially when it comes to protecting her children. This incident is merely anecdotal, and likely did not represent the norm, yet, in any case, it does offer an image of women that is not passively dependent upon men.

Apart from this document concerned with state history, we find that women in medieval Assam generally exercised some rights and that their movements were not especially restricted. Women did not veil themselves in Assam.[164] Nor was there a strong dowry system in place.[165] One consequence of the lack of a strong dowry system was that the birth of female children was not considered a financial liability. In contrast, in medieval Assam we find more commonly the practice of paying a bride-price to the family of the woman.[166] In fact, a common practice was that if the groom or his family could not pay the bride-price, then he had to serve the family of the bride for one to two years as payment.[167]

In addition to these general practices, it is also likely that tribal traditions influenced general attitudes and practices regarding women. A number of tribes in the Assam region were matrilineal, with property being inherited by daughters. Here we can include the Tiwas, the Jayantias—who were especially known as worshipers of the goddess—the Khasis, the Dimacha Kachāris, and a modified form of matrilineality among the Rabhas.[168] Some tribes like the Mikirs also considered women to have higher divinatory powers than men.[169] It is interesting, and may not be unconnected, that the fourteenth-century Brahmin writer, Mādhava Kandali, who translated into Assamese the *Rāmāyaṇa* has Kauśalyā uttering protective *mantras* for Rāma, Sītā, and Lakṣmaṇa as they leave for their forest exile.[170] This is suggestive in light of the idea we find in the group of texts used for this study—that women should be initiated because they have special skill with *mantras*. It suggests that this notion may have been part of a generally accepted idea of women for Assam in the medieval period.

We also find that women were taught at home to read and write, and we find mention of several women who were literate, including Śaṅkaradeva's granddaughter, Kanaklata; Bhubaneshwari, who headed one the branches of the Vaiṣṇava movement; and another woman named Padmapriyā.[171] We know about these women because they were mentioned in the annals that writers in the Vaiṣṇava movement kept. It is not improbable that other women were also educated. Other evidence for this is that the chief queen of Śiva Simha, Prathameśvarī/Phuleśvarī was herself educated.[172] She was also initiated into the Śākta cult by the Śākta guru Kṛṣṇarāma Bhaṭṭācāryya Nyāyavāgīśa, brought from Bengal by the Ahom king, Rudra Simha. Further, she established a school for girls in the palace grounds during her reign.[173] All this suggests that at least some women were literate. We do not have statistics, however one might conjecture that literate women would probably have only come from families where it was also a practice to educate men, including Brahmins and also the Kayasthas, the Kalitas and Ganaks.

Prathameśvarī herself was reportedly originally a *devadasī*, a temple dancer at the Jaysāgar temple, and was likely educated in the course of her training as a temple dancer.[174] She seems to have placed a premium on education and consequently established the school for girls during her reign. She came into power because the king, her husband Śiva Simha, was told by astrologers that his reign would come to a disasterous end if he continued as king. The astrologers' remedy for this was that after only reigning for two years, he "transferred his kingly duties and powers to his chief queen Prathameśvarī."[175] The total length of Śiva Simha's reign was thirty years, and after Prathameśvarī died, her sister Ambikā took her place as head of state. Prathameśvarī was, however, not a mere figurehead for the king. She engaged in policy-making and building as well. An ardent worshiper of the goddess, she especially tried to popularize the goddess's worship. One incident we hear about, in part because it invoked the ire of some groups of the then fairly well-established Vaiṣṇava movement, was that she invited a number of *śūdra* heads of the Vaiṣṇava *sattras* to an annual celebration of the goddess Durgā and in the course of the celebration the Vaiṣṇavas were given the traditional marks of the goddess, including the red powder mark on the forehead and the mark of the blood from the goat sacrificed to the goddess.[176] This, of course, offended the Vaiṣṇavas who as a matter of practice refused to worship any god other than Viṣṇu. The Vaiṣṇavas were also, in general, less liberal in their practices toward women than the Śāktas. For instance, in the religious dances performed in the *sattras*, boys played the part of women.[177] In general though, we see that in Assam attitudes toward women were typically more open to the suggestion of women in roles of leadership. This may have played a part in the particular attitudes we find toward women in the texts consulted for this study.

Appendix 2

Synopsis of Contents of the Bṛhannīla Tantra

Introductory Comments

The BT, which forms the primary text used in this study, has not yet been translated from Sanskrit into English or any European language, though as I mention earlier, it has been published, in its various versions as many as five times since the 1880s. This synopsis is presented to give some sense of the contents of this text. This synopsis will attempt to cover the major themes and topics addressed in the BT. The BT is a comparatively large text, some 256 pages of Sanskrit and the bulk of the text focus on the minutiae of precise ritual details—by far the majority of the text's verses simply consist of ritual instruction. Probably, in its original Indian context these details made the text a valuable ritual compendium, a handbook for the practitioner. More information about the text is located in appendix 1.

The BT is framed throughout as a dialogue between the god Śiva and the goddess Pārvatī, mostly with the goddess asking questions and the god, who speaks for the bulk of the text, replying with answers, stories, and ritual prescriptions.

The last chapters of the text, 18, 20, 22–24, diverge from this general format in that they present a series of long hymns that are known as *nāmastotrams*, a litany of names of a particular deity. Included here are the *sahasranāma*-s of Kālī, and the Blue Goddess of Speech (Nīlasarasvatī)/Tārā, that is, the one thousand names of Kālī, Nīlasarasvatī/Tārā (the two are equated here), along with the hundred-name hymns of these and Annapūrṇā. Since these are simply a list of names, without authorial reflection and not directly relevant to the study carried out here, these are mentioned but not included in the synopsis.

In addition to ritual prescriptions, however, in much smaller proportion, we find stories and occasional philosophical explanations. This element of the BT presents the greatest amount of authorial reflection—the "voice" of these authors—and, consequently, I rely extensively upon these stories and philosophical speculations for culling out the view of women that the BT presents. There are also stories that, even though they offer much food for thought, nevertheless address topics not directly relevant to the discussion of women, for instance, the story of why the preceptor of the demons, Śukra, cursed liquor. These also I do not draw upon for this study.

In general, I also do not present here in the synopsis a complete recounting of the details of ritual procedure, since this would take a great deal of space and would likely not interest most of my readers. Additionally, much of this ritual material is repetitive, with minor variations (though it was likely of great importance and prized by the practitioner who employed this text for mapping out how to do the specific rites). For considerations of space and in the interests of the probable readers of this book, this synopsis will include some ritual elements, especially those that are pertinent to the treatment of women, but will not focus extensively on this element of the BT. Nor do I take the space here to present the various *mantras* that the text reveals, which also take up a fairly substantial portion of the text, and are often embedded in a secret code, since these are also not relevant to the study at hand, and neither are the secret codes entirely clear to me.

The synopsis is presented chapter by chapter, in order, and following the sequence of verses within each chapter.

Who Is the Goddess?

The BT focuses on a particular set of images of the goddess, a four-armed goddess who is dark, and though the visualizations of her vary somewhat throughout the text, a certain coherency pervades. This goddess is called Kālī, Mahākālī, Kālikā, Nīlā, Nīlasarasvatī, with the text consistently equating these names as though they were different names of the same goddess. That is, for example, one sentence says, "Now I will describe the worship of Kālī," followed by ritual procedure and concluded with "this then is the procedure for Nīlā's worship." Frequently, the text also equates these four names with Tārā and Tāriṇī, and also, though less frequently, with Sundarī, Tripurā, Mahādevī,

Parameśvarī, Annapūrṇā and Mahāmāyā. I give here the text of one of the lengthier visualizations of the Blue Goddess of Speech taken from the second chapter of the BT:

> Beginning with [the sound] OM and ending with the word "homage," the wise man should worship with great effort. Then one should perform the purification of the elements [air, water, earth, fire, and space], with the sequence of breath control. After having placed [in oneself] the purified elements, now one should think that the universe is empty. One [should contemplate] one's own self as without qualities, without stain, as pure and as made up of the Goddess Tāriṇī. Then, in the intermediate region one visualizes the letter "āḥ" in a red lotus. Again, above that one visualizes the letter "ṭāṃ" on a white lotus situated above that. Above that, again one visualizes the letter "hūṃ" with a blue color. Then from the letter "hūṃ" [one visualizes] a scissors adorned with syllables.[1] Moving above the scissors, one should visualize one's own self as the Goddess Tāriṇī. Standing with the left foot forward, fierce and adorned with a garland of skulls; she is crippled, dwarfish. She has a hanging big belly and a tiger skin around her waist. She has the freshness of new youth and is adorned with the five gestures: the happy face, the four corners, the circle, the cow face and the female organ gesture. Thus these are well-known as the gestures in the five acts of bowing. She has four arms and a lolling tongue; She is profoundly terrifying and she gives boons. She holds a sword and a scissors in her two right hands, and a skull and a lotus in her left hands. One should visualize her with a single matted lock of hair which is yellowish-brown and the top of her head is adorned with [the Buddha] Akṣobhya. She has blue snakes in the matted locks piled on top of her head, white snakes forming her earrings, yellow snakes as bracelets and smoky colored snakes on her arms. She is adorned with snakes the color of the rain-clouds, and snakes shining like a strand of pearls. She has white snakes as a shining girdle and rose-colored snakes on her two feet. Covering both sides of her body is a long garland made of blue lotuses. She stands in the middle of a burning cremation ground; she has fangs. Her left and right foot are the duality standing upon the Sapida plant on the corpse. She has a smile on her face, revealing that she is inwardly absorbed in a trance state. She gives fearlessness to the devotees. O Goddess [Pārvatī], one should meditate[2] with this procedure on the Blue Goddess of Speech.[3]

This goddess is fierce looking, but with a smile on her face and she gives fearlessness to her devotees. She is covered in snakes and is also youthful in appearance, even as she is typically portrayed with a distended belly. The text tends to equate the Blue Goddess of Speech with Tārā/Tāriṇī, here at one point in the visualization calling her Tāriṇī, and then telling the reader at the end of the description that this is the visualization for the Blue Goddess of Speech. Other visualizations in particular in the BT are similar to this one, though not as elaborate in general and we also find other elements, such as that she is asked to "please bathe me in the rain of the nectar of good fortune"[4] and that in one place she has blue eyes, "adorned with three eyes, the color of blue lotuses."[5] Also we see that this Blue Goddess of Speech is a Ruler of Speech (*vācāmīśvarī*) and that she "gives the attainment which fulfills all desires through bestowing the ability to compose eloquent poetry in meter and natural, unaffected prose.[6]

On a couple of occasions (which may be interpolated) the BT refers to a scheme of three goddesses, Parā, Parāparā, and Aparā, associated with earlier Trika and Śrī Vidyā traditions; however, this is more rare. Especially Kālī, Tārā, and Nīlasarasvatī throughout this text confer the power of eloquence. This is a theme repeated constantly throughout the BT. Specific rites for specific gains appear throughout the text but the attainment of eloquence remains a consistent focus.

The BT appears to be influenced by other Tantric texts, notably Śākta texts, and yet takes an interesting position on women at various places throughout. So, for instance, the story related in the twelfth chapter of the BT, where the goddess saves the gods, echoes the recounting of the episode in the *Kālikā Purāṇa* where the goddess kills the demon Mahiṣa for the sake of the gods, even to the extent that both texts record what appears to be an initial victory but where the gods are again constrained to have to wait for the goddess to fully, finally, kill the demon (KP 62.54ff.; BT 12.23–85). However, the BT departs in its figuring of the goddess. In the KP recounting the goddess is formed out of the energies (*śaktis*) that the gods in their rage emit; the energies come together to form the body of the goddess whose various weapons are the particular energies associated with each of the various gods. This is also how the story is told in the (presumably) earliest version, in the *Devī Māhātmya*. However, the BT differs first in that the goddess is not formed out of the energies emitted from the gods. She is conceived as entirely independent and notably clearly more powerful. Second, it is she who emits the weapons out from her body, as *vidyās, mantras* that are fierce, dancing goddesses, which then defeat the demons, who in this version remain nameless and plural

(12.83). It is probably important in the representation of woman that in the earlier version, the fierce goddess appears as a psychological displacement of the male gods' impotent rage. This no doubt feeds into a mostly unarticulated but pervasive construction of the ugly half of the bifurcated feminine as the emblem of fierce, irrational rage—the powerful destructive rage of Kālī. The independent Blue Sarasvatī of the BT appears to be less a raging, destructive goddess and more a compassionate, if somewhat disinterested, omnipotent/female who deigns to appear into the thick of worldly wars, to help the gods because she is moved by their worship (12.48, 66ff., especially 12.76). She herself divines their needs when they are inarticulate in her presence (12.78f.). Also the myth of how Blue Sarasvatī turns blue portrays this goddess as not entirely omnipotent. In this story she is vulnerable to the violence of the demons.

Chapter 1

The first chapter, with sixty-six verses, addresses the root *mantra*, the primary *mantra* of the practitioner, along with the rules for the twilight offerings. The chapter begins by extolling the BT, declaring it should be kept secret, and listing the subjects that the BT will cover, including the procedures for worship, recitation of *mantra*, practice of seasonal rituals, and those engaged in for a specific purpose, as well as for the fire ceremony, and states of devotion and trance (*bhāva*). The text also declares it will discuss the hidden worship ceremony, secret *mantras*, and the secret mode of reciting the *mantra*. Other subjects include the use of gold, silver, and mercury ash; a description of mercury; and the definition of the six acts (the six goals and procedures in Tantric ritual, including killing, paralyzing, driving away, creating enmity, controlling others, and rites that bring peace and prosperity). In this chapter Śiva tells the goddess the *mantra* for Blue Sarasvatī, which functions primarily to bestow eloquence. This chapter also gives the ritual procedure for taking a bath. This chapter also makes reference to the doubling of the ritual in the prescription of Vedic rites and the Tantric equivalent, which a Tantric practitioner was often expected to perform. That the text prioritizes the Vedic ritual, enjoining its performance before the Tantric ritual, may indicate a tendency toward an orthodoxy, that is, the writer of this first chapter tends to be more orthodox. This continues through the fifth chapter after which point the BT shifts to a less orthodox position, including describing the sex rite and rites to be performed upon corpses.

Chapter 2

Entitled the "Description of the 16 Offerings of the Ritual Along with Hymns," this chapter contains 156 verses and focuses on the ritual of worship and where it should be performed. The deities that should be included in the preliminary worship include Gaṇeśa, Baṭuka, the local spirits guarding the area (*kṣetrapāla*), and the accomplished female practitioners (*yoginī*), and then other deities, mostly goddesses, such as Lakṣmī, Puṣṭi, Tuṣṭi, and so on. This chapter also stresses the role of the teacher. It also contains a hymn to the goddess (2.119ff.), which contains a refrain "*trāhi mām śaraṇāgatam*" reminiscent in style of the *Durgā Saptaśatī*. This hymn is also found in the *Nīlasarasvatī Tantra* 7.12–25 with numerous minor variations.

This chapter also gives three visualizations of the goddess. I give this first one in detail above, and have translated it because it is quite interesting, and appears to suggest some affinities with Buddhist Tantric mediations through the use of a meditation on letters. This first visualization (2.43ff.) involves first a meditation on three seed syllables successively, first the letter letter āḥ in a red lotus, then one meditates on an ṭāṃ on a white lotus situated above that.[7] After this is meditation on the syllable hūṃ in blue above the white lotus, situated near it. After that, from the "hūṃ" bījā one meditates on the "kartrikām" the scissors, adorned with letters, the bījā.[8] The practitioner should then think of emptiness, of the universe as empty; one's own self is visualized as consisting of Tāriṇī, without qualities (*guṇa*), without stain. The BT then gives the visualization.

The second visualization occurs in conjuction with the *cakras*, the psychic wheels in the body associated with the *kuṇḍalinī*, here with only five *cakras* rather than the more well-known six, plus the space at the top of the head (*brahmarandhra*). The fifth here is the tongue (2.112ff.). The nomenclature of *svādhiṣṭhāna* for the second cakra indicates in this case probably some influence from the Kubjikā tradition most likely via the Śrī Vidyā (though the number of *cakras* differs), especially given the references to *bindu, ardhacandra*, and *suṣumṇā* in 2.136ff. Also, this section (2.136ff.) offers a relatively sophisticated use of language, compared with much of the rest of the BT, suggesting that it is likely an interpolation. In any case it reflects a certain hodgepodge quality that we tend to find in this text, likely pointing to more than one author, with some authors adding piecemeal material from a variety of traditions.

The third visualization is similar to the first presented above with a somewhat fierce representation of the goddess, with a garland of skulls, adorned in snakes, but notably, here as well shown as smiling, in the bloom of youth and "raining the nectar of good fortune" (2.40ff. and 2.136ff.). Interestingly, in this third visualization she is depicted with blue eyes. In both she holds a scissors.

Chapter 3

The third chapter is fairly short, only fifty-six verses. It focuses primarily upon initiation and appears fairly orthodox with, as one might expect in a chapter titled "Description of the Procedures for Initiation" an especial attention to the importance of the guru. The list of items given to the guru in the worship of the guru includes an appropriately adorned seat, water for washing the feet, the offering of scented water, water for sipping, frankincense as incense, a well-lit lamp, tasty food, different types of fruits together with a variety of juices, an offering of a handful of flowers smeared with sandalwood paste, and a well-decorated bed and couch (3.49–54). One should worship the guru's wife as well; however, one should not massage her feet, as one is enjoined to do with the guru, because a young wife, the text tells us, doesn't know the difference between vice and virtue (3.56), and presumably might be susceptible to an indiscretion.

Chapter 4

The fourth chapter is about the "preliminary" ritual required for perfecting a *mantra*, (*puraścaryāvidhi*). This chapter, with 113 verses, focuses primarily on the procedure for reciting a *mantra*, including a discussion of the merits of the various types of rosaries (*mālā*). For instance, a rosary made from the skulls of outcastes killed in battle spontaneously gives one the magic power one desires (4.25ff.). (There may still be some preference given to this choice of rosary, given a recent news item in April 2004, which described several smugglers who were captured by the Nepali police as they were bringing in sacks of skulls from India.) The text also gives the procedure for *mantra* repetition where the counting is done on one's fingers (4.52ff.). The text then gives directions for the ancillary procedures, including reciting the *mantra* while making an offering into the ritual fire, making a water offering with the *mantra* (*tarpaṇa*), and pouring milk on the image of the deity while reciting the *mantra* (*abhiṣekha*). In addition to these three, the fifth element of *puraścaraṇa* includes feeding sages (*vipra*). Instead of the word *brahmaṇa* to refer to a Brahmin, the text uses uses the word *vipra* (4.71).[9]

Interestingly, in the description of the appropriate method for repeating the *mantra*, which includes, for instance, that one should always have a lamp lit while performing the repetition, the text also says "whoever does not know the vagina gesture (*yoni mudrā*), which is the enlivening power of the mantra, how can [that person] perfect the mantra, even with a hundred thousand repetitions?" (*mantrārthaṃ mantracaitanyaṃ yonimudrāṃ na vetti yaḥ| śatakoṭijapenāpi kathaṃ siddhir varānane ||* 4.74).

The text proceeds here in a fairly technical discourse upon the proper procedure for *mantra* repetition until the goddess interjects with an entirely new topic: whether the (male) practitioner should go to (i.e., have sexual contact) with the wives of other men (4.92ff.). Here again, as in the preceding chapters, the god's response to the goddess helps us to map the text's relation toward the transgressive elements of Tantra. With a style reminiscent of classical *mīmāṃsā* exegesis, the author delineates a method for interpreting contradictory statements in the Vedas, first stating that there are four Vedas, and listing the "Sāma, Yajus and Ṛg, etc.," then declaring that the Vedas are the absolute Brahman itself, and have no author, but are self-existent (*svayambhū*). Because, for this author, the Vedas prohibit relations with other men's wives, the text's author declares that the sex rite should be performed with one's wife. The author is aware that some Tantric texts prescribe going to other men's wives, but corrects these as meaning simply that in imagination only, one practices this, not in actuality (*parastriyam maheśāni manasā bhāvayañ japet,* 4.105a). The author here offers the view of performing the sex rite only with one's own wife. (This position is elsewhere in the BT both reversed and also incorporated into an indifference to the issue of whether the woman in the rite is one's own or another man's wife, suggesting more than one author for the text.) The text at this point continues with superlative praise of the Tantric sex rite, that it gives one a rebirth in heaven, or else final enlightenment (4.106ff.), and that one should in fact go to another man's wife (*tasmāt kuryāt sādhakendraḥ paradārāgamaṃ śubhe,* 4.109b), albeit, presumably, only through visualizing the rite in one's mind.

Chapter 5

This chapter contains 258 and one-half verses. After giving specific details for the daily worship (*nitya pūjā*), this chapter proceeds with a long discussion on liquor. Like the fourth chapter, this one also reveals a fundamental tension regarding the transgressive practices of left-handed Tantra. In response to a question by the goddess, Śiva replies that the twice-born should not drink liquor, and then continues with a thorough differentiation of eleven different types of liquor. Drinking liquor is censured (*nindā*) the god explains; a penance is prescribed for one who breaks the rule. And here the same word *vaidhetara*, "rule-breaker," literally, one who practices otherwise than what is enjoined is used as in chapter 4 with respect to those who go to the wives of other men.

The author then tells the story of how liquor became prohibited (5.27ff.). The guru for the demons, Śukra (lit., "semen"), had been reciting a *mantra* for thousands of years with no result. At a certain point, disgusted with his lack of progress and tempted by the celestial nymph Urvaśī, he united with the nymph and at the point of ejaculation had a flash of insight. He realized that the barrier to perfection of the *mantra* was the rum he imbibed each day. Furious, he cursed liquor so that no one could perfect a *mantra* ever if the person drank liquor. After a hundred more years, the goddess Kālī appeared to him and upbraided him for cursing liquor, explaining to him that the *mantra* could not be perfected because he did not say *mantras* over the wine before drinking it. The curse on liquor was then modified, so that one could drink liquor and still perfect the *mantra* if one recited a *mantra* over the liquor before drinking it. The text also prescribes substituting other substances for liquor. For instance, the practitioner can offer sugar mixed with fresh or dried ginger.

The text also gives an extensive list of holy sites for worshiping the goddess. Preeminent among places conducive to worship of the goddess is Kāmākhyā, Kāmarūpa (5.69), which the author extols for several verses (5.69–73).

Chapter 6

This chapter entitled "The Description of the Rules for the Clan (*Kula*) Worship and the conduct of the worshipper of the Goddess and so on" forms the longest in the text, with 398 verses. This chapter in particular contains much of significance for this study (so I give greater detail for this chapter), and presents a shift toward the left, that is, toward the transgressive. With this chapter the text moves toward an unabashed promulgation both of the worship of women generally, and includes at parts also the worship of women in conjunction with the sex rite. Here also, the author displays an indifference toward whether one performs the rite with one's own wife or with the wife of another person (6.21, 76).

What is also interesting in this chapter is that the author here places stress on knowledge of the written texts associated with transgressive traditions. The goddess places as a precondition for the practice of the transgressive sex rite that the aspirant must know the textual traditions (*kula śāstra*) and be worthy (*arhas*) (6.2).

This chapter also breaks the divide whereby ordinary women and goddesses are two different categories, where the goddess should be worshiped, but not an ordinary woman. Here the BT assimilates the form of goddess to the living woman who is worshiped as an instantiation of the goddess. "If a young woman is worshipped, then all the supreme Goddesses are worshipped" (6.4). Also, "One is smeared with many obstacles if he does not worship a beloved woman" (6.5).

By worshiping nine women and five women the aspirant gains the same fruits as gifting a Brahmin who is versed in the Vedas land that yields a good crop of corn and grain, and the same fruit as feeding one thousand and one hundred people, and that of donating a well, a water tank, and a water reservoir for Śiva and Kṛṣṇa (6.7–11a).

The text also gives the procedure for worshiping a woman in conjunction with the sex rite, whether his own or someone else's (*svakāntāṃ vā parastriyam*, 6.21). The rite includes feeding her; bowing to her; making offerings of water, of scents, delightful flowers with scent, frankincense incense; a light made with ghee, in a copper dish; a coconut; as well as different fruits along with the Indian version of after-dinner mints—the mild intoxicant betel nut, "which is tasty and well-dressed" (6.28). Further, one should give to the woman one is worshiping whatever she desires so that she will become especially pleased (6.30b). After this one writes with sandalwood paste a variety of "seed" *mantras* on the body of the woman. He offers her cloth and flowers on her sex organ. Then he bows to her with a gesture of submission, lying flat on the ground. The text enjoins this gesture three times, or so long as the *dṛṣṭi, the* sight or vision of the goddess does not arise (6.40b). After this the text describes the procedure of the sex rite, which it notes should be accompanied by the recitation of the aspirant's main *mantra* (*mūla mantra*). This procedure, which is named as "the Kālī method," affords magical perfection (*siddhi*) (6.44). (Notably, this preliminary procedure of worshiping a woman as a deity is often missing or strikingly curtailed and brief in other Tantric texts, which espouse the performance of the rite of sexual union, in the KCT, for instance, or the MNT, or the YT.)

The rite should be performed in a lonely place, and the text prescribes the use of meat in the food offering (*naivedyam*) (6.49). The leftover meat should be fed to any stray animal that happens by; the aspirant should call out "Kāli, Kāli" (in the vocative) to bring the goddess in the form of a stray animal.

The BT likens the worship of women (*kulapūjā*) to the orthodox rites for the ancestors; both should be performed regularly (6.53).

This chapter also delineates the prescribed daily conduct of the worshipers of the goddess. This includes arising in the morning and bowing to the tree of the clan (*kula*) (following this the text lists eight types including neem tree and lemon tree, among others), meditating on the guru in the head, and mentally worshiping the guru as free from disease. Then he imagines the root feminine *mantra* (*mūla vidyā*—the *mantra* associated with a goddess that is the main *mantra* of the aspirant's practice). He visualizes it as a light, shining like ten million suns flooding his body with nectar from root cakra at the base of the spine up to the soft spot on the skull at the top of the head (6.68ff.).

Following this the aspirant should bow to a woman (or women) with the text emphasizing the importance of bowing to women. With this the text lists a variety of women one should bow to, including a little girl, an intoxicated young woman, a beautiful woman, and also a contemptible, vile woman, a wicked woman. Having bowed to any of these, the aspirant should reflect upon the notion that blame or criticism of women and lying to women and hitting women should be avoided; women do not like it. Consequently, one should not engage in this type of behavior. As a further incentive the text notes that acting in these undesirable ways prevents the attainment of perfection (*siddhi*) (6.73b–75a). Interestingly, this particular act of bowing is also not performed in conjunction with, or as a part of, the sex rite but exists as an independent activity. It serves to inculcate a general attitude toward women independent of the attitude toward women taken in the course of the rite.

At this point in the text the BT emphatically encodes this veneration of women. "Women are Gods; women are one's life-breath" (6.75b). After this the text also recommends the inverted posture for the sexual intercourse (6.76b), which places the woman physically in the upper position, on top of the male. The text also lists general practices the aspirant should avoid, which appear to be mostly sectarian, such as smearing the path up to a holy site with cow dung (a practice of the Rāmānuja sect), but also, more generally, with the exception of the ritually prescribed animal sacrifice, the aspirant should avoid harming other creatures at all times (6.80f.).

In general, the aspirant should behave civilly and peacefully, be slow to revile others, be externally engaged in Vaiṣṇava conduct, that is, conduct that tends to accommodate others rather than engage in dispute with others (or so this seems to be the import here). One should be always engaged in helping out (6.87f.). This Vaiṣṇava element suggests a northeastern provenance for the BT; it also presents a model of behavior that combines an appreciation for women and a socially agreeable practitioner, which suggests a moment in the historical movement of this Śāktaism where this author was attempting to galvanize a public persona of the Śākta, the follower of the goddess as a socially responsible member of the community.

This chapter also delineates a variety of omens indicating that a particular goddess has accepted the aspirant's worship. So, for instance, if one sees a red cloth or a red flower this signals that the goddess Tripurāmbikā has accepted his worship (6.94).[10] Following this the text gives a number of ritual prescriptions, including the sequence for installing the *mantra* and its seer (the sage who revealed the *mantra*) in the aspirant's body, as well as *mantras* for Kālī and a visualization of Kālikā Bhuvaneśvarī. The text also outlines the procedure for purifying the elements in the body (the earth, water, air, etc., which make up the human body), known as *bhūta śuddhi*, along with a secret *mantra* for the goddesses Kālī, procedures for worshiping the goddesses Annapūrṇā, Tārā, and Sundarī, and additional ritual prescription, including a rite enabling a king to conquer his enemy.

In a lengthy section this chapter also delineates the *kāmya* rites, rites engaged for a specific purpose. Definitions of each of the six types (*ṣaṭkarmāṇi*) of *kāmya* rites are given along with the appropriate times, colors, postures, and ritual accoutrements for performing each.

Notably, the author also makes a plea for an expansive attitude toward a variety of other Hindu traditions without placing his own, the Kaula dharma, above these others: "Listen to the knowledge of everything which is situated within. The Vaiṣṇava, the Gāṇapatya, the Śaiva, and the Śāmbhava, yoga, *saṃnyāsin*, all these religious paths and the Kaula path; all are to be commended" (6.240f.). Without digressing too extensively, I will note here that given the general pattern of what Diana Eck calls "inclusivism" in Indian traditions, where other groups are tolerated but only to be subordinated to one's own preeminent tradition, this remarkable easiness with other groups displayed here in the BT is noteworthy.[11]

Intermixed within the external ritual prescriptions are occasional references to inward meditation on the goddess, such as "now, in the middle of the space between the eyebrows, one should see with one's own eyes your shining luster, in the middle of the upper part of the nose your light, which is salubrious, free from disease (*anāmayam*), white, shining with the light of ten million moons, and sharp, equal to the radiance of ten million suns" (6.250f.). Here one finds also references to the goddess as the *kuṇḍalinī*, rising through the subtle channels in the spine (6.70 and also earlier, 4.49ff.).

At times we see stress on the importance of the inner attitude, focusing on making the mind happy, pleased: "How does the mind (*cetas*) become pleased?" (6.254). This attention to the inner attitude of the aspirant also appears elsewhere (4.112f.; 21.24ff.).

In this context in this chapter, the focus on the mind, on the inner attitude, functions to inculcate a faith in a theistic scheme. The cause for the transformation of the mind is the action of the gods upon the mind (6.256). At the same time at this point in the text, the BT emphasizes a nondual philosophical stance (6.245, 264).

This chapter also includes a number of short hymns to the goddess, one in particular praising her as the absolute both with form and without form (6.272f.) and praise of the sacred syllable "om," which frees one from the sin of killing a Brahmin and from the curse of Śukra (6.281; presumably the curse Śukra placed on those who drink wine, found in the preceding chapter). Also contained in this chapter are instructions for the rite performed upon on a corpse.

In conjuction with the rite upon the corpse, the aspirant should hope to see Satī (6.289). In this context also one makes the water offering (*tarpaṇa*) with liquor (6.293).

Interestingly, the text asserts that the aspirant should not ever insult the food, which is used as the offering for the ritual. "If one insults the food then Kālī will chew him up" (6.296). At this point a list of animals suitable for the animal sacrifice (*bali*) is given.

Following this the text steps outside of a delineation of ritual procedures and presents a clear outline of behavior toward women. Perhaps what may be one of the most salient aspects of this section is that it moves beyond the mere ritual treatment of woman—in the limited confines of the rite. This move controverts the more common assertion that the woman may be treated like a deity during the rite, but that this does carry over into the everyday attitudes toward women. Here the text prescribes a permanent reverence toward woman. Interestingly, this extends beyond the woman worshiped in the rite to include "the females of beasts, of birds, and of humans" (6.301). So the BT asserts, "Women are not to be harmed [even] mentally, and especially [this applies to] his own women" [i.e., his female dependents, the women one interacts with on a daily basis.] "The form of the feminine is everywhere you, made manifest, O Goddess" (6.300–301). Indeed virtue arises from the worship of women (6.302), and further, one should not ever hit women. When the śakti (here this may refer to women in general or it may mean his partner in the ritual) is pleased then she [the goddess] is pleased (6.303).

When the goddess is pleased, she manifests by signs; she appears as a variety of animals, especially including the jackal (6.305f.). We also see that when the śakti, the woman, is pleased then the goddess is pleased, and then the mind is pleased (6.310). With this attitude the god Śiva becomes pleased (6.312).

Following this the text engages in a bit of philosophic discourse that sounds somewhat like the world-denying attitudes we find in Advaita Vedanta. The author declares, "Know that the body is made of impurity and the mind is fickle. There is no getting rid of impurity, so how can meditation happen?" (6.317), and "Fear, shame, hatred, etc., deep sleep, illusion, etc., unripened illusion, grief and worry, etc.—these are the various states of mind which those who have bodies have to bear" (6.319f.). This apparently rather untantric life-denying position is immediately followed by a praise of liquor as "the very form" of the goddess. It can give everything and removes a number of faults such as weakness, sickness, and timidity (6.322ff.). Given the fourth chapter's tentative and ambivalent acceptance of liquor, the shift here suggests more than one author.

The BT also makes a significant and interesting departure from the usual presentation of transgressive behavior. In listing the notorious Five Ms, the five substances that make up a transgressive ritual—which in the Sanskrit all begin with the letter *m*, the BT presents a different list. Perhaps appropriately so, given this text's radical, attitude toward women, the fifth transgressive element is women. Unlike other Tantric lists that can present varying degrees of fluidity, the list of Five Ms doesn't typically vary. The list is typically presented as wine (*madya*), meat (*māṃsa*), fish (*matsya*), parched grain (*mudrā*),[12] and sexual intercourse (*maithuna*). The list in the BT replaces parched grain with woman (*mahilā*) and uses the highly respectful form of the Sanskrit word, *mahilā*, which is best translated as "lady" (6.329). So the BT's list includes sexual practice *and* women, suggesting with this list that sexual practice is a different transgression than the transgression involving women. This digression is all the more interesting since the text presents these five as normative, when in fact this list in the BT is unusual.

Following this the text outlines a procedure for a left-handed rite performed at night with liquor (6.335ff.). This rite adheres to the prescriptions given earlier, including flowers, incense, and so forth, and also specifies that the food quantity should be equal to the liquids. One particular form of this rite, like the *cakra pūjā*, the sex rite involving numerous couples,[13] involves a number of men and women, though the rite here with a group, as I note in appendix 1, does not culminate in the rite of sexual union. The BT also prohibits using force of any sort, physical or mental, to coerce a woman's participation in the rite of sexual union (6.343).

At this point the author again reminds the reader that the aspirant should at all times act with compassion toward others and should, with the exception of the ritual sacrifice (*bali*), avoid harming others, human and nonhuman (6.345f.). Here the BT advises normative behaviors according to caste and veneration of Brahmins and the *śāligrāma*, the fossilized stone sacred to Viṣṇu. However, while these general rules of orthodoxy, including partaking of ritually consecrated food, and not touching members of other castes, apply during the day, at night when one meets with the members of the clan of goddess devotees, these rules do not apply. The BT extols this particular worship of the goddess. Immensely salvific, it should be kept secret, only divulged to devotees (6.351ff.).

The final verses of the chapter continue with precise ritual procedures and the results they bring; for instance, if one makes the water libation (*tarpaṇa*) mixed with coconut water, one attains all one's goals (6.369); with pepper mixed in the water, one's enemies are destroyed (6.370); and so on in like fashion, including also a rite for making an enemy army sick (6.383).

Chapter 7

This chapter, entitled "The Procedure for Subjugation, etc., and a Description of the Sequence for Worship of the Young Girl" is also lengthy, containing 293 verses. The chapter focuses on a description of a variety of ritual procedures for the infamous six acts, that is, creating enmity, causing death, forcing a person to leave town, and so forth, as well as controlling others (*vaśīkaraṇa*), and bringing about general welfare (*puṣṭi*).

In addition, the text also supplies *mantras* that give wealth and protection, knowledge and children, and that should be written and worn on the body, on a woman's left arm and on the right arm for a man, and around the neck for a child (7.20ff.). Ritual procedure abounds in this chapter; also given is a rite of passage for a young boy, which involves writing a *mantra* on the child's tongue with either a gold stick or a blade of *durva* grass. This gives the child poetic ability (7.45ff.).

At one point in the rite, the person performing the rite for the child sings a hymn into the left ear of the mother (7.64–72). The hymn, which is borrowed from the earlier KCT (3.35–44), is similar to the celebrated Devī Sūktam of the *Devī Māhātmya* with its litany of names of the goddess and similar stylistically with its repetitive refrain "By your compassion, take away my obstacles and give me all perfection" (*kṛpayā hara me vighnaṃ sarvasiddhiṃ prayaccha me*). It also tends to philosophize the goddess both as the supreme, impersonal, absolute Brahman—"O Mother, O Goddess, honor to you, sinless, who has the form of the absolute Brahman" (7.64) and who "comprise the object and the subject, who makes both subject and object manifest externally [in the world]" (*miti-mātṛ-maye devi miti-mātṛ-bahiṣkṛte*, 7.72).

After this the goddess asks the god Śiva to tell her the procedure for the transgressive sex practice (*mahācīna krama*, 7.82). The god initially complies, and in the process reveals a secret: a reversal in the usual cosmic order of sentient spirit and insentient matter—that the goddess is spirit (*dehin*) and the male god is matter (*deha*).

Following this Śiva appears to think better of his agreement to reveal the practice, since he would not only be revealing this to her but also to the rest of creation. Presumably she would pass this knowledge on to humans as well as other beings, gods, demons, and the Indian equivalent of fairies, among others. The god's objection to the revelation of this powerful truth is that most of the world's inhabitants—whether human, divine, or semidivine, animal or demonic—are "engaged in bad deeds." Most are very stupid (*jaḍatara*); "the nature of all these is such that all are mutually fighting in battle" (7.89f.).

The goddess then cajoles him with a hymn praising his compassion (7.92ff.), which causes him to relent. This dramatic device serves to psychologically frame the author's agenda: the textually necessary revelation of the procedure for the rite. The god then reveals the secret rite (*mahācīna krama*), elsewhere referred to as the "practice of Kālī." The procedure abandons the otherwise ubiquitous proliferation of precise rules regulating ritual praxis. So there are no fixed times (7.104), and in a striking contrast to nearly all ritual performance elsewhere on the subcontinent, no concern or need for purity (7.107), nor is there any impiety attached to this practice (*adharma*, 7.116). Contrary to normative ritual expectations, without having bathed, the practitioner can eat and worship, and without having worshiped, the practitioner can eat (7.109). "The rules are according to his will in this practice of the great *mantra*" (7.115). The praxis also emphasizes a mental performance rather than an external performance (7.103f.). One single element is obligatory: the practitioner should never criticize women (7.110). His love of women should increase and even if women hurt him tremendously, one should not direct ill will or hatred toward them, but should rather worship them (7.111).

When the author describes something transgressive, as here, as if to apologize, the author reminds the readers "there is no wrong doing (adharma); this path (dharma) is great" (7.116a), in this case followed with an emphasis on the inner state of the aspirant: "One should be mentally filled with joy, whatever one does" (7.116b).

This practice also presumably involves the sexual encounter with a woman. In this context also, if the aspirant sees a menstruating woman, one should recite a *mantra* one thousand times. Following this, in describing the particularities of the rite, the text then engages in coded figurative language, which, as a guess here, may be referencing bodily fluids (cf. White, *The Kiss of the Yoginī: Tantric Sex in Its South Asian Contexts* (Chicago: University of Chicago Press, 2003). The "flower" of the tree of the *mahācīna* may refer to menstrual fluid (7.128, 132).[14] Most of this section of the text (7.128–42) involves a figurative and coded language, which would probably be best deciphered with the help of an oral tradition. Night is an optimal time for doing *mantra* repetition (7.135), as well as the eighth and fourteenth days of the lunar cycle, reversing the earlier expressed disavowal of any adherence to rules of timing, and so forth.

One point of interest, however, is that the text declares that entering into the house of the female partner (*latā*, lit., the creeper, vine) gives a greater result than the rite that involves sitting upon and worshiping a corpse (7.142b). In this context also the text prescribes that the aspirant offer *bilva* leaves, the root of the tree of the *mahācīna*, that is, probably the menstrual fluid, along with marrow, or fat (?) (majja) in the cremation ground in the company of a woman. If she does not run away then he acquires great merit. The rites with corpses, the text declares, are not worth one-sixteenth of a portion of the potency of this rite with a woman in the cremation ground (7.140–42). These rites also include offering one's own flesh, and one's blood (7.1.49b). Sexual union is salutary (7.145).

This particular section of the seventh chapter comprising verses 7.120–70 most resembles the *Yoni Tantra* (see also the thirteenth chapter of the BT). The voice of the author shifts and the style of language shifts somewhat also. We also find things like a reference to the woman's pubic hair (notably discussed in several places in the *Yoni Tantra* but otherwise absent in the BT, except in one other section of the BT that resembles the YT, in the thirteenth chapter). However, unlike the *Yoni Tantra*, we find also a simultaneous increase in cryptic, codified speech (7.128ff.). Along with this, the text more exclusively focuses on the magical results especially attained from menstrual fluid. After describing the procedure for making an offering with the sexual fluids of the male and the female, the text enjoins the aspirant to abandon his disgust, his aversion, and worship the sex organ of the woman (7.170).

Following this, the author focuses on the inner workings of the goddess as energy, the mystical feminine force of the *kuṇḍalinī* (7.172–87).

Then a remarkable section occurs that extols the spiritual capacities and attainments of women as a class. "The restrictions which hamper men are not [a problem] for women. Anything whatsoever, by any means and moreover, always, from all sides, simply by meditating, women acquire perfection, magic power (*siddhi*), without a doubt" (7.188b–89). The text goes on to list a series of metaphors that are apparent truisms, that is, "just as by drinking milk, joy arises for a hungry person" (7.192), "just as by merely remembering the

Gaṅgā, one is freed from sin" (7.196), which are similes illustrating by example, that women, just by mere contemplation, acquire perfection, even the power to confer boons upon others (7.198a). The even more remarkable conclusion of this encomium on women is the logical conclusion the text reaches. That is, the only reasonable thing to do is to initiate the women in one's clan.[15]

After this the author recounts a story that Nārada, the celestial and paradigmatic devotee of the god Viṣṇu, tells the goddess Pārvatī (7.203ff.). The story recounts how Indra lost a battle with demons and then took refuge in the guru of the gods, Bṛhaspati. Bṛhaspati counsels him on how to protect himself, and explains that the demons cannot be conquered while on the surface of the earth. Bṛhaspati then relates the method for acquiring mastery over the demons (7.209ff.). One of the ostensible morals of the story is the power of the Blue practice, that is, the meditative practice directed to the Blue Goddess Sarasvatī (the Blue Goddess of Speech) (7.210).[16]

Along with this the guru of the gods emphasizes the importance of providing a livelihood for teachers (7.217f.). The story continues with the powerful demons abandoning right conduct, and as a consequence, eventually themselves falling on hard times (7.223f.). The text then provides instructions for the worship of a young girl, including the construction of the altar area (7.229ff.).

Following this a more elaborate description of the worship of a young girl (*kumārī*) ensues, a rite that is ostensibly not connected with the sex rite. In this rite, which occurs during the waxing half of the lunar month, a girl child the same age as the corresponding lunar day is worshiped (i.e., a one-year-old on the first day, a two-year-old on the second day) up to the full moon with a sixteen-year-old girl (7.246ff.). If we take *puṣpa* to mean menstrual fluid as Schotermann does with the *Yoni Tantra*, then none of the young girls should have commenced menstruation in order to participate in the ritual (7.250).

This section of the text also presents a curious shift to a tripartite form of the goddess as Parā, Parāparā, and Aparā incarnate as the young girl (7.243f.). This tripartite scheme is associated with the much earlier nondual tradition of the tenth-century writer, Abhinavagupta,[17] and as we might expect in this context, the text references here terminology associated with the speculative yoga of this tradition (*bindu* 7.255ff.), which the BT in general tends not to draw upon.

The text continues with ritual details and presents the benefits of worshiping the young girl (7.256ff.). The young girl is the visible form of the *yoginī*, the female ascetic.[18] She is the incarnate form of all the gods (7.275). Consequently, when the young girl is worshiped, all the gods, as well as lesser spirits and demons, become pleased (7.278f.). This elevation of the young girl apparently for this author should translate into social action. That is, the text enjoins that the young girl should receive financial benefits. The aspirant should pay for her wedding (7.283), a considerable and costly affair in the Indian context. The chapter concludes with profuse praise of the worship of the young girl.

Chapter 8

The eighth chapter has 210 and one-half verses and begins with a description of a magical diagram for the attainment of the power to fly (*khecaratām* 8.2—also sometimes construed as an elevated state of awareness), with the diagram written on copper with red and other powders (8.5f.).[19] In this chapter also the goddess is philosophically assimilated to subject and object (8.15). This section appears to be a slightly corrupted and condensed paraphrase of the section I referred to earlier in the KCT., which describes the *cakra* rite that also includes the "Karṇejapa Stotram," the hymn recited into the ear of the woman to initiate her into the rite of sexual union for the KCT. The stotram is not given here. We see here praise of Kālī, and then after having praised her (*stutvā*) and bowed, the "mixing" (*saṃmelana*) occurs, which likely refers to a *cakra* rite, and after this the gods are fed and then the participants are fed (*saṃbhoga*). We find also that the goddess (*devī*) is made to depart (*viṣṛjya*) before the feasting. The condensed and not entirely clear descriptions given here appear to echo the KCT 3.48. We also find here an odd rendering of three forms to be worshiped, the subject (*mātrā*), the *mudrā*, and the object (*mitām*). This appears to echo the part of the Karṇejapa Stotram, which declares the woman to be the subject and object, but confusedly inserts the unlikely and obscure *mudrām* in tandem with the subject and the object. In this context the BT seems to refer to the inward rise of the feminine energy known as *kuṇḍalinī* with a description of a yogic breath practice (8.10f.).

Following this, the chapter contains a description of the transgressive rite employing liquor and intercourse (8.19ff.). In this context the text especially emphasizes a pure attitude (8.29) and steadiness of mind (8.28). The text here also offers suitable substitues; so the products of a cow put in a copper vessel are equivalent to wine (8.21).[20]

The text at this point also relates a story, which it reveals as a secret. In the story the god Viṣṇu comes across a group of sage/ascetics (*muni*) engaging in transgressive sexual practices and drinking wine. He is disturbed by this apparently inappropriate behavior. Indignant, he asks "What path is this?" (8.41). Śiva explains to him that this is a secret path, that the sages are in fact mentally repeating the *mantra* of Kālikā who is also the Unobstructed Goddess Sarasvatī. This secret path, Śiva explains, leads to liberation (8.43). Following this he gives a list of examples taken from Purāṇic and epic sources, each of which is glossed against the grain of its usual interpretation, and each of which stands as a proof of the efficacy of a path involving transgression. So, Śiva explains, Dattātreya was enlightened through drinking liquor; Vasiṣṭha became enlightened through sexual relations with an outcaste woman; Soma, the moon, became enlightened by having an adulterous affair with the wife of the guru of the gods, Bṛhaspati. Even that paradigm of righteous conduct, Rāma, gains enlightenment by transgressive behavior, in this case, by the murder of a Brahmin—the demon Brahmin Rāvaṇa (8.47).

Notably, here the examples span the list of heinous sins, including the murder of a Brahmin, drinking liquor, and engaging in sexual relations with the wife of the teacher. Stylistically, this list of transgressive feats appears similar to the fourth chapter of the *Yoni Tantra*, which gives a similar list of figures and ascribes their success to the performance of the worship of the *yoni* of the goddess; that is, Rāma defeats the demon Rāvaṇa in the YT by virtue of the worship of the *yoni*.

The god Śiva then reveals to Viṣṇu the secret *mantra*, which must accompany this transgressive practice (8.47ff.). The text then discusses the transgressive rite, but here, in an interesting literary move, the text invokes a motif from the Upaniṣhads, where the aspirant and the elements of the rite are metaphorically connected with the elements of the fire sacrifice: "The mind is the ladle" [for offering butter to the fire], "in the fire of the self" (8.55). The text configures the rite in mental and philosophically nondual terms: "[The aspirant] should engage in ritual copulation, with the light which is the offering of both what is good and what is sinful (*dharma* and *adharma*) (8.55).

Another point of interest: in ritual copulation the semen should not be withheld, but should rather be emitted (contrary to popular Western conceptions of Tantra and to some Buddhist practice). However, note that Narasiṃha, who adopts a conservative position, rejecting the use of the Five Ms in his *Tārābhaktisudhārṇava*, also, like the Buddhists, enjoins nonemission by the male.[21] The emission is likened to the moment of offering with the ritualistic utterance "svāhā" at the end of the *mantra* recited at the time of emission (8.57). This emission (as elsewhere; 7.128ff., for instance) forms part of the ritual offering.

The text goes on to list appropriate places for the worship of the goddess, with Kāmarūpa as preeminent. This list favors northeastern India in its list, including the Karatoya River and Lauhitya, both in the northeast region (8.78). It also prioritizes the cremation ground for the worship of the goddess Tārā

(8.83). Following this the text again extols the special "Kālī Practice," which has no rules regarding time, place, and so forth (8.93f.), except for the rule that the aspirant should revere women (8.91). Here again the text repeats "women are Gods; women are life breath" (8.90). "Striking women, hitting them, criticizing them, and not being straightforward with them is not pleasing to them. In every way possible one should not do that" (8.91). After this the text prescribes the inverted posture for ritual copulation (8.97), and with this again, as we saw earlier, a cryptic poetic speech that "the bow should be rubbed with the arrow of love" (8.98). This is followed with more ritual detail.

After this the text presents a description of the inner mystical feminine energy that rises up the central channel in the spine, with a system of fourteen psychic centers (8.120ff.). In this system of the inner-coiled goddess who rises up the central path, the goddess takes the form of a point of light. This form appears to be inclusive: she is Nārāyaṇī, Kālī, Tārā, as well as She-who-dwells-in-Emptiness, as well as comprising male gods, including Rāma, Viṣṇu, and Śiva, and also the Supreme Self (8.129ff.).

Following this the text presents ten methods for writing out *mantras* that render them free of faults. These methods incorporate a variety of procedures, such as separating the vowels from the consonants, writing out the *mantra* and striking it with water scented with sandalwood paste, inserting potent seed syllables at specific places in the recitation, or writing out the *mantra* with *karavīra* flowers (8.143ff.).

After this the text engages in a philosophic speculation that is based on gender. The supreme, it says, is without form, is of the nature of light. When it arises with form, it takes one of three forms (8.155f.). The text proceeds to discuss a feminine form (*bhagākāra*) and a masculine form (*liṅgākāra*). "Everywhere," the text continues, "in all bodies, the form of the feminine is that which is the creator" (8.158b).[22] This, the god Śiva says, is the highest convention (*saṃketa*), indicating both an essentialist view of gender, as well as an understanding of the ultimately arbitrary nature of this convention. Then again the text offers an allusion to the Upaniṣadic coding of the sacrificial rite, declaring "the female organ is the sacrificial fire pit and the male organ is the ladle" (8.160). Here the fire is the feminine season; the semen is the ghee, and the mind is the priest (*hotṛ*).

Following this the text continues with more discussion of the mystical feminine energy within the body, the coiled goddess Kuṇḍalī (8.167ff.), reiterating what was discussed earlier regarding this goddess and the forms she takes, including her forms as a pure point of light (8.174) as well as the forms of the masculine gods Rāma, the Great Viṣṇu, Kṛṣṇa, the Great Śiva, and Tāriṇī (8.177). The text continues this mystical exploration with a description of this inner light connected with the breath, culminating in a vision that the author shares (via the voice of the god Śiva) of the goddess Tripurasundarī, sitting on a couch that is made of the god Sadāśiva, and holding five arrows in one of her four hands. This long section reveals influence from the south Indian Śrī Vidyā tradition, both in the metaphysical speculation it engages in as well as with the discussion of the coiled goddess inside the human body.

At this point the text abruptly shifts the subject to *nyāsa,* the ritual placement of the deity in the body. This suggests that perhaps the previous section may have been interpolated, especially since the section does not properly conclude and neither does the goddess Tripurasundarī figure elsewhere so prominently in the BT.

On the heels of this is a visualization of the god Sadāśiva (8.200ff.), also unusual since elsewhere in the BT the visualizations of goddesses Kālī and Nīlasarasvatī mostly predominate.

Then, the text shifts to the goddess Kālī, reminding its readers, "You should understand that the form of Kālikā which is light—that indeed is Nature (*prakṛti*)" (8.209), stressing that the transcendent goddess is also especially immanent in the world. This chapter then ends with Śiva declaring that he remained in meditation for one hundred thousand years. It is not clear if this is meant to refer to the vision of the goddess Tripurasundarī some thirty verses earlier.

Chapter 9

The ninth chapter, entitled "The Procedure for the Hero's Practice," is short, with only thirty verses. Details are given for the performance of the hero practice, which in this context involves sitting upon a corpse. Most of this practice occurs at night; ritual offerings are made and the aspirant sits upon the corpse, offering to the deity. The best choice for a corpse is an outcaste who has died a violent death (9.23).

Chapter 10

The tenth chapter is also short, thirty verses, and is titled "Other Procedures for Practice." This chapter focuses on two practices: a worship of the highest goddess (Parameśvarī), and a practice for attracting the powerful and fierce form of the god Śiva called Bhairava. The latter practice occupies the greater part of the chapter. In this practice one buys a corpse from the corpse marketplace, and lovingly offers the skin of a fish to the corpse. After this, one offers marijuana on the eyelid and on the mouth and then recites the *mantra* silently (10.16ff.). This causes the fierce god Bhairava, who hangs around the corpse marketplace, to come to the aspirant (10.19). At a certain point one throws the fish skin into the mouth of the corpse (10.21). This chapter's practice also emphasizes the importance of the guru (10.29), suggesting a connection with the Siddha tradition, and strikingly unlike the special "Kālī Practice" where the guru is not important (13.5ff).

Chapter 11

The eleventh chapter, comprising ninety-nine verses, tells the story of how the goddess Sarasvatī took on a dark form to became Blue Sarasvatī. The story takes up thirty-nine verses, a good portion of which shifts from the common *anuṣṭubh* stanza form with eight syllables, to the quarter verse, to an elaborate metrical form, *upajāti*, with each quarter verse containing eleven syllables.

This remarkably metaphysical action adventure begins with a war between the demons and the gods, with the demons being defeated. They take refuge underneath the ocean. The defeated demons enlist the aid of two demons, Horse-neck and Moony, who do intense austerities in order to please Sarasvatī, the goddess of Speech (11.60; lit., "The Goddess who attracts words).

Pleased by their intense practice, the goddess grants them a boon. They ask for the boon of being able to attract all the words. She grants it, and the two demon brothers immediately deprive the world of words, leaving the Brahmins tongue-tied (11.61ff.). They kidnap the Goddess of Speech and tie her up in a poisonous underwater pit, a mixture of the deadly poison *halāhala* and dark blue water, securing the prison with mountains.

The two demons then return to the surface of the earth and shoot an arrow, which draws all the words from the surface of the earth, making the Brahmins forget the Vedas (11.68). The god Viṣṇu then comes to the rescue of the goddess. Taking the form of a large fish, he goes to the underwater residence of the demons and after a long war defeats them in battle.

He then sings a song of praise to the Goddess of Speech, who is not harmed; she is smiling, but with her skin turned dark due to the effects of the poison (11.81). Viṣṇu consoles her; in fact, his speech is a striking example of the ethic toward women that characterizes the BT. The goddess feels shame, consternation over the way she looks (11.83ff.); however, Viṣṇu gently tells her, "Don't feel grief. . . . So you've become blue by the force of the poison. What's the problem? How is that any fault?" (11.85). Viṣṇu is primarily concerned with the goddess's welfare, that she is alive and unharmed, not with how she looks. Relieved, he says, "Your limbs are perfect, a smile plays on your lotus face" (11.81); "what fault is there in the color blue?" (11.87); "you are alive!" (11.90).

To allay her feelings of shame regarding her dark skin, he presents a litany of examples of dark-skinned gods, extolling the beauty of blackness. So, he tells the goddess, the great god Śiva's throat was made blue by the poison *halāhala*; Indra, the king of the gods is blue; and the clouds that give rain to the earth are blue. "I, myself, [Viṣṇu] who is the abode of purity (*sattva*) am dark" (11.88), and the goddess Sāvitrī, the soft kind one who is the light of the world is dark. Indeed "a dark color makes the world thrive" (11.86–88).

The chapter concludes with instructions regarding the *mantra* of Blue Sarasvatī, along with the results it gives.

Chapter 12

This chapter, with ninety-eight verses, also employs stories to convey specific attitudes toward the feminine. It begins with the declaration that the goddess Kālī is, on the one hand, transcendent, without form, existing as pure light, and that she is the form of the absolute impersonal transcendent Brahman, and, on the other hand, that she is capable of overriding the split between the world and the transcendent. She is also immanent (*jaganmayī*) (12.1f.).

Following this is a description of her celestial residence, situated above Goloka, the abode of the god Viṣṇu, by implication suggesting her superiority with respect to this great god (12.2ff.). After this the chapter tells a story that parallels an episode in the *Yoginī Tantra*, where the goddess Kālī gives the god Brahmā the power to create the world, along with the power of will to Viṣṇu, and the power of knowledge to Śiva, by entering into these gods (YogT 10.19ff.). With this power that is the goddess Kālī's, the god Brahmā is then able to create the world (YogT 10.33ff.). The YogT presents the goddess Kālī with a vaster imperial power and majesty absent in the BT (YogT 10.49ff.).

In the BT's more abbreviated version, the gods discover the goddess Kālī moving on the path (*pathagā*) and sing a hymn of praise to her (12.12ff.). The hymn the gods sing to her, as with others in the BT, stylistically echoes the well-known *Devī Sūktam* from the sixth-century *Devī Māhātmya*, and with a direct reference to that text praises the goddess as the destroyer of the demons Madhu and Kaiṭabha, and destroyer of the demon Nisumbha [*sic*].[23]

She offers them a boon and then gives them the power to create the world (12.20). The god Brahmā appears confused and asks for guidance regarding the form creation should take. At this point, in a philosophical twist on the more usual presentation of material creation, the goddess replies, "Follow the dust (*rajas*) emanating from my feet" (12.21). With this the text at once suggests that the goddess is transcendent, as well as that the material substance of creation comes from her, from that which is the lowest part of her, her feet. Rather than simply reversing the roles assigned to the genders in the classical tradition, where the male god wills the creation and the female nature (*prakṛti*) composes its material essence, this episode plays upon the notion of the feminine as the source of material creation. The gods take the dust from her feet and with this begin the cycle of creating, maintaining, and withdrawing the world (12.23ff.).

Following this the gods need protection from the demons; so they go to the goddess and praise her. This hymn presents the goddess as composing the totality of the world, containing within herself the polar oppositions that structure the world. She is the subject and the object, the enjoyer and that which is to be enjoyed (12.32–34).

After a modicum of bureaucratic runaround that serves the purpose of establishing that the highest gods, Śiva and Viṣṇu, are not capable of helping the gods, the goddess appears to the gods and agrees to help them. After a wait of five years the goddess appears again to the gods when they pray to her. At this point, out of her body she manifests the *vidyā-s*, feminine *mantras*, who are also goddesses, and who then win the war against the demons for the gods (12.79–85).

The chapter concludes with a description of ritual procedures for the last eleven verses.

Chapter 13

This short chapter (thirty-six verses) again discusses the special "Kālī Practice," which has no rules for time or place (13.5ff.). Interestingly, here this lack of ritual regulation is extended even to the guru. "And here in this practice (*sādhana*) of the Great Kālī, there isn't any thinking or contemplation on the guru" (13.7). The text gives the *mantra* for Kālī and then gives a visualization of the goddess. The visualization itself suggests a late medieval date for the text. Kālī here is not the fierce, ugly goddess of the earlier tradition. Rather, she is beautiful, fierce still, with limbs dark like rain clouds, naked with four arms and three eyes and a garland of skulls, wearing a pair of boys as her earrings, standing astride the corpse that is the god Śiva, bearing a club, holding a decapitated male head, and displaying with gestures no fear and the act of boon-giving (13.13ff.). This image is popular on lithographs today in Bengal, without, however, displaying the earrings. This is also the image that has been imported into the West.

Following this, the chapter reiterates the procedure discussed earlier for the rite of worshiping the woman (6.34ff., 73ff.; 7.104ff.; 8.93f.). The chapter concludes with praise of the pilgrimage site of Kāmarūpa in northeast India.

Chapter 14

The fourteenth chapter, containing sixty-one and one-half verses, opens with the revelation of the *mantra* of Kāmākhyā. The *mantra* is given, along with praise of it (14.3ff.), and then this chapter focuses on ritual procedures. A list of goddesses to be worshiped is given (14.39ff.) along with a reference to the *Kālikā Tantra* (14.50).[24] The text follows this with a discussion of the symbolism of the number three as it connects with the goddess Tripurā ("the triple-city Goddess" 14.53ff.). The chapter concludes with additional ritual detail.

Chapter 15

This chapter entitled "The Description of Other Places for Practice" contains 134 and one-half verses. This chapter functions primarily as a *sthāna māhātmya*, describing and extolling various places for worship. The region described is a hilly, or mountainous region, that is, the place called Darpaṇa is a mountain (15.2); however, the region is not located in the Himalayas (15.4, "*himālayena sadṛśaḥ*), rather, there is reference throughout to Kāmākhyā.

Most of the sites praised and described are associated with a mountain or a sacred pool of water (*kuṇḍa*), and a few are associated with rivers. Also given are instructions for worship of the various gods associated with a particular place.

Included is a visualization of the goddess Ugra Tārā, who in this form plays, that is, is located at a Bhūmipīṭha in the center of the principality of Kāmākhyā (*Kāmākhyānābhimaṇḍalam*). In this visualization the goddess has skinny limbs (not voluptuous ones as usual with Tārā); she has red teeth, four arms, and a belly that hangs down. She has a garland of snakes on her matted hair and stands upon a corpse. She is laughing with a loud and boisterous laugh.

After this visualization the text continues with a description of places and short ritual prescriptions for the various places described.

Chapter 16

This chapter, with seventy-three and one-half verses, focuses on the rituals pertaining to the annual ritual calendar. The chapter opens with a discussion of proper conduct in an uncharacteristic voice, echoing the Gītā, with the prescription that each person should perform his or her own dharma, not the dharma of another, or face the penalty of a fine (16.5f.). After this the text shifts into a description of the annual worship of the goddess Durgā on the Great Eighth Day (*mahāṣṭamī*) in the fall. In the course of this calendrical ritual prescription, which occupies this chapter, is also a seven-day ritual with a horse. This rite was obviously designed for a royal patron, serving the purpose of ascertaining whether one would conquer a foreign country or, depending upon the horse's actions, whether the king's son dies, or whether the king conquers his enemies after some struggle (16.17ff.). The rest of the chapter continues the discussion of specific ritual prescriptions for specific days in the calendar.

Chapter 17

This chapter, 148 and one-half verses long, opens with a description of the procedure for a nighttime repetition of the *mantra*, which brings a capacity for knowing all (17.1ff.).[25] After more ritual prescription, the text presents another visualization of the goddess Kālī. Similar to the visualization given in the thirteenth chapter, here also the goddess stands on the corpse, which is the god Śiva; she has a smiling face and dark limbs, with three eyes and four arms. Her long ears are adorned with young boys (i.e., these are her earrings). She holds a decapitated head and makes the gestures of boon-giving and having no fear. Here, however, in her upper-left hand she holds a scissors, as in the visualization in the second chapter (17.12ff.). Following this the text gives instructions on how to construct her altar and what to offer in worship (17.17ff.).

After this, a long discussion of the fire rite ensues, which takes up the bulk of the chapter (17.25–115). This discussion includes how to construct the pit for the fire as well as the ritual enlivening of the fire pit, and also a long visualization of the God of Fire (17.83–92).

Following this the text presents more ritual procedure for the goddess including a short visualization of a four-armed goddess Mahādevī residing in the fire of the cremation ground (17.116ff.). After this the text also gives the ritual procedure for the twilight offering, with a visualization for this goddess (17.123ff.). The chapter concludes with more ritual prescription.

Chapter 18

This chapter, comprising 206 verses, contains the thousand names of Tārā. Here the goddess Pārvatī requests the god Śiva to reveal the one thousand names of the Blue Goddess of Speech (Nīlasarasvatī) (18.2). He responds that the names are too secret; he can't reveal them. They have a lover's spat and the god relents saying to the goddess, "You are my life; without you I'm just a dead corpse" (18.13f.).[26] The rest of the chapter reveals the one thousand names of Tārā (here equating Tārā with Nīlasarasvatī).

Chapter 19

This chapter in forty-one verses reveals the hymn that is used as an armor of the goddess Tārā. The god reveals the hymn with instructions to keep it appropriately guarded or risk death (19.20ff.). Following this, secret *mantras* are revealed (19.26ff.).

Chapter 20

This chapter, with fifty verses, opens with the goddess requesting and Śiva revealing the one hundred names of Tārā. Following this the text engages in philosophical and metaphysical speculation on the process that brings forth the world. Here, the author places the feminine (*śakti*) as the first emanation to come out of the supreme being that is the impersonal "being-consciousness-bliss" (20.33).[27] Interestingly, this feminine being arises as with form (*sakala*). A progressive cosmology that draws from the Śrī Vidyā tradition ensues, including the use of terminology associated with this tradition, such as the *bindu*, which here is the form of time (20.34) and sound (*nāda*). The chapter continues this philosophic discourse, stressing a nonduality: that the one Self takes a variety of different births (20.42), and that this Self has no gender whatsoever, neither male, nor female, nor neuter (20.43).

The rest of the chapter continues with a praise of nature, the feminine *Prakṛti*, because it is by means of nature that one can discover the Self. At a point in this discussion, the text abruptly disjointedly shifts into the voice of nature speaking (20.47), instead of the god Śiva, suggesting that this section was incorporated from an earlier text where the feminine nature was the revealer of the doctrine. Interestingly, the text here also discounts the efficacy of all ritual acts. "Not by the application of ritual procedures, not by knowledge [plural here], not by the Vedas, nor by the lineage of gurus (*gurukrama*); Not by ritual baths, nor by *tarpaṇa*, nor by giving charity—none of these whatsoever. The self is only known by Prakṛti" (20.47f.). This latter section of the chapter is glossed as "the principle of the essence of everything" (20.50).

Chapter 21

The first twenty verses of this chapter focus on alchemical ritual procedures for turning various metals into gold. The second half of the forty verses talks about the three Tantric attitudes (divine attitude, hero attitude, and bound beast attitude), focusing really only on the attitude of the hero (despite the fact that the text explicitly considers the divine attitude [*divya*] the best [21.23]). The text asserts the necessity of *bhāva*, the attitude, and here it appears that the attitude translates into a habitual pattern of feeling or being, rather than a ritual course of action (21.24ff.). This chapter concludes with a brief discussion of the hero's worship that partially assimilates it to the special Kālī sādhana, where any time is fine for worship and *mantra* repetition (21.37ff.).

Chapter 22

This chapter with 172 verses gives the 1,000 names of Kālī. The style of the hymn is eloquent, with much alliteration. Following this the text gives the praise of the hymn with its results (*phalaśruti*). In the final portion the author explicitly asserts the unity of Mahākālī, Mahādevī, and Nīlasarasvatī (22.171).

Chapter 23

This chapter in twenty-eight verses gives the one hundred names of Kālī along with the fruits of its recitation.

Chapter 24

This chapter, with fifty-five verses, gives the one hundred names of the goddess Annapūrṇā, along with a long litany of the results of reciting them, one of which is that one's family for generations will not have to worry about getting food (24.31).

Notes

INTRODUCTION

I am grateful to the Wabash Center for a Lilly Grant, which allowed my research in Kāmākhyā over the summer of 2004.

1. "Īśvarakṛṣṇa," in *The Sāṃkhya Kārikā of Īśvarakṛṣṇa*, ed. with introduction by Radhanath Phukan (Calcutta: Firma K. L. Mukhopadhyay 1960), verses 59-66. See also Gerald Larson, *Classical Sāṃkhya: An Interpretation of Its History and Meaning* (Delhi: Motilal Banarsidass, 1969), 222, 278.

2. See Sree Dharanikanta Devsharma, *The Holy Shrine of Kamakhya*, 5th ed. (Guwahati: Ganesh Bhawan, 1999), passim, for the particular equation of the goddess at Kāmākhyā and Mahā-Māyā.

3. In one version, she beheads him.

4. The story of Kāmākhyā also addresses another issue, the problem of the male gaze, which will not be dealt with in this study, or rather, will be dealt with only indirectly. That is, we deal with this issue only insofar as the idea of the gaze, especially the male gaze, also encodes a notion of subjectivity and who has it.

5. This story was told to me by three separate informants during research in Kāmākhyā in the summer of 2004. A brief and slightly different version may also be found Devsharma, *The Holy Shrine of Kamakhya*, 45–47.

6. Cynthia Humes, in an insightful analysis of the role of the *Devī Māhātmya* in the lives of ordinary women, conjectures that the "issue of women's agency lies at the crux of female empowerment and feminism in Hinduism." See Cynthia Humes, "Is the *Devī Māhātmya* a Feminist Scripture?" in *Is the Goddess a Feminist?* ed. Alf Hiltebeitel and Kathleen Erndl, 147, (New York: New York University Press, 2000). A number of other

writers, Julia Leslie and also Rajeshwari Sunder Rajan, with some caveats, for example, concur. See Julia Leslie, ed., *Roles and Rituals for Hindu Women* (Cranbury, N.J.: Fairleigh Dickinson University Press, 1991), 9; Rajeshwari Sunder Rajan, *Real and Imagined Women: Gender, Culture and Postcolonialism* (London: Routledge, 1993). Whether women did enact a greater sense of agency much earlier in India's Vedic history, and to what degree and how this became attenuated, are important issues that have also only begun to be addressed, for example, in Frederick Smith, "Indra's Curse, Varuṇa's Noose and the Suppression of the Woman in the Vedic Śrauta Ritual," in *Roles and Rituals for Hindu Women*, ed. Julia Leslie (Cranbury, N.J.: Fairleigh Dickinson University Press, 1991); Werner Menski, "Marital Expectations as Dramatized in Hindu Marriage Rituals," in *Roles and Rituals for Hindu Women*, ed. Julia Leslie (Cranbury, N.J.: Fairleigh Dickinson University Press, 1991); and especially Stephanie Jamison, *Sacrificed Wife/Sacrificer's Wife: Women, Ritual and Hospitality in Ancient India* (New York: Oxford University Press, 1996).

7. *Manusmṛti*, ed. Taranath Vidyaratna with an introduction by Arthur Avalon (Sir John Woodroffe) (Madras: Ganesh and Company, 1965), 5, 147–148.

8. For my understanding of the idea of subjectivity and the distinctions between a subjectivity and agency I have found Sunder Rajan, *Real and Imagined Women*, 10–12. and passim, especially helpful. In general, for this study I leave aside the question of agency since this work deals solely with textual sources for which we have very little corroborative evidence in the form of archival or historical records, and hence the notion of women as agents and women in their own voices is not easily accessible from the textual vantage point here. It may be that we could recover this type of agency if we could read some of these texts, or portions of them as authored by women. And, given the caveat that authorship of these texts has not been determined, we cannot entirely rule out the possibility that some of these authors may have been women. However, this also cannot readily be proved and the texts appear to address men more than women. Consequently, I focus expressly on representations of subjectivity.

9. In Hegelian terms, in the Sāṃkhya story her dance is for-another, whereas in the Kāmākhyā story, the dance is for-herself.

10. See Susan Wadley, "Women and the Hindu Tradition," in *Women in India: Two Perspectives*, ed. Doranne Jacobson and Susan S. Wadley (Columbia, Mo.: South Asia, 1977), 118–119; Tracy Pintchman, *The Rise of the Goddess in the Hindu Tradition*, 203–206. (Albany: State University of New York Press, 1994); Wendy Doniger, *Women, Androgynes and Other Mythical Beasts* (Chicago: University of Chicago Press, 1980), 90–91.

11. For Tantra especially, one might imagine that powerful goddesses would translate into empowered women, and we find this suggestion at times, for instance, in Rita Sherma, "'Sā-Ham—I Am She': Woman as Goddess," in *Is the Goddess a Feminist?* ed. Alf Hiltebeitel and Kathleen Erndl, 187–202 (New York: New York University Press, 2000). Particularly anthropological sources suggest this translation between goddesses and women. Exemplary is Kathleen Erndl, "Is *Shakti* Empowering for Women? Reflections on Feminism and the Hindu Goddess," in *Is the Goddess a Feminist?* ed. Alf Hiltebeitel and Kathleen Erndl, 91–103. However, for contrasting

views see June McDaniel, *Offering Flowers, Feeding Skulls: Popular Goddess Worship in West Bengal* (New York: Oxford University Press, 2004); and, to some degree, Sarah Caldwell, *Oh Terrifying Mother* (New Delhi: Oxford University Press, 1999). See also Humes's interesting "Is the *Devī Māhātmya* a Feminist Scripture?"

12. To cite only a small selection of very interesting analyses on this phenomenon: Rachel Fell McDermott's "Kālī's New Frontiers: A Hindu Goddess on the Internet," in *Encountering Kālī*, ed. Rachel Fell McDermott and Jeffrey Kripal, 273–296 (Berkeley and Los Angeles: University of California Press, 2003); Rachel Fell McDermott, "Introducing Kālī Studies," in *Encountering Kālī*, 1–22; as well as McDermott's "The Western Kālī," in *Devī: Goddesses of India*, ed. John Stratton Hawley and Donna Wulff, 281–314 (Berkeley and Los Angeles: University of California Press, 1996). Also, Erndl's "Is *Shakti* Empowering?" 91–103; as well as Rita Gross's "Is the Goddess a Feminist?" 104–112; and Tracy Pintchman's thoughtful "Is the Hindu Goddess a Good Resource for Western Feminism?" all found in *Is the Goddess a Feminist?* Also see Lina Gupta's "Kali, the Savior," in *After Patriarchy: Feminist Transformation of the World Religions*, ed. Paula Cooey and William Eakin 124–42 (Maryknoll, N.Y.: Orbis, 1991). On a more personal level, Roxanne Gupta's "Kālī Māyī: Myth and Reality in a Benares Ghetto," in *Encountering Kālī at the Margins*, ed. Jeff Kripal and Rachel Fell-McDermott, 124–142 (Berkeley and Los Angeles: University of California Press, 2003); as well Caldwell's very moving personal encounter with the Keralite Kālī in *Oh Terrifying Mother*. This represents only a small fraction of the very interesting work being done in this area, without including topical literature that engages the broader arena, for instance, Wendy Doniger's interesting cross-cultural studies dealing with issues of gender, in *The Bedtrick: Tales of Sex and Masquerade* (Chicago: University of Chicago Press, 2000); and *Splitting the Difference: Gender and Myth in Ancient Greece and India* (Chicago: University of Chicago Press, 1999).

13. See Humes, "Is the *Devī Māhātmya* a Feminist Scripture?" For a more positive view of the translation into women's social empowerment see n. 11 above. Also see Narendra Nath Bhattacarya, *Indian Mother Goddess* (New Delhi: Manohar, 1977), and Narendra Nath Bhattacarya, *History of the Śākta Religion*, 2nd rev. ed. (New Delhi: Munshiram Manoharla, 1996). See also Miranda Shaw, *Passionate Enlightenment: Women in Tantric Buddhism* (Princeton, N.J.: Princeton University Press, 1994) for a rereading of the Tantric appraisal of women; and Elinor Gador's "Probing the Mysteries of the Hirapur Yoginis," *Revision* 25, no. 1 (Summer 2002): 33–41.

14. For a more textually oriented perspective, see David White, *The Kiss of the Yoginī: Tantric Sex in Its South Asian Contexts* (Chicago: University of Chicago Press, 2003); and Ronald Davidson, *Indian Esoteric Buddhism* (New York: Columbia University Press, 2002) for an idea of how women figure more typically and normatively in textual Tantric contexts. Hugh Urban, *Tantra: Sex, Secrecy, Politics and Power in the Study of Religion* (Berkeley and Los Angeles: University of California Press, 2003), also takes a similar view, although we should note that while White and Davidson work with Sanskrit texts, Urban here, rather, addresses Western presentations of Tantra. S. C. Banerji, *Brief History of Tantra Literature* (Calcutta: Naya Prokash, 1988), 501, concludes that "women were looked upon as objects of enjoyment, however, [*sic*]

much the Tantras may try to put a spiritual significance to such unions of males and females." Also again, see n. 13 above; Shaw, *Passionate Enlightenment*, 7ff., for her critique of what she sees as a bias in much current scholarship on Tantra.

15. From the side of Hindu studies, one sees the issue resurfacing in a number of places: in Erndl's thoughtful renditions of actual women who present with their lives models of an autonomous and socially influential guru; in Leslie Orr, *Donors, Devotees, and Daughters of God: Temple Women in Medieval Tamilnadu* (New York: Oxford University Press, 2000); in much of Wendy Doniger's work, especially in *Splitting the Difference: Gender and Myth in Ancient Greece and India* in Doniger, *Women, Androgynes and Other Mythical Beasts*; in Stephanie Jamison's comments on the role and place of women as subjects in Vedic life in *Sacrificed Wife*, 8; in Pintchman, *The Rise of the Goddess*, 178ff., especially; in Humes's research into contemporary responses to the goddess and her relationship to ordinary women in her "Is the *Devī Māhātmya* a Feminist Scripture?"; in Shaw's assiduous recovery of the subjectivity of the female Buddhist practitioner. Susie Tharu and K. Lalita, eds., *Women Writing in India*, vol. 1 (Delhi: Oxford University Press, 1991) attempts this same recovery from a different perspective. This list does not intend even remotely to be exhaustive but simply to point out the pervasiveness of the issue in its various guises.

16. The information available for studying this period includes records compiled by the British, by Muslims, the Assamese historical chronicles called *Buranjis*, and writings from the Assamese medieval Vaiṣṇava movement. I discuss the historical context in appendix 1.

17. Anne Feldhaus, *Water and Womanhood: Religious Meanings of Rivers in Maharashtra* (New York: Oxford University Press, 1995), 11f., 166.

18. That is, to posit that women may have authored some of these texts or sections of these texts. And while I laud the efforts of others to reclaim the voices of women through spotlighting women's writing, an approach successfully pursued by a number of authors—notably Tharu and Lalita, *Women Writing*; Shaw, *Passionate Enlightenment*; as well as the careful work with inscriptions pursued by Orr, *Donors, Devotees and Daughters of God*—to mention a few, it would be, as I note, difficult to prove female authorship for these texts.

19. For instance, in authors like Abhinavagupta and Kṣemarāja, two well-known Tantric thinkers from the eleventh century.

20. See Alf Hiltebeitel, "Draupadī's Question," in *Is the Goddess a Feminist?* 116ff., for an engaging discussion of the gendered implications of matter and spirit.

21. I should also note here that most of my texts do not exclude the wife as a partner, but offer the option of either one's wife or another woman. I discuss this in greater detail in chapter 3.

22. See Raia Prokhovnic, *Rational Woman: A Feminist Critique of Dichotomy* (New York, London: Routledge, 1999). Along these lines also see the recent research in biology and genetics of Anne Fausto-Sterling, "The five sexes," *The Sciences*, (March/April 1993): 65–69, where she suggests a model of five sexes as biologically more apt.

Her model has nothing to do with caste, but the rescripting of how we think of categories is salient.

23. See n. 13 in this introduction.

24. It was pointed out to me that Madhu Khanna also has documented this shift in a number of Tantric texts. See her fine piece, "The Goddess–Woman Equation in Śākta Tantras" in *Gendering the Spirit: Women, Religion and the Post-colonial Response,* ed. Durre S. Ahmed, 35–59 (London: Zed, 2002).

25. *Sarvavijayi Tantra* (verses 95–103), in the *Tantrasaṅgraha,* edited by Vrajvallabha Dvivedi, Yogatantragranthamālā Series 8, part 5 (Varanasi: Sampurnand Sanskrit University, 1996).

26. One finds this also in Miranda Shaw's *Passionate Enlightenment,* 39. Rita Gross, *Feminism and Religion: An Introduction* (Boston: Beacon, 1996), 192, also notes this in Tibetan Buddhism, where one of the vows of Vajrayana Buddhism is to not disparage women.

27. See Alexis Sanderson, "Śaivism and the Tantric Tradition," in *The World's Religions,* ed. Stewart Sutherland et al., 660–705 (London: Routledge, 1988).

28. In this sense she is not "heroic," nor with masculine qualities like the goddess in the *Devī Māhātmya* that Humes, "Is the *Devī Māhātmya* a Feminist Scripture?" 133, describes.

29. In the list of texts used that I give below, the *Sarvavijayi Tantra* ("*Complete Hashish Tantra*") diverges somewhat from the other texts in that it focuses extensively upon the ritual manipulation of substances, herbs especially, to effect its results.

30. The *ṣaṭkarmāṇi,* a term referring to the sixfold division of goals in Tantric praxis, including those in most lists (there is some variation); *śānti,* rites of pacification; *vaśīkaraṇa,* rites that mentally subjugate another; *māraṇa,* rites that kill another; *stambhana,* rites that paralyze another; *uccāṭana,* rites that drive another person away; and *puṣṭi,* rites that nourish; or, alternatively, *vidveṣa,* rites that cause enmity.

31. Teun Goudriaan and Sanjukta Gupta, *History of Indian Literature, Vol 2: Hindu Tantric and Śākta Literature* (Wiesbaden: Harrassowitz, 1981); Gopinath Kaviraj, *Tāntrika Sāhitya* (Benares: Bhargava Bhushan, 1972).

32. For information on attitudes toward women in Vedic Sanskrit texts, see, for example, especially Stephanie Jamison, *Ravenous Hyena and the Wounded Sun* (Ithaca, N.Y.: Cornell University Press, 1991); Jamison, *Sacrificed Wife*; and also Laurie Patton, "Mantras and Miscarriage: Controlling Birth in the Late Vedic Period," in *Jewels of Authority,* ed. Laurie Patton, 51–66 (New York: Oxford University Press, 2002); Smith, *Indra's Curse*; and Menski, "Marital Expectations." This list does not attempt to be exhaustive.

33. (BT) *Bṛhannīla Tantra,* edited by Madhusudhana Kaul (Delhi: Butala and Co., 1984). There is also a version of the Nīla Tantra mentioned by Goudriaan and Gupta in *Tantrasāra,* ed. Rasik Mohan Chattopadhyaya (Calcutta: 1877–1884), in Goudriaan and Gupta, *History of Indian Literature,* 88. I discuss in appendix 1 the similarities and differences between the BT and the Nīla Tantra version published

by Kalyana Mandir under the title, *Nīla Tantra*. Edited by Bhadrasheel Sharma. Guptāvatāra Durlabha Tantramālā Series, varṣa 2, maṇi 6 (Prayag: Kalyana Mandir, 2022 samvat [1965 or 1966]).

34. The *Cīnācāra Tantra* (CT), *Gupta Sādhana Tantra* (GST), *Māyā Tantra* (MT), and *Sarvavijayi Tantra* (SVT), a text that I reference at one point, are all located in *Tantrasaṅgraha*, ed. Vrajvallabha Dvivedi. Yogatantragranthamālā Series, vol. 8, part 5 (Varanasi: Sampurnand Sanskrit University, 1996); the Gandharva Tantra (GT) is located in *Tantrasaṅgraha*, ed. Rāmprasāda Tripāṭhī. Yogatantragranthamālā Series, vol. 5, part 3 (Varanasi: Sampurnand Sanskrit University, 1992); *Nīlasarasvatī Tantram*, edited by Brahmananda Tripathi, Hindi commentary by S. N. Khandelwal (Varanasi: Chaukhamba Surbharati Prakashan, 1999); *Phetkāriṇī Tantra* (PhT) is located in *Tantrasaṅgraha*, 3rd ed., ed. M. M. Gopinath Kaviraj, in Yogatantragranthamālā Series, vol. 4, part 2 (Varanasi: Sampurnand Sanskrit University, 2002); *Yoni Tantra*, ed. with an introduction by J. A. Schoterman (Delhi: Manohar, 1980). Again, this list does not attempt to be exhaustive. Given the very large number of Tantric texts that have not yet been examined, in all likelihood other texts from this region probably exist that also exhibit the patterns I point out here. Other Tantras that were not available in published versions, such as the *Vīratantra*, may also follow the pattern presented here. My point is merely to establish that a sufficient number of texts share these features, suggesting a particular historical pattern.

35. As Jan Schoterman points out, the *Yoni Tantra*, 6, poses a curious exception.

36. That is, BT 15.68, and also for Kāmākhyā, BT 5.69ff.; 7.197; 14.1ff. This is a possible reference, but not one that may be proved with no uncertainty. There is also a tradition of Nīlā in Kashmir, which looks not to be related to the Nīlasarasvatī of the BT, although it cannot be entirely ruled out.

37. Nearly all of these texts, however, date much later, to probably not earlier than the fifteenth century at the earliest, suggesting a late date for this signature verse. The *Gandharva Tantra* and *Phetkāriṇī Tantra* are both cited in Brahmānanda Giri's sixteenth-century *Śāktānandataraṅgiṇī* (in Goudriaan and Gupta, *History of Indian Literature*, 145), suggesting an earlier date for these two texts, especially for the *Gandharva Tantra*, which Brahmānanda Giri cites extensively. Although we also must not rule out the possibility that this particular verse in any case could be a later addition. The verse is discussed in chapter 1.

38. The *Cīnācāra Tantra* presents an exception. In addition to Marion Meisig's German translation of the *Mahācīnācāra Tantra, Die "China-Lehre" des Śaktimus: Mahācīnācāra Tantra* (Wiesbaden: Harrassowitz, 1988), I heard of a popular nonscholarly English translation of the *Cīnācāra Tantra*, but was not able to track it down.

39. See Vrajvallabha Dvivedi's Sanskrit introduction to the fifth part of the *Tantra Saṅgrahaḥ*, Edited by Vrajvallabha Dvivedi. Yogatantragranthamālā Series 8, part 5, (Varanasi: Sampurnanand Sanskrit University, 1996) that contains a number of the texts consulted here and where he cites the popularity (*lokapriyatā*) of the related Tantric texts already published earlier in this series (1996:1).

40. David White, *The Kiss of the Yoginī*, passim.

41. As I note in appendix 2, this is perhaps useful in dating these texts and indicates a feature of northeastern Indian Śāktism, which Schoterman pointed out for the YT—its curious link with Vaiṣṇavism rather than Śaivism.

42. For instance, see the GT, fortieth chapter.

43. We find this for instance in the twelfth chapter of the MT where the frame narrator/teacher is designated as the goddess, who nevertheless appears to either be instructing a woman, or, more likely, to be the god instructing the goddess.

44. Elsewhere, Gudrun Buhnemann, *The Iconography of Hindu Tantric Deities.* 2 vols. (Groningen: Egbert Forsten, 2000), 1:102, notes the equation of these two goddesses. The Blue Goddess of Speech is pictured with blue eyes at BT 2.138.

45. Madhu Khanna also documents this shift in attitudes toward women in her piece, "Goddess," 35–59.

46. Gloria Goodwin Raheja and Ann Grodzins Gold, *Listen to the Heron's Words: Reimagining Gender and Kinship in North India* (Berkeley and Los Angeles: University of California Press, 1994), 14.

47. In Wendy Doniger, *Implied Spider: Politics and Theology in Myth* (New York: Columbia University Press, 1998), 112–115.

48. Doranne Jacobson and Susan S. Wadley, eds. *Women in India: Two Perspectives,* 8.

49. For instance in BT 7.182ff., the author(s) explicitly suggests an inner ritual involving the *kuṇḍalinī* and the use of the breath.

50. In this respect I agree with and follow David White's illuminating literal reading of much of the ritual in his *The Kiss of the Yoginī.*

51. Miranda Shaw, *Passionate Enlightenment,* 12–13.

52. Doniger, *Implied Spider,* 110. Her argument on this topic extends from 109–25.

53. Gloria Goodwin Raheja and Ann Grodzins Gold, *Listen to the Heron's Words,* 21.

54. Ibid., 22.

55. Jamison's *Sacrificed Wife* is noteworthy. See especially 10–12 for her comments on the importance of attention to texts.

56. Kathleen M. Erndl, *Victory to the Mother: The Hindu Goddesses of Northwest India in Myth, Ritual and Symbol* (New York: Oxford University Press, 1993); Raheja and Gold, *Listen to the Heron's Words.* Also see McDaniel, *Offering Flowers, Feeding Skulls*; Caldwell, *Oh Terrifying Mother*; Tharu and Lalita, *Women Writing*; Leslie Orr, *Donors, Devotees, and Daughters of God*; Feldhaus, *Water and Womanhood*; Madhu Khanna, "Parallel Worlds of Madhobi Ma, 'Nectar Mother': My Encounter with a Twentieth-Century Tantric Saint" in *Gendering the Spirit: Women, Religion and the Post-colonial Response,* ed. Durre Ahmed, 136–154 (London: Zed, 2002); Joyce Flueckiger, *Gender and Genre in the Folklore of Middle India* (Ithaca, N.Y.: Cornell University Press, 1996). This list is by no means exhaustive.

57. While I do not address Gayatri Spivak's work here, nor follow her model for scholarship in this book, this project, in its exploration of the issues of "talk" about women may be seen as an expanded reflection upon the question she poses in

"Can the Subaltern Speak?" in *Marxism and the Interpretation of Culture*, ed. Cary Nelson and Lawrence Grossberg (Urbana: University of Illinois Press, 1988).

58. Rajeshwari Sundar Rajan, *Real and Imagined Women*, 10.

59. Judith Butler, *Excitable Speech: A Politics of the Performative* (New York: Routledge, 1997), 80.

60. Ibid., 28.

61. *Yoni Tantra*, 11f.

CHAPTER 1

1. *Yoni Tantra* 5.23. "svayam vā pūjayed yonim athavā sādhakena ca |.

2. The word *yoni* here may refer to the woman or it may refer to the female sex organ. In this case, the reply appears to suggest that it refers to the sex organ, since the symmetry of males worshiping female sex organs and females worshiping male sex organs is thereby established. That the word for female sex organ at times also just refers to the woman as a being suggests that woman's identity is intricately intertwined with, and constructed upon, the notion of her sex organ.

3. *Yoni Tantra* 5.23, "svayam vā pūjayed yonim athavā sādhakena ca |; 5.24a–b, sādhakena pūjitavyā yonirūpā jaganmayī | tayā liṅgaṃ ca; 5.25b, tayoḥ pūjānamātreṇa jīvan mukto.

4. The god replies with a heterosexual arrangement where men worship women and women worship men. Recently, Roxanne Gupta (at the Society for Tantric Studies Conference, Flagstaff 2002) presented her contemporary anthropological research based on a south Indian Śrī Vidyā practitioner who apparently also includes as a Tantric praxis women worshiping women.

5. I discuss in greater detail the views of these and other texts on women in appendix 1.

6. This is what one finds in writers like Abhinavagupta. Contemporary scholarship such as the fine work of Paul Muller-Ortega and Alexis Sanderson reflects this attitude of the primary sources in their discussions.

7. David White's argument in *The Kiss of the Yoginī* (Chicago: University of Chicago Press, 2003) for the position that women especially were the suppliers of fluids is convincing. One sees the focus on women as an inner principle in work such as that of Paul Muller-Ortega, *Triadic Heart of Śiva* (Albany: State University of New York Press, 1989), which focuses on esoteric, inner forms of worship. Miranda Shaw, in particular, sees the representation of women as being excluded from Tantric practice as symptomatic of male scholarship and her own scholarship works to refute the relegation of women to the sidelines of Tibetan Buddhist Tantric practice, while other scholars, such as Ronald Davidson, suggest that women did not play substantial roles in early medieval Buddhist Tantra. See Davidson, *Indian Esoteric Buddhism* (New York: Columbia University Press, 2002), 92ff., especially 97, in response to Shaw, *Passionate Enlightenment: Women in Tantric Buddhism* (Princeton, N.J.: Princeton University Press, 1994), 7 and passim, which stresses a blind spot in modern and contemporary Western scholarship on Tantra with regard to recognizing

women's roles in classical Tantra. Davidson draws upon texts that date several centuries earlier than the Hindu Sanskrit sources from the fifteenth through eighteenth centuries I use here. The other side of the coin is that often (particularly in the context of studies of Sanskrit Tantric texts of "right-handed" Tantra), in a number of excellent studies, the question does not arise, and is not addressed. Compare Alexis Sanderson, "Meaning in Tantric Ritual," in *Essais sur le Rituel* 3, ed. Anne-Marie Blondeau and Kristofer Schipper (Louvain-Paris: Peeters, 1992), 15–95; Alexis Sanderson, "Śaivism and the Tantric Tradition," in *The World's Religions*, ed. Stewart Sutherland et al. (London: Routledge, 1988); Teun Goudriaan, ed., *Ritual and Speculation in Early Tantrism: Studies in Honor of Andre Padoux* (Albany: State University of New York Press, 1992); Andre Padoux, *Vāc: The Concept of the Word in Selected Hindu Tantras*, trans. Jacques Gontier (Albany: State University of New York Press, 1989), as a by no means exhaustive list. Apart from the presence of women as actors in Sanskrit texts, in the larger Hindu and Śākta context a variety of positions has emerged, some suggesting greater agency (especially Kathleen Erndl, *Victory to the Mother: The Hindu Goddesses of Northwest India in Myth, Ritual and Symbol* (New York: Oxford University Press, 1993), and others suggesting less agency for women. For more information on this, see Erndl, *Victory to the Mother*; Tracy Pintchman, *The Rise of the Goddess in the Hindu Tradition* (Albany: State University of New York Press, 1994); Cynthia Humes, "Is the *Devī Māhātmya* a Feminist Scripture?" in *Is the Goddess a Feminist?* ed. Alf Hiltebeitel and Kathleen Erndl (New York: New York University Press, 2000); Stephanie Jamison, *Sacrificed Wife/Sacrificer's Wife: Women, Ritual and Hospitality in Ancient India* (New York: Oxford University Press, 1996); Leslie Orr, *Donors, Devotees, and Daughters of God: Temple Women in Medieval Tamilnadu* (New York: Oxford University Press, 2000); Rita Sherma, "Hinduism," in *Sex and Religion*, ed. Christel Manning and Phil Zucherman, 18–40 (Belmont, Calif.: Wadsworth, 2005); Sarah Caldwell, *Oh Terrifying Mother* (New Delhi: Oxford University Press, 1999); Julia Leslie, ed., *Roles and Rituals for Hindu Women* (Cranbury, N.J.: Fairleigh Dickinson University Press, 1991); June McDaniel, *Making Virtuous Daughters and Wives: An Introduction to Women's Brata Rituals in Bengali Folk Religion* (New York: State University of New York Press, 2002); and especially Erndl for ethnographic instances that controvert textual findings excluding women as active participants. This list is by no means exhaustive.

8. YT 5.25. See n. 2 above for the relevant Sanskrit text. The text does not explicitly state either that both will attain enlightenment or that only one gender or the other attains it. It does, however, imply that both of them will attain it by worshiping the opposite sex.

9. Edwin Dimock, *Place of the Hidden Moon* (Chicago: University of Chicago Press, 1989), 215–216, suggests the same. In this case, following Moriz Winternitz (in Dimock), he goes even further, citing in particular Lakṣmīmkarā as an authoress of a Tantric text. Winternitz concludes that "indeed it is no rare thing to find women among the writers of Tantric works" (216). Neither Winternitz nor Dimock pursue this inquiry and my own research on the texts consulted here does not supply conclusive evidence supporting Winternitz's claim. One more suggestion along these

lines may be found in S. C. Banerji, *Brief History of Tantra Literature* (Calcutta: Naya Prokash, 1988), 316, where he says that a woman named Prāṇamañjarī, the wife of Premanidhi Pāntha wrote a commentary on the Tantrarāja Tantra. However, I was not able to corroborate this claim.

10. As, for instance, as Goudriaan translates it in Teun Goudriaan and Sanjukta Gupta, *History of Indian Literature,* vol. 2, *Hindu Tantric and Śākta Literature* (Wiesbaden: Harrassowitz, 1981), 153.

11. On an interesting side note, V. V. Dvivedi in his 1978 Sanskrit introduction to the *Śaktisaṅgama Tantra* notes that the description of the "Chinese Way" approximates Muslim practice. He tells us, in Sanskrit, "Here the description of the Chinese bath and bowing resembles the action of namaz [daily practice], following along with the Muslim religion." I give here also Dvivedi's original Sanskrit for this quote: "ityatra varṇitau cīnasnānanamaskārau islāmadharmānuyāyināṃ vaju-namaj-karmaṇī anuharataḥ" in *Śaktisaṅgama Tantra,* vol. 4, Chinnamastākhaṇḍa, ed. B. Bhattacharyya and V. V. Dvivedi (Baroda: Oriental Institute, 1978), 42.

12. In chapter 3, I describe the rite of sexual union in detail.

13. White's brilliant, detailed analysis is probably one of the best representations of this view, but his is not isolated. Agehananda Bharati, *The Tantric Tradition* (London: Ryderand Co., 1965; reprint, New York: Grove, 1975), 304ff., also presents this picture as does Davidson's recent study of Buddhist Tantra (Davidson, *Indian Esoteric Buddhism,* 92ff., especially 97). For the attainment of magic powers, especially the power of flight, see White, *The Kiss of the Yoginī,* 196ff. White, in particular, admirably pays attention to historical shifts and nuances in the use of Tantric sex, contrasting, for instance, the view of the *Kulārṇava Tantra* and other Kaula texts with Abhinavagupta's school; although his examination of texts does not include the group of texts I examine here. So, while in a number of cases, the *Kaulajñānanirṇaya,* for instance, even in the *Kulacūḍāmaṇi Tantra,* from which the BT borrows considerably, I would concur with this assessment of women's role in Tantra, the point here is that we should not understand this as always being the case. Even keeping this in mind, a greater diversity within and between texts needs to be noted. So, for instance, the BT tends on the whole to neglect the use of fluids as a practice, something that White notes as key, whereas, on the other hand, it does figure in the CT and the YT, two other texts used for this study. The CT and the YT also present more of a mixture of what we find in the "Kālī Practice" along with what we find in earlier Tantric texts that White notes, this in contrast to the BT. On an anthropological front, see, for instance, Cynthia Humes's excellent study involving field research at a popular goddess site in Uttar Pradesh, near Benares. Her research focuses on the contemporary understandings of the sixth-century *Devī Māhātmya* and she comes to a similar conclusion, that women are not empowered by the goddess in this popular Śākta (though not necessarily Tantric) text, in her interviews of contemporary worshipers of the goddess at the goddess's shrine in Vindhyacal (Humes, "Is the *Devī Māhātmya* a Feminist Scripture?").

14. And in the case of some anthropological research, contemporary views, i.e., Humes's ("Is the *Devī Māhātmya* a Feminist Scripture?") conclusions, as well as to some degree Caldwell's (*Oh Terrifying Mother*) conclusions.

15. McDermott, "*The Western Kālī*," in *Devī: Goddesses of* India, ed. John Stratton Hawley and Donna Wulff (Berkeley and Los Angeles: University of California Press), 291.

16. McDermott, "Kālī's New Frontiers: A Hindu Goddess on the Internet," in *Encountering Kālī*, ed. Rachel Fell McDermott and Jeffrey Kripal (Berkeley and Los Angeles: University of California Press, 2003), 276ff.

17. Khanna, "The Goddess—Woman Equation in Śākta Tantras," in *Gendering the Spirit: Women, Religion and the Post-colonial Response*, ed. Durre Ahmed (London: Zed, 2002), 35–59.

18. Dimock, *Place of the Hidden Moon*, 215–216.

19. I especially appreciate Miranda Shaw's reconfiguration in precisely this direction. And while I think it would be premature to rule out the possibility that some of these texts may have had female authors, following Dimock or Winternitz (see n. 9 above), given the historical and archival limitations of this project, I do not have sufficient evidence to substantiate this claim.

20. In her generally thoughtful study of women in Tantric Buddhism, Shaw (*Passionate Enlightenment*, 10) suggests that it is a mistake to read a gendered binary along Cartesian lines of a mind/body dualism into Tantric texts. However, in the Tantric texts encountered here, as well as elsewhere (and elsewhere in classical Indian texts), the legacy of Sāṃkhya with a gendered dualism where the feminine is matter and the male is spirit pervades. This model of spirit/body is quite similar to the Cartesian mind-body split. We do at points in the "transgressive" Tantric texts I consult here encounter a conscious opposition to this model, but this is clearly an exception—not only for classical sources, but even for most Tantric texts.

21. Anjali Bagwe, *Of Woman Caste: The Experience of Gender in Rural India* (London: Zed, 1995), vi.

22. See Smith, "Indra's Curse, Varuṇa's Noose and the Suppression of the Woman in the Vedic Śrauta Ritual," in *Roles and Rituals for Hindu Women*, ed. Julia Leslie (Cranbury, N.J.: Fairleigh Dickinson University Press, 1991), 18; and Jamison, *Sacrificed Wife/Sacrificer's Wife*, 261n21. Also we find this in GST 11.13.

23. Luce Irigaray is probably one of the best examples of the articulation of this model, especially her *This Sex Which Is Not One*, trans. Catherine Porter (Ithaca, N.Y.: Cornell University Press, 1985), though its proponents are numerous.

24. See, for instance, Raia Prokhovnic, *Rational Woman: A Feminist Critique of Dichotomy* (New York: Routledge, 1999).

25. Lacan suggests this dynamic of male identity established upon an exclusion of the female particularly in linguistic terms, with his exclusion of woman from the order of the "symbolic." This is a theme that surfaces again in a number of contemporary thinkers, with some interesting permutations especially in a thinker like Judith Butler. See her *Psychic Life of Power: Theories in Subjection* (Stanford, Calif.: Stanford University Press, 1997).

26. BT 12.13–12.16: namastubhyaṃ maheśāni paramānandarūpiṇi | asmākaṃ prāṇarakṣārthamāgatāsi jalopari || namastubhyaṃ namastubhyaṃ namastubhyaṃ namo namaḥ | namaste >stu mahāraudri kālarātri namo >stu te || tvāṃ vinā parame

raudri pretatvaṃ gatavān bhavaḥ | rakṣa rakṣa pare vidye trailokyabhuvanodare || madhukaiṭabhasaṃhantri nisumbhāsuramardini | devaiṣvaryaprade devi namaste śaṅkarapriye ||.

27. BT 12.20: kena rūpeṇa deveśi sṛṣṭisthityādikaṃ bhavet |.

28. BT 12.21: mama pādarajo nītvā upādānātmakaṃ śivaṃ ||. Literally, "having followed the dust of my feet."

29. Doniger, *Women, Androgynes and Other Mythical Beasts* (Chicago: University of Chicago Press, 1980), 90f.

30. GST 6.6: etatprakāraṃ deveśa yadi me na prakāśitam | prāṇatyāgaṃ kariṣyāmi purataste na saṃśayaḥ |. Literally, this last portion is "there is no doubt."

31. She threatens again in the next chapter, GST 7.6, to commit suicide unless he reveals to her the principle that is supremely difficult to obtain (tattvaṃ paramadurlabham, GST 7.2).

32. GST 5.16b: sarvaṃ tyaktvā maheśāni strīsaṅgaṃ yatnataścaret ||.

33. GST 5.13b: sa śivo >ham mahādevi kevalaṃ śaktiyogataḥ ||. Also YT 1.8.

34. YT 4.6–8: rādhāyoniṃ pūjayitvā kṛṣṇaḥ kṛṣṇatvam āgataḥ || śrīrāmo jānakīnāthaḥ sītāyoniprapūjakaḥ | rāvaṇaṃ sakulam hatvā punar āgatya sundari || ayodhyānagarīṃ ramyāṃ vasatim kṛtavān svayam |.

35. BT 7.111b: strīdveṣo naiva kartavyo viśeṣāt pūjayet striyaḥ. Also for the worship of women see BT 6.5; YT 7.14–15; PhT 11.17; GT 35.54–57; CT 2.31; NST 16.9; MT 11.15ff.; GST 4.4. One of the variations we can note where the BT makes a subtle shift in the text that shifts the attitudes toward women can be seen in this line that is found slightly modified in the YT and in the clearly much earlier PhT where the verse reads, "One should not at all have hatred towards women, especially not the woman one is worshipping" strīdveṣo naiva kartavyo viśeṣāt pūjanaṃ striyāḥ.

36. BT 7.110b: strīnindāṃ ca na kurvīta tāsāṃ prema vivarddhayet |.

37. I discuss the rite of sexual union at much greater length in chapter 2.

38. BT 6.74–75; NT p. 28, line 14; also BT 6.300; NST11.120–21; CT 2.23–24; the same idea with a different expression in MT 11.35–38. Literally, the second line says "hitting them, criticizing them, dishonesty and that which is disagreeable to them—in every way these are not to be done"; bālāṃ vā yauvanonmattāṃ vṛddhāṃ vā kulasundarīm || kutsitāṃ vā mahāduṣṭāṃ namaskṛtya vibhāvayet | tāsāṃ prahāro nindā vā kauṭilyamapriyaṃ tathā || sarvathā ca na kartavyam. See note 41 for the Sanskrit preceding this quote. The translation there follows this Sanskrit.

39. What is also interesting about these lines is the way that they echo, even perhaps mockingly, the well-known verse in Manu's Law book. Compare the line given in the footnote above, beginning with "bālām . . ." with Manu's line 5.147: "bālyā vā yuvatyā vā vṛddhayā vāpi yoṣitā . . ." and we notice that the same nouns are used in the verse above. In the recitation of this verse, it likely called to mind, and reversed, Manu's line.

40. BT 6.75: striyo devāḥ striyaḥ prāṇāḥ.

41. NST 11.116–22 is nearly identical to these verses in the BT. BT 6.69–72: prātarutthāya mantrajñaḥ kulavṛkṣaṃ praṇamya ca | śiraḥpadme guruṃ dhyātvā tatsudhāplāvitaṃ smaret || mānasairupacāraistu tamārādhya nirāmayaḥ |

mūlādibrahmarandhrāntaṃ mūlavidyāṃ vibhāvayet || sūryakoṭipratīkāśāṃ sudhāplāvitavigrahām | tatprabhāpaṭalavyāptaṃ svaśarīraṃ vicintayet || śleṣmātaka karañjākṣa nimbāśvattha kadambakāḥ | bilvo vāpyathavā >śoka ityaṣṭau kulapādapāḥ ||.

42. BT 6.301–2; paśuśaktiḥ pakṣiśaktir naraśaktiśca śobhane | viguṇaṃ pūjitā karma saguṇaṃ jāyate sadā ||. Also see BT 6.57.

43. Loriliai Biernacki, field research notes, Summer 2004. Note also an extensive discussion regarding the worship of a young girl, which does not involve the rite of sexual union, also in the *Rudrayāmala*, beginning from the seventh Paṭala, p. 89, especially 7.36ff., p. 92.

44. This more common practice of worshiping a young girl takes us afield from the discussion of the "Kālī Practice," and, due to space constraints, will not be discussed here except to note that, just as in the "Kālī Practice," the young girl is also viewed as a goddess, and is especially given a *dakṣinā*, a gift of money, which, for the BT (7.280ff.) and the NST (15.27ff.), is quite substantial.

45. We find also that a more sexually, and we might say socially, conservative text like the *Yoginī Tantra* (YgT), also associated with the northeast region in the late medieval period, focuses extensively on this rite, the worship of the young girl. However, we should note that the sexual conservatism of the YgT is not like the conservatism of the Mahānirvāṇa Tantra (MNT) in that it's clear that the author of the MNT was greatly influenced by British opinions, whereas this is not in evidence in the YgT. Also the MNT still advocates the rite of sexual union, but not in a way that is especially empowering for women. In this context, the *Tārābhaktisudhārṇava*, a late text from northeast India, which focuses on devotion to Tārā, also like the YgT, tends toward a conservative exclusion of the rite of sexual union.

46. GT 35.54–56: cintanaṃ yoṣitā sārddhaṃ pūjanaṃ ca tathaiva hi | tayā virahito mantrī na sidhyati kadācana | bhāvayed yoṣitā sārddhaṃ juhuyācca tayaiva hi || tayā virahito mantrī na sidhyati kadācana | striyo devāḥ striyaḥ prāṇāḥ.

47. GST 5.11b: śaktiyuktaṃ japenmantraṃ na mantraṃ kevalaṃ japet |.

48. I describe the rite in detail in chapter 2, so I will not go into it here, except to mention that, as we find in the MT's version here, 11.12–16, which is here named as "latā sādhana," a recurring feature in different texts' representations of the element of sexual union involves reciting *mantras* on the various parts of the woman's body, either a hundred or three hundred times. In chapter 2 I mention this in the sequence of the elements of the rite.

49. MT 11.17: athānyat sādhanaṃ vakṣye sāvadhānā >vadhāraya | parakīyalatācakre sampūjya sveṣṭadevatām ||.

50. See Abbe Dubois, *Hindu Manners, Customs and Ceremonies* (Oxford: Clarendon, 1906; reprint, New Delhi: Asian Educational Services, 1986), 286ff.; and for our own century, Bharati, *The Tantric Tradition*. For the verse in the MT see note 49.

51. KuT 8.71b: dhṛtvāśirasi nṛtyanti madyabhāṇḍāni yoginaḥ.

52. KuT 8.73–74: yogino madamattāśca patanti pramadorasi | madākulāśca yoginyaḥ patanti puruṣopari || manorathasukhaṃ pūrṇaṃ kurvanti ca parasparam |.

53. The guru may optionally be present, and it appears was probably a necessary presence when the couple first began performing the rite. See YT 1.19.

54. I discuss this durable reverence in detail in chapter 2, which addresses the rite of sexual union.

55. CT 3.16; again at YT 1.16. The Sanskrit for CT 3.16 is *tatra cāvāhanaṃ nāsti.* The line in the YT is identical (shifting slightly in the next portion of the verse). The emphatic use of the verb ✓*as* in these cases emphasizes that this runs counter to a more usual practice of possession. Hence my italics for *not* is actually marked in the text, as the use of the verb ✓*as* is reserved mostly for when one wishes to add emphasis.

56. See, for instance, Kathleen Erndl, *Victory to the Mother: The Hindu Goddesses of Northwest India in Myth, Ritual and Symbol*; or Mary Hancock, "The Dilemmas of Domesticity: Possession and Devotional Experience among Urban Smarta Women," in *From the Margins of Hindu Marriage*, ed. Lindsey Harlan and Paul Courtright, 60–87 (New York: Oxford University Press, 1995).

57. Minus, of course, what the priest takes as his or her share. (I say "her" because I noticed on a recent trip to the Annapūrṇā temple in Benares that one young girl also served as a priest to the goddess.)

58. MT 11.34: vṛthā nyāso vṛthā pūjā vṛthā japo vṛthā stutiḥ | vṛthā sadakṣiṇo homo yadyapriyakaraḥ striyāḥ.

59. CT 2.24: tāsāṃ prahāranindāñca kauṭilyamapriyantathā || sarvathā naiva kartavyam |; CT 2.24; NST 11.121; NT p. 28, line14; BT 8.91 as well as 6.74; GT 35.8; PhT 11.17 for no hatred toward women; and GST 5.17–20 cautioning the practitioner to worship and feed women, and if one out of anger or delusion neglects to worship women, the practice is useless.

60. GT 35.8a: kadācid darparūpeṇa puṣpeṇāpi na tāḍayet |; NST 16.7: śatāparādhasaṃyuktāṃ puṣpeṇāpi na tāḍayet. As I discuss in appendix 1, this line in the NST, though not that in the GT, is lifted from KuT 11.65.

61. BT 6.300b: strīṇāṃ mano na hantavyaṃ |. The line here continues "especially not the women who are his." See also *Tantrarājatantra*, ed. Mahāmahopādhyāya Lakshmana Shastri, introduction by Arthur Avalon (Delhi: Motilal Banarsidass, 1997; originally published in 1926), an earlier text with a seventeenth-century Kashmiri commentator, Subhagānandanātha, which also states that the practitioner should not get angry at women: 5.80b, strīṣu roṣaṃ prahāraṃ ca.

62. BT 7.111: atyutkaṭāparādhe >pi na tasyādveṣamācaret | strīdveṣo naiva kartavyo viśeṣāt pūjayet striyaḥ ||. Also, NST 16.7: śatāparādhasaṃyuktāṃ puṣpeṇāpi na tāḍayet.

63. NST 16.11b–16.12a: kruddhāyāṃ yoṣiti kruddhaḥ sadāhaṃ kulanāyakaḥ || duḥkhitāyāṃ sadā devī duḥkhitā śāpadāyinī |.

64. MT 11.33: durgāmantraratā puṃso yoṣid bhūtivivarddhinī | sā ced bhavati saṃkruddhā dhanamāyuśca nāśayet ||.

65. *Cilappatikaram.* See Lakshmi Holmstrom, *Kannagi: A Modern Version of Silappadikaram* (Bombay: Sangam, 1980). Thanks to Ginni Ishimatsu for supplying this reference.

66. See especially Lindsey Harlan's interesting discussion of the cursing power of the *satī*, in "Satī: The Story of Godāvarī," in *Devī: Goddesses of India*, ed. John S. Hawley, 227–49 (Berkeley and Los Angeles: University of California Press, 1996).

67. BT 7.188–89: niyamaḥ puruṣairjñeyo na yoṣitsu kadācana || yadvā tadvā yena tena sarvataḥ sarvato > pi ca | yoṣitāṃ dhyānamātreṇa siddhayaḥ syur na saṃśayaḥ ||. BT 7.198: yoṣiccintanamātreṇa tathaiva varadāyinī | tasmāt sarvaprayatnena dīkṣayed nija kaulikīm |. Here "siddhi" is plural, but for the sake of syntax I translate it as singular, "magical attainment." Also, an alternative reading in the text is "dvija" instead "nija," meaning he should initiate the twice-born woman.

68. GT 36.5b–6a: na snānaṃ na tathā pūjā na dhyānaṃ nyāsameva vā || mantrasmaraṇamātreṇa yoṣitāṃ varadāyinī |.

69. *Chāndogya Upaniṣad* 4.4.3ff. in Patrick Olivelle, *Early Upanishads: Annotated Text and Translation* (New York: Oxford University Press, 1998).

70. In chapter 4, on women and *mantra*, I discuss in greater detail the affinity of women with *mantras*.

71. Kathleen Erndl, "Is Shakti Empowering for Women? Reflections on Feminism and the Hindu Goddess," in *Is the Goddess a Feminist?* ed. Alf Hiltebeitel and Kathleen Erndl, 92 (New York: New York University Press, 2000); Sherma, "Hinduism," 31; Shaw, *Passionate Enlightenment*; and Karen Pechilis, ed., *The Graceful Guru: Hindu Female Gurus in India and the United States* (New York: Oxford University Press, 2004).

72. See Carol S. Anderson, "The Life of Gauri Ma" in *Graceful Guru*, 65–84.

73. See Rebecca Manring, "Sītā Devī: An Early Vaiṣṇava Guru" in *Graceful Guru*, 51–64 (New York: Oxford University Press, 2004).

74. H. K. Barpujari, *Comprehensive History of Assam*, vol. 3 (Guwahati: Publication Board Assam, 1990–94), 236–237.

75. NST 5.70: ānandanāthaśabdāntā guravaḥ sarvasiddhidāḥ | striyo 7 pi gururūpāśced ambāntāḥ parikīrtitāḥ |. Literally, the second line reads "women also, if they are gurus are known by 'mother' attached to the end [of their names]."

76. GST 2.18b–20: striyā dīkṣā śubhā proktā sarvakāmaphalapradā || bahujanmārjitāt puṇyād bahubhāgyavaśād yadi | strīgururlabhyate nātha tasya dhyānaṃ tu kīdṛśam || kulīnastrīgurordhyānaṃ srotumicchāmi sāmpratam | kathayasva mahābhāga yadyahaṃ tava vallabhā ||. We should also note here that the god Śiva initially does not want to reveal the visualizations to Pārvatī because women's natures are wavering, and they might tell the secret. See GST 2.9b.

77. A variant reading the editors give here is prasannavadanāṃ, "a smiling face."

78. GST 2.21–26: śṛṇu pārvati vakṣyāmi tava snehapariplutaḥ | rahasyaṃ strīgurordhyānaṃ yatra dhyeyā ca sā guruḥ || sahasrāre mahāpadme kiñjalkagaṇaśobhite | praphullapadmapatrākṣīṃ ghanapīnapayodharām || sahasravadanāṃ nityāṃ kṣīṇamadhyāṃ śivāṃ gurum | padmarāgasamābhāsāṃ raktavastrasuśobhanām || ratnakaṅkaṇapāṇiṃ ca ratnanūpuraśobhitām | śaradindupratīkāśavaktrodbhāsitakuṇḍalām || svanāthavāmabhāgasthāṃ varābhayakarāmbujām | iti te kathitaṃ devi strīgurordhyānamuttamam || gopanīyaṃ prayatnena na prakāśyaṃ kadācana ||.

79. The verses giving the visualization of the male guru are GST 2.12–15.

80. Rāmatoṣaṇa Bhaṭṭācārya, *Prāṇatoṣiṇī*, part 1, ed. Harivansh Kumar Pandey, 473, 475ff. (Varanasi: Sampurnanand Sanskrit University, 2000), for the hymn of "armor" and for the song sung to the woman as a guru (*strīgurugītā*). This stotram in

the *Kaṅkālamālinī Tantra* in *Tantrasaṅgraha*, ed. Ramprasād Tripāṭhī. Yogatantragranthamālā Series, vol. 6, part 4 (Varanasi: Sampurnanand Sanskrit University, 1996), 3.27–34, is not framed in this text as a hymn to a female guru, but rather as a hymn to Pārvatī as the guru. For the worship of the wife of the guru see 479 in the *Prāṇatoṣiṇī*; I address in appendix 1, on sources, that the *Kaṅkālamālinī Tantra* contains some elements of the "Kālī Practice," but not enough to include it as one of the sources for this study.

81. Rāmatoṣaṇa Bhaṭṭācārya, *Prāṇatoṣiṇī*, 479. This is called the *sapatnīkaguru-pūjanam*.

82. Here GST 2.14a, but also often generally as well.

83. Banerji cites this verse in his *Brief History*, 184. He, however, reads the compound, "svanāthavāmabhāgasthām" (GTS 2.25a; *Prāṇatoṣiṇī*, 473) as "she who is situated on the left side of her lord" (reading the second half of the compound in *tatpuruṣa* relationship to the first half instead of reading it as a *karmadhāraya* compound, which would instead render the compound as "she who has her lord seated on her left side"). I suggest that given the parallel structure in visualization of the male guru—GST 2.14a: "suraktaśaktiṃ saṃyuktavāmabhāgamanoharam," "who is attractive, united with his beloved śakti on his left side," which also uses "vāmabhāga," "the left side," to indicate that his śakti is on his left—may be read in its parallel structure to indicate that both should be visualized with partners on their left side. I also found this visualization on the Web site of Mike McGee, cited as a selection taken from the *Brahmayāmala* (www.religiousworlds.com/mandalam/guru.htm). In the translation given on this Web site, as in mine, the male is placed to the left of the female guru. Curiously, this Web site also gives on a separate page a summary of the contents of the GST, but seems to miss that this visualization is taken directly from the second chapter of the GST.

84. GST 2.19.

85. *Rudrayāmala* 2.107: svapne tu niyamo nāsti dīkṣāsu guruśiṣyayoḥ | svapnalabdhe striyā datte saṃskāreṇaiva śuddhyati ||; *Rudrayāmala (Uttara Tantra)*. Prathama and Dvitīya Vibhaga, 2 vols., ed. Rāmaprasāda Tripāthī. Yogatantra-Granthamālā Series 7 (Varanasi: Sampurnananda Sanskrit University, 1991). One could also possibly read the locative absolute in the second line as the "mantra given by a woman in a dream," but given the lines following this verse, the reading I offer makes more sense.

86. *Rudrayāmala*, 2.108–11: sādhvī caiva sadācārā gurubhaktā jitendriyā | sarvamantrārthatattvajñā suśīlā pūjane ratā | sarvalakṣaṇasampannā jāpikā padmalocanā | ratnālaṅkārasaṃyuktā varṇābhuvanabhūṣitā | śāntā kulīnā kulajā candrāsyā sarvavṛddhigā | anantaguṇasampannā rudratvadāyinī priyā || gururūpā muktidātrī śivajñānanirūpiṇī | guruyogyā bhavet sā hi vidhavā parivarjitā || striyā dīkṣā śubhā proktā mantrāścāṣṭaguṇāḥ smṛtāḥ | putriṇī vidhavā grāhyā kevalā ṛṇakāriṇī || ("bhūvana emended to read "bhuvana"; "mantraś" emended to read "mantrāś").

87. But note that the verses that immediately follow this, 2.113–14, make exceptions for some widows and mothers.

88. This text is the *Uttara Tantra* version of the *Rudrayāmala*.

89. Brahmānanda Giri, *Śāktānandataraṅgiṇī*, ed. Rājanātha Tripāthī (Varanasi: Sampurnanand Sanskrit University, 1987), 2.31.

90. *Rudrayāmala* 2.113; also, 2.115 for more praise of the *mantra* given by one's mother.

91. *Śāktānandataraṅgiṇī*, 2.31–33. We might also note here that the medieval writer Jayaratha also refers to three women as esteemed teachers, gurus, in his lineage (Navjivan Rastogi, *Introduction to the Tantrāloka* (Delhi: Motilal Banarsidass, 1987), 114.

92. BT 7.198b: tasmāt sarvaprayatnena dīkṣayed nija kaulikīm; and also GT 36.2. An alternative reading given by Kaul in the notes, *dvija* for *nija* (BT, p. 110), would suggest that one ought to initiate women belonging to the upper castes. See also NST 14.50.

93. BT 7.199b–200: anenaiva krameṇaiva yaḥ karoti kriyāṃ śubhām || tasya vaṃśe maheśāni bṛhaspatisamaḥ pumān | jāyate nātra sandehaḥ satyaṃ satyaṃ surārcite.

94. GST 5.11b: śaktiyuktaṃ japenmantraṃ na mantraṃ kevalaṃ japet |.

95. GST 5.12: sāvitrī sahito brahmā siddho >bhūn naganandini | dvārāvatyāṃ kṛṣṇadevaḥ siddho >bhūt satyayā saha ||. Once initiated, women engage in the practice of *mantra* repetition (MT 11.33) and worship (*kulapūjā*, GT 36.8). We also find in the Sarvavijayi Tantra (SVT) in *Tantrasaṅgraha*, ed. Vrajvallabha Dvivedi, Yogatantragranthamālā Series 8, part 5. (Varanasi: Sampurnanand Sanskrit University, 1996), a rite for women that is textually marked as a woman's rite, since it affords a woman control over her husband (SVT 95–103).

96. GT 36.6a; also BT 7.189ff.

97. BT 7.196: gaṅgāsmaraṇamātreṇa niṣpāpo jāyate yathā ||.

98. BT 7.193: puṣpadarśanamātreṇa gandharvaśca sukhī bhavet |.

99. BT 7.192b: kṣudhārtaḥ kṣīrapānena yathā tṛpto >bhijāyate ||.

100. BT 7.195: tripurādhyānamātreṇa bhuktirmuktiryathā bhavet |.

101. BT 7.189b: yoṣitām dhyānamātreṇa siddhayaḥ syur na saṃśayaḥ |.

102. GT 36.2–5; NST 14.45–50.

103. BT 7.188b–89: niyamaḥ puruṣairjñeyo na yoṣitsu kadācana || yadvā tadvā yena tena sarvataḥ sarvato > pi ca | yoṣitāṃ dhyānamātreṇa siddhayaḥ syur na saṃśayaḥ ||.; BT 7.198: yoṣiccintanamātreṇa tathaiva varadāyinī | tasmāt sarvaprayatnena dīkṣayed nija kaulikīm.

104. This section is similar to KCT 5.50ff., with some minor differences. This may be read in two ways: as meditation on women, or meditation by women. Here I explain why I think it can only be read as meditation by women—based on two pieces of evidence, the context and the parallel structure we find in the verses that offer the analogies. To present Louise Finn's translation, taking the genitive "belonging to women" to mean "on women," Finn translates this as mere meditation *on* women rather than *by* women. However, the whole point of this section's poetic analogies is to urge the practitioner to initiate a woman in his family. If it were simply by meditation *on* a woman that one acquired *siddhi*, there would be no need to initiate women. Only by *her* meditating does one acquire *siddhi*. Hence *she* should be

initiated. Note also that GT 36.2–5 and NST 14.45–50 offer a similar set of analogies to argue for women's initiation, including some of the ones we find in the BT. All these texts conclude that one should initiate women, which would be totally unnecessary if it were merely a case of meditation on women. Also the genitive is used for *nṛnām* (of men, humans) to note that men acquire *siddhi* by serving the guru. So again, it makes sense to take the genitive applied to women in the same sense of ownership, attainment, as we see in the genitive of *nṛ*. While I suggest that the KCT differs from the BT and NST and GT with respect to women, this is one of the incidents I refer to in appendix 1 on sources where we do find a precursor in an earlier text to the attitudes toward women in the later texts.

105. Finn ascribes a date of the ninth through eleventh centuries for the KCT (*Kulacūḍāmaṇi Tantram and Vāmakeśvara Tantra, with the Jayaratha Commentary*, introduced, translated, and annotated by Louise Finn, 21 (Wiesbaden: Harrassowitz, 1986). To point out a number of these: KCT 3.53–55 = BT 6.4–6; KCT 5.41 = BT 5.74; KCT 3.30 approximates BT 6.20; KCT 7.45–52 is very similar to BT 6.54–66. In reference to this description, KCT call this the right-handed path (*dakṣiṇācāra*), where the BT calls this conduct for occasional rites (*naimittika*). The pattern of repetition, often not exact, with a greater attention to meaning than to the form of the earlier version, tends to indicate that the BT's author or authors were aware of the KCT and synthesized elements of it to suit their own understanding. One could also conjecture that much of the KCT had, over the course of six or so centuries, become a part of a common oral tradition, which was utilized by the author or authors of the BT in their composition. Kāmākhyā is especially referenced at KCT 5.1, 36–42, and also in connection with other *pīṭhas* at 3.60ff., 6.4ff. Other texts in the group of texts from the fifteenth through eighteenth centuries that I examine also bear similarities and borrow from earlier sources like the KCT, especially, for instance, the GT. Since many of the myths and stories I focus on come from the BT, however, it especially makes sense to use it as a particular point of comparison.

106. KCT 3.35–44 = BT 7.64–73. Finn follows Avalon (*Kulacūḍāmaṇi Tantram*, ed., Girīsha Candra Vedāntatīrtha, in *Tantrik Texts*, vol. 4, ed. Arthur Avalon [London: Luzac and Co., 1915; reprint, New Delhi: Aditya Prakashan, n.d], 9) in noting the title of this hymn as the "karṇejapa stotram," literally, the "Hymn for Recitation of the Mantra in the Ear" (*Kulacūḍāmaṇi Tantram*, 98). Pratapaditya Pal also references a line from this hymn in his discussion of the *Tantrasāra* of Kṛṣṇānanda Āgamavāgīśa in *Hindu Religion and Iconology* (Los Angeles: Vichitra, 1981), 18.

107. It is not explicitly clear from this section of the KCT that ritual sex is involved, but the text seems to suggest it. See, for instance, KCT 3.5–12, 49ff.

108. KCT 3.11: dīkṣitā na ca yoṣā cet kathaṃ syāt kulapūjanam |. That is, in the KCT the hymn likely serves to make available women for the rite of sexual union, an act one might suspect to be simply a mechanism for fulfilling the desires of the male participants.

109. KuT 7.38: adīkṣitāṃ striyaṃ kuryāt sadyaḥ saṃskāramambike |.

110. BT 7.72: miti-mātṛ-maye devi miti-mātṛ-bahiṣkṛte. The seventh verse also differs slightly; the KCT imagines the woman covered in the blood of severed heads,

while the BT gives her the more iconographically stylized "wearing a garland of skulls."

111. KCT 2.29–30; 3.4–10.

112. KCT 2.21ff.; 5.28.

113. Especially KCT 3.4–10; 4.22–34; 5.25–31. I discuss the similarities to James Bond in chapter 3 in the context of the rite of sexual union.

114. I address these in chapter 3 so I will not elaborate more here. The references are "gazing at him with a sideways glance, the composure of her mind is broken by her longing" (KCT 4.22); "flustered, she reveals her body by adjusting the end of her garment" (KCT 4.27); "she goes here and there, unable to bear the sexual desire" (KCT 4.31); and so on.

115. BT 6.73ff., 300ff.; 7.283ff.; in contrast to KCT 7.75, which enjoins not insulting only the *kula* woman.

116. See also, for instance, GT 36.2. The GT follows the same principle of necessary initiation for female participants, and GT 36.3ff. presents a list of analogies similar to the BT in this context, also arguing for the initiation of women.

117. PhT 11.20: dikkālaniyamo nāsti sthityādiniyamo na ca | jape na kālaniyamo nārcādiṣu baliṣvapi ||. Also see BT 7.104ff.; CT 2.21f.; GST 3.4; NST 13.21ff.

118. BT 7.107: nātra śuddhyādyapekṣāsti na cāmedhyādidūṣaṇam |. Also see CT 2.21; NST 13.23; BT 8.93ff.; PhT 11.11f., 20ff.; GST 3.4.

119. BT 7.109.

120. Sanderson, "Śaivism and the Tantric Tradition," 662.

121. S. C. Banerji, *Tantra in Bengal: A Study in Its Origin, Development and Influence*, 2nd rev. and enl. ed. (New Delhi: Manohar, 1992), also takes note of this practice, with no rules except that of regarding women with great respect, which he designates as "kulācāra" and "kaula." The terms *kulācāra* and *kaula*, however, do appear in a variety of texts from other periods and places without this particular stipulation. And while these terms also appear in these texts, this practice is not specifically designated by these terms. To avoid confusion I note only the terms here used by the texts in this study.

122. Louis Dumont, *Homo Hierarchicus: The Caste System and Its Implications*, 2nd ed., trans. Mark Sainsburg, Louis Dumont, and Basia Gulati (Chicago: University of Chicago Press, 1980).

123. Veena Das, *Structure and Cognition: Aspects of Hindu Caste and Ritual*, 2nd ed. (London: Oxford University Press, 1982).

124. Abhinavagupta, *Tantrāloka of Abhinavagupta with Commentary by Rājānaka Jayaratha*. 12 vols., edited with notes by Mukund Ram Shastri et al. (Allahabad: Indian, 1918–38; reprinted with introduction and notes by R. C. Dwivedi and Navjivan Rastogi. 8 vols. (Delhi: Motilal Banarsidass, 1987), 4.213ff.

125. An idea, by the way, that Jacques Derrida has explored to great length.

126. CT 2.25; NST 11.122; 16.6; GT 35.56; BT 6.75b; 8.90. The Sanskrit here is "*striyo devāḥ striyaḥ prāṇāḥ striya eva vibhūṣaṇam*": "Women are Gods; women are the life-breath; women in this way are a splendor, a beauty." "*Vibhūṣaṇam*" alternatively

means "ornament." NST 16.6 reverses the word order with "*striyaṃ* [*sic*] *prāṇāḥ striyo devāḥ striya eva vibhūṣaṇam.*"

127. GST 1.9: śakti mūlaṃ jagat sarvaṃ śaktimūlaṃ parantape |.

128. NST 16.12b–14a: mātāpitrorgurostyāgo brahmā śambhustathā hariḥ || varañcāhaṃ parityājyo nāvamānyā tu kāminī. vṛthā nyāsaṃ vṛthā pūjā vṛthā jāpo vṛthā stutiḥ | vṛthā sadakṣiṇo homo yadyapriyakaraḥ striyāḥ.

129. Gloria Goodwin Raheja and Ann Grodzins Gold, *Listen to the Heron's Words: Reimagining Gender and Kinship in North India* (Berkeley and Los Angeles: University of California Press, 1994), 121.

130. NST 16.12b–14a. See n. 128 above for the Sanskrit for this.

131. NST 16.15: varaṃ prāṇaparityāgo na kuryādapriyaṃ striyāḥ |.

132. MT 11.36b: varaṃ devī parityājyā naiva tyājyā svakāminī ||. For the sake of smooth English, I supply the word *the* here, making the goddess into a singular universal. However, this universalizing article "the" is not a feature of Sanskrit. Literally, the text reads "better to abandon Goddess. . . ."

133. MT 11.37b–38a: na dhātā nācyutaḥ śambhur na ca vāmā sanātanī || yoṣidapriyakartāraṃ rakṣituṃ ca kṣamo bhavet |. This appears to echo a popular verse lauding the guru, which states that the guru can save someone from the wrath of the god Śiva, but no one can save one from the wrath of the guru. Here the verse is co-opted to express a different sentiment.

134. GT 35.8: tvatsvarūpiṇī.

135. We should also note here that the text uses the term *God,* rather than the feminine abstractive *devatā,* which tends to carry a diminished importance in relation to the term *deva.* In this context see also Catherine Weinberger-Thomas, *Ashes of Immortality: Widow Burning in India* (Chicago: University of Chicago Press, 1999), 172, for a contemporary instance of women, in this case, the *satī,* designated with the male term *dev* (the Hindi version of the Sanskrit), rather than the female form *devī.*

136. CT 5.7.

137. The *pañcatattva* in these texts usually refers to the Five Ms discussed earlier. However, it may also refer to the five elements or five principles of the cosmos.

138. GST 7.15ff. This reading comes from two manuscripts the editors titled "k" and "ṅ." Recension "g" also lists women as a fifth group, though here they do not get absorbed in the body of the goddess. The editors printed an alternative version that lists the fifth category as "army generals" (apparently the "kha" manuscript). Now as far as the logic of categories goes, it seems rather far-fetched to list the four well-known castes and then as a fifth add the category of "army generals"—apart from the fact that most of the manuscripts (the other three listed) give the fifth category as women. This editorial decision likely reflects an uneasiness on the part of this text's editors and one of this text's redactors to the more symmetrical idea of women as constituting a fifth caste. Also, "army generals" as a category is generally subsumed under the warrior caste. Finally, given that what the fifth caste obtains, absorption into the body of the goddess (*devīdehe pralīyate, GST 7.20a*), it appears rather more likely that women would attain this state than would army generals.

139. CT 4.23b: sarve >pi jantavo loke muktāḥ syuḥ strīniṣevaṇāt ||. Also see 2.44 (the first verse) in the extra set of verses attached to the end of the second chapter called the "Adhika Pātha."

140. See Smith, "Indra's Curse," 18. We should note also GST 11.13 where women are still conceived of as a group like the four castes, however here they, rather than being treated more like Brahmins, are again lumped together with Śūdras, as being prohibited from pronouncing the syllable "Om."

141. Jacques Lacan, *On Feminine Sexuality: The Limits of Love and Knowledge.* 20th Seminare, Encore 1972–73, trans. Bruce Fink (New York: Norton, 1998); Julia Kristeva, *Powers of Horror: An Essay on Abjection*, trans. Leon S. Roudiez (New York: Columbia University Press, 1982).

CHAPTER 2

1. This section in the CT borrows from the *Kulārṇava Tantra*, ed. Taranatha Vidyaratna with an introduction by Arthur Avalon (Sir John Woodroffe), 2.117–19 (Madras: Ganesh and Company, 1965; reprint, Delhi: Motilal Banarsidass, 1975). In fact, the CT borrows extensively from the *Kulārṇava Tantra* and reworks it, modifying it and adding some new material. One also notices here that this assumes that women are not in the loop of getting enlightenment through sex (unless the text assumes that women are also having intercourse with women). The Buddha's response to Vasiṣṭha's question here is elusive; he simply praises the *kula* path as the highest and as leading to liberation.

2. David White's brilliant, detailed analysis is probably one of the best analyses of this, but his is not isolated. Agehananda Bharati also presents this picture (*The Tantric Tradition* [London: Ryder and Co., 1965; reprint, New York: Grove, 1975], 304ff.) as does Ronald Davidson's recent study of Buddhist Tantra (*Indian Esoteric Buddhism* [New York: Columbia University Press, 2002], 92ff., especially 97). For the power of flight, see White, *The Kiss of the Yoginī:Tantric Sex in Its South Asian Contexts* (Chicago: University of Chicago Press, 2003), 196ff. Also I address in greater detail differences between the earlier texts and texts used in this study in appendix 1.

3. The texts used are those cited in the introduction. The specific version I focus on for the rite of sexual union derives especially from the BT (6.21ff.; 7.84ff.; 7.112ff.), with similar versions in PhT (11.18ff.), MT (11.5ff.), CT (3.13ff.), YT (7.10ff.), GT (35.54ff.), which I also draw upon. In appendix 1 I examine in greater detail this set of texts. For this chapter in general I focus mostly upon the BT and the CT, using also occasionally the tenth-century KCT as a point of contrast.

4. See n. 2 above. Also see Dimock, *Place of the Hidden* Moon (Chicago: University of Chicago Press, 1989), 210ff.; White, *The Kiss of the Yoginī*, passim; and Urban, *Tantra: Sex, Secrecy, Politics and Power in the Study of Religion* (Berkeley and Los Angeles: University of California Press, 2003), 49f.

5. See Catharine Mackinnon, *Only Words* (Cambridge, Mass.: Harvard University Press, 1993); Catharine Mackinnon and Andrea Dworkin, eds., *In Harm's Way: The Pornography Civil Rights Hearings* (Cambridge, Mass.: Harvard University Press,

1997); and Catharine Mackinnon, *Feminism Unmodified: Discourses on Life and Law* (Cambridge, Mass.: Harvard University Press, 1987).

6. KCT 3.5–8: Kūlākula [*sic*?] japaṃ kṛtvā samānayati tatkṣaṇāt || yannāmnā likhitaṃ yantraṃ tamānayati tatkṣaṇāt [*sic*?]| śatayojanadūrasthāṃ nadīparvatamadhyagām || dvīpāntarasahsreṣu rakṣitāṃ nigaḍādibhiḥ | payodharabharakṣubdhamadhyamāṃ lolalocanām... sādhakākāṅkṣihṛdayāṃ. This whole section runs from KCT 3.4–10. The lines I left out were more graphic than this project calls for and the reader in any case gets the idea here.

7. It also differs, coincidentally, from the slightly later and Western influenced *Mahānirvāṇa Tantra*, which also tends toward what I read as a less empowering vision of women, even as the *Mahānirvāṇa Tantra* incorporates Western notions of a chivalric protection of women.

8. KuT 8.103: cakramadhye tu mūḍhātmā jātibhedaṃ karoti yaḥ taṃ bhakṣayanti yoginyas. Also see, for instance, 11.38. David White, *The Kiss of the Yoginī*, passim, also expatiates at length on this image of woman as *yoginī*.

9. Recent television series, such as those of the epics *Rāmāyaṇa* and the *Mahābhārata*, aptly enforce this image with a benign and pious Vasiṣṭha as the epitome of brahminical propriety. For a good literary example of the popular representation of Vasiṣṭha as the calm and pure Brahmin, see R. K. Narayan's *Gods, Demons and Others*, 2nd ed. (Chicago: University of Chicago Press, 1993), 64–84.

10. CT 1.34b–35a: ārādhayanmahāmāyāṃ Vaśiṣṭho <tijitendriyaḥ || athārādhayatastasya sahasraṃ parivatsarān |. The spelling of Vasiṣṭha's name with the ś in this text likely indicates the northeast region for the text's location.

11. From ten thousand years in CT 1.14, the figure is reduced to one thousand years in his subsequent conversation with Brahmā (CT 1.24). Bharati (Agehananda Bharati, *The Tantric Tradition* [London: Ryder and Co., 1965; reprint, New York: Grove, 1975], 69) cites a similar, though somewhat different story as derived from the *Brahmayāmala*, though without giving an indication of where in the *Brahmayāmala* one might find this. White cites an earlier version of this story found in the *Rudrayāmala*, which differs from the version in the CT, especially in that in the *Rudrayāmala* version, Vasiṣṭha comes across sages drinking (menstrual) blood (White, *The Kiss of the Yoginī*, 75–76), whereas in the CT, after Vasiṣṭha's story is told, Śiva relates a similar parallel story, but where the god Brahmā comes across the sages, they were not drinking blood but were drinking wine (*madyapāna* CT 5.17). Below I offer a similar version with the sages from the BT.

12. CT 1.14b: nānugrahaṃ cakārāsau Tārā saṃsāratāriṇī.

13. CT 1.16b–18: Brahmā sa ca muniṃ prāha śṛṇu putra vaco mama || tattvajñānamayīṃ vidyāṃ tārāṃ bhuvanatāriṇīm | ārādhaya tvaṃ śrīcaraṇaṃ siddhiyuktena cetasā || asyāḥ prasādādevāhaṃ bhuvanāni caturdaśa | sṛjāmi caturo vedān kalpayāmi.

14. CT 1.36b–37a: tadā roṣeṇa mahatā jajvāla sa munīśvaraḥ || tato jalaṃ samādāya tāṃśaptumupacakrame |.

15. CT 1.41.

16. CT 1.40–43: tato devī mahāmāyā tāriṇī sarvasiddhidā | uvāca sādhakaśreṣṭhaṃ vaśiṣṭhaṃ munināṃ varam || roṣeṇa dāruṇamanāḥ kathaṃ māmaśapad bhavān

| madīyārādhanācāraṃ buddharūpī janārdanaḥ || eka eva vijānāti nānyaḥ kaścana tattvataḥ | vṛthaiva yāmabāhulyaḥ kālo >yaṃ gamitastvayā || viruddhācāraśīlena mama tattvamajānatā | tadbuddharūpiṇo viṣṇoḥ sannidhiṃ yāhi samprati ||.

17. Pintchman, *The Rise of the Goddess in the Hindu Tradition* (Albany: State University of New York Press, 1994), 201. Susan Wadley also articulates this view, connecting it to the married or unmarried state of a woman or goddess, with the former being auspicious and the latter dangerous ("Women and the Hindu Tradition," in *Women in India: Two Perspectives*, ed. Doranne Jacobson and Susan S. Wadley [Columbia, Mo.: South Asia, 1977], 118f.), as does William Sax, *Mountain Goddess: Gender and Politics in a Himalayan Pilgrimage* (New York: Oxford University Press, 1991), 31f.

18. One might suggest she acts more like the finicky guru Marpa, who repeatedly rejects Milarepa's architectural efforts, than like the terrific and beneficent goddess we find in the *Devī Māhātmya*.

19. The quote I cite from Monier-Williams below is a good example of this nineteenth-century consternation over a perceived impropriety and prurience discovered in Tantric practice. Also see Urban, *Tantra*, for attention to nineteenth-century European reactions to Tantra.

20. CT 2.5b: madirāpānasañjātaṃ raktamantharalocanam.

21. CT 2.3b: vilāsollasitena ca.

22. CT 2.6–7: dūrādeva vilokyaivaṃ vaśiṣṭho buddharūpiṇam | vismayena samāviṣṭaḥ smaran saṃsāratāriṇīm || kimidaṃ kriyate karma viṣṇunā buddharūpiṇā | vedavādaviruddho >yamācāraḥ sammato mama ||.

23. CT 4.23: strīsambhogena lokānāṃ yadi mokṣo bhavediha | sarve >pi jantavo loke muktāḥ syuḥ strīniṣevaṇāt ||.

24. CT 2.8–9a: iti cintayatastasya vaśiṣṭhasya mahātmanaḥ | ākāśavāṇī prāhāśu maivaṃ cintaya suvrata || ācāraḥ paramārtho >yaṃ tāriṇīsādhane mune |.

25. CT 2.11b–13: vaśiṣṭho daṇḍavadbhūmau papātātīva harṣitaḥ || tathotthāya praṇamyāsau kṛtāñjalipuṭo muniḥ | jagāma viṣṇoḥ sānnidhyaṃ buddharūpasya pārvati || athāsau taṃ samālokya madirāmodavihvalaḥ | prāha buddhaḥ prasannātmā kimarthaṃ tvamihāgataḥ ||.

26. The CT, of course, names the special practice "the Chinese Conduct" or "the Tibetan Conduct" (*cīnācāra*). For the sake of consistency I keep the English nomenclature of the "Kālī Practice" throughout this book.

27. CT 2.20a and 2.22b: sarva eva śubhaḥ kālo nāśubho vidyate kvacit |; and, sarvathā pūjayed devīmasnātaḥ kṛtabhojanaḥ ||.

28. CT 2.23b–24b: strīdveṣo naiva kartavyo viśeṣāt pūjanaṃ striyaḥ || tāsāṃ prahāranindāñca kauṭilyamapriyantathā sarvathā naiva kartavyam. The quote continues on to say that these activities obstruct the attainment of the practitioner.

29. In appendix 1 I note how the KuT rather suggests that one should dissemble, and not tell a woman she is ugly in order to make sure she stays for the rite.

30. CT 2.25. Again, I discuss this in detail in chapter 1.

31. CT. 2.44. *Adhika pātha* also CT 4.23: sarve >pi jantavo loke muktāḥ syuḥ strī niṣevaṇāt ||. That is, Vasiṣṭha learns precisely the lesson that he mockingly makes fun

of, when he suggests that everyone ("sarve," here presumably all male creatures) ought to be enlightened from serving women. The Sanskrit word here, *niṣevana*, from the root *sev*, carries a double connotation of serving, worshiping, and also having sexual intercourse with someone.

32. I discuss in greater detail in chapter 1 this special "Kālī Practice." In the BT see 6.73f.; see also, for instance, NST 11.120f.

33. In a number of cases, the *Kaulajñānanirṇaya* for instance, I would concur with this assessment.

34. Curiously, Vasiṣṭha's attitude is oddly reminiscent here of much of the way that contemporary science—genetic manipulation of crops, for instance—suggests that more and greater scientific manipulation of Nature will force Nature to submit to human will.

35. And perhaps even for Vasiṣṭha, as his question to Buddha in the epigraph here suggests. I discuss the "pornographic" element ascribed to Tantra by the West below.

36. CT 3.16: tatra cāvāhanam nāsti.

37. In chapter 1 I discuss the ordinary, nonpossessed woman as goddess, in contrast to a more typical Tantric ritual worship of a woman as goddess who is *possessed* by a goddess.

38. What is probably the most important and striking aspect of this practice is that it counters what we find in an earlier Tantric text such as the KCT, by explicitly extending this rule to the treatment of women all the time; see BT 6.73f.; also NST 11.120f.; CT 2.23ff.

39. Monier Monier-Williams, *Hinduism* (London: SPCK, 1906), 126ff.

40. Ibid., 127.

41. Ibid., 126.

42. Ibid.

43. Ibid.

44. For instance, see www.tantra.com; www.kundalini-tantra.com; www.tantramagic.com; www.tantra-sex.com; www.sexuality.org/tantra.html. This list is by no means exhaustive, nor does it include the variety of Tantric workshops offered in local and regional resource magazines, such as the "Tantra" workshops designed to improve sexual relationships, offered by Charles and Caroline Muir as advertised in *Nexus* in the Denver/Boulder area.

45. Paul Muller-Ortega, "Aspects of *Jīvanmukti* in the Tantric Śaivism of Kashmir," in *Living Liberation in Hindu Thought*, ed. Andrew Fort and Patricia Mumme, 187–217 (Albany: State University of New York Press, 1996); Muller-Ortega, *Triadic Heart of Śiva* (Albany: State University of New York Press, 1989).

46. Muller-Ortega, "Aspects of *Jīvanmukti*," 197f.

47. See also Muller-Ortega, "Tantric Meditation: Vocalic Beginnings," in *Ritual and Speculation in Early Tantrism: Studies in Honor of Andre Padoux*, ed. T. Goudrian (Albany: State University of New York Press, 1992); as well as Douglas Brooks, *Auspicious Wisdom: The Texts and Traditions of Śrī Vidyā Śākta Tantrism in South India* (Albany: State University of New York Press, 1992); the work of European scholars

like Andre Padoux, *Vāc: The Concept of the Word in Selected Hindu Tantras,* trans. Jacques Gontier (Albany: State University of New York Press, 1989); Gudrun Buhnemann, *The Iconography of Hindu Tantric Deities.* 2 vols. (Groningen: Egbert Forsten, 2000); especially Alexis Sanderson's ("Śaivism and the Tantric Tradition," in *The World's Religions,* ed. Stewart Sutherland et al. [London: Routledge, 1988]) insightful historical research; Helene Brunner, "The Sexual Aspect of the *Liṅga* Cult according to the Saiddhāntika Scriptures," in *Studies in Hinduism 2: Miscellanea to the Phenomenon of Tantras,* ed. G. Oberhammer, 87–103 (Vienna: Osterreichischen Akademie der Wissenschaften, 1998); Raffaele Torella, *The Īśvarapratyabhijñākārikā of Utpaladeva with the Author's Vṛtti: Critical Edition and Annotated Translation* (Rome: Istituto Italiano per il medio ed estremo oriente, 1994); Sanjukta Gupta, "The Worship of Kālī according to the *Toḍala Tantra*" in *Tantra: In Practice,* ed. David Gordon White, 463–88 (Princeton, N.J.: Princeton University Press, 2000); and especially Sanjukta Gupta, Teun Goudriaan, and Dirk Hoens, *Hindu Tantrism* (Leiden: Brill, 1979); Mark S. G. Dyczkowski, *The Canon of the Śaivāgama and the Kubjikā Tantras of the Western Kaula Tradition* (Albany: State University of New York Press, 1988); and Hugh Urban, *Tantra: Sex, Secrecy, Politics and Power in the Study of Religion* (Berkeley and Los Angeles: University of California Press, 2003), also attempts to historically locate and diffuse Western Orientalist constructions of Tantra's association with sexuality.

48. *Yoginī Tantra,* ed. Biswanarayan Shastri (Delhi and Varanasi: Bharatiya Vidya Pradashan, 1982), xii.

49. S. C. Banerji, *Tantra in Bengal: A Study in Its Origin, Development and Influence.* 2nd rev. and enl. ed. (New Delhi: Manohar, 1992), 247.

50. One also might read this as an internalization of earlier critiques of Tantra by Westerners being proffered forth by indigenous scholars, even as they distance themselves and revision the critiques given.

51. Wendy Doniger, "Tantric Bodies," *Times Literary Supplement,* May 20, 2004. http://www.svabhinava.org/friends/rajivMalhotra/WendyWhite-frame.html. The issues involved in this critique are clearly far more complex than I have the space to present here, involving a politics of representation and authenticity; interesting for our purposes, however, is that the critique focuses on a misreading of sexuality.

52. Doniger herself takes these terms from White, who uses these terms, not innappropriately, to distinguish between different forms and degrees of a Tantric praxis' use of sex.

53. Rae Langton, "Speech Acts and Unspeakable Acts," *Philosophy and Public Affairs* 22, no. 4 (Autumn 1993): 293–294.

54. Judith Butler, *Excitable Speech: A Politics of the Performative* (New York: Routledge, 1997), 82ff., especially 85.

55. Langton, "Speech Acts and Unspeakable Acts," 321ff.

56. Butler, *Excitable Speech,* 3 and passim.

57. White, *The Kiss of the Yoginī,* xiff.

58. Kripal, *Kālī's Child: The Mystical and the Erotic in the Life and Teaching of Ramakrishna,* 2nd ed. (Chicago: University of Chicago Press, 1998). Kripal's

thoughtful study and the response to it especially illustrates a process whereby identity is interpellated and internalized to the point that the cultural gap reinforces a problematics of sexual identity. In terms of a liberatory politics, something like a double bind ensues. Sara Suleri's articulation of the competing bind between race and gender in a postcolonial context nicely expresses the implications and ramifications of this sort of bind (though in a different context) (Suleri, "Woman Skin Deep: Feminism and the Postcolonial Condition," in *Contemporary Postcolonial Theory*, ed. Padmini Mongia (London: Arnold, 1996), 340.

59. BT 8.37–47: idānīṃ śṛṇu deveśi rahasyamidamuttamam || purā dāruvane ramye unmattā rāgamohitāḥ | parastriyaṃ gharṣayanti madyaṃ svādanti nityaśaḥ | tad dṛṣṭvānucitaṃ karma viṣṇunā samupasthitam | śrīviṣṇuruvāca | devadeva mahādeva sarvadeva dayānidhe || devadāruvane pāpā madyapānaratāturāḥ | parastriyaṃgharṣayanti munayo rāgamohitāḥ || digambarāstathā muḍhāḥ samprayāsyanti kām gatim | iti tasya vacaḥ śrutvā tamuvāca tvahaṃ priye || kālikā yā mahāvidyā hyaniruddhasarasvatī | vidyārājñīti yā proktā ete tanmantrajāpakāḥ || paraṃ muktā bhaviṣyanti tadgāyatrīṃ japanti ca | etasyāstu prabhāveṇa sarve devā vimocitāḥ || nijamātṛvadhāt so >pi paraśurāmo vimocitaḥ | dattātreyaścātriputraḥ surāpānād vimocitaḥ || gotamastrīgharṣaṇācca devendro >pi vimocitaḥ | cāṇḍālīgamanāt pūrvaṃ vaśiṣṭhaśca vimocitaḥ || gurudārāgharṣaṇācca candramāśca vimocitaḥ | brahmaṇastu śiraśchedāc śivaḥ so haṃ vimocitaḥ || rāvaṇasya vadhāccāpi rāmacandro vimocitaḥ | tameva gūḍhaṃ vakṣyāmi śrutvā gopyaḥ sadā budhaiḥ ||.

60. The fifth case endings here for this sequence of examples are ambigous; they may be read either as "liberated because of" or "liberated/freed from." In the latter interpretation, they are freed from the sin they commit. I read this section mostly with the latter interpretation, though the text does suggest that the transgressive acts may be an integral and necessary component triggering these characters' subsequent liberation.

61. YT 4.6ff.

62. Elaine Scarry, *The Body in Pain: The Making and Unmaking of the World* (New York: Oxford University Press, 1985).

63. Copjec, *Imagine There's No Woman: Ethics and Sublimation* (Cambridge, Mass.: MIT Press, 2002), 58.

64. As Mackinnon and Langton suggest, as I note above.

65. With this I am indebted to Judith Butler's formulation of identity as that which is continuously performed in our relations with others on a daily basis (Butler, *Psychic Life of Power: Theories in Subjection* (Stanford, Calif.: Stanford University Press, 1997); Butler, *Excitable Speech*). What I would add to Butler here is that, in addition, the rite especially seeks to consciously channel this performing of identity.

66. There have also been a number of studies on mystics in Western traditions, which take up sexual imagery and have helped us to rethink sexual imagery. One thinks immediately of the work of Caroline Walker Bynum, for instance, *Holy Feast and Holy Fast* (Berkeley and Los Angeles: University of California Press, 1987), 153ff.

67. KuT 8.70a: mukhe āpūrya madirāṃ pāyayanti striyaḥ priyān.

68. KuT 8.71b: dhṛtvāśirasi nṛtyanti madyabhāṇḍāni yoginaḥ.

69. KuT 8.73–74: yogino madamattāśca patanti pramadorasi | madākulāśca yoginyaḥ patanti puruṣopari || manorathasukhaṃ pūrṇaṃ kurvanti ca parasparam |.

70. KCT 4.22: bhāvaika bhinnahṛdayā vakradṛṣṭyā vilokya ca . . . ; KCT 4.25: kravyādāḥ pala māṃsādya tṛṣṇārttā stoyadarśanāt. . .[māsādya emended to māṃsādya]; KCT 4.26: cañcalā nijavaṃśācca ced bhāvanā mūḍhamānasā utkṣipya bhujamūlañca vasanaṃ kṣipyate punaḥ . . . ; KCT 4.31: kāmāsahiṣṇuhṛdayā dūre vā cāntike sthitā. See also KCT 3.4–10; 4.22–34; 5.25–31.

71. This word, like the "Om," is a word used ritually, which does not have a general semantic meaning.

72. "Pala" here can also refer to meat.

73. BT 6.21: ādāvānīya deveśi svakāntāṃ vā parastriyam | prathamaṃ cāsanaṃ dattvā pādyaṃ dadyāttataḥ param || arghyaṃ dadyānmaheśāni yathoktavidhinā śive | ācamanīyaṃ ca tathā dadyācca sudhayā priye || snānīyaṃ parameśāni vauṣaḍantena dāpayet | gandhaṃ dadyānmaheśāni gandhānāmaṣṭakaṃ tathā || puṣpaṃ dadyādvarārohe gandhayuktaṃ manoharam | dhūpaṃ guggulunādadyāt mahādaivyai manoharam || dīpaṃ ca sarpiṣā dadyāt tāmrādhāraṃ suśobhanam | naivedyaṃ paramaṃ dadyāt susvādu sumanoharam | nānādravyayutaṃ dadyānnārikelayutaṃ tathā | rambhāphalaṃ bījapūraṃ śrīphalaṃ śrīniketanam | madhu dadyānmaheśāni paladvayamitam śubhe | ghṛtaṃ dadyānmaheśāni nūtanaṃ palamānataḥ || nānopahārasaṃyuktaṃ dadhidugdhayutaṃ tathā | tāmbūlaṃ paramaṃ dadyāt susvādu ca suvāsitam || karpūrādi samāyuktaṃ guvākena samanvitam | carvyaṃ coṣyaṃ tathā lehyaṃ peyaṃ dadyānmaheśvari || jalaṃ dadyādvarārohe karpūrādisuvāsitam | yadyadicchati tasmin vai kāle suragaṇārcite || tattad dadyādviśeṣeṇa yena tuṣyati sundarī |.

74. BT 6.34: keśasaṃskaraṇaṃ kuryānnānādravyairmanoramaiḥ |.

75. BT 6.35: stanadvandve ramābījaṃ hanudvaye bhaga dvayam | kakṣādhaḥ parameśāni likhet gaṅgādhara dvayam ||.

76. It would take us too far afield to explore this, but one difference here is salient. In typical performance of nyāsa for the male practioner on his own body, the syllables are inserted orally, not written down. That they are written down in the case of the woman offers a suggesting parallel to the argument Jacques Derrida makes in *Of Grammatology* (trans. Gayatri Chakravorty Spivak [Baltimore: Johns Hopkins University Press, 1976; reprint, Delhi: Motilal Banarsidass, 1994]), where he suggests that the written is conceived as inferior to the spoken (something we find in the case of India as well, especially with regard to the Vedas). Derrida argues that the written as the inferior secondary member of a binary reflects a repressed inversion of an arrangement where the spoken in fact is always existent with the written. Suggestive for our purposes here is that the binary reflects other binaries, especially the binary of gender, and one wonders whether writing the letters, rather than speaking them, in the case of the woman has to do with the fact that both writing and female are secondary members of binaries. There is not space to reflect more deeply on this here. I do, however, address stereotypes of women's speech as inferior in chapter 4.

77. See, for instance, BT 6.41 and 6.43. BT 6.41, which suggests one thousand recitations of the primary *mantra* while massaging the woman's "mountain," which

may perhaps be understood as ensuring that the male practitioner does not prematurely lose his seed or neglect the woman's enjoyment; BT 6.41: mūlamantraṃ maheśāni japet parvatamastake | sahasrasya pramāṇena japet tatra maheśvari ||. Likewise, BT 6.43 says, "For the sake of the desired attainment, he should massage her 'mountain' "; BT 6.43a: tāsāmabhīṣṭasiddhyarthaṃ kuryāt parvatamardanam |. Interestingly, analogous verses do not appear in the KuT or the KCT.

78. And perhaps it encodes, as Judith Butler suggests, in an indirect assimilation of the Hegelian portrayal of the relationship between master and bondsman (Butler, *Psychic Life of Power*, 32).

79. BT 6.30b.

80. Bṛhannīla Tantra 6.343b–44a: parīvādaḥ parābhūtir haṭhād ākarṣaṇaṃ striyāḥ || manasāpi na kartavyaṃ devi siddhiṃ yadīcchati |.

81. BT: 6.40: praṇamed daṇḍavadbhuvi.

82. BT 6.73f.; also NST 11.120f.; CT 2.23ff.

83. Alfred Collins, "Dancing with the Goddess," in Alf Hiltebeitel and Kathleen Erndl, eds., *Is the Goddess a Feminist?* ed. Alf Hiltebeitel and Kathleen Erndl, 66 (New York: New York University Press, 2000).

84. The closest we get to seeing the KCT practitioner bow to women is KCT 3.58, where we don't quite see him bow, but at least know that women of all castes are worthy here of being bowed to (namasyāḥ). This apparently, however, is a mental operation, which he carries out presumably not in front of actual women, but while taking a bath or rising in the morning. I suspect that even this gesture from the tenth century presents earlier incipient and inchoate beginnings of the more developed tradition we find in the "Kālī Practice" by the fifteenth through eighteenth centuries, which I describe in chapter 1.

85. In the classical, orthodox view he is the subject desiring the world, which he must ultimately reject as illusion in a gesture of renunciatory asceticism.

86. Specifically, here I refer to the Sāṃkhya view, which underlies nearly all of Indian cosmology.

87. Here this is literally the Great Chinese Practice, "mahācīnakramaṃ."

88. BT 7.85b–87: idānīṃ parameśāni nidhāraya manaḥ śive || mahācīnakramaṃ devi kathitavyaṃ varānane | ahaṃ deho maheśāni dehī tvam sarvarūpadṛk || mīnoyathā mahādevi payasi prahṛto tathā | sadātmā tvaṃ maheśāni akathyaṃ nāsti sundari ||. I have emended the Sanskrit from yathā to tathā in 7.87a. The metaphor of a fish thrown in water is not entirely clear to me.

89. Butler, *Excitable Speech*, 39.

90. BT 6.301: "Everywhere what takes the form of the feminine, that is the visible manifestation of you, [in] the female of animals, the female of birds and the female of humans, O auspicious lady."

91. See also n. 92 below.

92. In her insightful and tantalizing article on Śaiva temple ritual Brunner reconstructs the original model for the establishment of the aniconic image of the god Śiva in the temple. While the central focus of her article is that the installation of the aniconic image, the liṅga (the phallic-shaped image of the god Śiva), in the

temple is a ritual replication of the sexual act, in the process, without dwelling at great length on it, she points out a feature relevant for our discussion here. She notes that the iconic positioning in the image of the liṅga and yoni (the pīṭham), which represents the male and female genital principles, upsets the normal hierarchy of the genders. The "sexual act," which the ritual installation of the icon replicates, reverses the normative male-on-top spatial relation between the sexes (Brunner, "The Sexual Aspect," 95f.). In a seemingly offhanded yet conspiratorial gesture, the image in the temple inverts the "missionary position," instead putting the woman on top—replicating in all those thousands of Śiva temples all over India what our Tantric texts call the highly potent and transgressive form of "perverse love-making" (viparītarata).

93. For instance, Dimock (*Place of the Hidden Moon*, 104) reads the transgression in the Tantric ritual, without addressing this gendered posture reversal, in terms of a liminal state, which reestablishes the normative order. This reverse posture occurs not only in this group of texts from the fifteenth through eighteenth centuries but also in a variety of texts dealing with the transgressive rite of sexual union. I suspect that like some of the inchoate turns toward a reverence toward women that we find in an earlier text like the KCT, this posture reversal represents an incipient direction, which the BT then develops further.

94. This extends also to the idea of "feminine" nature (*prakṛti*) and "feminine" earth (*bhūdevī*).

95. "Kālī Practice" here is *mahācīnakrama*.

96. BT 7.81–82: devadeva mahādeva sthitisaṃhārakāraka | praśnamekaṃ karomyatra sakāśāt tava suvrata || kaitavaṃ ca parityajya tat kathyaṃ bhavanāśana | mahācīnakramaṃ deva kathitaṃ na prakāśitam | kathayasva tadidānīṃ yadi sneho >sti māṃ prati ||.

97. BT 7.84–86: Na vaktavyaṃ maheśāni bhuvanatritaye śive | śuddhabhāvena deveśi vaktavyaṃ tava gocare || nānyo >sti me priyaḥ ko >pi tvadanyaḥ suravandite | idānīṃ parameśāni nidhāraya manaḥ śive || mahācīnakramaṃ devi kathitavyaṃ varānane | ahaṃ deho maheśāni dehī tvam sarvarūpadṛk ||.

98. BT 7.87b–91: sadātmā tvaṃ maheśāni akathyaṃ nāsti sundari || kecid devā narā kecid dānavā yakṣarākṣasāḥ | nāgalokāḥ kinnarāśca gandharvāpsarasāṃ gaṇāḥ || ye vā paśumṛgāḥ pakṣā ye kecijjagatigatāḥ || ete jaḍatarāḥ sarve parasparakhalātmakāḥ || kukarmaniratāḥ sarve kumārgadarśanotsukāḥ | eteṣāṃ brahma vijñānamānandaṃ brahma citsukham || na jānāti maheśāni tat kathaṃ kathayāmi te |. I emended "jagatī" to "jagati."

CHAPTER 3

1. Edwin Dimock, *Place of the Hidden Moon* (Chicago: University of Chicago Press, 1989), 210ff.; see also David White, *The Kiss of the Yoginī: Tantric Sex in Its South Asian Contexts* (Chicago: University of Chicago Press, 2003), passim; and Urban, *Tantra: Sex, Secrecy, Politics and Power in the Study of Religion* (Berkeley and Los Angeles: University of California Press, 2003), 49f.

2. While Dimock notes the eventual victory of the *parakīyā* position in Bengali Vaiṣṇava circles, he also notes the considerable support that the *svakīyā* position, where the favored partner is one's wife, had as well (*Place of the Hidden Moon*, 208f.). And while much of the scholarly literature after Dimock focuses on the *parakīyā* position, one hardly finds mention of the *svakīyā* position.

3. Michael McGee on his Web site, discussing the Kaṅkālamālinī Tantra, notes that when a Tantric text offers the suggestion that one's own wife or another woman is prescribed for the rite that, "this is an example of tantrik code. The 'other woman,' according to tantrik insiders, is one's wife or woman, while one's own woman here refers to the Devī. within. From this point of view, sex with one's own woman is adultery. On the other hand, this tantra may well be speaking literally." See http://www.religiousworlds.com/mandalam/kankala.htm, which suggests with this that the practice of the wife as the partner is much more ubiquitous.

4. On this see n. 24 below.

5. KCT 3.5–8: Kūlākula [*sic*?] japaṃ kṛtvā samānayati tatkṣaṇāt || yannāmnā likhitaṃ yantraṃ tamānayati tatkṣaṇāt | śatayojanadūrasthāṃ nadīparvatamadhyagām || dvīpāntarasahsreṣu rakṣitāṃ nigaḍādibhiḥ | payodharabharakṣubdhamadhyamāṃ lolalocanām . . . sādhakākāṅkṣihṛdayāṃ. This whole section runs from KCT 3.4–10. Again, as I mentioned earlier, the lines I left out were more graphic than this project calls for and the reader in any case gets the idea here.

6. KCT 5.28–29: jñātavyā purabhāvastu yatnataḥ kulasādhakaiḥ | kenāpi vyapadeśena kulacūḍāmaṇiṃ svataḥ || gṛhītvā svarṇa pātre vā tāmre vā kulasaṃjñake |. Here female fluids are the translation of kulacūḍāmaṇi, literally, "crest jewel," a reading borne out by the text. I follow Louise Finn's translation of *Kulacūḍāmaṇi*, 117, in reading purabhāvas as residents of the household. One may construe *pura* here to relate to the human body as well, however. In either case, the general sense of the argument remains the same. In this context, KCT 4.22–34 also supports the argument I make here.

7. White, *The Kiss of the Yoginī*, passim.

8. We may also note the general Indian tendency to view the wife in an agonistic relation to the husband and his family, which may also play into the equation of the general preference for the "other" woman. See Gloria Goodwin Raheja and Ann Grodzins Gold, *Listen to the Heron's Words: Reimagining Gender and Kinship in North India* (Berkeley and Los Angeles: University of California Press, 1994), 122–148. Raheja notes this view and seeks to controvert it. In chapter 2 I discuss the rite of sexual union, and in particular how the notion of "talk" about sex, that is, discussion, figures within the equation of titillation.

9. See n. 15 below.

10. Sanderson, "Purity and Power among the Brahmins of Kashmir," in Michael Carrithers, Steven Collins, and Steven Lukes, *The Category of the Person* (Cambridge: Cambridge University Press, 1985).

11. It may not be out of place here to suggest that the alliterativeness involved in this list itself points to an element that Julia Kristeva sees as naturally aligned in the history of the West with the degraded and rejected element of the binary male/

female. That is, the language of the sensory in poetry, the "semiotic" in Kristeva's terms, including alliteration and so on, is aligned with the feminine. She encodes these as the semiotic and the symbolic in *Revolution in Poetic Language*, trans. Margaret Walker (New York: Columbia University Press, 1984). While the similarity appears to be only coincidental, it is interesting to note that the use of alliteration when speaking of the transgressive, especially the transgressive as linked with the female, echoes this binary structuration.

12. We sometimes find, often in earlier Tantric texts, only three "Ms," in a list that excludes fish and parched grain.

13. We should also note that apart from this list, ritual practice enacted on corpses is frequently included within transgressive Tantric practice as well, though, due to space constraints, this aspect is not addressed here.

14. Monier Monier-Williams, *Hinduism* (London: SPCK, 1906), 126ff. See especially the work by Rachel Fell McDermott, "The Western Kālī," in *Devī: Goddesses of* India, ed. John Stratton Hawley and Donna Wulff (Berkeley and Los Angeles: University of California Press, 1996); Rachel Fell McDermott, "Kālī's New Frontiers: A Hindu Goddess on the Internet," in *Encountering Kālī*, ed. Rachel Fell McDermott and Jeffrey Kripal (Berkeley and Los Angeles: University of California Press, 2003); and Urban, *Tantra*, for contemporary Western attitudes toward Tantra.

15. Does it echo, as Dimock suggested (*Place of the Hidden Moon*), a carnivalesque reversal where society is overturned in order to reestablish normative order? Dimock's notion derives from the work of Bahktin, Turner, and others and suggests that social hierarchies engender internal mechanisms for releasing social tensions. In this view, the antinomian practice of Tantra represents a partial and temporary reversal that releases social tensions while it ultimately asserts the dominant order. On the other hand, in 1974 Narendra Nath Bhattacarya provocatively suggested that we see Tantrism as an indigenous Indian form of Marxist social resistance. See Bhattacarya, *History of the Śākta Religion*. 2nd rev. ed. (New Delhi: Munshiram Manoharla), 1996, passim. The use of a Marxist framework for understanding the evolution of a variety of religious traditions in India remains a theme throughout his work. The antinomian practices entailed by the "left-handed," "transgressive" way of worshiping God were, in Bhattacarya's view, an organic folk resistance against the political hegemony of an elite minority. Apart from the political appeal Communism held in Bengal in the 70s (an appeal still somewhat present today), Bhattacarya's theory highlighted a lingering and problematic aspect of Tantra—one even embarrassing from the view of a fledgling nation attempting to measure itself by internalized standards of Victorian propriety. Using a fundamentally different lens, White sees the transgressive, especially sex, as a form of a spiritual technology, a means of harnessing the latent hydraulic potency of bodily fluids as a means for ecstatic psychic flight in *The Kiss of the Yoginī*, 73ff. White's view moves away from understanding transgression in terms of a structural play of social forces; rather, his view suggests that Tantric practitioners developed something like a scientific technology involving the body. On the other hand, Paul Muller-Ortega understands the transgressive as a metaphoric representation for an inner meditative process in Muller-Ortega, *Triadic Heart of Śiva* (Albany: State

University of New York Press, 1989). This view is taken by numerous scholars, from India and the West, too many to enumerate here. Muller-Ortega presents one of the most eloquent and sophisticated renditions of this view. In his view Tantrics encoded an inner spiritual life in terms of social representations of freedom and conformity. Certain traditions in particular emphasize a spiritual-somatic force, the *kuṇḍalinī*, an inner goddess whose movement in the human body reconfigures human consciousness. David Kinsley suggests that the transgressive is a means whereby one breaks away from a limited and limiting social identity, including caste identity, in *Tantric Visions of the Divine Feminine: The Ten Mahāvidyās* (Berkeley and Los Angeles: University of California Press, 1997). I cite Kinsley here, however this view is also, like the previous, generally accepted by numerous scholars as a motive for the transgressive element in Tantra. Especially, one could point to the work of Alexis Sanderson, "Śaivism and the Tantric Tradition," in *The World's Religions*, ed. Stewart Sutherland, Leslie Houlden, Peter Clarke and Friedhelm Hardy (London: Routledge, 1988) for this view. This view bears some similarities to Bhattacarya's cited above. In this respect the liberatory impetus Tantra offers is reflected in the social order to some degree, even if the transgressive remains publicly obscured. Urban, on the other hand, suggests that the image of Tantric sex ritual derives especially from a prurient Western reading of Tantra, and is, in this sense, more a fabrication of the West, in *Tantra*, 41f. See also Caldwell, *Oh Terrifying Mother* (New Delhi: Oxford University Press, 1999); and Jeffrey Kripal, "Why the Tantrika Is a Hero: Kālī in the Psychoanalytic Tradition," in *Encountering Kālī*, ed. Rachel Fell Mcdermott and Jeffrey Kripal, 212ff. (Berkeley and Los Angeles: University of California Press, 2003), in contrast, explore the psychological ramifications of Tantric transgression, understanding it in terms of a deeper psychological dynamic.

16. Satyendranath Sarma, *Socio-economic and Cultural History of Medieval Assam, 1200–1800 A.D.* (Gauhati: Government of Assam, 1989), 245.

17. Alexis Sanderson, "Meaning in Tantric Ritual," in *Essais sur le Rituel* 3, ed. Anne-Marie Blondeau and Kristofer Schipper. Colloque du Centenaire de la Section des Sciences Religieuses de l'Ecole Pratique des Hautes Etudes (Louvain-Paris: Peeters, 1995); also, Navjivan Rastogi, *The Krama Tantrism of Kashmir* (Delhi: Motilal Banarsidass, 1979), 242; White, *The Kiss of the Yoginī*, 82f.). *Mudrā* also refers to hand gestures used in the context of the rite and in this context may be similar to the interpretation set forth by Sanderson in "Śaivism in the Tantric Tradition," since these gestures are supposed to elicit inner psychic and psychological states. For N. N. Bhattacarya, *mudrā* refers to the woman (*History of the Śākta Religion*, 121).

18. Edward Gait, *History of Assam*, rev. and enl. by B. K. Barua and H. V. S. Murthy (Calcutta: Thacker Spink, 1963; originally published in 1905), 123; H. K. Barpujari, ed. *Comprehensive History of Assam*. 5 vols. Guwahati: Publication Board Assam, 1990–94), 3:193.

19. In this context it may be interesting to note that in Tibet, where there is also an official state-sanctioned cult of oracular possession, the word *mudrā* also tends to mean the woman rather than a state of possession.

20. Sanderson, "Meaning in Tantric Ritual," 67.

21. KuT 11.55: kṛṣṇāṃśukāṃ kṛṣṇavarṇāṃ kumārīñca kṛśodarīm | manoharāṃ yauvanasthāmarcayeddevatādhiyā. That she is thin here likely reflects the image of Kālī, since thinness was not an especially attractive quality as it is for the modern West.

22. CT 5.6: kanyāyoniṃ paśukrīḍāṃ nagnāṃ strīṃ prakaṭastanīm | . . . sarvathā na vilokayet.

23. CT 5.27: parastriyaṃ gharṣayanti madyaṃ khādanti nityaśaḥ | nirvāṇaṃ te ca yāsyanti bhagavatyāḥ prasādataḥ ||. This verse is part of a longer panegyric to "other" women and wine from verses 5.17–30.

24. Not all the texts used in this study take this position. Some texts favor the "other woman" (*parastrī*), for instance, the *Cīnācāra Tantra* (CT) 5.23; also the *Māyā Tantra* (MT) 11.17; and also the *Kāmākhyā Tantra* (KamT) 2.72 in Tripāṭhī, *Tantrasaṅgraha, series 6,* part 4, 115–173. Others favor one's own wife as the ritual partner, for instance the BT (4.95ff.) and GT (34.97ff.). The majority of texts, however, are mostly indifferent; either will do, as we see in the *Yoni Tantra* (YT) 1.14.

25. BT 6.21: ādāvānīya deveśi svakāntāṃ vā parastriyam | prathamaṃ cāsanaṃ dattvā pādyaṃ dadyāttataḥ param.

26. BT 4.96–97: paradāravidhau vedanindāvādaḥ pravartate | tāsāṃ saṅgānmaheśāni tāmisraṃ narakaṃ bhavet || vedārthamiti vijñāya katham kuryācca sādhakaḥ | paradārān naiva gached. Following this the author employs an argument reminiscent of a *Mīmāṃsā*-like exegesis explaining what the Vedas are and their authority. We should also note, however, that in the end, taking a Jimmy Carter-like approach to adultery over a Bill Clinton-like approach, by accommodating other Tantric schools' assertions of the importance of the other woman, this author allows that one could in imagination *only* have sex with women other than one's wife while reciting the *mantra*: BT 4.104–5: paradārāgamaṃ vede tanniṣiddhaṃ sureśvari | yaddhi vaidhetaraṃ devi tanniṣiddhaṃ maheśvari || parastriyaṃ maheśāni manasā bhāvayañjapet [vede emended from vade].

27. GT 34.98: ekāpativratā bhāryā sādhvī cet sahacāriṇī | kimanyābhirmaheśāni yathaivāhaṃ tvayā prabhuḥ.

28. GT 34.103a: parakāntāṃ maheśāni sa yāti cādhamāṃ gatim.

29. See "Female Sexuality in the Hindu World," in *Immaculate and Powerful: The Female in Sacred Image and Social Reality*, ed. Clarissa Atkinson, 239ff. (Boston: Beacon, 1985). Also S. C. Banerji notes the practice of the wife as ritual partner for the rite of sexual union as well, here he classifies this practice as part of the *dakṣiṇācāra*, the "right-handed" path, which he notes in William Ward's account of nineteenth-century practices of Tantra in Bengal (*Tantra in Bengal: A Study in Its Origin, Development and Influence.* 2nd rev. and enl. ed. [New Delhi: Manohar, 1992], 247). I have not seen this particular explanation of the "right-handed" path elsewhere, however.

30. While it is the case that the Tantric rite is still practiced secretly, this aspect appeared to be not problematic for the three male practitioners I interviewed in Assam who talked about the sex rite. It was taken for granted that one's wife would be the optimal choice of a partner. Another point of interest, of the several practitioners

I located, none spoke English, suggesting a lesser degree of both awareness and influence of Western media in their self-representations to me (although one English-speaking priest at Kāmākhyā temple expressed a desire to get initiated in the left-handed *pūjā* in the future along with his wife). I hope to conduct further research in the future that would include interviewing the wives of these practitioners.

31. Dimock, *Place of the Hidden Moon*, 217 and passim; Banerji, *Tantra in Bengal*, 167; White, *The Kiss of the Yoginī*, 72ff. and passim; also, for instance, KCT 3.17.

32. Dimock, ibid., 211ff.

33. This section is lifted from the *Kulārṇava Tantra* 2.117–19. In fact, the CT borrows extensively from the *Kulārṇava Tantra* and reworks it, modifying it and adding some new material. One also notices here that this assumes that women are not in the loop of getting enlightenment by intercourse with women. The Buddha's response here is elusive; he simply praises the *kula* path as the highest and as leading to liberation.

34. The path outlined here is particularly that of the BT and the GT. The CT, which is more heavily indebted to the earlier tradition found in, for instance, the *Kulārṇava Tantra* generally prefers the "other woman" (5.17) though most of the texts consulted for this study suggest both as an option. While the *Mahānirvāṇa Tantra* also suggests the wife as partner, its indebtedness to Western ideas makes it not especially reliable.

35. Manu, however, neither mentions nor enjoins the practice of *satī*, the immolation of wives on their husbands' funeral pyres.

36. While the literature on *satī* is too voluminous to list here, a few important recent works include John S. Hawley, *Sati, the Blessing and the Curse* (New York: Oxford University Press, 1994); also Rajeshwari Sunder Rajan, "Real and Imagined Goddesses: A Debate." In *Is the Goddess a Feminist?* ed. Alf Hiltebeitel and Kathleen Erndl, 15–39 (New York: New York University Press, 2000); Lata Mani's *Contentious Traditions: The Debate on Sati in Colonial India* (Berkeley and Los Angeles: University of California Press, 1998); Catherine Weinberger-Thomas's *Ashes of Immortality: Widow Burning in India*, trans. Jeffrey Mehlman and David Gordon White (Chicago: University of Chicago Press, 1999). Also see Julia Leslie's discussion in *Roles and Rituals for Hindu Women* (Cranbury, N.J.: Fairleigh Dickinson University Press, 1991), 173–a91; and Arvind Sharma, *Sati: Historical and Phenomenological Essays* (New Delhi: Motilal Banarsidass 1988).

37. *Mahābhāgavata Purāṇa*, ed. Pushpendra Kumar. (Delhi: Eastern Book Linkers, 1983), 9.79, cited in Kinsley, *Tantric Visions of the Divine Feminine*, 25. Also see Hawley, ed., *Sati, the Blessing and the Curse*, 14.

38. Sharma, *Sati*, xii. One should also keep in mind the economic impetus for the male relatives of the dead man to convince his wife to commit *satī*, especially, for instance, in the region of Bengal during the nineteenth century with the British adoption of Dāyabhāga's law code, which stipulated that the wife of a dead man had inheritance rights to his property.

39. K. R. van Kooij, *Worship of the Goddess according to the Kālikāpurāṇa* (Leiden: Brill, 1972), 35. Van Kooij takes this from Albert Grunwedel, *Der Weg nach Śambhala*

(Abh. Kon. Bayerischen Ak. Wiss. Phil.- Philol. und Historische Klasse, 29, 1918), 18ff.

40. So, for instance, the eyes fall in Varanasi and the wide-eyed goddess (*Viśālākṣī*) resides there. Each place where a body part falls, a form of a goddess is venerated with a name and a history that recognizes the affiliation with the particular bodily organ.

41. But note also Weinberger-Thomas's fieldwork, which, as she notes, contains contradictory practices. Against the textual prescriptions, she notes that the bones of the *satī* are separated from the husband's and separately either disposed of at a *tīrtha* site, or else kept in the house (*Ashes of Immortality*, 81). I suspect that in this case the wife's remains signify a liminal being partaking of two identities—that of the wife of the dead husband, who will not be given a separate offering at the *śhraddha* ceremony because she has merged with her husband, and that of a being apotheosized into a goddess, whose divinity must somehow be marked. In this context it may be interesting to do a comparative study of funerary practices of *satīs* in Bengal and Rajasthan, given that that *satī* functions more prominently as deity in Rajasthan than in Bengal.

42. Sanderson, "Śaivism and the Tantric Tradition."

43. Ibid., 669.

44. There is not space here to explore the psychological dynamic behind this reversal. It may elicit psychological memories of the omnipotent mother; it may be a compensation for the power a male has over his mother and women in the public arena. Here I refer the reader to Kripal, "Why the Tantrika Is a Hero; Caldwell, *O Terrifying Mother*"; and Sudhir Kakar, "The Maternal-Feminine in Indian Psychoanalysis," *International Review of Psychoanalysis* 16 (1989), 335–62.

45. Cynthia Humes, "Is the *Devī Māhātmya* a Feminist Scripture?" in *Is the Goddess a Feminist?* ed. Alf Hiltebeitel and Kathleen Erndl (New York: New York University Press), 2000. See also Dimock, *Place of the Hidden Moon*, 200ff., for a detailed discussion of the debate over the comparative Tantric efficacy of the "other" woman over one's own wife. Keeping in mind the historically conservative tenor of Dimock's Vaiṣṇava sources in contrast to Śākta circles, it should not be too surprising that the outcome mostly favors the "other" woman.

46. In most cases that is. Certainly in the Indian context some devotees hear her talking back and their lives shift dramatically; however, this mystical transformative experience lies outside the purview of the argument presented here.

47. However, we find an example that contradicts this in the story mentioned briefly in chapter 4 where the goddess at Kāmākhyā about sixty years ago did "talk back" to the road engineer whose dynamite blew up her "body" as the mountain rocks.

48. So, for instance, the list of the six acts that are a key feature of Tantra sometimes includes *puṣṭi*, rites for the sake of increase in welfare, and sometimes does not.

49. This list in much earlier incarnations includes only three items; however, when it reaches a total of five these elements remain steady. This may in part be attributable to the alliteration of the list.

50. This is iterated as well in a different way in the *kumārī pūjā* where a young girl is worshiped without the use of the rite of sexual union. Also, one important point of interest is that the BT tends to differ from numerous Tantric texts in that it does not pay quite so much attention to bodily fluids as earlier texts. (The earlier *Kulārṇava Tantra* presents a good example in contrast.) Otherwise, texts that tend to neglect body fluids also tend to metaphorize the sexual elements into internal states. The BT, interestingly, does neither.

51. BT 6.329: pañcamī tvatsvarūpiṇī ||.

CHAPTER 4

1. Teresa De Lauretis, *Alice Doesn't: Feminism, Semiotics, Cinema* (Bloomington: Indiana University Press, 1984), 19.

2. P. C. Bagchi, *Studies on the Tantras* (Calcutta: Ramakrishna Mission, 1989), 48.

3. Andre Padoux, *Vāc: The Concept of the Word in Selected Hindu Tantras,* trans. Jacques Gontier (Albany: State University of New York Press, 1989), xiii.

4. Advaita Vedānta most obviously draws upon this dualism, where the secondary term becomes the illusory Māyā; however, one can find it throughout, including bhakti traditions as well and in many forms of Tantra also.

5. As Frits Staal construes the *mantra,* "*Mantra*s and Bird Songs," *JAOS* 105, no. 3 (1985): 549–558.

6. Bharati, *The Tantric Tradition* (London: Ryder and Co., 1965; reprint, New York: Grove, 1975), 111.

7. Particularly, Bharati's clearly pre-Wittgensteinian idea of a definition reflects the disjuncture: "a definition . . . is a set of formal propositions of exceptionless validity. If there is a single exception to a statement, then that statement forfeits its claim to being a definition" See Bharati, ibid., 111.

8. A subsequent and recent session at the annual meeting of the American Academy of Religion devoted to working toward a definition of *mantra,* by its own assessment found the task's complexity nearly insurmountable.

9. Note also Larsen's reference to the bījā *mantra* as "non-sense," cited by Muller-Ortega (*Triadic Heart of Śiva* [Albany: State University of New York Press, 1989], 279). To give a sense of other notions of *mantra*: Jan Gonda more informally defines *mantra* as "a general name for the formulas, verses or sequences of words in prose which contain praise . . . , are believed to have magical, religious, or spiritual efficiency, are recited, muttered or sung in Vedic ritual and which are collected in the methodically arranged corpora of Vedic texts . . . [along with] comparable 'formulas' of different origin used in the post-vedic cults" (Jan Gonda, "The Indian mantra," Oriens 16 (1963): 244–297; reprinted in *J. Gonda Selected Studies* 4:251 (Leiden: Brill, 1975). And we should note here the distinction he makes between Vedic *mantras* and Tantric *mantras.* Alternatively, for Gonda the term *mantra* "covers also all potent (so-called magical) forms of texts, words, sounds, letters, which bring good luck to those who know or 'possess' them and evil to their enemies" (Gonda, "The Indian

mantra, 271f.). Bagchi notes in particular the brevity, "compression" of meaning, that occurs in the transition from the vedic *mantra* to the Tantric *mantra* (P. C. Bagchi, *Studies on the Tantras* [Calcutta: Ramakrishna Mission, 1989], 48). Recently, much thoughtful work has been devoted to the *mantra*, particularly with Alper's edited volume (*Understanding Mantras* [Albany: State University of New York Press, 1989; reprint, Delhi: Motilal Banarsidass, 1991]. Alper himself seeks to shift the discussion away from questions of definition, noting, for instance, that the phenomenon and the terms used to indicate it are divergent and various (Alper, *Understanding Mantras*, 4). In this important work he also offers, with a nod to the fourteenth-century Vedic commentator Sāyaṇa, the plastic notion that a *mantra* is whatever a person in a position to know might designate as *mantra*, a useful heuristic device for this collection of articles whose topics span across genres and centuries.

10. Wade T. Wheelock, "The Mantra in Vedic and Tantric Ritual"; Frits Staal, "Vedic Mantras"; and Ellison Banks Findley, "*Mantra Kaviśasta*: Speech as Performative in the Ṛgveda," all in *Understanding Mantras* stress the performative element of *mantra*, what Andre Padoux in his summary of these articles identifies as the idea of the *mantra* as language with a "use rather than a meaning" (Padoux, "*Mantras*," 302). Wheelock in particular notes its creative aspect, its capacity to "create and allow participation in a known and repeatable situation" (Wheelock, "The Mantra in Vedic and Tantric Ritual," 99). Padoux in his comprehensive survey stresses the fact of the *mantra*'s location within a particular cultural milieu, its efficacy intimately linked with the cultural beliefs about the potency of sound, apart from its communicative aspects (Padoux, *What Are They*, 306).

11. Paul Muller-Ortega's insightful if brief analysis along cosmological lines using the work of the physicist David Bohm presents a coherent and tangible representation of the function of *mantra* not along social lines, nor semantic lines, but rather imbricating the *mantra* in a generative logic (Muller-Ortega, "Tantric Meditation: Vocalic Beginnings," in *Ritual and Speculation in Early Tantrism: Studies in Honor of Andre Padoux*, ed. Teun Goudriaan, 228–240 (Albany: State University of New York Press, 1992). From this certainly one gathers that the idea of the *mantra* is complex, amenable to multivalent interpretation, but more than this that in the Tantric context speech itself has already deconstructed the myth of a transparent sign, faithfully, objectively mirroring the "real" "out there." The mirror of language is itself generatively transforming. See also Muller-Ortega's *Triadic Heart of Śiva* (173), where he also proposes the transformative impetus of *mantra*, citing Abhinavagupta, however, in this instance, in a more general sense than in the article noted above.

12. Laurie Patton, "Mantras and Miscarriage: Controlling Birth in the Late Vedic Period," in *Jewels of Authority*, ed. Laurie Patton (New York: Oxford University Press, 2002), 55.

13. BT 4.74: mantrārthaṃ mantracaitanyaṃ yonimudrāṃ na vetti yaḥ | śatakoṭijapenāpi kathaṃ siddhirvarānane ||.

14. BT 12.38–41: yayau brahmāmahendreṇa golokaṃ sahito mudā | nānāvidhair maheśāni vākyaiśca parameśvaram || tuṣṭāva paramānandaṃ svakāryoddharaṇāya ca | iti tasya vacaḥ srutvā brahmaṇaḥ parameṣṭhinaḥ || uvāca sādaraṃ viṣṇurna

mayāśakyate vibho | brahmaviṣṇū maheśāni āgatau mama gocare || stavairbahuvidhair divyaistuṣṭuvatuḥ paraṃ śubhe | mayoktaṃ parameśāni etān hantuṃ na śakyate.

15. BT 12:57b–59a: gacchata yatra te >surāḥ || aham tatra gamiṣyāmi sarvathā sannidhau surāḥ | ityuktvā sā mahādevī tāriṇī kāmacāriṇī || antarhitā mahāmāyā māyārūpavatī ca sā |.

16. BT 12:67: pañcavarṣaṃ gataṃ tatra devānāṃ divyajanmanām | bhraṣṭarājyāḥ parātaṅkā martyā iva nagopari ||. "Gods born from the light" reflects a notion we find elsewhere in this text that both the "good guys" and the "bad guys" are "gods," "deva-."

17. The Sanskrit here is Nīlasarasvatī. She is also in this myth, which forms part of the twelfth chapter of the BT, called "Nīlavāṇī," "the Blue Goddess of Speech; "Nīlarūpā Devī," "The Blue Goddess"; "Tāriṇī," "the Saviouress"; "Mahāmāyā," "the Great Goddess of Illusion"; and simply "Goddess" (Devī, Bhagavatī).

18. BT 12.52: sṛṣṭasarvavimohinī.

19. Bṛhannīla Tantra 12.69–75: āsanaṃ svāgataṃ pādyam arghyam ācamanīyakam | madhuparkācamasnānavasanābharaṇāni ca || gandhapuṣpe dhūpadīpau naivedyaṃ vandanaṃ śive | ṣoḍaśair upacāraiś ca devīṃ nīlasarasvatīm || pūjayitvā baliṃ dattvā śivāyai vividhaiḥ śubhaiḥ | japaṃ cakāra deveśi devavṛndaḥ surottamaḥ || mahāmantraṃ pūrvamuktaṃ lakṣaṃ japtvā maheśvari | ayutaṃ cājuhodajyaiḥ padmapuṣpairmanoramaiḥ || homaṃ cakrustilayuktaiḥ śarkarāsahitairapi | evaṃ hutvā mahādevi daśāṃśenābhiṣecanam || daśāṃśaistarpaṇaṃ devi kṛtaṃ sarvairmaheśvari | samāpte ca tato devīṃ pūjayitvā mahāniśi || baliṃ dattvā mahādevyai surāhārāḥ surāstathā | evaṃ niyamamānena kṛtaṃ karma manoramam ||.

20. BT 12.76–77: tato bhagavatī devī devaiḥsmṛtā maheśvari | santuṣṭā sā mahādevī nīlarūpā mahodarī | devāgre parameśāni pratyakṣatvamupāgatā | kiṃ karomi kva gacchāmi brūta devāḥ samāhave ||.

21. BT 21.24: bahujāpāt tathā homāt kāyakleśādivistaraiḥ | na bhāvena vinā devi mantravidyā phalapradā ||.

22. BT 21.27b–29a: bhāvena labhate muktiṃ bhāvena kulavarddhanam || bhāvena gotravṛddhiḥ syād bhāvena kulasādhanam | kiṃ nyāsavistareṇaiva kiṃ bhūtaśuddhivistaraiḥ || kiṃ tathā pūjanenaiva yadi bhāvo na jāyate |. See also BT 4.112; 21.24–30.

23. It is by *re-membering,* in a sense, by bringing to consciousness her existence as a whole entity rather than as part and object, seeing the Blue Goddess of Speech, which constitutes something like a reintegration of a feminine sense of being, that they can connect with the power she affords. One can read an astute psychological sophistication in the Hindu notion of a reintegration of elements back into the psyche. One sees this also especially in the portrayal of demons, not just in this text, but in a variety of others as well insofar as the "demon" is never ultimately relegated to a realm of pure evil, but rather nearly always understood as a fragmentation of egoity that seeks its destruction in order to ultimately attain a fuller sense of self. The paradigmatic demon, Rāvaṇa, who is killed by Rāma, the incarnation of the god Viṣṇu, exemplifies this principle. When he is killed, he transforms back into his inherent original purity, and attains ultimate salvation. After all, in a psychological register what is a demon except that part of the psyche that must be separated off and rejected

as other? One could read the time on the mountain for the gods as the process of integrating that part of the self, in this case, the feminine goddess, back into the psyche.

24. BT 12.78–83: prasannā bhava ceśvari | tato bhagavatī devī nīlarūpā manoramā || dṛṣtvā surasamūhān sā tāriṇī sarvakāmadā | svadehataḥ parāḥ sṛṣṭā vidyā dvādaśa īritāḥ || kālī caiva mahādevī mahāvidyā tathaiva ca | ṣoḍaśī bhuvaneśānī bhairavī cchinnamastakā || dhūmāvatī ca bagalā mātaṅgī kamalātmikā | etā vidyā mahādevi siddhividyāḥ prakīrtitāḥ || mahādevyāḥ sarasvatyā dehodbhūtā varānane | anyāśca mātarastasyā dehājjātā varānane || sarvā devyāḥ parānande nṛtyanti caraṇāntike |.

25. The text lists eleven names; that is, Kamalātmikā is probably one name, but in order to get twelve, one of the names has to split and this is the best choice. We could also just have only eleven names here.

26. BT 12.83a: sarvā devyāḥ parānande nṛtyanti caraṇāntike |. There is clearly a reference here to the ten goddesses who also are called the *Mahāvidyā*, and many of the names that the BT gives are referenced in other lists. See David Kinsley, *Tantric Visions of the Divine Feminine: The Ten Mahāvidyās* (Berkeley and Los Angeles: University of California Press, 1997).

27. This English word is perhaps curiously illustrative of the point I'm making here. It suggests a mental stopping, a pause or rupture in the ordinary flow of time. One is "spellbound" and the mind stops, and so consequently time seems to stop, or does stop psychologically. Interestingly, its origin refers to magic, the use of a "spell" to bind someone, that is, the use of a language that is not semantically oriented.

28. BT 8.152: kuśodakena japtena pratyarṇaṃ prokṣayed manoḥ | tena mantreṇa vidhivadetadāpyāyanaṃ matam.

29. BT 8.147b: mantravarṇān samālikhya tāḍayeccandanāmbhasā ||.

30. See, for example, BT 6.43, and also YT 2.10. The BT also uses other words to describe sexual intercourse during the rite of sexual union, for instance "*saṃkṣipya liṅgaṃ tadyonau ghātaṃ kuryāc*" (BT 13.29) and in the YT "*maithunam ācaret*"; however, "*tāḍayet*" is the most frequent.

31. Dhātupāṭha xxxiii, 126, cited in Monier Monier-Williams, *A Sanskrit-English Dictionary*, 10th ed. (Oxford: Oxford University Press, 1988), 432.

32. "Mahālakṣmyaṣṭaka Stotram" 4b: "mantra mūrte sadā devi Mahālakṣmi namostute" in *Bṛhatstotraratnākara*, ed. Śivadatta Miśra Śāstrī (Varanasi: Jyotiṣa Prakāśana, 1997), 258.

33. Harlan, "Satī: The Story of Godāvarī" in *Devī: Goddesses of India*, ed. John S. Hawley (Berkeley and Los Angeles: University of California Press, 1996).

34. Ibid., 244–245.

35. Ibid., 229.

36. Harlan notes that the story of Godāvarī is exceptional; the more common *satī* story involves one, or two, or maybe three curses. However, Godāvarī's story presents an excess, a sort of cursing binge. We could analyze this negativity psychologically, as a sign of male fear mixed with guilt, or ethically as the moral result of

the extreme abrogation of the woman's voice, so that when she does speak, all she can utter is her pain offered to others.

37. In a sense this effusion of curses is similar to what Butler sees as the force of hate speech (Butler, *Excitable Speech: A Politics of the Performative* [New York: Routledge, 1997]), only the dread, or perhaps guilt encoded in the soon-to-be sacrifice of this bride never misfires. Of course it may make most sense to read this omnipotent cursing rage of the *satī* as a male projection of guilt surrounding an uneasy and unnecessary sacrifice of another's life, something Harlan alludes to in her thoughtful discussion of the psychology behind the depiction of the *satī*'s cursing spree (Harlan, "Satī," 240ff.).

38. In Hindi we find "hath," but also "*kām karne wala*" for hand, explicitly linking the hand with a notion of performing/doing things.

39. Rajeshwari Sunder Rajan, "Real and Imagined Goddesses: A Debate," in *Is the Goddess a Feminist?* 88.

40. Ibid., 86.

41. Ibid., 88.

42. Ibid.

43. Butler, *Excitable Speech,* 83ff.

44. Catharine Mackinnon, *Only Words* (Cambridge, Mass.: Harvard University Press, 1993). Rae Langton offers a philosophical backing for the notion of pornography as silencing women in "Speech Acts and Unspeakable Acts," *Philosophy and Public Affairs* 22, no. 4 (Autumn 1993): 321ff.

45. Butler, *Excitable Speech,* 83ff.

46. Ibid., 77.

47. For Butler, if I am reading her correctly, this imputation of the performative in Hill's speech signals a deeper manipulation enacted by the state, ultimately, in its assuming the somewhat disingenuous role of neutral arbiter, and Butler focuses as well on racial elements in the proceedings. Butler suggests that the Thomas proceedings "[permit] for a purification in prurience for the white imaginary. African-American status permits for a spectacularization of sexuality and a recasting of whites as outside the fray, witnesses and watchers who have circuited their own sexual anxieties through the publicized bodies of blacks." See ibid., 83.

48. *Devī Māhātmyam,* 10.3–8.

49. Judith Butler, *Bodies That Matter: On the Discursive Limits of "Sex"* (New York: Routledge, 1993), 53.

50. Here I am referencing the Lacanian notion that the "self" is constructed upon an act that excludes that which is "other." The excluded other is the hidden repressed foundation for the identity of self. This occurs for Lacan in the mirror stage, and in his view, the mirror stage in his conception precedes the formation of the symbolic, the power of language to represent the world in its absence. See Jacques Lacan, *Ecrits,* trans. Alan Sheridan (New York: Norton, 1977), 1–8, 171ff.

51. This story was told to me by several informants during research conducted in the summer of 2004 in Kāmākhyā.

52. BT 20.45–46a: "avyaktaśca sa ca vyaktaḥ prakṛtyā jñāyate dhruvam | tasmāt prakṛtiyogena vinā na jñāyate kvacit || vinā ghaṭatvayogena na pratyakṣo yathā ghaṭaḥ |" ("dhruvam," "firmly" is something of a filler for the meter here).

53. Jamison, *Ravenous Hyenas and the Wounded Sun* (Ithaca, N.Y.: Cornell University Press, 1991), 211, 237.

54. Mādhava Vidyāraṇya, *Śaṅkaradigvijaya* (Śrīrangam: Śrīvaṇivilasamudranālayaḥ, 1972), 10.59, 2:82.

55. We see this especially in the rite where the goddess takes a variety of forms.

CHAPTER 5

1. An exploration of this lies beyond the scope of the present project, but I address it at greater length in a work in progress. See Gayatri Spivak, "Can the Subaltern Speak?" in *Marxism and the Interpretation of Culture*, ed. Cary Nelson and Lawrence Grossberg (Urbana: University of Illinois Press, 1988).

2. This myth codifies in narrative form some of the insights that Elaine Scarry brings up regarding torture and speech in *The Body in Pain: The Making and Unmaking of the World* (New York: Oxford University Press, 1985).

3. Speech separates humans from animals, especially for that early, seminal thinker of Enlightenment thought, Rousseau, who begins his *Essay on the Origin of Languages* with this iteration, in Jacques Derrida, *Of Grammatology*, trans. Gayatri Chakravorty Spivak (Baltimore: Johns Hopkins University Press, 1976; reprint, Delhi: Motilal Banarsidass, 1994), 183. For India, one sees this also exemplified in a popular story of the master poet Kālidāsa, who was initially scorned by his educated wife for his lack of civilized breeding because he could not pronounce the three consonants clustered in the Sanskrit word for camel.

4. Jenny Sharpe, *Allegories of Empire: The Figure of Woman in the Colonial Text* (Minneapolis: University of Minnesota Press, 1993), 77.

5. The BT is not written in English and predates 1857, the date that Sharpe and others propose as inaugurating the beginning of a British discourse around rape (as well as 1919—the date marking a resurgence of the British fear of the rape of white women after the brutal Amritsar massacre). See Sharpe, *Allegories of Empire*, 61; and also Revathi Krishnaswamy, *Effeminism: The Economy of Colonial Desire* (Ann Arbor: University of Michigan Press, 1998). Both of these studies point out the use of rape as a trope within colonial discourse. So while it may not be possible to entirely rule out British influence in this textual representation of male violence toward women, a best guess suggests that British influence is not likely. In other words, these authors at this time period were likely independently, without British influence, aware of the problems of sexual harassment of women and of the pernicious and pervasive social response that blamed the woman for her harassment. This text's author(s) attempt to offer a different response to this problem.

6. BT 7.86: "dehin." This is the word used for "spirit." See the discussion in chapter 2, 87, 90.

7. BT 7.89–91: ete jaḍatarāḥ sarve parasparakhalātmakāḥ || kukarmaniratāḥ sarve kumārgadarśanotsukāḥ . . . tat kathaṃ kathayāmi te |. Perhaps in this case, the use of the male gender marker that the author uses to list the categories of beings, human, and so on, may not, after all, be intended to be inclusive of both genders. That he lists also the generally female water-spirits (*apsaras*) separately could perhaps be read to support this.

8. BT 11.56.

9. BT 7.89: ete jaḍatarāḥ sarve parasparakhalātmakāḥ |

10. BT 11.60: śabdākarṣaṇikā devī.

11. BT 11.60–63: tāvubhau bhrātarau duṣṭau turaṅgagrīvasomakau | śabdākarṣaṇikāṃ devīṃ samuddiśyātapasyatām || tayorghoratapaḥprītā śabdākarṣaṇidevatā | provāca vriyatāmatra vāñchito varavallabhaḥ || tābhyāmuktā bhagavatī varaprārthanahetave | sarvaśabdākarṣaṇārthaṃ varo >smabhyaṃ pradīyatām || tathāstviti tayā proktau dānavāvatidarpitau |.

12. BT 11.64b–67: sā śabdarūpiṇī devī śubhrarūpā sarasvatī || mukhāni sarvaviprāṇāṃ tyaktvā divyavapurdharā | āyātā daityavarayor duṣṭagṛhamupāgatā || krandantīṃ tāṃ ca vivaśāṃ nītvā pātālagolake | hālāhalaviṣaiḥ kṛtvā kuṇḍaṃ nīlajalaprabhaiḥ || tatra tāṃ vinimajyaiva baddhvā pannagarajjubhiḥ |.

13. Viewed through a semiotic classification system of signifier and signified, that the goddess as *vidyā*, magical speech is nonsemantic sound, suggests that in this equation there is no signified, only goddess-word as Signifier.

14. Note here the visualization of the Blue Goddess of Speech (BT 2.49ff.), given in appendix 2, which depicts her with a variety of different-colored snakes.

15. BT 11.68b–70: śabdākarṣaṇabāṇena daityānāṃ pṛthivītale || niḥśabdāścaiva bāṇena vedavismāriṇo dvijāḥ | mantravismaraṇenaiva yajñavidyā nirāsitā || tannāśato havirbhāgavarjitā balahānitaḥ |.

16. BT 11.71–72: itthaṃ vidrāvya vibudhāṃstau hayagrīvasomakau | viṣṇucakrāṅkitau tau ca samudrāntargṛhe sthitau || tato viṣṇurmahāmatsyarūpadhārī sadā prabhuḥ |.

17. It is similar perhaps to the Vedic notion of sacrificing the seasons, where time takes on the same substantive aspect as more corporeal elements such as the earth, and so forth.

18. BT 11.74: varāharūpeṇa yathābdhimagnāṃ yuge yuge proddhṛtavān dharitrīm | tathaiva matsyākṛtirambujākṣo viloḍayāmāsa samudrapuram ["puram" emended from "pūram"] ||.

19. BT 11.74–76.

20. It is not entirely clear who is singing here, the Goddess of Speech or Viṣṇu, though a few lines down Viṣṇu speaks to her, seemingly in reply, so a good guess is that she is speaking here. And it makes sense that she would be singing the *mantras* related to Tārā.

21. BT 11.79–81: hariḥ smitāṃ prāha sarasvatīṃ tām | tritāravidyāṃ prathamaṃ jagāda samastamantraprakarasya mūlam || tenāpi no saṃvidamāpa devī . . . nīlāsi jātā viṣakuṇḍamadhye sarvāṅgapūrṇā smitavaktrapadme || ["smitaṃ" emended to

"smitāṃ"]. The last word is an epithet, "o smiling lotus faced one" which to avoid awkwardness I translate into his statement to her.

22. BT 11.83: matsyāvatāreṇa surakṣitāhaṃ bhayaṃ bhavennaiva phalam samāptam | kiṅtvasya śobhākṛtiranyathā me nīlatvamāpteti nitāntacintā ||.

23. BT 11.90: hi jīvitāsi vinaṣṭaceṣṭā viṣakuṇḍamadhye ||.

24. BT 11.85: mā tvaṃ śucaṃ . . . ugreṇa hālāhalakarṣaṇena nīlatvamāptāsi kuto >tra doṣaḥ ||.

25. BT 11.86.

26. BT 11.86–88: puṣṇanti nīlaḥ khalu deva eva | nīlā mṛḍānī jagatāṃ sāvitrī nīlaṃ ca kaṇṭhe puraśāsanasya || nīlo mahendraḥ suracakravartī nīlā jagajjīvanadāśca meghāḥ | nīlaṃ nabhaḥ sarvajanāvakāśo nīlaḥ kalaṅkaḥ śaśidīptihetuḥ || nīlo >pyahaṃ sattvaguṇāśrayaśca nīlasya varṇasya kuto >sti doṣaḥ | (savitrī emended to sāvitrī).

27. BT 11.85–87.

28. BT 11.84. In the context of this story, she is also called as "Kāmeśvarī," the Goddess of Love, referencing Kāmākhyā, Vāṇī, "Speech," and Sarasvatī, the "Goddess of Speech."

29. Sharpe, *Allegories of Empire*, 70f.

30. Ibid., 69.

31. BT 11.86–88.

32. Alice Walker, *The Color Purple: A Novel* (New York: Harcourt Brace Jovanovich, 1982).

33. BT 11.92: tataḥ prabhṛtyeva jagatpratītā mokṣapradā nīlasarasvatīti.

34. Perhaps we may also read it as answering Spivak's question of whether the subaltern can speak.

CONCLUSION

1. Slavoj Zizek, *Looking Awry: An Introduction to Jacques Lacan through Popular Culture* (Cambridge: Massachusetts Institute of Technology Press, 1991), 10–12. Zizek continues in this passage to link Shakespeare's image of "looking awry" with Lacan's notion of *objet petit a*, where "looking," which is distorted by desire, enables the construction of the object, where it was not "seen" before.

APPENDIX I

1. *Bṛhannīla Tantra [BT]*, ed. Madhusudhana Kaul, (Delhi: Butala and Co., 1984). The Nīla Tantra version is found in *Tantrasāra*, ed. Rasik Mohan Chattopādhyāya (Calcutta: 1877–84), cited in Goudriaan and Gupta, *History of Indian Literature*, vol. 2: *Hindu Tantric and Śākta Literature* (Wiesbaden: Harrassowitz, 1981), 88.

2. The *Cīnācāra Tantra* (CT), *Gupta Sādhana Tantra* (GST), *Māyā Tantra* (MT), and *Sarvavijayi Tantra* (SVT), a text that I reference at one point, are all located in *Tantrasaṅgraha*, ed. Vrajvallabha Dvivedi. Yogatantragranthamālā Series 8, part 5

(Varanasi: Sampurnanand Sanskrit University, 1996). The Gandharva Tantra (GT) is located in Tantrasaṅgraha, ed. Ramprasāda Tripāṭhī. Yogatantragranthamālā Series 5, part 3 (Varanasi: Sampurnanand Sanskrit University, 1992). *Nīlasarasvatī Tantram*, ed. Brahmananda Tripathi, with Hindi commentary by S. N. Khandelwal (Varanasi: Chaukhamba Surbharati Prakashan, 1999). *Phetkāriṇī Tantra* (PhT) is located in *Tantrasaṅgraha*, 3rd ed., ed. M. M. Gopinath Kaviraj, in Yogatantragranthamālā Series 4, part 2 (Varanasi: Sampurnanand Sanskrit University, 2002). *Yoni Tantra*, edited with an introduction by J. A. Schoterman (Delhi: Manohar, 1980).

3. Teun Goudriaan and Sanjukta Gupta, *History of Indian Literature*, vol. 2: *Hindu Tantric and Śākta Literature* (Wiesbaden:Harrossowitz, 1981), 88.

4. BT 13.7a: gurucintā na caivātra mahākālyāśca sādhane.

5. S. C. Banerji, *Brief History of Tantra Literature* (Calcutta: Naya Prokash, 1988), 248–257.

6. Rāmatoṣaṇa Bhaṭṭācārya, *Prāṇatoṣiṇī*, ed. Harivansh Kumar Pandey (Varanasi: Sampurnanand Sanskrit University, 2000). He mentions the NT throughout; a couple of examples include 1:453, and 1:455; for the BT, which he also mentions throughout, 15, 478, and 480; and for the Mahānīla Tantra, 3.

7. This, according to Worldcat.

8. Banerji, *Brief History*, 468.

9. Goudriaan and Gupta, *History of Indian Literature*, 88n.

10. Dvivedi, ed., *Tantrasaṅgraha* 8, part 5, p. 1 of the "Prāstāvikam."

11. Goudriaan and Gupta, *History of Indian Literature*. For Banerji's ascription to Bengal, see Banerji, *Brief History*, 256.

12. Gudrun Buhnemann, *The Iconography of Hindu Tantric Deities*. 2 vols. (Groningen: Egbert Forsten, 2000), 1:102.

13. Kinsley, *Tantric Visions of the Divine Feminine: The Ten Mahāvidyās* (Berkeley and Los Angeles: University of California Press, 1997), 96.

14. See Schoterman, ed., *Yoni Tantra*, 10, for a discussion of this phenomenon in the YT.

15. The *Tārā Tantra*, in Goudriaan and Gupta, *History of Indian Literature*, 87, also located in the northeastern India region and likely from late medieval times, also employs a tripartite scheme of goddesses, including Ugratārā, Ekajaṭā (a name for Tārā specifically associated with Buddhist texts), and Nīlasarasvatī; again there is evidence supporting a late medieval date for the BT, and a northeastern Indian regional affiliation for the BT.

16. Rai K. L. Barua Bahadur, *Early History of Kāmarūpa* (Shillong, 1933), 294; also, for instance, 64 where the king Nīlāmbar flees to the hills.

17. S. Sarma, *Socio-economic and Cultural History of Medieval Assam, 1200–1800 A.D.* (Gauhati: Government of Assam, 1989), 248–249.

18. Goudriaan and Gupta, *History of Indian Literature*, 74n67.

19. Schoterman, ed., *Yoni Tantra*, 6.

20. Ibid., 9, and 84 in appendix.

21. Ibid., 18.

22. Ibid., 6; Shastri, ed., *Yoginī Tantra*, xxxixff.

23. Narasiṃha, *Tārābhaktisudhārṇava*, ed. Pañcānana Tarka-Sāṃkhya-Vedānta-Tirtha (Delhi: Bhāratīya Vidyā Prakāśana, 1983), 388f.

24. Cited in Banerji, *Brief History*, 256. Banerji gives Sarvānanda a date of ca. 1425, while Goudriaan and Gupta, *History of Indian Literature*, 146, cite his date as sixteenth century. Banerji also notes that the NT is cited elsewhere, for instance, in Pūrṇānanda's *Śyāmārahasya*, in Brahmānanda Giri's *Tārārahasya*, in his *Śāktānanda Taraṅginī*—which we note below—in Kṛṣṇānanda's *Tantrasāra*, and in Raghunātha Tarkavāgīśa's *Āgamatattvavilāsa*, among others.

25. Rāmatoṣaṇa Bhaṭṭācārya, *Prāṇatoṣiṇī*, ed. Harivansh Kumar Pandey, vol. 1 (Varanasi: Sampurnanand Sanskrit University, 2000), 1:4, where he lists both the NT and the BT; 272–73, 478, for the discussion of the guru; 300, on not massaging the feet of the guru's wife; 570, for the inclusion of both Vedic and Tantric *sandhyā*; and, for instance, in volume 2 (Varanasi: Sampurnanand Sanskrit University, 2002) 2:35, for the worship of the goddess in the cremation ground and where there is only a single *liṅga* established; 2:252f., for the *kumārī pūjā vidhi*; 2:549 and 2:555, for discussion of the *Kumārī pūjā*; and 2:577, for the praise of Brahmins, to mention only some of his citations.

26. Goudriaan and Gupta, *History of Indian Literature*, 82.

27. Ibid., 80.

28. Ibid.

29. Banerji, *Brief History*, 255.

30. Barpujari, *Comprehensive History of Assam* (Guwahati: Publication Board Assam, 1990–1994), 2:13.

31. Ibid.

32. K. R. Van Kooij, *Worship of the Goddess according to the Kālikāpurāṇa* (Leiden: Brill, 1972), 3.

33. Goudriaan and Gupta, *History of Indian Literature*, 86.

34. Buhnemann, *The Iconography of Hindu Tantric Deities*, 35.

35. S. Sarma, *Socio-economic and Cultural History*, 161.

36. Schoterman, *Yoni Tantra*, 5–9.

37. White, *The Kiss of the Yoginī: Tantric Sex in Its South Asian Contexts* (Chicago: University of Chicago Press, 2003).

38. Davidson, *Indian Esoteric Buddhism* (New York: Columbia University Press), 2002.

39. However, I should emphasize that the portrait I am painting right here is speculative.

40. See Brahmānanda Giri, *Śāktānandataraṅgiṇī*, ed. Rājanātha Tripāṭhī (Varanasi: Sampurnanand Sanskrit University, 1987), for NT, p. 59; GT, pp. 38, 58. He does not reference the BT, the MT, the CT, or the GST, which leads one to surmise a later date for these texts, though even the texts he does cite may have changed through different recensions.

41. In *Vāmakeśvarīmatam, with the Commentary of Jayaratha*, ed. Madhusudan Kaul Shastri (Srinagar: Kashmir Series of Texts and Studies, 1945), 36.

42. *Kulārṇava Tantra*, ed. Taranatha Vidyaratna with an introduction by Arthur Avalon (Sir John Woodroffe) (Madras: Ganesh and Company, 1965; reprint, Delhi: Motilal Banarsidass, 1975).

43. See White's *The Kiss of the Yoginī*, passim.

44. Goudriaan and Gupta, *History of Indian Literature*, 227. See also Goudriaan's statement in this text that the KuT is "without doubt the most important of its class" (93).

45. KuT 8.52: yoginyaḥ kṣtrepālāśca mama dehe vyavasthitāḥ.

46. KuT 8.46.

47. KuT 8.103: cakramadhye tu mūḍhātmā jātibhedaṃ karoti yaḥ | taṃ bhakṣayanti yoginyas. Also, for instance, 11.38.

48. KuT 11:62a: nāpriyaṃ nānṛtaṃ brūyāt kasyāpi kulayoginaḥ |.

49. KuT 11.62b: kurūpā ceti kṛṣṇeti na vadet kulayoṣitam.

50. KuT 9.52a: svecchācāraparāyaṇaḥ.

51. KuT 9.57a: apeyamapi peyaṃ syādabhakṣyaṃ bhakṣyameva ca.

52. KuT 9.58: na vidhirna niṣedhaḥ syānna puṇyaṃ na ca pātakam | na svargo naiva narakaṃ kaulikānāṃ kuleśvari ||.

53. BT 6.341b–42a śaktiśca kusumaiḥ pūjyā sindūrairgandhacandanaiḥ || atha mālyairalaṅkāraiḥ kevalaṃ mātṛbhāvataḥ |.

54. KuT 8.71b: dhṛtvāśirasi nṛtyanti madyabhāṇḍāni yoginaḥ.

55. KuT 8.73–74: yogino madamattāśca patanti pramadorasi | madākulāśca yoginyaḥ patanti puruṣopari || manorathasukhaṃ pūrṇaṃ kurvanti ca parasparam |.

56. *Kaulāvalīnirṇaya*, ed. Arthur Avalon (Varanasi: Bharatiya Vidya Prakashan, 1985; reprinted with permission of M/s Ganesh and Co. [Madras, n.d]).

57. KuT 11.65: striyaṃ śatāparādhāñcet puṣpeṇāpi na tāḍayet | doṣānna gaṇayet strīṇāṃ guṇāneva prakāśayet ||.

58. P. C. Bagchi suggests a northeastern location for the KJN. See *Kaulajñānanirṇaya and Some Minor Texts of the School of Matsyendranātha*, edited with an introduction by Prabodh Chandra Bagchi. Calcutta Sanskrit Series, no. 3 (Calcutta: Metropolitan Printing and Publishing House, 1934), 16–20. White, however, in contrast to Bagchi's assertion of a northeastern provenance for this text, has pointed out to me that there is no evidence to give a northeastern provenance to the KJN (correspondence-mail message to author, May, 4, 2006).

59. *Kaulajñānanirṇaya* [KJN], edited with an introduction by P. C. Bagchi, translated by Michael McGee. Tantra Granthamala, no. 12 (Varanasi: Prachya Prakashan, 1986), 56.

60. Ibid., 57; KJN 3.24.

61. Ibid., KJN 5.20: satatamabhyasedyogī siñcyamānaśca viṣaiḥ | valīpalitanirmuktaḥ sarvavyādhivivarjitam [*sic*]. Bagchi here inserts "śe" to make "viśeṣaiḥ." This changes the meaning from "poisons" to "special substances"; however, the point I make with this verse remains the same. That is, that the KJN offers practices toward attaining immortality. Also the previous and succeeding verses, 5.18–19, indicate that the practice here is an inner meditation with its focus on the *cakras*, and the following verses, 5.21–23, indicate the same with the use of *dhyatvā* in 5.22.

62. White notes that the sex rite is described here, and while his thesis of the use of fluids I think is certainly borne out by this passage, the sex rite itself is not described; KJN 18.21: "Having offered, one gives respect to the guru, especially through the guru-worship. Then, having done the worship of the hero, by which he (the hero? The Goddess? The guru? The practitioner?) should be made happy again and again"; nivedya gurave mānaṃ gurupūjā viśeṣataḥ | vīrapūjāṃ tataḥ kṛtvā yena tuṣyet punaḥ punaḥ |.

63. KJN 21.8–9: pūrṇimāyāṃ amāvasyāṃ aṣṭamī ca caturddaśī [*sic*] || sajīvaṃ matsyamadyañca māṃsañcaiva baliṃ da[det] | vyākhyā caiva tu kartavyā ācāryaḥ śaṅkavarjitaḥ ||.

64. KJN 8.7–8a: vivāhaṃ tu kṛtaṃ yasya sahajā sa tu ucyate | kulajā veśyamityāhurantyajā varṇa antyajā || bahisthākathitā devi ādhyātmyāṃ śṛṇu sāmpratam.

65. KJN 23.11: kopantu naiva karttavyaṃ bhāṣamāṇaṃ surādhipe | kumārikā striyo vāpi bhāṣamāṇe kadācana ||.

66. This is not to discount the reading of the "mouth to mouth" initiation that White discusses in *The Kiss of the Yoginī*, especially 94–122, which may refer to sexual relations between the male and female who "imparts" the teaching through her "lower" mouth, which we do find in the KJN. For our purposes here, what is significant especially are the differences that we find between the KJN and the BT, and other texts used for this study.

67. *Kālikā Purāṇam*, introduction and translation by B. N. Shastri. Delhi: Nag, 1991–1992.

68. K. R. Van Kooij, *Worship of the Goddess according to the Kālikāpurāṇa* (Leiden: Brill, 1972), 30.

69. KP 84.127b–28a: asvatantrāḥ striyaḥ kāryāḥ satatam pārthivena tu || tāḥ svatantrāḥ striyo nityaṃ hānaye sambhavanti hi |.

70. J. A. Schoterman, *Ṣaṭsāhasra Saṃhitā* (Leiden: Brill, 1982), 12.

71. Goudriaan and Gupta, *History of Indian Literature*, 81.

72. *Toḍala Tantra* in *Tantrasaṅgraha*, ed. Ramprasād Tripāṭhī. Yogatantragranthamālā Series 4, part 2 (Varanasi: Sampurnanand Sanskrit University, 2002), 3.28.

73. *Mahānirvāṇa Tantra*, with the commentary of Hariharananda Bharatī, ed. Arthur Avalon (Sir John Woodroffe). Tantrik Texts 13 (Delhi: Motilal Banarsidass, 1989; originally published in 1929), 8.106: tiṣṭhet pitrorvaśe bālye bharttuḥ samprāptayauvane | vārddhakye patibandhūnāṃ na svatantrā bhavet kvacit ||. One wonders whether this shift from "son" to "husband's relatives" had anything to do with Bengali inheritance laws for the nineteenth century.

74. *Yoginī Tantra* [YogT], ed. Biswanarayan Shastri (Delhi and Varanasi: Bharatiya Vidya Prakashan), 1982.

75. YogT, xxxii, xxxviiif., xliii.

76. YogT 1.6.37b–38a: brāhmaṇī brāhmaṇasyaiva kṣatriyā kṣtriyasya ca || vaiśyāvaiśyasya deveśi maithune yadvidhiḥ smṛtaḥ |.

77. YogT 1.6.39b: śūdrā vā brāhmaṇādīnāṃ trivarṇānāmabhāvataḥ ||.

78. YogT 1.6.44: mātṛyoniṃ parityajya maithunaṃ sarvayoniṣu | kṣatayonistāḍitavyā akṣatāṃ naiva tāḍayet ||. Schoterman also discusses this exclusion of mothers and virgins in his introduction to the Yoni Tantra. See *Yoni Tantra*, edited with an introduction by Schoterman, 18f.

79. YogT 1.4.30–31a: padminī śāntidā proktā vaśye ca śaṅkhinī matā | stambhanoccāṭane devi praśastā nāgavallabhā || māraṇe ca tathā śastā ḍākinī śatrumṛtyudā.

80. YogT 1.4.31b–32a: gaurāṅgī dīrghakeśī yā sadā sāmṛtabhāṣiṇī || raktanetrā suśīlā ca padminī sādhane śubhā |.

81. YogT 1.4.35: hrasvakeśī dīrghaghoṇā sadā niṣṭhuravādinī | sadā kruddhā dīrghadehā mahārāvaparāyaṇā ||.

82. One instance may be found at YogT 1.13.35–39.

83. For instance, especially Kāmākhyā Tantra 2.66ff., in Tantrasaṅgraha, 3rd ed., ed. M. M. Gopinath Kaviraj, in Yogatantragranthamālā Series 4, part 2 (Varanasi: Sampurnanand Sanskrit University, 2002).

84. KāmT 2.68: āvāhanādikarmāṇi na tatra sarvathā priye.

85. KāmT 2.72b: parastrīyonimāsādya viśeṣeṇa yajet sudhīḥ.

86. KāmT 2.73a: veśyāyoniḥ parā devi sādhanaṃ tatra kārayet.

87. In Tantrasaṅgraha, ed. Gopinath Kaviraj.

88. *Devī Rahasya with Pariśiṣṭas*, ed. Ram Chandra Kak and Harabhatta Shastri (Delhi: Butala Publications, 1985; reprinted from the 1941 edition of Kashmir).

89. *Niruttara Tantram: Mūla Saṃskṛta tathā Bhāṣānuvāda.* (Sanskrit Text with Hindi Translation.) Hindi, trans. S. N. Khandelwal (Varanasi: Bharatiya Vidya Prakashan, 1996).

90. KMT 5.7: nātra śuddhyādyapekṣāsti na niṣiddhādi dūṣaṇam | dikkālaniyamo nātra sthityādiniyamo nahi ||. This train of thought continues through KMT 5.9.

91. Rāmatoṣaṇa Bhaṭṭācārya, *Prāṇatoṣiṇī*, 477; the hymn is in KMT 3.27–34.

92. *Rudrayāmala (Uttara Tantra), Prathama Vibhaga* (part 1), ed. Rāmaprasāda Tripāṭhī. Yogatantra-Granthamālā Series 7 (Varanasi: Sampurnananda Sanskrit University, 1991).

93. *Rudrayāmala (Uttara Tantra), Dvitīya Vibhaga* (part 2), ed. Rāmaprasāda Tripāṭhī. Yogatantra-Granthamālā 7 (Varanasi: Sampurnand Sanskrit University, 1996), 64.55b and 64.56b, respectively: cīnācāraṃ rākṣasīnāṃ kulīnānāṃ sadāśiva; cīnācāraṃ rākṣasīnāṃ sādhanādeva siddhyati.

94. Brahmānanda Giri, *Śāktānandataraṅgiṇī*, ed. Rājanātha Tripāṭhī (Varanasi: Sampurnanand Sanskrit University, 1987); Rāmatoṣaṇa Bhaṭṭācārya. *Prāṇatoṣiṇī*, ed. Harivansh Kumar Pandey (Varanasi: Sampurnanand Sanskrit University, 2000; 2002).

95. Brahmānanda Giri, *Śāktānandataraṅgiṇī*, 4.147–49; 5.31–32.

96. Ibid., 15.5–10.

97. Ibid., 2.27–30; 9.139–40.

98. Ibid., 2.31: striyodīkṣā śubhā proktā mātuścāṣṭaguṇā smṛtā | svapnalabdhā ca yā dīkṣā tatra nāsti vicāraṇā ||. I have emended "spapna" to read "svapna" in this line.

99. Ibid., 2.32: sādhvī caiva sadācārā gurubhaktā jitendriyā | sarvatantrārthasārajñā sadhavā pūjane ratā | guruyogyā bhavedeṣā vidhavāṃ parivarjayet ||.

100. Brahmānanda Giri, *Tārā Rahasyam* Saṭippaṇa "Vidyā" Hindīvyākhyopetam, ed. Sarayuprasad Shastri. Kashi Sanskrit Series 199 (Varanasi: Chowkamba, 1970). The first version is explained from TR 3.23–53; the concluding verse is TR 3.53.

101. TR 3.70–73.

102. TR 3.63b: sādhakāṃścāpi śaktīṃśca praṇamya ca punaḥ punaḥ ||.

103. Rāmatoṣaṇa Bhaṭṭācārya. *Prāṇatoṣiṇī*, ed. Harivansh Kumar Pandey (Varanasi: Sampurnanand Sanskrit University, 2000; 2002).

104. To get a sense of his citations I mention several here: p. 4, where he lists both the NT and the BT; pp. 273, 478, for the discussion of the guru; p. 300, on not massaging the feet of the guru's wife; p. 570, for the inclusion of both Vedic and Tantric *sandhyā*; and, for instance, in vol. 2 (Varanasi: Sampurnanand Sanskrit University, 2002) p. 35, for the worship of the goddess in the cremation ground and where there is only a single *liṅga* established; p. 252f. for the *kumārī pūjā vidhi*; pp. 549 and 555 for discussion of the *Kumārī pūjā*; and p. 577 for the praise of Brahmins to mention some of his citations.

105. PT pp. 472–473.

106. PT pp. 473, 475–479.

107. Narasiṃha, *Tārābhaktisudhārṇava*, ed. Pañcānana Tarka-Sāṃkhya-VedāntaTirtha (Delhi: Bhāratīya Vidyā Prakāśana, 1983).

108. Tantrarāja Tantra 5.80b: strīṣu roṣam prahāraṃ ca duṣṭāsvapi na yojayet.

109. S. Sarma, *Socio-economic and Cultural History*, 193; and Edward Gait, *History of Assam* (Calcutta: Thacker Spink, 1963), 7, 9.

110. S. Sarma, ibid., 123.

111. H. K. Barpujari, ed. *Comprehensive History of Assam* 3:59.

112. Even to the extent that we find an Ahom king, Rajeśvara Simha, in 1760 patronizing Muslim holy places. See Barpujari, *Comprehensive History of Assam*, 3:244.

113. Ibid., 3:249.

114. S. Sarma, *Socio-economic and Cultural History*, 58.

115. Naliniranjan Sarma, *Kāmarūpa School of Dharmaśāstras* (Calcutta: Punthi Pustak, 1994), 15–16, 66–67, 165.

116. Barpujari, *Comprehensive History of Assam*, 3:107, 3:111.

117. S. Sarma, *Socio-economic and Cultural History*, 18.

118. Ibid., 211.

119. Edward Gait, *History of Assam*, 287; N. Sarma, concurs in N. Sarma, *Kāmarūpa School of Dharmaśāstras*, 17.

120. Gait, ibid., 59.

121. M. M. Sharma, "Religion," in Barpujari, *Comprehensive History of Assam*, 3:224.

122. S. Sarma, *Socio-economic and Cultural History*, 197. Similarly, the regions of Tripura and Jayantia were known for Śākta Tantric practices mixed with tribal practices. See Barua Bahadur, *Early History of Kāmarūpa*, 304.

123. *Tungkhungia Buranji: A History of Assam, 1681–1826 A.D.* by Srinath Duara Barbarua, compiled, edited, and translated by S. K. Bhuyan (Calcutta: Humphrey

Milford; Oxford University Press, 1933), 13. Unfortunately for the minister, the young man hears of the plan and kills the minister first and then flees.

124. *Ahom Buranji: From the Earliest Time to the End of Ahom Rule*, translated and edited by Rai Sahib Golap Chandra Barua (Guwahati: Spectrum, 1985), 100.

125. S. Sarma, *Socio-economic and Cultural History*, 245.

126. Ibid.

127. Ibid., 58. Rites of worshiping Śiva with wine and meat have also been connected to earlier tribal rites as well; see also, Barpujari, *Comprehensive History of Assam*, 3:217.

128. See Alexis Sanderson's insightful, "Meaning in Tantric Ritual," in *Essais sur le Rituel* 3, ed. Anne-Marie Blondeau and Kristofer Schipper. Colloque du Centenaire de la Section des Sciences Religieuses de l'Ecole Pratique des Hautes Etudes (Louvain-Paris: Peeters, 1995), 67.

129. Ibid., 15–95; and Alexis Sanderson, "Purity and Power among the Brahmins of Kashmir," in *Category of the Person: Anthropology, Philosophy, History*, ed. Michael Carrithers, Steven Collins, and Steven Lukes (Cambridge: Cambridge University Press, 1985), 191–216.

130. Hugh Urban, "Path of Power: Impurity, Kingship, and Sacrifice in Assamese Tantra" in *Journal of the American Academy of Religion* 69, no. 4 (2001): 777–816.

131. Sanderson, "Meaning in Tantric Ritual," 67.

132. GT 34.98: ekāpativratā bhāryā sādhvī cet sahacāriṇī | kimanyābhirmaheśāni yathaivāham tvayā prabhuḥ.

133. YT 1.14: svakāntāṃ parakāntāṃ vā suveśāṃ sthāpya maṇḍale | prathame vijayāṃ datvā pūjayed bhaktibhāvataḥ ||.

134. BT 6.21: ādāvānīya deveśi svakāntāṃ vā parastriyam | prathamaṃ cāsanaṃ dattvā pādyaṃ dadyāttataḥ param.

135. S. Sarma, *Socio-economic and Cultural History*, 164.

136. Barpujari, *Comprehensive History of Assam*, 3:171.

137. S. Sarma, *Socio-economic and Cultural History*, 159; and ibid., 3:299.

138. S. Sarma, ibid., 207.

139. Barua Bahadur, *Early History of Kāmarūpa*, 307.

140. Barpujari, *Comprehensive History of Assam*, 2:28.

141. Barua Bahadur, *Early History of Kāmarūpa*, 311.

142. BT 6.80b–81: bhūtahiṃsā na kartavyā paśuhiṃsā viśeṣataḥ || balidānaṃ vinā devyā hiṃsāṃ sarvatra varjayet | balidānāya yā hiṃsā na doṣāya prakīrtitā ||. The argument for killing animals for the sake of ritual continues through 6.84.

143. In addition to the instance cited above, we also find an injunction against harm at 6.103, 346; and 22.169.

144. Urban, "Path of Power," 809.

145. The culmination of this rite is not sexual union, but rather the seeker "should worship the woman with lotus flowers, red powder and scents, with ornaments and garlands, only with the attitude towards a mother"; BT 6.341b–42a:

śaktiśca kusumaiḥ pūjyā sindūrairgandhacandanaiḥ || atha mālyairalaṅkāraiḥ kevalaṃ mātṛbhāvataḥ |.

146. BT 6.56: ekayā bhujyate yatra śivayā devi bhairavi | tatraiva sarvadevānāṃ prītiḥ paramadurlabhā ||.

147. BT 10.14: tāṃ prapūjya namaskṛtya svayaṃ japtvā susaṃyataḥ | prātaḥ strībhyo baliṃ dattvā mantrasiddhirbhaven.

148. That the BT does not support Urban's argument alerts us to the need to distinguish between different Tantric texts. Urban relies on the earlier Kālikā Purāṇa, a text from the ninth through eleventh centuries. The author of the BT, writing after the Vaiṣṇava movement, had different concerns and attitudes toward a variety of issues.

149. S. Sarma, *Socio-economic and Cultural History*, 206; Barua Bahadur, *Early History of Kāmarūpa*, 314.

150. Barpujari, *Comprehensive History of Assam*, 3:188–189.

151. S. Sarma, *Socio-economic and Cultural History*, 206.

152. Barpujari, *Comprehensive History of Assam*, 3:232, 3:236.

153. Ibid., 3:177.

154. Ibid., 3:236–237.

155. S. Sarma, *Socio-economic and Cultural History*, 104.

156. Ibid., 216; also Barua Bahadur, *Early History of Kāmarūpa*, 305.

157. We also see what may be construed as a Buddhist trace in some terminology. For instance, initiation is termed "saraṇa," corresponding to the Buddhist vow of refuge, "śaraṇa." See Barpujari, *Comprehensive History of Assam*, 3:187.

158. *Tungkhungia Buranji*, 15.

159. Barua Bahadur, *Early History of Kāmarūpa*, 329.

160. Barpujari, *Comprehensive History of Assam*, 3:166–167.

161. For instance, see *Ahom Buranji*, 53, 66, 68, 77.

162. Ibid., 10.

163. Ibid., 87–88; also, Barua Bahadur, *Early History of Kāmarūpa*, 294.

164. S. Sarma, *Socio-economic and Cultural History*, 243; Barpujari, *Comprehensive History of Assam*, 3:194–195.

165. Barpujari, ibid., 3:183.

166. Ibid., 3:184.

167. Ibid., 3:185.

168. Ibid., 3:178, 3:198; S. Sarma, *Socio-economic and Cultural History*, 84.

169. Barpujari, ibid., 3:255.

170. S. Sarma, *Socio-economic and Cultural History*, 270.

171. Barpujari, *Comprehensive History of Assam*, 3:299–300.

172. Ibid., 3:300.

173. Lila Gogoi, *Buranjis, Historical Literature of Assam: A Critical Survey* (Guwahati: Omsons, 1986), 267; also S. Sarma, *Socio-economic and Cultural History*, 161.

174. S. Sarma, ibid., 298.

175. Barpujari, *Comprehensive History of Assam*, 3:193.

176. Ibid., 2:288; S. Sarma, *Socio-economic and Cultural History*, 31.

177. S. Sarma, ibid., 300.

APPENDIX 2

1. Gudrun Buhnemann, *The Iconograpy of Hindu Tantric Deities* (2 vols. [Groningen: Egbert Forsten, 2000]), also notes a scissors associated with Nīlasarasvatī, the Blue Goddess of Speech.

2. Literally, here, "having meditated or visualized"; "dhyātvā."

3. 2.42–55a: praṇavādinamo >ntena pūjayed yatnataḥ sudhīḥ [avagrah inserted] | bhūtaśuddhiṃ tataḥ kuryāt prāṇāyāmakrameṇa tu || bhūtaśuddhiṃ vidhāyātha śūnyaṃ viśvaṃ vicintayet | nirlepaṃ nirguṇaṃ śuddhaṃ svātmānaṃ tāriṇīmayam [text emended from "tāriṇamiyam"] || antarikṣe tato dhyāyet āḥkārādraktapaṅkajam | bhūyastasyopari dhyāyet ṭāṃkārācchetapaṅkajam [śeta emended here to śveta = white] || tasyopari punardhyāyet hūṃkāraṃ nīlasannibham | tato hūṃkārabījāttu kartrikāṃ bījabhūṣitāṃ || kartrikoparigaṃ dhyāyet svātmānaṃ tāriṇīmayam | pratyālīḍhapadāṃ ghorāṃ muṇḍamālāvibhūṣitām || kharvāṃ lambodarīṃ bhīmāṃ vyāghracarmāvṛttāṃ kaṭau | navayauvanasaṃpannāṃ pañcamudrāvibhūṣitām || sumukhaṃ caturasraṃ ca vṛttaṃ gomukhameva ca | yonimudreti vikhyātā mudrāḥ pañca namaskṛtau || caturbhujāṃ lalijjihvāṃ mahābhīmāṃ varapradām | khadgakartrisamāyuktasavyetarabhujadvayām || kapālotpalasaṃyuktasavyapāṇiyugānvitām | piṅgograikajaṭāṃ dhyāyenmaulāvakṣobhyabhūṣitām || nīlanāgajaṭājūṭāṃ śvetāhikṛtakuṇḍalām | pītāhikaṅkaṇopetāṃ dhūmrāhibāhubhūṣaṇām || śyāmanāgopavītāṃ ca śubhrāhihārabhūṣaṇām || śvetanāgalasatkāñcīṃ pāṭalāhipadadvayām || pārśvadvaye lambamānanīlendīvaramālikām | prajvalatpitṛbhūmadhyasthitāṃ daṃṣṭrākarālinīm || śavakaṇṭapadadvandvavāmadakṣapadadvayām | sāveśasmeravadanāṃ bhaktānāmabhayapradām || krameṇānena deveśi dhyātvā nīlāṃ sarasvatīm |.

4. 2.138d: saubhāgyāmṛtavarṣaṇena kṛpayā siñca tvamasmādṛśam ||.

5. 2.138c: nīlendīvaralocanatrayayute.

6. 2.138b: gadyaprākṛtapadyajātiracanāsarvārthasiddhiprade.

7. I emend the text here to śveta = white, from śeta.

8. See for this also Buhnemann, *The Iconography*, 101ff. and plate 20, where Nīlasarasvatī is pictured with a scissors, which Buhnemann notes may be the *kartrikā* in the visualization.

9. Perhaps this is to suggest flexibility, a slightly wider interpretive net in the choice of the meal's recipients, to include perhaps, for instance, an itinerant practitioner who might not come from the Brahmin caste.

10. This is a feature found in other earlier Tantras as well, in the Kālikā Purāṇa and in the Kulārṇava Tantra (K. R. Van Kooij, *Worship of the Goddess according to the Kālikāpurāṇa* [Leiden: Brill, 1972], 30).

11. Eck, *Encountering God: A Spiritual Journey from Bozeman to Banaras* (Boston: Beacon, 1993).

12. Note that in Buddhist Tantra *mudrā* can refer to the female ritual partner of the male Tantric practitioner.

13. Agehananda Bharati, *The Tantric Tradition* (London: Ryder and Co., 1965; reprint, New York: Grove, 1975), 257ff.

14. See also J. A. Schotermann's analysis of the *Yoni Tantra* (*Yoni Tantra,* edited with an introduction by J. A. Schoterman[Delhi: Manohar, 1980], 31), a text that bears similarities to the left-handed chapters of the BT.

15. Here I follow the reading of M. S. Kaul's emendation choice of *nija* over *dvija* (BT 7.198, p. 110).

16. Here I emend "*akaror*" to "*akarod.*" This particular section contains a few obvious scribal errors, that is, "*samāpayet*" for "*samārpayet*" (7.237). Also, the Blue Goddess of Speech is also considered synonymous with the goddess Tārā and Kālī (7.211).

17. See, for instance, the *Parātrīśikā Vivaraṇa.* This tripartite form of the goddess is also evidenced in the Śrī Vidyā practice and has remained part of the tradition even today. On this see Douglas Brooks's excellent study, *The Secret of the Three Cities: An Introduction to Hindu Śākta Tantrism* (Chicago: University of Chicago Press, 1990).

18. In this context the *yoginī* is perhaps the female equivalent of the mythical, magically powerful male *siddha,* or perhaps to a semihuman, half-divine female magician or sorceress.

19. The *kuṇḍagola* mentioned here may refer to menstrual blood. This seems likely, especially since this section appears to be taken from an earlier text without careful attention by the redactor at this point. See Schotermann for the elucidation of the terms *kuṇḍagola* and *svayambhū* (*Yoni Tantra,* pp. 31f.).

20. The standard list of five products coming from a cow include milk, yogurt, clarified butter, urine, and feces. The text bars ghee from being included in the substitute for wine (8.21).

21. See Narasiṃha's *Tārābhaktisudhārṇava*[1], 271, for rejection of the Five Ms and 268 for nonemission.

22. The Sanskrit here is strījātirūpā sarvatra sarvadeheṣu jānatā (8.158b).

23. This textual misspelling of Niśumbha as Nisumbha suggests also a northeastern provenance for the text, since this is a common morphological shift in the vernaculars of this region.

24. This may be a reference to the *Kālikā Purāṇa,* or the word *tantra* could in this instance simply mean "method." Given the context of the verse, the former interpretation is more likely.

25. In Sanskrit, "*sarvajña.*" This word is often translated as "omniscience," which doesn't, in my opinion, accurately capture the sense of "*sarvajña,*" which is more of an ability to know things by concentrating upon them and not the more outlandish claim to absolute knowledge.

26. This refers to the notion that it is the goddess who enlivens Śiva; phonetically encoded as the letter *i,* which is the goddess, this makes the word *śava* = "corpse" into the god "Śiva."

27. The "*saccidānanda*" of the Vedantic tradition.

Bibliography

SANSKRIT TEXTS

Abhinavagupta. *Īśvara Pratyabhijñā Vivṛti Vimarśinī*. 3 vols. Edited by Paṇḍit Madhusudan Kaul Shāstrī. Delhi: Akay Reprints, 1985.

——— *Parātrīśikā Vivaraṇa*. Translated by Jaidev Singh. Edited by Bettina Baumer. Delhi: Motilal Banarsidass, 1988.

——— *Parā-Trimshikā, with the Commentary by Abhinavagupta*. Edited with notes by Mukunda Rāma Shāstrī. Reproduction of the KSTS text, no. 18. New Delhi: Aroma, 1918. Reprint 1991.

———. *Tantrāloka of Abhinavagupta with Commentary by Rājānaka Jayaratha*. 12 vols. Edited with notes by Mukund Ram Shastri et al. Allahabad: Indian Press, 1918–38; reprinted with introduction and notes by R.C. Dwivedi and Navjivan Rastogi. 8 vols. Delhi: Motilal Banarsidass, 1987.

Aṣṭaprakaraṇam. Edited by Vrajavallabha Dvivedi. Yogatantra-Granthamālā, vol. 12. Varanasi: Sampurnanand Sanskrit University, 1988.

Bhūtaḍāmaramahātantram, with the Hindi commentary "Paminī." Edited by Ajaya Kumāra Uttama. Varanasi: Bhāratīya Vidyā Saṃsthāna, 2002.

Bhūtaśuddhitantra in *Tantrasaṅgraha*. Edited by Vrajvallabha Dvivedi. Yogatantra-Granthamālā Series 8, part 5. Varanasi: Sampurnanand Sanskrit University, 1996.

Brahmānanda Giri. *Śāktānandataraṅgiṇī*. Edited by Rājanātha Tripāṭhī. Varanasi: Sampurnanand Sanskrit University, 1987.

Brahmānanda Giri. *Tārā Rahasyam. Saṭippaṇa "Vidyā" Hindīvyākhyopetam*. Edited by Sarayuprasad Shastri. Kashi Sanskrit Series 199. Varanasi: Chowkamba, 1970.

Bṛhannīla Tantra. Edited by Madhusudan Kaul. Delhi: Butala and Co., 1984.

Bṛhatstotraratnākara. Edited by Śivadatta Miśra Śāstrī. Varanasi: Jyotiṣa Prakāśana, 1997.

Chāndogya Upaniṣad. In Early Upanishads: Annotated Text and Translation. Patrick Olivelle. New York: Oxford University Press, 1998.

Cīnācāra Tantra in *Tantrasaṅgraha.* Edited by Vrajvallabha Dvivedi. Yogatantra-Granthamālā Series 8, part 5. Varanasi: Sampurnanand Sanskrit University, 1996.

Ḍāmara Tantra. Edited and translated by Ram Kumar Rai. Tantra Granthamala 13. Varanasi: Prachya Prakashan, 1988.

Devīkālottarāgamaḥ. Commentary in Sanskrit by Nirañjanasiddha. Edited with Hindi translation by Pt. Vrajavallabha Dwivedi. Varanasi: Shaiva Bharati Shodha Pratishthanam, 2000.

Devī Māhātmyam: 700 Mantras on Sri Durga. Translated by Swami Jagadiswarananda. Madras: Sri Ramakrishna Math, n.d.

Devī Rahasya with Pariśiṣṭas. Edited by Ram Chandra Kak and Harabhatta Shastri. Delhi: Butala Publications, 1985. Reprinted from the 1941 edition of Kashmir.

Dikṣit, Rajesh. *Mahākālī Siddhi.* Delhi: Dehati Pustak Bhaṇḍar, n.d.

Gandharva Tantra in Tantrasaṅgraha. Edited by Ramprasāda Tripāṭhī. Yogatantra-Granthamālā Series 5, part 3. Varanasi: Sampurnanand Sanskrit University, 1992.

Gāyatrī Tantram, with the Hindi Commentary "Tattvadīpikā." Edited by Śrī Tārakanātha Bhaṭṭācārya. Commentary by Śrī Śivadatta Miśra Śāstrī. Varanasi: Chaukhambha Sanskrit Bhawan, 2003.

Girvāṇendra Sarasvatī. *Prapañcasārasārasaṅgraha: Uttaro Bhāgaḥ*, part 2. Edited by K. S. Subramania Sastri. Thanjavur: Administrative Committee of T. M. S. S. M. Library, 1980.

Guptasādhana Tantra, in *Tantrasaṅgraha.* Edited by Vrajvallabha Dvivedi. Yogatantra-Granthamālā Series 8. part 5. Varanasi: Sampurnanand Sanskrit University, 1996.

Īśvarakṛṣṇa. *Sāṃkhya Kārikā.* Edited with introduction by Radhanath Phukan. Calcutta: Firma K. L. Mukhopadhyay, 1960.

Jñānānanda, Paramahaṃsa. Kaulāvalīnirṇaya. Edited by Arthur Avalon. Varanasi: Bharatiya Vidya Prakashan, 1985. Reprinted with permission of M/s Ganesh and Co. Madras, n.d.

Kālīkalpadruvallarī. Edited by Rāma Nārāyāṇa Tripāṭhī. Varanasi: Sampurnand Sanskrit University, 1996.

Kālikā Purāṇam. Introduction and translation by B. N. Shastri. Delhi: Nag, 1991–92.

Kālikāpurāṇe Mūrtivinirdeśaḥ. Edited by Biswanarayan Shastri. Kalāmūlaśāstra Series, vol. 9. New Delhi: Indira Gandhi National Centre for the Arts; Delhi: Motilal Banarsidass, 1994.

Kaṅkālamālinī Tantram. Hindīṭikopetam, with Hindi Commentary. Translated by S. N. Khandelwal. Varanasi: Bharatiya Vidya Prakashan, 1993.

Kaṅkālamālinī Tantram in *Tantrasaṅgraha.* Edited by Ramprasād Tripāṭhī. Yogatantra-Granthamālā Series 6, part 4. Varanasi: Sampurnanand Sanskrit University, 1996.

Kaulajñānanirṇaya. Edited with an introduction by P. C. Bagchi. Translated by Michael McGee. Tantra Granthamala, no. 12. Varanasi: Prachya Prakashan, 1986.

Kaulajñānanirṇaya and Some Minor Texts of the School of Matsyendranātha. Edited with an introduction by Prabodh Chandra Bagchi. Calcutta Sanskrit Series, no. 3. Calcutta: Metropolitan Printing and Publishing House, 1934.

Kṛṣṇānanda Āgamavāgīśa. *Bṛhat Tantrasāraḥ*. Edited and put into Devanagari script by Ram Kumar Rai. Varanasi Sanskrit Texts 3. Varanasi: Prachya Prakashan, 1985.

Kubjikāmatatantra: Kulālikāmnāya Version. Edited by Teun Goudriaan and Jan Schoterman. Orientalia Rheno-Traiectina 30. Leiden: Brill, 1988.

Kulācāra, Rāmacandra. *Śilpa Prakāśa. Medieval Orissan Sanskrit Text on Temple Architecture*. Translated and annotated by Alice Boner and Sadasiva Rath Sarma. Leiden: Brill, 1966.

Kulacūḍāmaṇi Tantram. Edited by Girīśa Candra Vedāntatīrtha. In *Tantrik Texts*, ed. Arthur Avalon 4. London: Luzac and Co., 1915. Reprint, New Delhi: Aditya Prakashan, n.d.

Kulacūḍāmaṇi Tantram and Vāmakeśvara Tantra, with the Jayaratha Commentary. Introduced, translated, and annotated by Louise M. Finn. Wiesbaden: Harrassowitz, 1986.

Kulārṇava Tantra. Edited by Taranatha Vidyaratna. Introduction by Arthur Avalon (Sir John Woodroffe). Madras: Ganesh and Company, 1965. Reprint, Delhi: Motilal Banarsidass, 1975.

Kulārṇavatantram, "Nīrakṣīraviveka" Bhāṣābhāṣyasamanvitam. Edited by Paramahansa Miśra. Chaukhamba Surabhāratī Granthamālā 353. Varanasi: Chaukamba, 2002.

Lakṣmaṇadeśikendra. *Śāradātilakam with Padārthādarśa Commentary by Rāghava Bhaṭṭā*. Edited by Mukunda Jha Bakhshi. Introduction by Mahāprabhu Lāla Gosvāmi. 3rd ed. Kashi Sanskrit Series, vol. 107. Varanasi: Chaukhambha Sanskrit Sansthan, 1986.

Luptāgamasaṅgrahaḥ. Edited by Gopinath Kaviraj. Part 1. Yogatantra-Granthamālā. Varanasi: Sampurnanand Sanskrit University, 1998.

Mādhava Vidyāraṇya, *Śaṅkaradigvijaya*. Śrīrangam: Śrīvaṇivilasamudranālayaḥ, 1972.

Mahābhāgavata Purāṇa, ed. Pushpendra Kumar. Delhi: Eastern Book Linkers, 1983.

Mahācīnācārasāra Tantra. Edited by Rāmadatta Śukla. Allahabad: Kalyāṇa Mandira Prakāśana, v.s. 2043 (= 1986?).

Mahānirvāṇa Tantra, with the commentary of Hariharananda Bharatī. Edited by Arthur Avalon (Sir John Woodroffe). Tantrik Texts 13. Madras: Ganesh Publishers. Originally published in 1929. Reprint, Delhi: Motilal Banarsidass, 1989.

Maheśvarānanda. *Mahārthamañjarī with the Auto-Commentary Parimala*. Edited by Vrajavallabha Dviveda. Yogatantra-Granthamālā Series 5. Varanasi: Sampurnanand Sanskrit University, 1992.

Makuṭāgama: Kriyāpāda and Caryāpāda. Edited by Vrajvallabha Dwivedi. Translated by Rama Ghose. Varanasi: Shaiva Bharati Shodha Pratishthanam, 1996.

Manu Smṛti. Edited by J. L. Shastri. Introduction by S. C. Banerji. Sanskrit commentary by Kullūka Bhaṭṭa. Delhi: Motilal Banarsidass, 1983.

Manusmṛti. Edited by Taranath Vidyaratna with an introduction by Arthur Avalon (Sir John Woodroffe). Madras: Ganesh and Company, 1965.

Māyā Tantra in *Tantrasaṅgraha*. Edited by Vrajvallabha Dvivedi. Yogatantra-Granthamālā Series 8, part 5. Varanasi: Sampurnanand Sanskrit University, 1996.

Meisig, Marion. *Die "China-Lehre" des Śaktimus: Mahācīnācāra Tantra*. Wiesbaden: Harrassowitz, 1988.

Narasiṃha. *Tārābhaktisudhārṇava*. Edited by Pañcānana Tarka-Sāṃkhya-Vedānta-Tirtha. Delhi: Bhāratīya Vidyā Prakāśana, 1983.

Nīla Tantra. Edited by Bhadrasheel Sharma. Guptāvatāra Durlabha Tantramālā Series, varṣa 2, maṇi 6. Prayag: Kalyana Mandir, 2022 samvat [1965 or 1966].

Nīlasarasvatī Tantram. Edited by Brahmananda Tripathi. Hindi commentary by S. N. Khandelwal. Varanasi: Chaukhamba Surbharati Prakashan, 1999.

Niruttara Tantram: Mūla Saṃskṛta tathā Bhāṣānuvāda. (Sanskrit Text with Hindi Translation.) Hindi Translation by S. N. Khandelwal. Varanasi: Bharatiya Vidya Prakashan, 1996.

Pheṭkāriṇī Tantra in *Tantrasaṅgraha*. Edited by Gopīnātha Kavirāja. 3rd Edition. Yogatantra-Granthamālā Series 4, part 2. Varanasi: Sampurnanand Sanskrit University, 2002.

Prapañcasāra Tantra. Edited by Aṭalānanda Sarasvatī. Introduction by Arthur Avalon. With commentary Vivaraṇa by Padmapādācārya and Prayogakramadīpikā—a Vṛtti on the Vivaraṇa. Parts 1, 2. Delhi: Motilal Banarsidass, 1981. Originally published in 1935.

Puṇyānanda. *Kāmakalāvilāsaḥ with Commentary*. Edited with notes by Mukunda Rāma Śāstrī. Kashmir Series of Texts and Studies 12. Bombay: Tatva-vivechaka Press, 1918.

Rāmatoṣaṇa Bhaṭṭācārya. *Prāṇatoṣiṇī*. Edited by Harivansh Kumar Pandey. Part 1. Varanasi: Sampurnanand Sanskrit University, 2000.

———. *Prāṇatoṣiṇī*. Edited by Harivansh Kumar Pandey. Part 2. Varanasi: Sampurnanand Sanskrit University, 2002.

Rudrayāmalam (Uttara Tantra). Prathama Vibhaga. (vol. 1.). Edited by Rāmaprasāda Tripāṭhī. Yogatantra-Granthamālā Series 7. Varanasi: Sampurnananda Sanskrit University, 1991.

Rudrayāmalam (Uttara Tantra). Dvitīya Vibhaga. (vol.2). Edited by Rāmaprasāda Tripāṭhī. Yogatantra-Granthamālā Series 7. Varanasi: Sampurnananda Sanskrit University, 1996.

Śaktisaṅgama Tantra. Vol. 4, *Chinnamastākhaṇḍa*. Edited by B. Bhattacharyya and V. V. Dvivedi. Baroda: Oriental Institute, 1978.

Śaktiviśiṣṭādvaita-Tattvatraya-Vimarśaḥ. Chandrashekhar Shivacharya Mahaswamiji. Varanasi: Shaiva Bharati Shodha Pratishthanam, 1996.

Saṃnyāsa Upaniṣads: Hindu Scriptures on Asceticism and Renunciation. Translated with an introduction by Patrick Olivelle. New York: Oxford University Press, 1992.

Ṣaṭsāhasra Saṃhitā. Chapters 1–5. Edited, translated, and annotated by J. A. Schoterman. Leiden: Brill, 1982.

Sarvavijayi Tantra. In *Tantrasaṅgraha*. Edited by Vrajvallabha Dvivedi. Yogatantra-Granthamālā Series 8, part 5. Varanasi: Sampurnanand Sanskrit University, 1996.

Śrīmad Devī Bhāgavatam, 4th ed. Translated by Swami Vijnanananda. Parts 1, 2. New Delhi: Munshiram Manoharlal, 1992. Originally published Allahabad: Panini Office, 1921-23.

Svātmārāma. *Haṭhayogapradīpikā, with the Commentary Jyotsnā of Brahmānanda and English Translation*. Madras: Adyar Library and Research Centre, 1984. Originally published in 1972.

Tantrarājatantra. Edited by Mahāmahopādhyāya Lakshmana Shastri Introduction by Arthur Avalon. Delhi: Motilal Banarsidass, 1997. Originally published in 1926.

Tantrasaṅgraha, 3rd ed. Edited by M. M. Gopinath Kaviraj. Yogatantra-Granthamālā Series 4, part 2. Varanasi: Sampurnanand Sanskrit University, 2002.

———. Edited by Ramprasāda Tripāṭhī. Yogatantra-Granthamālā Series 5, part 3. Varanasi: Sampurnanand Sanskrit University, 1992.

———. Edited by Ramprasāda Tripāṭhī. Yogatantra-Granthamālā Series 6, part 4. Varanasi: Sampurnanand Sanskrit University, 1996.

———. Edited by Vrajvallabha Dvivedi. Yogatantra-Granthamālā Series 8, part 5. Varanasi: Sampurnanand Sanskrit University, 1996.

Tārā Tantra Śāstra. Edited by Rajesh Dīkṣhit. Agra: Dīpa Publications, 1995.

Toḍala Tantra. In *Tantrasaṅgraha*. Edited by Ramprasāda Tripāṭhī. Yogatantra-Granthamālā Series 4, part 2. Varanasi: Sampurnanand Sanskrit University, 2002.

Tripurārṇavatantram. Edited by Śītalā Prasāda Upādhyāya. Introduction by Sītārāma Shastri Kavirāja. Yogatantra-Granthamālā Series 12. Varanasi: Sampurnanand Sanskrit University, 1992.

Vāmakeśvarīmatam, with the Commentary of Jayaratha. Edited by Madhusudan Kaul Shastri. Srinagar: Kashmir Series of Texts and Studies, 66, 1945.

Vīṇāśikhatantra. Edited with translation and introduction by Teun Goudriaan. Delhi: Motilal Banarsidass, 1985.

Vidyāraṇya, Mādhava. *Śaṅkaradigvijaya*. 2 vols. Śrirangam: Śrīvāṇivilāsamudranālayaḥ, 1972.

Yoginī Tantra. Edited by Biswanarayan Shastri. Delhi and Varanasi: Bharatiya Vidya Prakashan, 1982.

Yoni Tantra. Edited with an introduction by J. A. Schoterman. Delhi: Manohar, 1980.

SECONDARY SOURCES

Agamben, Giorgio. *The Coming Community*. Translated by Michael Hardt. Minneapolis: University of Minnesota Press, 1993.

———. *Homo Sacer*: Sovereign Power and Bare Life. Translated by Daniel Heller-Roazen. Stanford, Calif.: Stanford University Press, 1998.

Ahom Buranji: From the Earliest Time to the End of Ahom Rule (with parallel English translation). Translated and edited by Rai Sahib Golap Chandra Barua. Guwahati: Spectrum, 1985.

Alper, Harvey, ed. *Understanding Mantras.* Albany: State University of New York Press, 1989.

Anderson, Carol S. "The Life of Gauri Ma." In *Graceful Guru: Hindu Female Gurus in India and the United States,* edited by Karen Pechilis. New York: Oxford University Press, 2004.

Apfel-Marglin, Frederique. "Female Sexuality in the Hindu World." In *Immaculate and Powerful: The Female in Sacred Image and Social Reality,* edited by Clarissa Atkinson. Boston: Beacon, 1985.

Bagchi, P. C. *Studies on the Tantras.* Calcutta: Ramakrishna Mission, 1989.

Bagchi, Subhendugopal. *Eminent Indian Śākta Centres in Eastern India.* Calcutta: Punthi Pustak, 1980.

Bagwe, Anjali. *Of Woman Caste: The Experience of Gender in Rural India.* London: Zed, 1995.

Banerji, S. C. *Brief History of Tantra Literature.* Calcutta: Naya Prokash, 1988.

———. *Tantra in Bengal: A Study in Its Origin, Development and Influence.* 2nd rev. and enl. ed. New Delhi: Manohar, 1992.

Barbarua, Srinath Duara. *Tungkhungia Buranji: A History of Assam, 1681–1826 A.D.* Compiled, edited and translated by S. K. Bhuyan. Calcutta: Humphrey Milford; Oxford University Press, 1933.

Barpujari, H. K., ed. *Comprehensive History of Assam.* 5 vols. Guwahati: Publication Board Assam, 1990–94.

Barua Bahadur, Rai K. L. *Early History of Kāmarūpa.* Shillong: n.p., 1933.

Benjamin, Jessica. *Bonds of Love: Psychoanalysis, Feminism, and the Problem of Domination.* New York: Pantheon, 1988.

Bharati, Agehananda. *The Tantric Tradition.* London: Ryder and Co., 1965. Reprint, New York: Grove, 1975.

Bhattacarya, Narendra Nath. *History of the Śākta Religion.* 2nd rev. ed. New Delhi: Munshiram Manoharla, 1996.

———. *History of the Tantric Religion: A Historical, Ritualistic and Philosophical Study.* 3rd ed. New Delhi: Munshiram Manoharlal, 1992.

———. *Indian Mother Goddess.* New Delhi: Manohar, 1977

Bhuyan, B. C., ed. *Tribal Woman.* New Delhi: Omsons, 1993.

Bhuyan, S. K. *Annals of the Delhi Badshahate: Being a Translation of the Old Assamese Chronicle Padshah-Buranji, with Introduction and Notes.* Gauhati: Government of Assam in the Department of Historical and Antiquarian Studies, 1947.

Biernacki, Loriliai. "Shree Maa of Kāmākhyā" in *The Graceful Guru: Hindu Female Gurus in India and the United States,* edited by Karen Pechilis. New York: Oxford University Press, 2004.

Bledsoe, Bronwen. "An Advertised Secret: The Goddess Taleju and the King of Kathmandu." In *Tantra in Practice,* edited by David White. Princeton Readings in Religion Series. Princeton, N.J.: Princeton University Press, 2000.

Brooks, Douglas. *Auspicious Wisdom: The Texts and Traditions of Śrī Vidyā Śākta Tantrism in South India.* Albany: State University of New York Press, 1992.

———. *The Secret of the Three Cities: An Introduction to Hindu Śākta Tantrism.* Chicago: University of Chicago Press, 1990.

Brown, C. Mackenzie. *Devī Gītā: The Song of the Goddess: A Translation, Annotation, and Commentary.* Albany: State University of New York Press, 1998.

———. *Triumph of the Goddess.* Albany: State University of New York Press, 1990.

Brunner, Helene. "The Sexual Aspect of the *Liṅga* Cult According to the Saiddhāntika Scriptures." In *Studies in Hinduism 2: Miscellanea to the Phenomenon of Tantras,* ed. G. Oberhammer. Vienna: Osterreichischen Akademie der Wissenschaften, 1998.

Brunner, Helene, G. Oberhammer, and A. Padoux, ed. *Tāntrikābhidhānakośa 1.* Vienna: Ostereichischen Akademie der Wissenschaften, 2000.

Buhnemann, Gudrun. *The Iconography of Hindu Tantric Deities.* 2 vols. Groningen: Egbert Forsten, 2000.

Butler, Judith. *Bodies That Matter: On the Discursive Limits of "Sex."* New York: Routledge, 1993.

———. *Excitable Speech: A Politics of the Performative.* New York: Routledge, 1997.

———. *Psychic Life of Power: Theories in Subjection.* Stanford, Calif.: Stanford University Press, 1997.

Bynum, Caroline Walker. *Holy Feast and Holy Fast.* Berkeley and Los Angeles: University of California Press, 1987.

Caldwell, Sarah. *Oh Terrifying Mother.* New Delhi: Oxford University Press, 1999.

Chaliha, Parag. *Aspects of Assamese Culture.* Calcutta: Bani Prokash Private, 1994.

Chattopadhyaya, Sudhakar. *Reflections on the Tantras.* Delhi: Motilal Banarsidass, 1990.

Coburn, Thomas. *Devī-Māhātmya: The Crystallization of the Goddess Tradition.* Delhi: Motilal Banarsidass, 1988. Originally published in 1984.

Collins, Alfred. "Dancing with the Goddess." In *Is the Goddess a Feminist?* ed. Alf Hiltebeitel and Kathleen Erndl. New York: New York University Press, 2000.

Copjec, Joan. *Imagine There's No Woman: Ethics and Sublimation.* Cambridge: MIT Press, 2002.

Courtright, Paul. *Gaṇeśa: Lord of Obstacles, Lord of Beginnings.* Delhi: Motilal Banarsidass, 2001. Originally published in 1985.

Coward, Harold, and David Goa. *Mantra: Hearing the Divine in India.* Chambersburg, Pa.: Anima, 1991.

Das, Veena. *Structure and Cognition: Aspects of Hindu Caste and Ritual.* 2nd ed. London: Oxford University Press, 1982.

Datta, V. N. *Sati: A Historical, Social and Philosophical Enquiry into the Hindu Rite of Widow Burning.* New Delhi: Manohar, 1988.

Davidson, Ronald. *Indian Esoteric Buddhism.* New York: Columbia University Press, 2002.

De Lauretis, Teresa. *Alice Doesn't: Feminism, Semiotics, Cinema.* Bloomington: Indiana University Press, 1984.

Deleuze, Gilles, and Felix Guattari. *A Thousand Plateaus: Capitalism and Schizophrenia*. Minneapolis: University of Minnesota Press, 1987.

Derrida, Jacques. *Of Grammatology*. Translated by Gayatri Chakravorty Spivak. Baltimore: Johns Hopkins University Press, 1976. Reprint, Delhi: Motilal Banarsidass, 1994.

Devsharma, Sree Dharanikanta. *The Holy Shrine of Kamakhya*. Guwahati: Ganesh Bhawan, 1999.

Dimock, Edwin. *Place of the Hidden Moon*. Chicago: University of Chicago Press, 1989.

Doniger, Wendy. *The Bedtrick: Tales of Sex and Masquerade*. Chicago: University of Chicago Press, 2000.

———. *Implied Spider: Politics and Theology in Myth*. New York: Columbia University Press, 1998.

———. *Splitting the Difference: Gender and Myth in Ancient Greece and India*. Chicago: University of Chicago Press, 1999.

———. "Tantric Bodies." *Times Literary Supplement*, May 20, 2004. http://www.svabhinava.org/friends/rajivMalhotra/WendyWhite-frame.html.

———. *Women, Androgynes and Other Mythical Beasts*. Chicago: University of Chicago Press, 1980.

Dubois, Abbe. *Hindu Manners, Customs and Ceremonies*. Oxford: Clarendon, 1906. Reprint, New Delhi: Asian Educational Services, 1986.

Dumont, Louis. *Homo Hierarchicus: The Caste System and Its Implications*. 2nd ed. Translated by Mark Sainsburg, Louis Dumont, and Basia Gulati. Chicago: University of Chicago Press, 1980.

Dyczkowski, Mark S. G. The *Canon of the Śaivāgama and the Kubjikā Tantras of the Western Kaula Tradition*. Albany: State University of New York Press, 1988.

———. *Doctrine of Vibration*. Albany: State University of New York Press, 1987.

———. *Stanzas on Vibration*. Albany: State University of New York Press, 1992.

Eck, Diana. *Darśan: Seeing the Divine Image in India*. 3rd ed. New York: Columbia University Press, 1998.

———. *Encountering God: A Spiritual Journey from Bozeman to Banaras*. Boston: Beacon, 1993.

Erndl, Kathleen M. "Is *Shakti* Empowering for Women? Reflections on Feminism and the Hindu Goddess." In *Is the Goddess a Feminist?* edited by Alf Hiltebeitel and Kathleen Erndl. New York: New York University Press, 2000.

———. *Victory to the Mother: The Hindu Goddesses of Northwest India in Myth, Ritual and Symbol*. New York: Oxford University Press, 1993.

Fausto-Sterling, Anne. The five sexes. *The Sciences 33:2* (March/April 1993): 65–69.

Feldhaus, Anne. *Water and Womanhood: Religious Meanings of Rivers in Maharashtra*. New York: Oxford University Press, 1995.

Findley, Ellison Banks. "*Mantra Kaviśastā*: Speech as Performative in the Rgveda." In *Understanding* Mantras, ed. Harvey P. Alper. Albany: State University of New York Press, 1989. Reprint, Delhi: Motilal Banarsidass, 1991.

Flood, Gavin. *Introduction to Hinduism*. New York: Cambridge University Press, 1996.

Flueckiger, Joyce. *Gender and Genre in the Folklore of Middle India*. Ithaca, N.Y.: Cornell University Press, 1996.

Fort, Andrew, and Patricia Mumme, eds. *Living Liberation in Hindu Thought*. Albany: State University of New York Press, 1996.

Foucault, Michel. *History of Sexuality, Volume 1: An Introduction*. Translated by Robert Hurley. New York: Vintage, 1978.

Freud, Sigmund. *Beyond the Pleasure Principle*. Translated by James Strachey. New York: Liveright, 1950.

Fuller, C. J. *Camphor Flame: Popular Hinduism and Society in India*. Princeton, N.J.: Princeton University Press, 1992.

Gador, Elinor. "Probing the Mysteries of the Hirapur Yoginis." *Revision* 25, no. 1, Summer 2002: 33–41.

Gait, Edward. *History of Assam*. Revised and enlarged by B. K. Barua and H. V. S. Murthy. Calcutta: Thacker Spink, 1963. Originally published in 1906.

Geertz, Clifford. *Interpretation of Cultures*. New York: Basic, 1973.

Gogoi, Lila. *Buranjis: Historical Literature of Assam: A Critical Survey*. Guwahati: Omsons, 1986.

Gold, Ann Grodzins. *Fruitful Journeys: The Ways of Rajasthani Pilgrims*. Long Grove, Ill.: Waveland, 2000.

Gold, Daniel. *Comprehending the Guru*. American Academy of Religion Series, no. 57. Atlanta: American Academy of Religion, 1988.

Gonda, Jan. *Change and Continuity in Indian Religion*. New Delhi: Munshiram Manoharlal, 1985.

———. "The Indian Mantra." *Oriens* 16 (1963): 244–97. Reprinted *in J. Gonda Selected Studies*, vol. 4. Leiden: Brill, 1975.

Goudriaan, Teun, ed. *Ritual and Speculation in Early Tantrism: Studies in Honor of Andre Padoux*. Albany: State University of New York Press, 1992.

Goudriaan, Teun, and Sanjukta Gupta. *History of Indian Literature*. Vol. 2: *Hindu Tantric and Śākta Literature*. Wiesbaden: Harrassowitz, 1981.

Goudriaan, Teun, Sanjukta Gupta, and Dirk Hoens. *Hindu Tantrism*. Leiden: Brill, 1979.

Gross, Rita. *Feminism and Religion: An Introduction*. Boston: Beacon, 1996.

———. "Is the Goddess a Feminist?" In *Is the Goddess a Feminist?* ed. Alf Hiltebeitel and Kathleen Erndl. New York: New York University Press, 2000.

Grunwedel, Albert. *Der Weg nach Śambhala*. Abh. Kon. Bayerischen Akademie der Wissenschaften Philosophisch-Philol. und Historische Klasse, 29, 1918.

Gupta, Lina. "Kali, the Savior." In *After Patriarchy: Feminist Reconstructions of the World* Religions, ed. Paula M. Cooey and William R. Eakin. Maryknoll, N.Y.: Orbis, 1991.

Gupta, Roxanne. "Kālī Māyī: Myth and Reality in a Benares Ghetto." In *Encountering Kālī at the Margins*, ed. Jeff Kripal and Rachel Fell-McDermott. Berkeley and Los Angeles: University of California Press, 2003.

Gupta, Sanjukta, Teun Goudriaan, and Dirk Hoens. *Hindu Tantrism*. Leiden: Brill, 1979.

———. "The Worship of Kālī according to the *Toḍala Tantra*." In *Tantra: In Practice*, ed. David Gordon White. Princeton, N.J.: Princeton University Press, 2000.

Hamilton, Walter. *East-India Gazetteer Containing Particular Descriptions of the Empires, Kingdoms, Principalities, Provinces, Cities, Towns, Districts, Fortresses, Harbours, Rivers, Lakes and c.* Complete and unabridged, two volumes in one. Delhi: Low Price Publications, 1993. Originally published in 1828.

Hancock, Mary. "The Dilemmas of Domesticity: Possession and Devotional Experience among Urban Smarta Women." In *From the Margins of Hindu* Marriage, ed. Lindsey Harlan and Paul Courtright. New York: Oxford University Press, 1995.

Harding, Elizabeth. *Kali: The Black Goddess of Dakshineshwar*. Delhi: Motilal Banarsidass, 1993.

Harlan, Lindsey. "Satī: The Story of Godāvarī." In *Devī: Goddesses of India*, ed. John S. Hawley. Berkeley and Los Angeles: University of California Press, 1996.

Harlan, Lindsey, and Paul Courtright. *From the Margins of Hindu Marriage*. New York: Oxford University Press, 1995.

Harper, Katherine, and Brown, Robert. *The Roots of Tantra*. Albany: State University of New York Press, 2002.

Hawley, John S. *Sati, the Blessing and the Curse*. New York: Oxford University Press, 1994.

Hawley, John S., and Donna M. Wulff. *Devī: Goddesses of India*. Berkeley and Los Angeles: University of California Press, 1996.

Hayes, Glen. "The Necklace of Immortality." In *Tantra in Practice*, ed. David White. Princeton Readings in Religion Series. Princeton, N.J.: Princeton University Press, 2000.

Hess, Linda. *Bijak of Kabir*. San Francisco: North Point, 1983.

Hiltebeitel, Alf. "Draupadī's Question." In *Is the Goddess a Femininst: The Politics of South Asian Goddesses*, ed. Alf Hiltebeitel and Kathleen Erndl. New York: New York University Press, 2000.

———. *Rethinking India's Oral and Classical Epics: Draupadi among Rajputs, Muslims, and Dalits*. Chicago: University of Chicago Press, 1999.

Holmstrom, Lakshmi. *Kannagi: A Modern Verson of Silappadikaram*. Bombay: Sangam, 1980.

Humes, Cynthia. "Glorifying the Great Goddess or Great Woman: Hindu Women's Experience in Ritual Recitation of the Devī Māhatmya." In *Women and Goddess Traditions*, ed. Daren L. King, with introduction by Karen Jo Torgesen. Minneapolis: Fortress, 1997.

———. "Is the *Devī Māhatmya* a Feminist Scripture?" In *Is the Goddess a Feminist?* ed. Alf Hiltebeitel and Kathleen Erndl. New York: New York University Press, 2000.

Irigaray, Luce. *Je, Tu, Nous: Toward a Culture of Difference*. Translated by Alison Martin. New York: Routledge, 1993.

———. *This Sex Which Is Not One*. Translated by Catherine Porter. Ithaca, N.Y.: Cornell University Press, 1985.

Jacobson, Doranne, and Susan S.Wadley, eds. *Women in India: Two Perspectives*. Columbia, Mo.: South Asia, 1977.

Jameson, Frederic. *Signatures of the Visible*. New York: Routledge, 1992.

Jamison, Stephanie. *Ravenous Hyenas and the Wounded Sun*. Ithaca, N.Y.: Cornell University Press, 1991.

———. *Sacrificed Wife/Sacrificer's Wife: Women, Ritual and Hospitality in Ancient India*. New York: Oxford University Press, 1996.

Kakar, Sudhir. *The Inner World: A Psychoanalytic Study of Childhood and Society in India*. 2nd ed. Delhi: Oxford University Press, 1981.

———. "The Maternal-Feminine in Indian Psychoanalysis." *International Review of Psychoanalysis* 16 (1989): 335–62.

Kakati, Banikanta. *The Mother Goddess Kamakhya*. Guwahati: Publication Board Assam, 2003. Originally published in 1948.

Kamrupa Anusandhana Samiti. *Readings in the History and Culture of Assam*. Guwahati: Assam Research Society, 1984.

Kapali Sastry, T. V. *Sidelights on the Tantra*. Pondicherry: Dipti Publications, Sri Aurobindo Ashram, 1985.

Katz, Steven. *Mysticism and Philosophical Analysis*. London: Sheldon, 1978.

Kaviraj, Gopinath. *Dīkṣā*. Edited by Jagadishwar Pal. Varanasi: Anuraga Prakashan, 1993.

———. *Tāntrika Sāhitya*. Benares: Bhargava Bhushan, 1972.

Khanna, Madhu. "The Goddess—Woman Equation in Śākta Tantras" in *Gendering the Spirit: Women, Religion and the Post-colonial Response*, ed. Durre Ahmed. London: Zed, 2002.

———. "Parallel Worlds of Madhobi Ma, 'Nectar Mother': My Encounter with a Twentieth-Century Tantric Saint" in *Gendering the Spirit: Women, Religion and the Post-colonial Response*, ed. Durre Ahmed. London: Zed, 2002.

King, Richard. *Orientalism and Religion: Postcolonial Theory, India and the Mystic East*. London: Routledge, 1999.

Kinsley, David. *Goddesses Mirror: Visions of the Divine from East and West*. Albany: State University of New York, 1989.

———. *Tantric Visions of the Divine Feminine: The Ten Mahavidyās*. Berkeley and Los Angeles: University of California Press, 1997.

Kripal, Jeffrey. "A Garland of Talking Heads for the Goddess." In *Is the Goddess a Feminist?* ed. Alf Hiltebeitel and Kathleen Erndl. New York: New York University Press, 2000.

———. *Kālī's Child: The Mystical and the Erotic in the Life and Teachings of Ramakrishna*. 2nd ed. Chicago: University of Chicago Press, 1998.

———. "Why the Tantrika Is a Hero: Kālī in the Psycholanalytic Tradition." In *Encountering Kālī*, ed. Rachel Fell Mcdermott and Jeffrey Kripal. Berkeley and Los Angeles: University of California Press, 2003Krishnaswamy, Revathi. *Effeminism: The Economy of Colonial Desire*. Ann Arbor: University of Michigan Press, 1998.

Kristeva, Julia. *Powers of Horror: An Essay on Abjection*. Translated by Leon S. Roudiez. New York: Columbia University Press, 1982.

———. *Revolution in Poetic Language*. Translated by Margaret Walker. New York: Columbia University Press, 1984.

Kurtz, Stanley. *All the Mothers Are One: Hindu India and the Cultural Reshaping of Psychoanalysis.* New York: Columbia University Press, 1992.

Lacan, Jacques. *Ecrits.* Translated by Alan Sheridan. New York: Norton, 1977.

———. *On Feminine Sexuality: The Limits of Love and Knowledge.* 20th Seminare, Encore 1972–73. Translated by Bruce Fink. New York: Norton, 1998.

Langton, Rae. "Speech Acts and Unspeakable Acts." *Philosophy and Public Affairs* 22, no. 4 (Autumn 1993): 293–330.

Larson, Gerald. *Classical Sāṃkhya: An Interpretation of Its History and Meaning.* Delhi: Motilal Banarsidass: 1969.

Leslie, Julia, ed. *Roles and Rituals for Hindu Women.* Cranbury, N.J.: Fairleigh Dickinson University Press, 1991.

Lopez, Donald, Jr. *Religions of India in Practice.* Princeton, N.J.: Princeton University Press, 1995.

Mackinnon, Catharine. *Feminism Unmodified: Discourses on Life and Law.* Cambridge, Mass.: Harvard University Press, 1987.

———. *Only Words.* Cambridge, Mass.: Harvard University Press, 1993.

Mackinnon, Catharine, and Andrea Dworkin, eds. *In Harm's Way: The Pornography Civil Rights Hearings.* Cambridge, Mass.: Harvard University Press, 1997.

Mani, Lata. *Contentious Traditions: The Debate on Sati in Colonial India.* Berkeley and Los Angeles: University of California Press, 1998.

Manring, Rebecca. "Sītā Devī: An Early Vaiṣṇava Guru" in *Graceful Guru: Hindu Female Gurus in India and the United* States, ed. Karen Pechilis. New York: Oxford University Press, 2004.

McDaniel, June. *Making Virtuous Daughters and Wives: An Introduction to Women's Brata Rituals in Bengali Folk Religion.* New York: State University of New York Press, 2002.

———. *Offering Flowers, Feeding Skulls: Popular Goddess Worship in West Bengal.* New York: Oxford University Press, 2004.

McDermott, Rachel Fell. "Kālī's New Frontiers: A Hindu Goddess on the Internet." In *Encountering Kālī,* ed. Rachel Fell McDermott and Jeffrey Kripal. Berkeley and Los Angeles: University of California Press, 2003.

———. *Mother of My Heart, Daughter of My Dreams: Transformations of Kali and Uma in the Devotional Poetry of Bengal.* New York: Oxford University Press, 2000.

———. "The Western Kālī." In *Devī: Goddesses of* India, ed. John Stratton Hawley and Donna Wulff. Berkeley and Los Angeles: University of California Press, 1996.

———. With Jeffrey J. Kripal. "Introducing Kālī Studies." In *Encountering Kālī,* ed. Rachel Fell McDermott and Jeffrey Kripal. Berkeley and Los Angeles: University of California Press, 2003.

Menski, Werner. "Marital Expectations as Dramatized in Hindu Marriage Rituals." In *Roles and Rituals for Hindu* Women, ed. Julia Leslie. Cranbury, N.J.: Fairleigh Dickinson University Press, 1991.

Michaels, Axel, Corelia Vogelsanger, and Annette Wilke. *Wild Goddesses in India and Nepal: Proceedings of an International Symposium Berne and Zurich, November 1994.* Bern and New York: Lang, 1996.

Monier-Williams, Monier. *Hinduism*. London: SPCK, 1906.

———. *A Sanskrit-English Dictionary*, 10th ed. Oxford: Oxford University Press, 1988.

Moniga, Padmini. *Contemporary Postcolonial Theory*. London: Arnold, 1997.

Muller-Ortega, Paul. "Aspects of *Jīvanmukti* in the Tantric Śaivism of Kashmir." In *Living Liberation in Hindu* Thought, ed. Andrew Fort and Patricia Mumme. Albany: State University of New York Press, 1996.

———. "Tantric Meditation: Vocalic Beginnings." In *Ritual and Speculation in Early Tantrism: Studies in Honor of Andre Padoux*, ed. T. Goudrian. Albany: State University of New York Press, 1992.

———. *Triadic Heart of Śiva*. Albany: State University of New York Press, 1989.

Narayan, Kirin. *Storytellers, Saints, and Scoundrels: Folk Narrative in Hindu Religious Teaching*. Philadelphia: University of Pennsylvania Press, 1989.

Narayan, R. K. *Gods, Demons and Others*, 2nd ed. Chicago: University of Chicago Press, 1993.

Niyogi, Tushar K. *Aspects of Folk Cults in South Bengal*. Calcutta: Anthropological Survey of India, 1987.

O'Flaherty, Wendy. *Asceticism and Eroticism in the Mythology of Śiva*. London: Oxford University Press, 1973.

Olivelle, Patrick. *Early Upanishads: Annotated Text and Translation*. New York: Oxford University Press, 1998.

Orr, Leslie. *Donors, Devotees, and Daughters of God: Temple Women in Medieval Tamilnadu*. New York: Oxford University Press, 2000.

Padoux, Andre. "Conclusion: Mantras—What Are They?" In *Understanding* Mantras, ed. Harvey P. Alper. Albany: State University of New York, 1989. Reprint, Delhi: Motilal Banarsidass, 1991.

——. *Vāc: The Concept of the Word in Selected Hindu Tantras*. Translated by Jacques Gontier. Albany: State University of New York Press, 1989.

Pal, Pratapaditya. *Hindu Religion and Iconology*. Los Angeles: Vichitra, 1981.

Pandit, M. P. *Studies in the Tantras and the Veda*. Madras: Ganesh Publishers, 1973.

Patton, Laurie. "Mantras and Miscarriage: Controlling Birth in the Late Vedic Period." In *Jewels of Authority*, ed. Laurie Patton. New York: Oxford University Press, 2002.

Pechilis, Karen, ed. *The Graceful Guru: Hindu Female Gurus in India and the United States*. New York: Oxford University Press, 2004.

Pintchman, Tracy. "Is the Hindu Goddess a Good Resource for Western Feminism?" In *Is the Goddess a Feminist?* ed. Alf Hiltebeitel and Kathleen Erndl. New York: New York University Press, 2000.

———. *The Rise of the Goddess in the Hindu Tradition*. Albany: State University of New York Press, 1994.

Prokhovnic, Raia. *Rational Woman: A Feminist Critique of Dichotomy*. New York, London: Routledge, 1999.

Raheja, Gloria Goodwin, and Ann Grodzins Gold. *Listen to the Heron's Words: Reimagining Gender and Kinship in North India*. Berkeley and Los Angeles: University of California Press, 1994.

Rastogi, Navjivan. *Introduction to the Tantrāloka.* Delhi: Motilal Banarsidass, 1987.

———. *The Krama Tantrism of Kashmir.* Delhi: Motilal Banarsidass, 1979.

Readings in the History and Culture of Assam. Compiled by Dharmeswar Chutia. Guwahati: Kamrupa Anasandhana Samiti, 1984.

Rhodes Bailley, Constantina. *Shaiva Devotional Songs of Kashmir: A Translation and Study of Utpaladeva's Shivastotravali.* Albany: State University of New York Press, 1987.

Rice, Stanley. *Hindu Customs and Their Origins.* Delhi: Daya, 1986. Originally published in 1937.

Sanderson, Alexis. "Meaning in Tantric Ritual." In *Essais sur le Rituel* 3, ed. Anne-Marie Blondeau and Kristofer Schipper. Colloque du Centenaire de la Section des Sciences Religieuses de l'Ecole Pratique des Hautes Etudes. Louvain-Paris: Peeters, 1992.

———. "Purity and Power among the Brahmins of Kashmir." In The *Category of the Person: Anthropology, Philosophy, History,* ed. Michael Carrithers, Steven Collins, and Steven Lukes. Cambridge: Cambridge University Press, 1985.

———. "Śaivism and the Tantric Tradition." In *The World's Religions,* ed. Stewart Sutherland, Leslie Houlden, Peter Clarke and Friedhelm Hardy. London: Routledge, 1988.

Sarma, Hemanta Kumar. *Socio-Religious Life of the Assamese Hindus: A Study of the Fasts and Festivals of Kamrup District.* Delhi: Daya, 1992.

Sarma, Naliniranjan. *Kāmarūpa School of Dharmaśāstras.* Calcutta: Punthi Pustak, 1994.

Sarma, Satyendranath. *Socio-economic and Cultural History of Medieval Assam, 1200–1800 A.D.* Gauhati: Government of Assam, 1989.

Satpathy, Sarbeshwara. *Dasa Mahāvidyās and Tantra Śāstra.* Calcutta: Punthi Pustak, 1992.

———. *Śakti Iconography in Tantric Mahāvidyās.* Calcutta: Punthi Pustak, 1991.

Sax, William. *Mountain Goddess: Gender and Politics in a Himalayan Pilgrimage.* New York: Oxford University Press, 1991.

Scarry, Elaine. *The Body in Pain: The Making and Unmaking of the World.* New York: Oxford University Press, 1985.

Sharma, Arvind. *Sati: Historical and Phenomenological Essays.* New Delhi: Motilal Banarsidass, 1988.

Sharma, Naliniranjan. *Kāmarūpa School of Dharmaśāstra.* Foreword by Biswanarayan Shastri. Calcutta: Punthi Pustak, 1994.

Sharpe, Jenny. *Allegories of Empire: The Figure of Woman in the Colonial Text.* Minneapolis: University of Minnesota Press, 1993.

Shaw, Miranda. *Passionate Enlightenment: Women in Tantric Buddhism.* Princeton, N.J.: Princeton University Press, 1994.

Sherma, Rita "Hinduism." In *Sex and Religion,* ed. Christel Manning and Phil Zuckerman. Belmont, Calif.: Wadsworth, 2005.

———. " 'Sa-Ham—I Am She': Woman as Goddess." In *Is the Goddess a Feminist?* ed. Alf Hiltebeitel and Kathleen Erndl. New York: New York University Press, 2000.

Silburn, Lilian. *Kuṇḍalinī: Energy of the Depths.* Translated by Jacques Gontier. Albany: State University of New York Press, 1988.

Sircar, D. C. *Śākta Pīṭhas.* Delhi: Motilal Banarsidass, 1998. Originally published in 1973.

Smith, Frederick M. "Indra's Curse, Varuṇa's Noose and the Suppression of the Woman in the Vedic Śrauta Ritual." In *Roles and Rituals for Hindu Women*, ed. Julia Leslie. Cranbury, N.J.: Fairleigh Dickinson University Press, 1991.

Spivak, Gayatri. "Can the Subaltern Speak?" In *Marxism and the Interpretation of* Culture, ed. Cary Nelson and Lawrence Grossberg. Urbana: University of Illinois Press, 1988.

Staal, Frits. "*Mantras* and Bird Songs," *Journal of the American Oriental Society*, 105, no. 3 (1985): 549–58.

———. "Vedic Mantras." In *Understanding* Mantras, ed. Harvey P. Alper. Albany: State University of New York Press, 1989. Reprint, Delhi: Motilal Banarsidass, 1991.

Suleri, Sara. "Woman Skin Deep: Feminism and the Postcolonial Condition." In *Contemporary Postcolonial* Theory, ed. Padmini Mongia. London: Arnold, 1996.

Sunder Rajan, Rajeshwari. "Real and Imagined Goddesses: A Debate." In *Is the Goddess a Feminist?* ed. Alf Hiltebeitel and Kathleen Erndl. New York: New York University Press, 2000.

———. *Real and Imagined Women: Gender, Culture and Postcolonialism.* London: Routledge, 1993.

Taylor, Mark C. *Critical Terms for Religious Studies.* Chicago: University of Chicago Press, 1998.

Tharu, Susie, and K. Lalita, eds., *Women Writing in India*, vol. 1. Delhi: Oxford University Press, 1991.

Thomas, P. *Hindu Religion, Customs and Manners: Describimg the Customs and Manners, Religious, Social and Domestic Life, Arts and Sciences of the Hindus.* 4th ed. Bombay: D. B. Taraporevala Sons, 1960.

Torella, Raffaele. *The Iśvarapratyabhijñākārikā of Utpaladeva with the Author's Vṛtti: Critical Edition and Annotated Translation.* Rome: Istituto Italiano per il medio ed estremo oriente, 1994.

Urban, Hugh B. "The Cult of Ecstacy: Tantrism, the New Age, and the Spiritual Logic of Late Capitalism" *History of Religions* 40, no. 2 (2000): 268–304.

———. " 'India's Darkest Heart': Kali in the Colonial Imagination." In *Encountering Kālī*, ed. Rachel Fell Mcdermott and Jeffrey Kripal. Berkeley and Los Angeles: University of California Press, 2003.

———. "Path of Power: Impurity, Kingship, and Sacrifice in Assamese Tantra." *Journal of the American Academy of Religion* 69, no. 4 (2001): 777–816.

———. *Tantra: Sex, Secrecy, Politics and Power in the Study of Religion.* Berkeley and Los Angeles: University of California Press, 2003.

Van Kooij, K. R. *Worship of the Goddess according to the Kālikāpurāṇa.* Leiden: Brill, 1972.

Vātsyāyana. Complete Kāma Sūtra: The First Unabridged Modern Translation of the Classic Indian Text by Vātsyāyana, Including the Jayamangalā Commentary from the Sanskrit by Yashodhara and Extracts from the Hindi Commentary by Devadatta Shāstrī. Translated by Alain Daniélou, prepared with the help of Kenneth Hurry. Rochester, Vt.: Park Street, 1994.

Viswa Shanti Devi Yajña. Compiled by the Viswa Shanti Devi Yajña Committee. Kamakhya Hill, Guwahati: Viswa Shanti Devi Yajña Committee, 2004.

Wadley, Susan. *Struggling with Destiny in Karimpur, 1925–1984*. Berkeley and Los Angeles: University of California Press, 1994.

———. "Women and the Hindu Tradition." In *Women in India: Two* Perspectives, ed. Doranne Jacobson and Susan S. Wadley. Columbia, Mo.: South Asia, 1977.

Walker, Alice. *The Color Purple: A Novel*. New York: Harcourt Brace Jovanovich, 1982.

Weinberger-Thomas, Catherine. *Ashes of Immortality: Widow Burning in India*. Translated by Jeffrey Mehlman and David Gordon White. Chicago: University of Chicago Press, 1999.

Wheelock, Wade T. "The Mantra in Vedic and Tantric Ritual." In *Understanding Mantras*, ed. Harvey P. Alper. Albany: State University of New York Press, 1989. Reprint, Delhi: Motilal Banarsidass, 1991.

White, David. *The Kiss of the Yoginī: Tantric Sex in Its South Asian Contexts*. Chicago: University of Chicago Press, 2003.

———, ed. *Tantra in Practice*. Princeton Readings in Religion Series. Princeton, N.J.: Princeton University Press, 2000.

———. "Transformations in the Art of Love: *Kāmakalā* Practices in Hindu Tantric and Kaula Traditions." *History of Religion* 38, no. 2 (1998): 172–98.

Woodroffe, Sir John. *Introduction to Tantra Śāstra*. 8th ed. Madras: Ganesh and Company, 1990.

———. (Arthur Avalon). *Serpent Power:Tthe Secrets of Tantric and Shaktic Yoga*. New York: Dover, 1974. Originally published in 1919.

Zizek, Slavoj. *Looking Awry: An Introduction to Jacques Lacan through Popular Culture*. Cambridge, Mass.: Massachusetts Institute of Technology Press, 1991.

Index

performative speech 18, 65, 76, 78, 112–13, 121–25, 129–30, 146
Phetkāriṇī Tantra 13, 150, 155, 158
Pintchman, Tracy 68
Plato 126
pornography 63, 71, 75–77, 81, 107, 124, 262 n. 44
  and language 75–77
possession 97–98
  of women by the goddess 43–44, 86
power
  of women through mantras 45–46
prakṛti 3, 4, 18, 22, 35, 87, 109, 113, 127–28
Prapañcasāra 179
Prāṇatoṣiṇī 48, 50, 152, 178
prasāda 44
Prathameśvarī 8, 159, 191
pratyakṣa 117, 128
prema 39
prostitute 164
pūjā 46, 52
purity 74, 80, 98
  in Kālī Practice 55–56
puruṣa 3, 4, 35, 87, 113, 161

Rādhā 39
Raheja, Gloria Goodwin 17, 22, 23, 57
rākṣasa 133
Rāma 39, 79, 137–38
Ramakrishna 47
Ramanujan, A.K. 19
Rāmatoṣaṇa Bhaṭṭācārya 48, 50, 152, 156–57, 178
Rāmāyaṇa 39, 137–39, 190, 244 n.9
Ram Mohun Roy 152
rape 81, 131–32, 135, 137–39
Rāvaṇa 39, 68, 79, 137,
reverse sex position *see* sex position, woman on top
rod (for penetration of partner) 88
Rudrayāmala 49–51, 175–76
sādhvī 49, 99, 176, 185
Śaiva 20, 74, 160, 179, 182, 204
Śākta 14, 31–33, 106, 159, 160, 177, 182–86
śāktācāra see Śākta Conduct
Śākta Conduct 31–32
Śāktānandataraṅgiṇī 50, 161, 175–76, 178
śakti 62, 112, 164, 168, 174, 177, 183, 188–89
Śambhu 57
Śāmbhava 204
Sāṃkhya 4, 34, 62, 86–87, 113, 123, 143, 233 n. 20
saṃskāra 56
Sanderson, Alexis 55, 96–97, 104
Śaṅkara 127–29
Śaṅkaradeva 157, 158, 182, 185–89
Śaṅkaradigvijaya 127–28
Śāradātilaka 179
Sarasvatī 16, 134–35, 137, 159 *see also* Blue Goddess of Speech
Sarvavijayi Tantra 11, 156
Sarvollāsa Tantra 157
satī 18, 45, 100–2, 111–13, 121–23, 125, 129, 131–32, 138, 141 *see also* wife
Satī (goddess) 14, 100–3, 105–6, 122–23
Ṣaṭkarmāṇi 227 n. 30
Ṣaṭsāhasra Saṃhitā 170
Satyakāma Jābala 46
Saundarya Laharī 179
śava *see* corpse
Scarry, Elaine 80
Schoterman, Jan 26–27
second sex 36
secret knowledge 87
Secret Practice Tantra 41, 47–50, 52, 57 *see also* Gupta Sādhana Tantra
self 34, 37, 56, 58–60, 69, 71, 73, 86–87, 90, 98, 100, 102, 104, 113, 118, 125, 127, 129, 140
Setubandha 179
sex
  enacting identity 81